THE COMPLETE PARENTING BOOK

Practical Help from Leading Experts

EDITED BY DR. DAVID STOOP AND DR. JAN STOOP

Revell
Grand Rapids, Michigan

© 2004 by David and Jan Stoop

Published by Fleming H. Revell
a division of Baker Publishing Group
P.O. Box 6287, Grand Rapids, MI 49516-6287

Printed in the United States of America

Library of Congress Cataloging-in-Publication Data
The complete parenting book : practical help from leading experts / edited by David Stoop and Jan Stoop.
     p.   cm.
    Includes bibliographical references (p   ).
    ISBN 0-8007-1866-6 (cloth)
    1. Child rearing—Religious aspects—Christianity. 2. Parenting—Religious aspects—Christianity. I. Stoop, David A. II. Stoop, Jan.
    BV4529.C587 2004
    248.8′45—dc22
                                                           2004015450

CONTENTS

INTRODUCTION

Being a parent is the most challenging role we will ever have as adults. It is an awesome responsibility to shape young lives as they develop and mature. Over the years as we have considered the ways we have parented and as we have talked with many other parents about their parenting styles—many of whom questioned their own parenting skills—we wanted to come up with a handbook to help today's parents face today's challenges with the skills and insights we wish we had had when our kids were little.

One day, during the time we were working on this project, we were sitting in an outdoor restaurant at a table next to two young couples who were enjoying themselves and talking loudly enough that we could hear all sides of their conversation. They talked on and on about their recent weddings and then went on about how one couple had remodeled their kitchen. And then one of them moved to the subject of kids and started talking about a neighbor of theirs who had two young children. As the couple described this young family, they were very critical of the parenting methods they saw being used. Then they launched into a lively discussion about how they would certainly do it differently and how they would correct the strategies of these parents. Then both couples started talking about having kids of their own.

"Well, I hear that you should find a nanny first," said one husband.

5

"Oh yes. That's important," agreed the other wife. "But have you thought about having some foster children first? I hear it's a good way to see if you're suited to being a parent. We have friends who did that."

"No, I haven't heard that, but we did get a dog," added the first wife. "We love her—she's delightful."

"I think it's good to practice on a dog," someone said. "It gets you ready for parenting."

And from there they went on to talk about their plans to have three children, what type of house they would need, and how big the yard would have to be. We smiled as we listened to them as they considered so many aspects of parenting. One thing seemed obvious—all four of them were more than a little anxious about the idea of becoming parents.

We agree it is an awesome task, and while it is awesome, it is a task that is designed for parents who will make mistakes. God has built into the parenting process some flexibility—we don't have to be perfect parents. As we will point out, the parent who strives for perfection in parenting creates a whole set of problems, both within the family and in the child. It is our hope and prayer that this handbook will alleviate some of your anxiety about parenting and that you will turn to it frequently to find some answers to your questions but also to see that there are many great resources that our authors have recommended on a given subject.

Our focus in this handbook is the parenting of children from birth until adolescence. Here's an overview of what's covered.

In part 1, we begin by looking at some of the basics of parenting. We call it "Parenting 101." Most of what's covered in this section has to do with you as the parent and how you as a parent affect your child. We then explore the different tasks related to raising sons versus raising daughters. We also look at what ingredients go into raising confident children. The importance of the role of the father is emphasized, and discipline is discussed in the context of attachment issues. Last, we explore ways to simply be "good enough" as a parent as opposed to trying to be a "superparent."

Part 2 considers some of the developmental tasks related to children. We begin this section with the issue of attachment, which is the foundation of all our relationships. We then consider how children develop spiritually, how their personalities emerge, what their learning styles are, why children play, and how to teach them about money. It's during this time that we prepare them for school and lay a foundation for building character and developing Christian values. Finally, we will look at how parents can guard their children's faith as they move into adolescence.

In part 3, we explore some special issues related to parenting. We look at anger, both in the child and in the parent. We consider how to evaluate the educational options available to us, including whether we should homeschool, send them to private school, or send them to public school. What about ADD and AD/HD? You will get some insights from one of the leading medical experts in this area. We also look at how parents can better understand what we call "spirited children," how to help children deal with loss and grief, how to understand what happens to children in divorce, and how to build a strong single-parent family or build a successful stepfamily.

Most chapters have a series of questions that will help you discuss together, or even with other parents, what is covered in that chapter. In addition, authors list what they believe to be the best resources available today about their particular subject.

All the authors speak from what they have studied, and they bring themselves into the chapter and share what they have experienced as well. We hope you will read, reread, discuss, question, and explore the information found here, and that in doing so, you will not only find parenting to be a challenge but also find that it is one of the most rewarding things we can experience as adults. Our prayer for you is that God will provide the strength and wisdom you need as you face the daunting task of parenting.

CONTRIBUTORS

Claudia Arp and **David Arp**, M.S.W., are cofounders and codirectors of Marriage Alive International, a groundbreaking ministry dedicated to providing resources and training to empower churches to help build better marriages and families. Their Marriage Alive seminar is popular across the United States and in Europe. The Arps are popular conference speakers, columnists, and best-selling authors of more than thirty books and video curricula, including the Gold Medallion Award–winning *The Second Half of Marriage* and the popular 10 Great Dates series. Their latest releases include *Answering the 8 Cries of the Spirited Child* and *Loving Your Relatives Even When You Don't See Eye-to-Eye*.

Frequent contributors to print and broadcast media, the Arps have appeared as empty nest experts on NBC's *Today*, *CBS This Morning*, and *Focus on the Family*. Their work has been featured in *USA Today*, the *Christian Science Monitor*, and *Reader's Digest*. David and Claudia have been married for forty years and have three married sons and eight grandchildren. The Arps live in Knoxville, Tennessee, and can be reached at www.marriagealive.org.

Jack and Judy Balswick are both professors of marriage and family therapy at the School of Psychology, Fuller Theological Seminary. Jack received his Ph.D. from the University of Iowa, and in addition to teaching he is the director of marriage and family research at Fuller.

Judy is the director of clinical training at Fuller and received her doctorate from the University of Georgia. Together they have written a number of books, including *The Dual Earner Marriage*, *Family Pain*, *The Family: A Christian Perspective of the Contemporary Home*, and the recently published *Relationship Empowerment Parenting: Building Formative and Fulfilling Relationships with Your Children*. Jack and Judy have two children and four grandchildren.

Lynda Hunter Bjorklund, Ed.D., holds a doctorate from the University of Cincinnati in curriculum. She is the founding editor of Focus on the Family's *Single-Parent Family* magazine and the author of six books. She is a speaker and the host of *The Lynda Hunter Show*, a nationally syndicated talk show for women.

Lauren Littauer Briggs is the author of *The Art of Helping: What to Say and Do When Someone Is Hurting*. Her passion for comforting those in crisis began with the deaths of her two younger brothers, the first occurring when Lauren was just seven years old. Lauren holds a degree in psychology and is the daughter of nationally known speaker and author Florence Littauer. Lauren has been helping hurting hearts for more than twenty years through peer support groups, medical seminars, and the Compassionate Friends Organization. Lauren is available to speak at women's luncheons, meetings, seminars, and conferences.

For additional information please visit www.laurenbriggs.com. Lauren may be reached at lauren@laurenbriggs.com. If you would like to have Lauren speak to your church or organization, please call CLASServices at 1-800-433-6633.

Jim Burns is the president of YouthBuilders, formerly the National Institute of Youth Ministry. His passion is communicating to young people and adults practical truths to help them live out Christian lives. Highly respected for his expertise in the area of youth ministry, family, and parenting issues, Dr. Burns is the author of many books and speaks to thousands of people around the world each year. Each month in the United States and abroad, people either use Jim's written or video materials, hear him speak, or tune in to his radio feature currently airing on more than 850 stations and outlets daily. Jim is also a frequent guest on radio programs dealing with parenting issues and youth culture. He and his wife, Cathy, and their teenagers, Christy, Rebecca, and Heidi, live in Dana Point, California.

Tim Clinton is president of the American Association of Christian Counselors, a licensed marriage and family therapist, and an ordained minister. Dr. Clinton is also professor of counseling and pastoral care at Liberty University's Center for Counseling and Family Studies. He is a columnist for *ParentLife* magazine and host of the national daily radio program *Christian Counseling Today*. He is the executive editor for the *Soul Care Bible* and coauthored with his wife, Julie, the book *The Marriage You Always Wanted*. The Clintons have two children.

Mark E. Crawford, Ph.D., received his B.A. in psychology from the University of Tennessee in Knoxville. He received an M.S. and Ph.D. in clinical psychology from Saint Louis University in Saint Louis. His graduate research in the area of religion and mental health won an award from the Missouri Psychological Association for graduate research and was published in a professional journal. He completed an internship in clinical psychology from the Emory University School of Medicine in Atlanta. Mark began his career in psychology working for the Rapha Inpatient Treatment Program at West Paces Ferry Hospital in Atlanta. He became the clinical director of their adolescent and adult treatment programs. He later cofounded Lyles & Crawford Clinical Consulting, P.C., with his partner, Michael R. Lyles, M.D. Mark is a consulting psychologist to the Westminster Schools in Atlanta. He is regularly requested as a speaker to churches, parent groups, professional groups, and schools. He is the author of *The Obsessive-Compulsive Trap* and has appeared on ABC's *Good Morning America* and ABC's *World News This Morning*. Mark is married to Dana Crawford, and they have two sons, Caleb and Ben.

Ron L. Deal, M.MFT., is family life minister for the Southwest Church of Christ, director of SuccessfulStepfamilies.com, a licensed marriage and family therapist, and a licensed professional counselor with the Better Life Counseling Center, Inc., in Jonesboro, Arkansas. He is author of the book *The Smart Step-Family* and presents his humorous and practical Building a Successful Stepfamily seminar regularly throughout the country. Ron has been a guest on numerous TV and radio programs including *Focus on the Family* and *FamilyLife Today*. Ron is a member of the Institute Faculty and Advisory Council of the Stepfamily Association of America.

Cheri Fuller is the author of thirty books on family, prayer, spiritual growth, and children's learning such as *When Children Pray, Opening Your Child's Spiritual Windows, When Mothers Pray*, and others. She is an inspirational speaker who has written hundreds of articles for magazines including *Focus on the Family, Family Circle, Today's Christian Woman, ParentLife*, and *CHILD*. Wife and mother of three grown children, she and her husband, Holmes, have five grandchildren. Her website, www.cherifuller.com, has resources on prayer, a column called "Mothering by Heart," information on her speaking ministry, and lots of inspiration for families.

William Gaultiere has been a clinical psychologist and spiritual director in private practice in Irvine, California, since 1987. He has an M.A. from Rosemead School of Psychology at Biola University and a Ph.D. from United States International University. He is also the executive director of the New Hope Crisis Counseling Center where he has trained more than a thousand Christian lay counselors. He cofounded New Hope Online, the first website in the world to offer twenty-four-hour live crisis counseling for free. He has appeared on television and radio shows including *The Hour of Power* and *Minirth-Meier New Life*. He has authored three books including *A Walk with Your Shepherd* and contributed to others including *The Spiritual Renewal Bible*. You can contact him at DrBill@ChristianSoulCare.com.

   Kristi Gaultiere has been a marriage and family therapist in private practice in Irvine, California, since 1988. She has an M.A. in marriage and family therapy and a doctorate in clinical psychology. She is a mentor mom with Mothers of Preschoolers (MOPS) and leads two "Moms in Touch" prayer groups for her children's schools. You can contact her at DrKristi@ChristianSoulCare.com.

   Bill and Kristi live in Irvine, California, with their three children. They speak together and separately at local churches and conferences. You can contact them at their website, ChristianSoulCare.com, which features a free semiweekly devotional by email that you can sign up for, encouraging articles on Christian psychology and spirituality, and seminar tapes and books that you can order.

Archibald D. Hart, Ph.D., specializes in psychotherapy from a Christian orientation and lectures widely to church groups and ministers on topics of stress management and how to handle emotions from a biblical perspective. He is professor of psychology and dean emeritus of Fuller Theological Seminary's Graduate School of Psychology. He also serves as the executive editor and director of international relations for the American Association of Christian Counselors. Dr. Hart is an internationally known speaker and author whose books include *Adrenaline and Stress, Children and Divorce, The Sexual Man,* and *The Anxiety Cure.*

Glen Havens, M.D., received his medical degree from the Medical University of South Carolina in Charleston. He completed his residency in psychiatry at Wright State School of Medicine while on active duty with the Air Force. He was chairman of the department of psychiatry at Wilford Hall in San Antonio, Texas, prior to leaving active duty in 1990 to go into private practice. He served as medical director for Rapha's adolescent unit in Atlanta from 1990 until 1997. Since then he has acted as medical director for The Ark Psychiatric Services in Atlanta. He is board certified in psychiatry and has served as an examiner for the American Board of Psychiatry and Neurology. Dr. Havens specializes in AD/HD and has lectured extensively on this subject.

Dr. John A. Huffman Jr. has been the senior pastor of the 4500-member St. Andrews Presbyterian Church in Newport Beach, California, for more than twenty-five years. He is a graduate of Wheaton College and received his master of divinity and doctor of ministry from Princeton Theological Seminary. He serves on the board of directors of Gordon-Conwell Theological Seminary and is vice chairman of the Christianity Today International board. He also recently chaired the board of directors of World Vision U.S. He and his wife, Ann, have three grown daughters. Their daughter Suzanne, a Princeton University graduate, died in 1991 at the age of twenty-three after a twenty-month battle with Hodgkin's disease.

Christopher McCluskey is a licensed psychotherapist, board-certified sex therapist, and Christian life coach. He serves on the adjunct faculties of Reformed Theological Seminary and Psychological Studies Institute and is director of the Christian Track at the Institute for Life Coach Training. He is a nationally known speaker and frequently appears on radio and television and in print.

Rachel McCluskey is Chris's wife and the homeschooling mother of their five children (with a sixth on the way). She holds a bachelor's degree and has postgraduate training in elementary education; she was a public school teacher before having children. Chris and Rachel are coauthors of the Christian marriage book *When Two Become One*. They operate their private coaching business, Coaching for Christian Living, from their family farm in rural Missouri. They can be found on the Web at www.christian-living.com.

Lisa Graham McMinn is the author of *Growing Strong Daughters* and *Sexuality and Holy Longing*. She is an associate professor of sociology at Wheaton College. To balance a life of teaching, writing, and speaking, Lisa enjoys long walks, backpacking, gardening, baking, and good books. She and her husband, Mark, are the parents of three grown or nearly grown daughters.

Kathy Collard Miller is a speaker and writer who portrays God's healing power through practical principles from God's Word. Her trademark teaching, "The 1% Principle," inspires her audience to "excel still more" and "never give up on God's ability to create change." Her message comes from the work God did in her life by delivering her from being an abusive mother. Even though she had been a Christian for ten years at the time, she couldn't grasp God's strength to control herself. She hated her life and wondered if she'd ever experience God's love and joy again. But God faithfully replaced her anger with patience, rebuilt her love for her two children, and restored the joy between Kathy and her husband. Today, they both are speaking to audiences—sometimes together—about their story of God's grace and healing.

Sharon Hart Morris, Ph.D., is the director of the Marriage, Family and Relationship Institute at La Vie Counseling Center in Pasadena,

California, specializing in relationship issues in marriage and family from an attachment perspective. She is a graduate of UCLA and received her master's in theology and her doctorate in marriage and family therapy from the School of Psychology, Fuller Theological Seminary. She and her husband were married for fifteen years. In 1995 he was killed in an automobile accident. With the strength of the Lord and an incredible support system consisting of her family, Sharon raised her two young sons and rebuilt her life. Sharon is the author of the book *Safe Haven Marriage*, and she conducts Safe Haven parenting seminars and marriage intensives around the world. She can be contacted at www.havenofsafety.com.

Gary Oliver is the executive director of the Center for Marriage and Family Studies and professor of psychology and practical theology at John Brown University in Siloam Springs, Arkansas. He is a graduate of Biola University, Talbot Theological Seminary, and Fuller Theological Seminary, and he received his doctorate from the University of Nebraska. He is a licensed clinical psychologist and is a clinical member of the American Association for Marriage and Family Therapy.

Carrie Oliver is a licensed professional counselor with PeopleCare Clinic, associated with John Brown University. In addition to her clinical work, she enjoys conference speaking, teaching, and conducting small groups.

Gary and Carrie have coauthored *Raising Sons and Loving It!* Gary has also authored several other books, including *Made Perfect in Weakness*, and coauthored a number of books with Norm Wright including *Raising Kids to Love Jesus*. Gary and Carrie have been married twenty-two years and have three sons.

Diana M. O'Neill is a licensed professional counselor with more than twenty years of experience working with children, adolescents, and adults in educational and private practice settings. She received her master's level training in counseling and school psychology at Georgia State University. Attention deficit/hyperactivity disorder continues to be her area of greatest interest.

Les and Leslie Parrott are codirectors of the Center for Relationship Development at Seattle Pacific University (SPU), a groundbreaking program dedicated to teaching the basics of good relationships. Dr. Les Parrott is a professor of clinical psychology at SPU, and his wife, Dr. Leslie Parrott, is a marriage and family therapist at SPU. The Parrotts are authors of the Gold Medallion Award–winning *Saving Your Marriage Before It Starts, Becoming Soul Mates, The Love List,* and *Relationships,* as well as numerous other books and video resources.

They have been featured on *Oprah, CBS This Morning,* CNN, and *The View* and in *USA Today* and the *New York Times.* They are frequent guest speakers and have written for a variety of magazines. They live in Seattle, Washington, with their two sons and have been married nineteen years. They can be reached at www.RealRelationships.com.

Randy Petersen is a freelance writer and author or coauthor of more than thirty books, including several on psychological themes. He is coauthor of *Stress Test, Victim of Love?* and *Angry with God.* He lives and works in New Jersey.

David Stoop is a licensed clinical psychologist in the state of California. He is a graduate of Stetson University and Fuller Theological Seminary and received his doctorate from the University of Southern California. He is also an ordained minister. He is the founder and director of the Center for Family Therapy in Newport Beach, California, is an adjunct professor at Fuller Theological Seminary, and serves on the executive board of the American Association of Christian Counselors.

Jan Stoop is a counselor, author, and seminar speaker, is a graduate of Fuller Theological Seminary, and received her doctorate in psychology from the California Graduate Institute. Jan is a frequent speaker at Mothers of Preschoolers (MOPS) groups.

Together David and Jan have authored more than twenty-five books, including *Forgiving the Unforgivable, Making Peace with Your Father, When Couples Pray Together, The Tenderhearted Mom,* and *The Complete Marriage Book.* They have three sons and five grandchildren.

Mike Stoop currently works as a software engineering manager. He is also a talented musician and arranger. **Terri Stoop** is currently a third-grade teacher at a private Christian school. Her gift of encouraging and motivating women through her heartwarming messages has made her a favorite speaker at women's retreats and MOPS groups. Mike and Terri have a passion for teaching children God's Word through music. Their children's worship ministry has taken them as far away as Samoa. They have three children and live in Aliso Viejo, California.

Daniel S. Sweeney, Ph.D., is an associate professor and clinical director in the graduate department of counseling at George Fox University (GFU) in Portland, Oregon. He is also the director of the Northwest Center for Play Therapy Studies at GFU. Daniel is a registered play-therapist supervisor and has a small private practice. He has extensive experience in working with children, couples, and families in a variety of settings, including therapeutic foster care, community mental health, private practice, and pastoral counseling. He has presented at numerous national and international conferences on the topics of play therapy, filial therapy, and sandtray therapy. He is an author or coauthor of several books, including *Play Therapy Interventions with Children's Problems, Counseling Children through the World of Play, Sandtray Therapy: A Practical Manual*, and *Handbook of Group Play Therapy*. Daniel lives with his wife and children in Newberg, Oregon.

Cynthia Ulrich Tobias, M.Ed., is founder, manager, and CEO of AppLe St. (Applied Learning Styles). In addition to maintaining a busy speaking schedule, she coordinates the AppLe St. education and commerce programs and administers various learning-styles projects throughout North America as well as internationally. A lifelong strong-willed child herself and now the parent of a strong-willed child, Cynthia is a graduate of Northwest Nazarene University and received her master of education degree from Seattle Pacific University. She is the best-selling author of *The Way They Learn, The Way We Work, Every Child Can Succeed*, and her newest book, *I Hate School! How to Help Your Child Love Learning*. Cynthia and her husband have twin boys and live in the Seattle, Washington, area.

Thomas A. Whiteman is founder and president of Life Counseling Services, through which he directs therapists, psychologists, and psychiatrists in fifteen locations throughout Pennsylvania and New

Jersey. He is also a director for Fresh Start Seminars, which conducts more than fifty divorce recovery seminars a year. He has authored or coauthored several books, including *The Marriage Mender*, *Adult ADD*, *Victim of Love*, and *The Complete Stress Management Workbook*. Dr. Whiteman and his wife have three children and live in Berwyn, Pennsylvania.

PART 1

PARENTING 101

The Basics

1

GIVING YOUR CHILD SOMETHING TO REBEL AGAINST

Dr. John A. Huffman Jr.

Hear, O Israel: The LORD our God, the LORD is one. Love the LORD your God with all your heart and with all your soul and with all your strength. These commandments that I give you today are to be upon your hearts. Impress them on your children. Talk about them when you sit at home and when you walk along the road, when you lie down and when you get up.

Deuteronomy 6:4–7

I once read the comment, "The modern home is where switches control everything but kids." This tongue-in-cheek bit of whimsy captures a myriad of questions about the modern family.

Pollsters are constantly at work, studying American homes. My four decades of pastoral ministry, from 1962 to the present, have been carried out in an environment of constant change. And I have been reflecting recently on the most noticeable changes I have observed during these four decades. The top four are as follows, not necessarily in order of intensity.

One change is the substantial increase in the percentage of couples who end their marriage by divorce. Another is the increased number of couples living together prior to marriage. A third is the substantial decrease in parental authority, with the peer group of friends having taken over some of the influences on behavior once held by parents. A fourth is the substantial decline in the percentage of meals families have together with everyone at the table.

In response to these changes, I want to make two simple but highly important points. The first is a biblical, philosophical principle that can undergird all of your parenting. The second is a list of the practical biblical gifts you can give your children.

Wise Parents Give Their Children Something to Rebel Against

No, I am not calling for rebellion on the part of children. The Bible instructs children to obey their parents. The apostle Paul wrote, paraphrasing one of the Ten Commandments, "Children, obey your parents in the Lord, for this is right. 'Honor your father and mother'—which is the first commandment with a promise—'that it may go well with you and that you may enjoy long life on the earth'" (Eph. 6:1–3).

In addition, the Old Testament book of Proverbs is filled with instructions for children to learn from their parents. Wise sons and daughters accept the counsel of their father. God's Word instructs children to obey.

I would not encourage rebellion among young people. At the same time, it leaves an optional opening. They are free to disobey. They can become rebels. We must objectively face the fact that every young person has the opportunity and the right to rebel. It is against God's very creation of the individual to expect the child to be a carbon copy of the parent. It is natural for the young person to want to get on his or her own two feet, independent of the parents. But rebellion often is carried out at great risk.

To avoid having their child rebel, all too often parents will take a relaxed, hands-off attitude. For example, a parent recently took me aside and informed me that he would never influence his child religiously. He said, "It is unfair to a young person to try to mold his religious thinking. Every child should make up his own mind."

I agree that every young person has the right to make his or her own moral, spiritual, and personal choices. I agree that God has created human beings with the freedom to make choices. However, let's not kid ourselves. If we do not influence our children, someone else will. You can't adopt a hands-off policy without somebody else putting his or her hands on your child. Then it's often too late. If you abdicate your leadership role in the home, you will lose your influence. There are plenty of people who are, for their own economic and personal gain, prepared to step in and fill any leadership vacuum you have left.

A father shared with me his agony of having a son who is involved in the drug scene. This father wanted some quick principles to extract his son from this problem. I couldn't give him any easy answers, for there are none. However, I did make one suggestion. I suggested that the father get his own life straightened out. The minute I began to talk to him about his life, he became quite defensive and resistant. I talked to him about Jesus Christ and the forgiveness and new beginning he offers through his life, death, and resurrection. The dad was turned off. His response was "I'm not religious." No, he's not. That's part of the problem. His son, who feels the vacuum of life, looks to a father whose life is also a vacuum. So why not turn to drugs?

I talked with another father. This man is busy. Business is front and center in his life. He doesn't want to pay the personal price of following through on a commitment he made to Jesus Christ. His kids are growing up pagan. They know little of the sincere childhood commitment this father made years ago but has not fleshed out in any visible, concrete fashion. This man doesn't want to pay the price of Christian growth.

These three parents have abdicated their responsibilities. Two are already reaping what they have sown. The other one will bring in the harvest soon. Albert Camus and Jean Paul Sartre wrote their observa-

tions about life and its emptiness, in essence saying, "What is there
to life? Does it have any meaning? Why are we here? Where do we
come from? Where are we going?"

These three fathers, two with no faith, and the other without a
willingness to flesh out his faith, have taken the hands-off policy and
have left their children in the existential vacuum so personified by
Camus and Sartre.

In contrast, God's Word commands us to provide strong leadership
as parents. The Bible says in Deuteronomy 5:32–33:

> So be careful to do what the LORD your God has commanded you; do not
> turn aside to the right or to the left. Walk in all the way that the LORD your
> God has commanded you, so that you may live and prosper and prolong
> your days in the land that you will possess.

In the next chapter, Deuteronomy 6:5–7, we read these words:

> Love the LORD your God with all your heart and with all your soul and
> with all your strength. These commandments that I give you today are
> to be upon your hearts. Impress them on your children. Talk about them
> when you sit at home and when you walk along the road, when you lie
> down and when you get up.

This leaves no room for wishy-washy relativistic parents. Yours is to
be a life of affirmation. Your children have a right to know where you
stand. Give them something to rebel against. This is not simply good
biblical teaching; it also squares with today's insightful, contemporary
psychological insight.

The late Jewish psychoanalyst Bruno Bettelheim was best known
for his innovative studies of children's emotional development based
on both his private practice and his work on the faculty of the University of Chicago. His considered conclusion was "American parents
and American society have not given today's youth the emotional
equipment for engaging in rational, constructive protest."[1]

During the student revolts of the 1970s, Bettelheim stated that the
political content of student revolt was most of all a desperate wish
that parents would have been strong in the convictions that motivated
their actions. He noted that many of the radical students embraced

Maoism and chanted, "Ho, Ho, Ho Chi Minh," in their demonstrations in the revelation of a deep yearning for strong fathers with strong convictions.

The fact that their fathers had abdicated the role of imparting positive, affirmative input into their lives, leaving them in a vacuum, produced a willingness to attach themselves to strong, totalitarian father figures who filled this yearning for direction.

So here we are, sitting back, determined not to present too strong an image for fear of losing our children, and we all too often end up losing them. Every child craves to know what his or her parents believe. It doesn't mean that the child will buy the total package. However, that child wants to see some absolutes against which to measure his or her own values.

I challenge you to integrate the timeless truths of God's Word into the very core of your holistic faith commitments. Let them be evident to your children. Then lovingly, caringly, prayerfully, in the spirit of unconditional love, you can release them to ultimately accept or reject the claims of God's Word as they have seen it operative in your life.

Some Practical Biblical Gifts to Give to Your Children

I beg you, in the name of Jesus Christ, to give your children something to rebel against. Here are six practical, biblical gifts you can give your child.

1. Let Your Child See a Healthy Love of Jesus Christ in Your Life

I'm not talking about just a belief in the Savior. I am talking about a personal relationship that transforms your own life. Moses commanded the people to "Love the LORD your God with all your heart and with all your soul and with all your strength" (Deut. 6:5). Do you love the Lord? Your child can tell. He or she can detect whether it is genuine emotion.

We can sing the hymn "Jesus, Lover of My Soul." That little one standing beside you knows whether or not you love Jesus. Children can detect the hypocrisy of a Sunday-go-to-meeting type of Christianity that doesn't carry the personal friendship of the Savior into the other six days of the week. We can blithely sing, "O for a thousand tongues to sing my great Redeemer's praise," and we don't use the one tongue we have to speak a good word on his behalf the rest of the week.

Do you love Jesus Christ? If he's truly your Savior, you ought to. If he's your Lord, you have to. It wouldn't hurt us one bit to have a healthy portion of good, old-fashioned piety. No, I'm not talking about fake piety. I'm talking about a healthy, vital, up-to-date love for Jesus. Are you involved in a romance with the Lord? Is there an excitement in your relationship with him? Are you trusting him to follow through on the more than eight thousand promises he makes to you in his Word?

Let your child see your healthy love of Jesus.

2. Let Your Child See Habits of Life That Are Affected by This Love Relationship

What do you do with your money? That reveals most about who you are as a person. Do you tithe? This lets your children know that first things are first in your life.

What do you talk about? Is gossip, the running down of other people, normative in your life? Your children will pick up on that if it is. Are you addicted to alcohol? Some of us who are absolutely opposed to drugs forget that alcohol is our nation's most abused drug. Frequent government studies all conclude that, directly or indirectly, alcohol-related problems affect the lives of tens of millions of men, women, and children. Yet we go blindly ahead with this particular kind of drug abuse, holding the tiger by the tail, cursing our children's experimentation with other kinds of drugs. It is all the same problem.

Do you respect your body? The Bible talks about your body as God's temple. His Holy Spirit resides there. You and I have an investment responsibility to use our bodies the way they were created to be used, free from addiction to anything. This isn't only God's way—it's the smart way. That's because you and I were created to function, not to be impaired.

Now, I'm not talking about setting up some "don'ts" we all have to follow—that doesn't work. Nor am I talking about developing some negative standards to follow and enforce. I am talking about a positive lifestyle. Set the standard high. Where the Bible is clear, live by it. Where the Bible is unclear, with your own conscience, before God, decide how you are going to use your body and the freedoms God has given you in terms of habits of life. And then let your kids know how you came by your decision.

When they begin to be exposed to experimentation with drugs, alcohol, and sex, they will know where you as their parents stand and why you stand there. Where you have failed, let them know that as well.

I am convinced that one of the reasons so many parents are afraid to give sex information to their kids is that they are afraid the kids might ask, "Dad, did you go all the way before marriage?" or "Mom, were you a virgin on your wedding day?" Thank God if you as the dad can say no, or you as the mom can say yes. But if you can't, have the guts to admit where you were wrong and share how you have received the forgiveness and love of Jesus Christ, which filled the gap between who you are and what you know you should have been. Let them see, worked out in your life, an integrity that will turn them on in their faith, not turn them off.

3. Let Your Child See Your Honest Trust of God's Word

You don't have to go it alone. There is much relativity in the world today. Yet there are some absolutes that you can know and trust. The Bible tells you some absolutes about yourself, the nature of human-kind, the constant struggle we have between good and evil in this world. The Bible gives you an ethical system by which to live. Grab it. Run with it. Let your children see you put it to work in your own life.

The challenges we face today are nothing new. The middle of the eighteenth century in England was marked by enormous social upheaval. In many ways, the institutional church was striking out as it is today. Along came a man named John Wesley. We could use thousands like him today. His Christian faith was not something spontaneous, something that happened all at once. For a period of years, he searched for truth until finally, through the witness of a group of Moravian Christians and through an encounter at Aldersgate in London, his heart was "strangely warmed."

Now a converted man who had repented of sin and put his trust in Jesus Christ alone, Wesley didn't simply move on the emotional high he received. He became a man of the Book. With a Bible in hand, he traveled all over England. God touched that man who believed in the authority of his Word, and, in spite of the secularistic cynicism of that day, Wesley was God's instrument of revival. He was a man armed with the Word of God and who spoke with authority because he had the authority of the Bible.

Do you have this kind of trust in the Word of God? Is this book a constant companion? Are you exposing yourself to its teaching? Or is it stiff and dusty, lying unused on the shelf? Do you have an implicit trust in what it has to say? Unless you discover the Word of God, "the only infallible rule of faith and practice," your life has no authority. Perhaps you are committed to a vague, humanistic concept of the fatherhood of God and the brotherhood of man, the great principle extracted from the Word of God, but follow it void of the full counsel of God's Word, divinely revealed.

4. Let Your Child See You as Deeply Committed to Your Marriage Partner

The Bible tells us to "rejoice in the wife of your youth" (Prov. 5:18). I have already noted the exponential increase in divorce in our society. Please know that divorce is not the unforgivable sin. There is life after divorce. Our God is in the business of offering forgiveness and new life. At the same time, divorce is not the answer.

One of the most recent changes we are seeing in our society is the notion of a "mini-trial marriage." This is a tentative step into marriage by two people who are frightened by the commmitment, so they give it a go for several years without children with the thought that they can break up and start over if it doesn't work.

An increasing number are not even choosing to get married. A friend of mine recently said to me that she used to go to a lot of bridal showers for her friends. Now she is noting there are few bridal showers that precede the baby showers she's invited to. Her friends have chosen simply to live with a partner, to do what comes naturally, without the benefit of marriage or any long-term, legal commitment.

This is the logical outgrowth of the past decade in which we have trivialized marriage, minimized the meaning of commitment, and offered casual, no-fault divorce. We have produced a couple of generations of children who are scared of marriage and fearful of long-term commitment. After all, you could have your heart broken.

But as followers of Jesus Christ, we can model what it is to make the commitment "till death do us part." We can work through the tough stuff with the help of the Lord. We can grant space to our partner to be who they are in their differences from us, and still love them and be nurtured and nourished by those differences while remaining faithful and even fulfilled by the synergy that comes when two people so different have blended themselves in a lifelong commitment.

Back in the 1970s, I was invited one day to be the teaching resource guest in a sociology course at one of the local high schools. I asked the students in that class to tell me about their families. I discovered that 80 percent of those teenagers had been raised in Newport Beach and that their parents had divorced. A number of their fathers were living with a new live-in or a new wife and her children in Newport Beach. Their mothers were trying to raise these kids in scaled-down economic conditions in nearby Costa Mesa, a more affordable community. That was a quarter of a century ago. And we wonder why that generation is so scared of long-term commitments.

5. Let Your Child See Your Unconditional Love toward Other People Who Are Different from Yourself

Perhaps God is in charge of your life. You love Jesus Christ. Your habits are under his scrutiny. You have an honest trust in the Word of God. You are living in deep commitment to your marriage partner. But maybe all of these things have never seeped through to your attitude toward other people.

Kids notice when you are critical of others. I know one woman who is blind to her own shortcomings but is quick to see every speck wrong in the life of a fellow Christian. Her children, and many of those around her, can see the hypocrisy in her attitudes. And your kids will see it in you, if it's there. Even those who don't accept Christ are to be loved in his name.

The Bible says, "If I speak in the tongues of men and of angels, but have not love, I am only a resounding gong or a clanging cymbal. If I have the gift of prophecy and can fathom all mysteries and all knowledge, and if I have a faith that can move mountains, but have not love, I am nothing. If I give all I possess to the poor and surrender my body to the flames, but have not love, I gain nothing" (1 Cor. 13:1–3).

There is one major complaint the younger generation levels against the older. It is that we fail to practice the love that we preach. What a loveless crew we are. It is so hard for us to love one another, much less those who are not our brothers and sisters in Christ. The world whispers, "Hypocrites!" and our own children, if they are honest, may very well be saying the same thing about us. We need to practice loving others, whether we agree with them or not.

In the same way, you and I don't have to agree with everything our children do. But we dare not withhold our love from them. Our love must be unconditional love. That's the kind of love God has for you and me. It is his unconditional love that has wooed us back to himself when we've strayed. It is that kind of love reflected in us that, ultimately, God will use to win our children, both to him and to us.

6. Let Your Child See and Hear Your Spiritual Teaching in the Home and in the Church

Did you notice the instruction given to us in that great passage in Deuteronomy 6? Moses charged parents, "These commandments that I give you today are to be upon your hearts. Impress them on your children. Talk about them when you sit at home and when you walk along the road, when you lie down and when you get up" (Deut. 6:6–7). You are to be a teacher in your home. That's where your children will learn the most. They are crying out, "Teach me of Christ—by your words and your everyday life."

An attractive college woman recently paid her mother the supreme compliment when she said, "My mother is the best Christian I have ever known." Your children want to hear something from your lips. And they want to see it backed up by your life.

A young man shared how he remembers only one time when his parents ever prayed with him. He called it one of the most significant days he could remember from his childhood. How long has it been since you last prayed with your spouse? When was the last time you prayed with your children? Perhaps you are missing one of your finest opportunities for bringing unity into your home.

Begin to pray together as a family, joining hands on those occasions when you are able to have meals together. Initially it will be difficult. There may be some embarrassment. Richard C. Halverson once said, "Pride is at the bottom of this—we all tend to shy away from situations we aren't sure we can handle—and this pride needs to be disciplined." Personal humiliation is a small price to pay for raising godly children. A few verses read from the Scriptures along with a discussion over the table will gradually bring growth.

There is also the teaching that comes through the church. Are you faithful in attendance? Do you go out of your way to take, not send, your children to Sunday school? Do you support, with your work and money, Christ's church? Your children will learn from your clear-cut identification with God's people. It's important business!

God's Word promises that if we bring up children in the way they should go, when they are old they will not depart from it. Raising our children this way means we must give them something to rebel against. Do it lovingly, do it prayerfully, do it humbly. Then let them go as God has let you go. And trust him and the Holy Spirit to do his work in their lives, in his time, and in his way.

I remember at the age of seventeen stalking out of the living room, flinging at my folks the words, "You don't understand. I can't stay around this place anymore!" And I slammed the door shut behind me. Inside that house, I was an uncontrolled giant of passion and rebellion. Outside in the night I was a tall, skinny, scared kid who ran down the street away from home, tears streaming down my face.

Thank God I had something to rebel against. I was a kid who was running away *not from nothing but from something*. I was running away from parents who loved Jesus Christ, whose habits backed their life, who were faithful to the Word of God, who were committed to each other, whose attitudes toward other people, to the best of their ability, reflected their faith—parents who had been faithful in teaching me at home and going with me to church.

Show me a kid who has not had the urge to run, and I'll show you one who hasn't got what it takes to live. Show me the parents who, with God's help, have done their best, and I'll show you a kid who, no matter how far away he runs, has something and someone to whom he or she can return. It is Jesus Christ who can redirect the rebel in us all.

Questions to Discuss

1. How do you think your children would evaluate the quality of your marriage? Could you possibly discuss this with them to see what observations and suggestions they might have for you?
2. What evidences might your children see of a healthy love of Jesus in your life?
3. Are there times when you may unintentionally convey a hypocritical lifestyle by the unloving attitude you express in front of your children toward people who are different from you?
4. Are you giving your children something to rebel against? If so, what? Be specific.

For Further Reading

Caldwell, Elizabeth F. *Making a Home for Faith: Nurturing the Spiritual Life of Your Children.* Cleveland: Pilgrim Press, 2000.

Cline, Foster W., and Jim Fay. *Parenting with Love and Logic: Teaching Children Responsibility.* Colorado Springs: Pinion Press, 1992.

Worthington, Kirby, and Everett L. Worthington Jr. *Value Your Children: Becoming Better Parental Disciple-Makers.* Grand Rapids: Baker Books, 1995.

Yorkey, Mike. *The Christian Family ANSWER BOOK.* Wheaton: Victor Books, 1996.

2

WHEN HUSBAND AND WIFE BECOME MOM AND DAD

Les and Leslie Parrott

I f ever there was a husband and wife ready to become a mom and dad, it was Kevin and Judy. With their first baby on the way, their excitement was palpable. They prepared the nursery right down to a neatly ordered stack of diapers, signed up for Lamaze courses, and were reading all the *What to Expect* books. Late at night as they lay in bed they'd talk about their future with a baby. What they didn't realize was that they were not only giving birth to a new human, they were giving birth to a new marriage. Ready or not, they were about to be sucked into a huge force that would propel them through a passage from which they would emerge changed. Every new mom and dad goes through it.

When you have a child, you are still yourself, but now, as a mother or father, you are some new version of yourself. And you are standing in the middle of some new version of your marriage. Make no mistake about it, the birth of each child signals a serious and permanent alteration in your marriage. The alteration is, of course, deeply enriching if not miraculous, but for the majority of couples it is also somewhat confusing if not downright challenging.

Shortly after the birth of our first child, a friend warned us—with a huge smile—of the changes ahead. He literally gave us a list of ways to know the next few years would not be what we were used to. Here are a few of our favorites:

- You both fall asleep by nine o'clock in the evening after watching the beginning credits of the video you rented for after the baby's asleep.
- You're late to an appointment because you've spent twenty minutes looking for your baby's binky.
- You put on your best black suit for an important engagement, and you have to change before getting out the door because your left shoulder is wearing the baby's formula.
- You measure your sleep in minutes instead of hours.
- You realize your CD player isn't broken; your toddler has simply placed a few pennies in the slot where the CDs go.
- You ask your wife about making love, and she just chuckles.
- You ask your husband about going out for a romantic dinner, and he asks, "Which bill would you like to *not* pay this month?"
- An exciting Friday evening is standing in the family room and watching your baby try to roll over.

We know all too well that these descriptors are not just tongue-in-cheek. As I (Les) write these words, it is late in the evening—very late. Our five-year-old son is sound asleep, and so is Leslie. The house could not be quieter or more still. But not for long. Why? Because we have a new little baby, just nine months old, who's not quite sleeping through the night, and I know that somewhere around two-thirty in the morning he's going to wake up crying. So I'm taking the late shift and getting some writing in before the alarm sounds. It's all part of the package when a husband and wife become a mom and dad.

When Baby Makes Three

Studies show that when baby makes three, conflicts increase eight-fold. Marriage takes a backseat, women feel overburdened, and men feel shoved aside. By the baby's first birthday, most mothers are less happy about their marriage, and some are wondering whether their marriage will even make it. Baby-induced marital meltdowns are not uncommon. With the help of researchers like Dr. John Gottman, at the University of Washington, here's what we know for sure. In the year after the first baby arrives, 70 percent of wives experience a precipitous plummet in their marital satisfaction. For the husband, the dissatisfaction usually kicks in later as a reaction to his wife's unhappiness.[1] It has little to do with whether a couple's baby is colicky or a good sleeper, whether she is nursing or bottle-feeding, or whether the mother is working or staying at home. It simply has to do with how a little addition shifts the whole dynamic within a household.

How can something as good as a baby turn a marriage so bad? We could point to a wide range of reasons: lack of sleep, feeling overwhelmed and unappreciated, the awesome responsibility of caring for such a helpless little creature, juggling chores and other economic stress, and lack of time to oneself, among other things. The root reason, however, is no big mystery. In plain language, children take time and attention away from a marriage. They suck all the hours out of the day and fill up every spare cell in your brain. Being a parent is wonderful, only somehow it has made being a spouse different.

"Before kids, I was thrilled to hear my husband's voice on the phone," said Judy a few years into motherhood. "Now after a day of meetings and phone calls and carpools and wet swimsuits, I sometimes wonder who is this guy who seems to want food, an audience, and—he's got to be joking—sex?"

Isn't it romantic?

Of course not. But a lack of romance and intimacy isn't inevitable during this phase of marriage. The fact is, these are the good times, and that guy leafing through his mail oblivious to the baby's cries is your partner. That woman who used to give you back rubs and is now busy cleaning peanut butter off door handles is your soul mate. Someday you're going to look back on this period fondly, but only if both of you can keep this good thing from turning bad.

A Task for Dad: Turning "Us" to "We"

Motherhood brings every new mom a bassinet full of new feelings. She has never felt a love as deep and selfless as the one she feels for her child. She almost always experiences a profound new meaning in her life. She discovers she is willing to make enormous sacrifices for her child. "The experience is so life-altering," says John Gottman, "that if her husband doesn't go through it with her, it is understandable that distance would develop between them."

So the key to keeping a good marriage good while Mom is experiencing an intensely wonderful transformation is for Dad to undergo the same thing. In other words, marital success has everything to do with whether the husband experiences the transformation to parenthood along with his wife. If not, he gets left behind, pining for the old "us," while his wife is embracing a new sense of "we" that includes their child.

A new father often resents how little time his wife has for him (especially in their sex life) now that they have a baby. He resents how tired she always is. He loves his child, but he wants his wife back the way she was. What's a husband to do? Get over his whining and follow her into the new realm she has entered. He has to become a father as well as a husband. He must cultivate feelings of pride, tenderness, and protectiveness for his offspring. In other words, he must see his journey into parenthood as a sign and an opportunity for significant personal growth.

A Task for Mom: Reframe Romance

All the responsibility for navigating a good marriage through the unknown channels of parenthood does not rest with the husband alone. A new mother often resents the lack of emotional romance her husband now brings to the marriage. *He's changed*, you may think. *He's more distant*. In actuality, his efforts to embrace this new "we" has probably sidetracked the energy he put into your old romance. And the more stock you put in romance before the baby was born, the more loss you will feel when your busy husband seems disconnected.

If you were taught to believe that happy couples must be romantic ones, you may mourn the loss of romance way out of proportion to its worth. "But it's so little to ask," you say. "Just a bunch of flowers once in a while to let me know he remembers." If you give romance more importance than it deserves, you may become even more troubled and say, "Maybe he's lost interest in me."

The problem for parents with this kind of reasoning is found in how they define romance. We tend to think of it as that knee-weakening, heart-pounding, earth-moving spasm that occurs with our spouse. But is it realistic to expect that kind of dazzle during motherhood? Maybe, but probably not to the degree you enjoyed it before kids came along. A moonlit stroll with your new husband, for example, is distinctly different from that same stroll six years later, when you've wrestled the kids to bed, the sink is filled with dirty dishes, and you still have laundry to do. Romance doesn't need to end with parenthood, but it may need to take a new form while your husband works to find his place as a father.

The bottom line? As a new mom and new dad, you each have your role in keeping a good marriage going. Dads need to work at entering their wives' new world, and moms need to give their husbands space to do so.

But there's more. Much more.

Having Kids and a Sex Life Too?

One of the biggest complaints we hear from parents in our counseling office is that passion and intimacy become quite a challenge. We certainly concur. While we were speaking at a large marriage conference not long ago, after our session we slid into a workshop whose topic caught our eye: "How to Have Kids and a Sex Life Too." Workshop leaders Pam and Rich Batten warmed up the group by asking couples which movie title best described their sex life: *The Fast and the Furious, What's the Worst That Could Happen?* or *The Mummy Returns.* There wasn't a show of hands, but *Dr. Doolittle* got the most chuckles.

In the discussion that followed, couples were quick to rattle off obstacles to a satisfactory love life: no energy, no privacy, no spontaneity, kids banging on doors, kids barging in, and so on. Each complaint engendered nods and groans of agreement. It seems nearly every couple who become parents understand the struggle to keep their sex life filled with passion.

What most couples don't understand is how an intentional effort can keep the flames of passion burning strong, even between changing diapers and making formula. It's a point Leslie and I underscore in our book *The Love List*, in which we set aside theory and fluff and cut straight to what you can do—starting today—to give your marriage a boost. Our list reveals eight little things that make a big difference, and firing up passion may be the most frequently neglected. So we dedicate the rest of this chapter on how to stay connected as husband and wife when you become a mom and dad, to helping you keep your sex life strong.

Does It Really Matter?

Let's make this clear. Sex is critically important for a quality marriage. We'll say it again. Sex makes a significant impact on whether you will rate your marriage as satisfying or not. It is an aspect of your marriage you can't afford to let fade into the background.

In one survey on the importance of sex for marriage, the results were compelling: Couples who rated their sex lives positively also rated their marriages positively, and those who rated their sex lives negatively rated their marriages negatively as well. In other words, if couples report that sex is unimportant to them, it is very likely that they view their entire marriage as unhappy. Both the quantity and quality of sex in marriage are central to a good overall relationship.

As parents, you might be relieved to know that a number of factors other than frequency of sexual interaction also have been linked to satisfaction with marital sex. Mutuality in initiating sex can be an important contributor to the sexual satisfaction of both wives and husbands. It also appears that women who take an active role during sexual sharing are more likely to be pleased with their sex lives than those who assume a more passive role.

No study states that a high-quality sex life is an absolute requirement for a high-quality marriage, nor that a good sex life guarantees a good marriage. Nonetheless, studies consistently suggest that quality of sex and quality of marriage do go together in most cases.

Contrary to popular opinion, a married couple's sex life does not have to dissipate after having children. If you are intentional, marriage provides the greatest sex life possible. You have the opportunity to make your love life better than you ever imagined, even after parenthood, by cultivating this healthy habit of firing up passion. We'll warn you that it requires intentional work, but the dividends are invaluable for loving couples. Here's how.

How to Heat Up Passion, Even When You're Parents

Okay, let me (Leslie) have a quick word with the women. So you've been tugged, pulled, pinched, and gummed all day. The last thing on your mind is sex. I know just how you feel. But you're not the only one in this marriage. Not that you should completely set aside your own desires and become hot to trot in a new negligee each night between making baby bottles and changing diapers on less than three consecutive hours of sleep. But in case you haven't noticed, your husband's sex drive, in spite of the same lack of sleep, hasn't diminished since your baby came home.

And let me (Les) preface our suggestions with a quick word to the guys. If you're relatively sensitive, you realize your wife is not thinking about sex as much as she used to, and maybe not at all! Good for you. And maybe you haven't even mentioned it to your wife. Congratulations. But I know you're thinking about it. And I know you're looking for some small signal that provides hope that your sex life may someday return. It will. If you two put this little plan into practice, it will return more quickly than you might guess.

The following ideas are designed to help you fire up passion in your bedroom, and we begin by suggesting that you start with the basics. Assume that your partner doesn't know how to satisfy you. It doesn't matter how long you've been married; beginning with this premise will help you set the stage for increasing passion by asking for what you'd like most. That's the key, and research bears it out. In one survey, 88 percent of the women who reported discussing their sexual feelings with their spouses described their sex lives as good or very good. In contrast, only 30 percent of the women who reported never discussing sex with their partners described their sex lives as good or very good.[2]

What makes each of you happy is not necessarily the same thing. Your needs may be dramatically different. And they may have changed since you had your baby. So don't make the mistake of assuming your partner knows how to meet your sexual needs if you do not talk to each other about it. This is rule number one for firing up passion in the bedroom.

The second rule sounds so cold and unromantic. But make no mistake, a fulfilling sex life for almost every busy couple depends on it. At least once a month, schedule a specific time when the two of you can enjoy a leisurely time of passionate sex. We know this sounds artificial. We can hear you groaning right now. But please do not make the mistake of thinking this advice is for other couples. Every busy couple with a family can benefit from this. You can obviously have spontaneous sex anytime you are so inclined, but this once-a-month rendezvous is key to firing up passion in the bedroom. The next few points will show you how it works.

Once you agree on a time that will work, protect it. Pick a time when you are not distracted by kids or projects, and a time when you are not exhausted. This time is specifically set aside for the two of you. Don't allow something "urgent" to steal it away. Let's face it, a dozen potential things could interfere with your schedules. But hold to this time, knowing that your marriage is going to be better for it. Besides that, it's going to be a lot of fun.

If you are meeting at home over a long lunch hour or on a weekend when the kids are at Grandma's, be sure you think through what will make this time the best it can be for each of you. Do you want music? A clean house? Silk sheets on the bed? A time to shower beforehand? A bath together? Candles? What would be your ideal of how to make this time everything you want it to be? Talk it through. Don't make your spouse guess what you like; say what's on your mind.

And go shopping. In the weeks preceding your time together, be on the lookout for lingerie and such that will make this time special. Before we got married, somebody gave me (Les) a copy of Charlie Shedd's book *Letters to Phillip*, and in it he suggested that a husband should never skimp on the lingerie budget. Pretty good advice, especially for parents. You don't have to break the bank, but for these once-a-month occasions, it's a good idea to splurge a little.

Finally, part of what makes this once-a-month experience so beneficial to couples is the anticipation of it. Just knowing that you will have this dedicated time to enjoy each other to the fullest will make it all the more special. So give in to the anticipation. Say things to each other like, "Only one more week," "I can't wait for the eighteenth," or "Have you been thinking about our time like I have?" The point is to conjure up expectancy and eagerness. Don't allow your appointment simply to roll around on the calendar like any ordinary meeting. Give it special attention and let the excitement mount.

Well, there you have it—a few suggestions for keeping your love alive and well. Oh, and one more thing. Never forget that the best thing you will ever do for your children is build a strong marriage. The more loving you two are as a husband and wife, the better you'll be at being a mom and dad.

Questions to Discuss

1. How has having children affected your marriage relationship?
2. What conflicts have you experienced that you didn't experience before you had children? How did having children feed into these conflicts?
3. How has having children changed your sexual relationship? Your emotional relationship? Your sense of intimacy?
4. Which of the suggestions made in this chapter could you begin doing soon?

For Further Reading

Morgan, Elisa, and Carol Kuykendall. *When Husband and Wife Become Mom and Dad*. Grand Rapids: Zondervan, 1999.

Parrott, Les and Leslie. *When Bad Things Happen to Good Marriages: How to Stay Together When Life Pulls You Apart*. Grand Rapids: Zondervan, 2000.

3

Raising
Emotionally
Healthy Sons

Gary and Carrie Oliver

I've been told that as a little boy I (Gary) was fascinated with the stories of Peter Rabbit. It had been over thirty years since I'd looked at one of the beloved books by Beatrix Potter, so on a recent trip to England with my son Matt, I picked up a copy of the one-hundredth anniversary edition of *The Tale of Peter Rabbit* to refresh my memory.

The story starts out with Mother Rabbit getting her four children ready to go out and play. She has three daughters, Flopsy, Mopsy, and Cotton-tail, and one son, Peter. It's helpful to remember that Mother Rabbit is a single mom whose husband was killed and put in a pie by Mrs. McGregor when he ventured into Mr. McGregor's garden. That tragic event gives extra significance to the fact that before they go outside she tells them that they can go play out in the field or down in the lane but they can't go into Mr. McGregor's garden.

As the story unfolds we discover that the three daughters were good little bunnies. They hopped down the lane to gather berries. But Peter, the only boy, was very naughty and hopped as fast as he could to Mr. McGregor's garden. By the end of the story, Peter loses his lovely new coat and his shoes, and he almost loses his life. Naughty Peter comes home at night sick and tired and has to be put to bed while good little Flopsy, Mopsy, and Cotton-tail enjoy bread and milk and blackberries for supper. It doesn't matter whether you are a rabbit or a human; it's not easy to be a boy.

Probably one reason Dave and Jan asked us to contribute this chapter on raising boys is that we are the parents of three sons and have written an entire book on parenting boys entitled *Raising Sons and Loving It!* Having written a book and spoken around the country on the topic of raising sons, we had numerous discussions on what we could say in just one chapter that you the reader would find helpful.

Based on our own twenty-one years of experience parenting boys, as well as the feedback we've received from our book and speaking, it's clear that there is at least one thing that every parent of boys needs to understand to help their sons become mature and healthy men. Before we share that with you, here is some general information on boys you need to know to help you understand some of the unique challenges they face growing up in today's world.

The Challenge of Growing Up Male

Many young boys find themselves confused by society's mixed messages about what's expected of them, of what it really means to be a man. Raised in a culture that glorifies violence and says there are no absolutes, they feel out of touch with emotions they don't understand and don't know how to deal with. We've worked with many young men who felt a sadness and disconnection they couldn't even name. Even if they understood it, most of them didn't have the tools to talk about it or people they felt comfortable talking to.

It is not an exaggeration to say that today there is a crisis of masculinity. The media and television tempt boys to be sucked into a culture that equates masculinity with sexual experience. We live in a culture that is increasingly violent and provides opportunity for boys to express violence at a young age via video games. In our own research and endeavor to learn more about the male, we have discovered information that will help you better understand the boys God has given you to raise.

Most men have been taught how to pursue excellence as breadwinners, unfeeling human machines, and performers. Meanwhile, everything else has suffered. It's become clear during the past few decades that growing up male can be hazardous to your health. The following list of male-specific inequities, inferiorities, and wounds describes the male world in which we are raising our boys:

- Infant boys receive fewer demonstrative acts of affection from their mothers and are touched less than infant girls.
- Boys are talked to less and for shorter durations.
- Infant boys are more likely to be held facing outward, toward the world and other people. Girls are held inward, toward the security, warmth, and comfort of the parent.
- Infant boys crawl, sit, and speak later and tend to cry more, yet girl toddlers are more likely to get a positive response when crying for help than boys.
- When a child complains of a minor injury, parents are quicker to comfort girls than boys.
- Because boys are considered by most people to be emotionally tougher than girls, they are more often reprimanded in front of the whole class for misbehavior, whereas girls are more likely to be taken aside and spoken to more softly.
- Young boys are admitted to mental hospitals and juvenile institutions about seven times more frequently than girls of similar age and socioeconomic background.
- Boys are much more likely to suffer from a variety of birth defects. About two hundred genetic diseases affect only boys, including the most severe forms of muscular dystrophy and hemophilia.

- Boys are twice as likely as girls to suffer from autism and six times as likely to be diagnosed as having hyperkinesis.
- Boys stutter more and have significantly more learning and speech disabilities than girls. Some research suggests that dyslexia is found in up to nine times as many boys as girls.
- When boys become teenagers, they are told they must be prepared to be mutilated or die in our armed forces in order to protect women and children and the ideologies of their nation.
- In Vietnam more than 58,000 American men died in the war, compared to only eight women.
- Men have a 600 percent higher incidence of work-related accidents, and men die from work-related injuries approximately twenty to one over women.
- Suicide rates are about four times higher for men than women.
- Men make up about 80 percent of all homicide victims, are victims of about 70 percent of all robberies, and make up 70 percent of all other victims of aggravated assaults.
- Men's life expectancy is as much as nine years less than women's.
- Ninety-nine percent of the prisoners on death row are males.[1]

For twelve years we lived only a few miles from Columbine High School. Right next to Columbine is a lovely regional park where we spent hundreds of hours playing with our sons. We were perhaps more shocked than many when the tragic murders at Columbine occurred. What is even more tragic is that this was not an isolated incident. It was but one of many senseless murders by adolescents across the country. These stories were staggering and unbelievable. However, one common thread made these incidents even more distressing. In every single one of these shootings, the murderer was a boy. Recently a major network broadcaster reported that there are sixty-three adolescents on death row, and all of them are boys.

The incidents in Littleton, Colorado, and around our nation are only one indicator that these are difficult and challenging days to be a boy and to raise a boy. New research shows that boys are doing worse in school than they did in the past. (The 2002 National Assessment of Educational Progress exam, also known as "The Nation's Report Card," measured the writing skills of more than 200,000 fourth-, eighth-, and twelfth-graders, and when examined by subpopulations the results showed that girls outperformed boys.)[2] In comparison to girls, many seemingly strong boys have remarkably fragile self-esteem, and the rates of both depression and suicide in boys are frighteningly on the rise.

In addition to these troubling facts, research tells us that boys and girls are taught very different ways to deal with their emotions. The reality is that parents, in general, discuss emotions—with the exception of anger—more with their daughters than with their sons. Daniel Goleman cites research showing that girls are exposed to more information about emotions than are boys. When parents make up stories to tell their preschool children, they use more emotion words when talking to daughters than to sons. It's significant that when mothers play with their infants, they display a wider range of emotions to daughters than to sons. When mothers talk to their daughters about feelings, they go into much more detail about the emotional state itself than they do when talking with their sons—though with the sons they go into more detail about the causes and consequences of emotions like anger.[3]

Boys enter adolescence with a marked developmental disability in the area of understanding, expressing, and dealing with their emotions, and this deficit affects every area of their lives, especially their most intimate relationships. It's clear that much of this deficit can be attributed to the impact of both sin and socialization. At the same time, based on our personal and clinical experience as well as the results of recent research, it's become clear that another one of the major reasons males struggle so much with the emotional area is due to physiology. Replicated medical research suggests that boys bring what some have called a "biologically hardwired emotional disadvantage" to emotional and relational development.

In some ways it all starts with the male brain. As science continues to grow in its ability to use neural imaging scans, we are learning more about the differences between the male and female brain. Let's take a closer look at some male distinctives as they relate to emotional and relational development.

- The male brain is hardwired to be better at spatial relationships than emotional ones.

- The frontal lobes of the male brain, which handle many social and cognitive functions related to emotional relationships, develop more slowly in the male brain than in the female brain.
- The female brain has more gray matter, the active brain cells that perform thinking, than does the male brain. The female brain activates both sides of the brain more often, while the male brain lateralizes more often—i.e., restricts activity to one side of the brain (hence males may look at computer or television screens and not hear what spouses or parents are saying).
- With their increased blood flow, higher gray matter content, increased electrical activity, and more dual-functioning brain, adolescent and adult females on average score higher on communication- and social-skills tests than do males, and higher on emotional-recognition tests.
- The male brain is tuned to relate to nonemotional objects with less tension than emotional objects.
- The male brain system is actually emotionally fragile and often chooses to avoid emotional stimulation; meanwhile, his testosterone compels him to take huge physical risks and the social/professional risks of climbing corporate ladders and dominating fields of play. Many males experience a deep conflict between the awareness of their internal fragility and the need for external aggression. When a boy becomes an adolescent, this conflict increases.
- The male brain tends to avoid processing emotive data intensely. The way men tend to use the TV remote control demonstrates their brain formation. Males do not spend as much time as females focused on one topic of emotional or relational depth. If he does linger, he is more likely than the female counterpart to seek a quick solution.[4]

These are difficult and even dangerous times to raise boys. There is a crisis in masculinity. That's the bad news. The good news is that this is also a *great* time to raise a son. These are times of tremendous opportunities in growing young men with a love for the Lord, with a passion for truth, and with a commitment to character and integrity. One of the most important things Christian parents can do for their sons is to help them understand the importance of and provide them with modeling in the healthy expression of our God-given emotions.

Why Are Emotions So Important?

The first reason emotions are important is that they are a significant part of who God designed us to be when he made us in his image. It's no exaggeration to say that our emotions influence almost every part of our lives. God speaks to us through our emotions. They are like a sixth sense. God designed emotions to help us monitor our needs, make us aware of good and evil, and provide motivation and energy for growth and change. Emotions give us the vigor, force, power, and impetus for living.

Throughout the Bible God has a lot to say about emotions. From Genesis through Revelation we read about God's emotions and the emotions of the men, women, and children he created. In the New Testament we find that Christ experienced and expressed a wide range of emotions including love, compassion, joy, fear, sorrow, disappointment, discouragement, frustration, hurt, rejection, loneliness, and anger.

Emotions help us understand ourselves and others. Our emotions warn us when we are in danger or when our boundaries are being crossed or our rights are being violated. Emotions communicate what we value and what is important to us. If you can tell me what brings a person joy or what brings him or her to tears, I can tell you a lot about that individual.

Emotions give flavor to our interaction. They take what can be cold and impersonal and make it warm and personal. The appropriate expression of emotions can take a class or a conversation that tastes like boiled Spam and turn it into something that tastes more like prime rib with all the fixings.

Emotions are to a person's life what batteries are to a toy. They can add power, conviction, and intensity. There are times when I ask one of my boys to do something, and he interprets the tone of my voice to mean, "It's not really that important. You can do it whenever you happen to feel like doing it. Whenever the spirit happens to move

Knowing Your Emotions: This includes growing in your ability to recognize and name your emotions as well as being better able to understand the causes of feelings.

Managing Your Emotions: This involves better frustration tolerance and anger management, the use of fewer verbal put-downs, fewer fights and classroom disruptions, increased ability to express anger appropriately without fighting, and the ability to soothe yourself when upset and to regulate your own emotional state.

Emotional Self-Control: This is the ability to delay gratification, control impulses, pay attention, and focus on the task at hand.

Recognizing Emotions in Others: This is the ability to sense how your own words and/or behavior impacts the emotions of the other person.

Empathy: This is when you have the ability to take another person's perspective, the desire and ability to listen to others, and an increased sensitivity to the feelings of others.

Handling Relationships: This is when you are concerned about others, are considerate and cooperative, integrate skills in being a peacemaker and managing conflicts, and are prosocial and harmonious in groups.

you, that will be fine with me." Then there are other times when, without raising my voice, I can communicate in such a way that he feels my strong emotion and is motivated to spring into action immediately.

Regardless of age, everyone's emotional experiences are important. But they serve an especially critical role in our children's developmental process. Emotions are linked to everything children do and who they are becoming. Healthy emotional development is essential for the process of separating from Mom and Dad and developing healthy independence. It also facilitates the process of individuation or becoming the unique person God designed them to become.

Another reason emotions are important is that in more than thirty years of working with families, we've discovered that there can be long-term consequences for boys and girls who grow up in an emotionally handicapped family. What are some of these consequences? Let's take a look at Rick and Lonnie, who experienced the painful consequences of growing up in homes with parents who modeled unhealthy responses to emotions.

Rick grew up in a home where the male was the most important person in the house. His father, Dean, had all the power, he was always right, his needs always came first. The purpose of Mom and the kids was to compliment, honor, and obey Dad. The theoretical reason given for this was that it was the biblical model. The functional reason was so that Dean could feel good about himself. Independence was squelched, questions were discouraged, disagreements weren't allowed, and there was little open display of affection.

Dean was the kind of father who needed his kids to succeed to feel good about himself. He didn't mind if they expressed socially acceptable emotions, emotions that made him feel good and look good. However, by his example and his words, he taught his kids to repress any "negative emotions." He either discouraged them from or punished them for expressing any emotion that communicated weakness or pain. He didn't know how to deal with these kinds of emotions. Besides that, it made the family look bad.

Dean's children learned that you can't or shouldn't experience certain emotions. If you do, something is wrong with you. You are weak, you are inferior, you are a failure. If people ever find out you have these emotions, they will criticize, humiliate, and reject you. You must be especially careful about someone of the opposite sex finding out about the real you. If you let them see too much, they will leave you.

Imagine a young boy who grows up with this kind of an education. He gets into college, falls in love with a delightful young woman, and gets married. With the pressures of finishing college, finding a job, climbing the ladder in the company, and becoming a parent, there are many new challenges he must face, many decisions he must now make on his own, many new threats to his sense of competence and worth.

This is exactly what happened to Rick. He went to college and met and married Lonnie. As he struggled with each new challenge, he responded as he had been trained—to suppress his fear, hide his worries, and deny his doubts. He was the man and he should know what to do. If he was confused or discouraged, he must not show it. He should pretend that everything was fine. If he didn't, if Lonnie found out what an insecure weakling he really was, she would probably lose all respect for him. She might even want to divorce him.

Lonnie's childhood was a lot different from Rick's. She grew up in a home where her dad was an alcoholic. When he was sober he was a sensitive and wonderful father. When he was drunk he was totally unpredictable. She remembers as a child listening for him to come home from work. If the car tires screeched as he came in the driveway, she knew that she needed to stay out of the way. Whereas Rick grew up in an emotionless home, Lonnie grew up in a home where the expressions of emotions were inconsistent and out of control. At a young age she learned that emotions couldn't be trusted.

Twenty-five years later Rick and Lonnie came in for counseling. Rick was burned out from his job and close to having a nervous breakdown. His way of dealing with his enormous fear was either to work longer and harder or to medicate himself with a little alcohol. In time, he began to use alcohol as a way to deal with the struggles and complexities of life. It became his friend. He never got drunk. He only had a couple of drinks every day.

Lonnie was also burned out. But her burnout had come from spending twenty-five years trying to have a relationship with someone who, from her perspective, as a child had "relational bypass surgery." She loved Rick, but early in the marriage she realized that he was capable of only so much intimacy. The warmth and emotional intensity he had expressed while they were engaged seemed to vanish.

When the children came along, Lonnie discovered that her intimacy needs could be met by her children. She kept hoping and praying that Rick would change, but as the years rolled by, they became married singles. They lived together, slept together, shared the same home, family, and friends. But they were strangers. Now that the kids were grown, they were in the empty nest stage. Suddenly the stark reality of their relational bankruptcy hit with a force she could no longer deny.

However, there is a root cause to what Rick and Lonnie experienced. Both of them grew up in homes where there was poor emotional modeling. As children, neither one had seen a balance between mind, will, and emotions. They grew up with undernourished souls. They were the victims of emotional malnutrition. And the cost was high. Not only did they endure unnecessary isolation, frustration, pain, and relational mediocrity, but without intending to do so, they also passed on to their children an equally unhealthy legacy.

As Rick and Lonnie began to understand the nature of emotions and the importance of balancing the emotions with the mind and the will, a lot of things began to fall into place for them. Rick grew up in a home where emotions were ignored, and Lonnie grew up in a home where emotions were out of control. They realized that many of their problems stemmed from opposite yet equally dysfunctional perspectives on dealing with emotions. The lack of healthy emotional education and inability to balance all three dimensions of personality had caused them enormous heartache and almost cost them their marriage.

Another reason emotions are important is that there can be painful consequences for ignoring and not dealing with our emotions. Dr. John Gottman cites a nationwide random sample of more than two thousand American children, rated by their parents and teachers—first in the mid-1970s and then in the late 1980s—that found a long-term trend for children, on average, to be dropping in basic emotional and social skills. According to this research, on average, they became more nervous and irritable, more sulky and moody, more depressed and lonely, more impulsive and disobedient—and they went down on more than forty indicators.[5]

For years we have worked with men who, as young boys, never learned how to understand and value their emotions, let alone deal with them. They have spent their entire life struggling with and trying to overcome the consequences of these unhealthy emotional habits. Their emotional illiteracy has been a major contributor to a wide range of problems that have complicated their lives and compromised their most important relationships.

When we ignore our emotions, we cut off one of the most important aspects of our lives. Many of the problems that plague and paralyze adults have their roots in unhealthy emotional habits that were developed in childhood. The good news is that we don't have to be adults to begin to develop healthy emotional habits. Even with our youngest sons we can send the message that in this family it is safe to feel. As they get older we can begin to give them a vocabulary so they can talk about and describe what they are feeling. Then they can learn how to differentiate between experiencing and expressing an emotion.

Some of the consequences of inadequate emotional development include a partial and inadequate knowledge of self; an increased tendency to find your identity, meaning, and purpose in life from getting approval and affirmation from other people; a blurred vision of what is normal; poor physical health; and an increased tendency to become codependent and become involved in unhealthy and one-sided relationships.

Arrested emotional development hinders our ability to relate to God and hear his voice. It hinders our ability to grow as individuals, and it hinders our relational development. We don't know who we are or what we need. It's harder to understand and thus appreciate others. We don't know what to give them, and even if we did know what they needed, we might not have it to give.

When we withhold our emotions, it can keep others from knowing who we really are. When we conceal our emotions, they become more complex and difficult for us to understand. If we never express sadness, sorrow, or grief, if we are "up" all of the time, if everything is perfect and wonderful, we are lying to ourselves and robbing our sons of a healthy model of emotions as well as an opportunity to develop healthy emotional skills.

When we don't share our emotions with others, they don't know what is most important to us. If we don't have an appropriate emotional response, we not only lose out on getting our needs met but rob others of the opportunity to give to us in our time of need. Concealing our emotions only increases isolation, leads to misunderstanding, and causes everyone to lose.

The final reason healthy emotional development is important is that it's essential for personal and professional success. We all want our children to be successful, so we send them to school, we insist that they do homework, and we work with them to get good grades so that they can get into good schools and get a good education and be successful. Between my wife and me, we have seven earned degrees, so we obviously believe that a formal education is valuable. However, that's only a part of the education our boys need.

For many years educators believed that IQ, the intellectual domain, was the key to success. In the last decade or so, science has discovered a tremendous amount about the role emotions play in our lives. Researchers have found that even more than IQ, our emotional awareness and ability to handle feelings will determine our success and happiness in all walks of life, including family relationships. We've seen people much smarter than we are with much more biblical knowledge than we have flounder on the shoals of unbridled passions and unruly impulses. The harsh reality is that people with high IQs can be remarkably poor pilots of their private lives.

Many people are surprised to learn that more than thirty years of research tells us that at best, IQ contributes about 20 percent to the factors that determine life success, which leaves 80 percent to other forces. These other forces or factors have been called emotional intelligence: abilities such as being able to motivate oneself and persist in the face of frustrations; to control impulse and delay gratification; to regulate one's moods and keep distress from swamping the ability to think; to empathize and to hope. Beyond any shadow of a doubt, learning how to give your sons a "heart start" will give them a "head start" on life.

We're not exaggerating when we say that an awareness of our God-given emotion is the foundation on which everything else builds. Our boys need to learn how to balance the emotional and rational mind, with their emotions feeding valuable information into the rational mind, and the rational mind learning how to integrate and weigh that information and sometimes choosing to veto the input from the emotions.

Six Steps to Cultivating an Emotionally Healthy Son

So far we've established the challenges facing boys as they navigate the rapids of becoming young men and the challenges facing the parents who love and care for them. We've established the significance of healthy emotional development

What Is Emotional Intelligence?	
1. Self-Awareness	Emotional Self-Awareness
	Accurate Self-Assessment
	Self-Confidence
2. Self-Management	Emotional Self-Control
	Transparency
	Adaptability
	Achievement Orientation
	Initiative
	Optimism
3. Social Awareness	Empathy
	Organizational Awareness
	Service Orientation
4. Relationship Management	Developing Others
	Inspirational Leadership
	Change Catalyst
	Influence
	Conflict Management
	Teamwork and Collaboration

as one of the core gifts we can give our boys. Now the question is, just how can we do it? How can we raise emotionally healthy sons?

While love is important, it's clear that love isn't enough. The parents of the two young male shooters in the Columbine tragedy loved their sons, but obviously that wasn't enough. Dr. John Gottman's research found that very concerned, warm, and involved parents often had attitudes toward their own and their children's emotions that got in the way of them being able to talk to their children when they were sad or afraid or angry.[6] His research team encountered a group of parents who did a few very simple things with their children when they were emotional. These children who received emotional coaching from their parents had more general abilities including:

- Being able to regulate their own emotional states
- Better at soothing themselves when they were upset
- Better at calming down their hearts faster
- Had fewer infectious illnesses
- Better at focusing and attending
- Relating better to other people, even in the tough social situations they encountered in middle childhood (such as getting teased, during which being overly emotional is a liability, not an asset)
- Better at understanding people
- Better at situations in school that required academic performance

Our own personal and professional experience is that this key to raising healthy children isn't found in rigid rules, complex theories, or convoluted formulas for behavior. It is based on your God-given feelings of love and affection for your child and is demonstrated simply through empathy and understanding. Good parenting begins in our hearts as we start each day in prayer for our kids. It continues throughout the day on a moment-to-moment basis as we learn how to engage our children when feelings run high, when they are sad, angry, or scared. We agree with John Gottman that "the heart of parenting is being there in a particular way when it really counts."[7]

Here are a few simple and practical steps that, in addition to the other great suggestions in this book, will help you grow emotionally and relationally healthy sons.

Step 1: Cultivate His Identity as an Image Bearer

One of the most important things we can teach our sons, one of the things that we must teach our sons at an early age, is that they have been made in the image of God. Knowing that you have been made in God's image can be a source of strength and encouragement for at least two reasons.

First of all, the fact that you are a redeemed image bearer is a powerful statement as to the position God has given you. It provides a solid basis for both your significance and security. The foundation of our identity is that we were created by God in his image. Understanding this allows our sons to escape from the cultural myths of masculinity and become free from the unrealistic expectations that have bound so many men. It provides a foundation for their growing sense of what being a man really means.

When Adam and Eve sinned, it damaged and distorted the image of God in man; it didn't destroy it. And the story doesn't end at the fall. After the fall come the cross and the empty tomb. Not only are we made in God's image, but our salvation was purchased with the blood of God the Son. Out of God's entire creation, only human beings were made in his image and redeemed by his blood.

If we help our boys develop a clear sense of what it means to be in Christ, to have been made in the image of God, and to have been redeemed by the Son of God, their identity will be person-based (who they are in Christ) and not performance-based (what they do on their own).

Step 2: Understand the Significance of Healthy Emotions for Spiritual, Intellectual, and Relational Growth

An occupational hazard of being human is that we will experience emotions. The experience of emotions may be positive or negative.

It may be pleasurable or painful. But it is not optional! When God created us in his image, he gave us a mind, a will, and emotions. We can acknowledge them or ignore them. We can control our expression of them or let them control us.

Emotions are intended by God, designed by God, and created by God to enrich and enhance our lives, to be a potentially powerful and positive force for good. Emotions enhance our ability to be in relationship with him and with one another. But due to the fall and the effects of sin in our lives, our emotions, like our mind and our will, have become damaged and distorted. For many, the emotions that God gave to make life more meaningful instead make life more miserable.

A recent massive survey of parents and teachers "shows a worldwide trend for the present generation of children to be more troubled emotionally than the last: more lonely and depressed, more angry and unruly, more nervous and prone to worry, more impulsive and more aggressive."[8]

One of the major reasons parents bring children to counselors is because of emotional problems. If these problems have been unidentified and ignored, they may be disguised as problems with performance in school or physical problems such as stomachaches, headaches, or sleep problems. But most of the time they are, at the core, emotional problems.

A key to helping children grow to mature adults is to help them understand the role of emotions in their lives. Many children carry around a deep inner turmoil that remains carefully hidden from view to all but the most trusted of companions. This turmoil can be caused by problems at home, separation or divorce, sibling rivalry, illness, parent criticism, loneliness or boredom, and family financial difficulties. Problems at school can include pressure to conform academically, being humiliated by the teacher or laughed at by students, intense competition in class or during after-school sports, being excluded from group activities, getting low or failing grades, and the threat of violence.

Some children are better equipped to deal with these problems than others. They show no clearly observable effects. Other children develop headaches and stomachaches, restlessness, decreased concentration, increased irritability, aggressiveness, tight muscles, anger, anxiety, and depression.

When you take the time to help your children understand their feelings, accept them, and express them in creative ways, you are doing them a big favor. The way we handle our feelings as children seems to be fundamental to how happy we are as adults. If a child learns how to face fear, rebound from rejection, and grow through grief, he or she is more likely to grow into a healthy adult.

The reality is that emotional development is vital to your son because it is the key to his becoming a whole person, to his happiness and fulfillment. Research tells us that emotionally mature people typically live realistic, positive, productive, and happy lives. On the other hand, emotionally immature people inevitably live self-centered, irresponsible, and unhappy lives.

Emotional problems can be the cause of or a major contributor to problems in the family. This is because emotions are a key to helping people understand each other. When we communicate our emotions, we have the opportunity to check out what we are feeling. We can let others know not only about our need but also the intensity or depth of our need. Our emotional responses serve as cues to others as to what's going on in our lives and how we need them to respond to us.

When people express their emotions, it helps us better understand who they are and what is important to them. It gives us a hint as to how they are interpreting and experiencing the world. If we can understand someone else's feelings, it is more likely that we will be able to understand them and empathize with their behavior.

Most of the parents we've worked with were surprised to learn that emotions are related to academic performance. Research tells us that emotions can facilitate or hinder learning. Feelings can hold the key to academic success. When children's emotions are ignored or hidden from sight, they can sabotage a child's efforts to succeed.

There is growing neuropsychological evidence supporting the central role that the emotions have in learning. Dr. Thomas Armstrong writes about the significant relationship between feeling and thinking in the learning process. "We tend to think of learning—at least academic learning—as a mental process. Yet recent evidence from the brain sciences suggests that the emotions are vital to higher abstract thinking processes." He concludes, "It's really this balance between feeling and thinking that's most important in the education of the child. . . . Emotionally flat classrooms fail to teach because they neglect the emotional brain."[9] When emotions are acknowledged as real and given an opportunity for appropriate expression, they can pave the way for effective learning to occur.

In terms of our children, what Dr. Armstrong is really saying is that children will often get more out of the *way* something is being taught than from *what* is being taught. Sometimes the emotional tone of the classroom has greater impact than the specific content of the curriculum. If information is taught to our children with anger, enthusiasm, lethargy, or sadness, how it was taught may stand out much more in children's minds than the specific facts or ideas contained in the lesson.

What is true in the classroom is also true in the home.

Step 3: Be Aware of Your Own Emotions

Unfortunately, many of us are like Rick and Lonnie in that we don't understand our emotions and don't know how to share them. The deeper the emotion the more difficult it is to share. We may cry at the wrong time, laugh at the wrong time, or get angry at the wrong time. We've had years of training on how to communicate our ideas with clarity yet precious little training in clearly communicating our feelings. When we do try to express our emotions, we may come on too strong or not strong enough. We get embarrassed. People misunderstand. We decide it's safer not to risk the humiliation of being rejected or laughed at, so we don't share.

Some people try to hide in their intellect to keep themselves from the pain of feeling what they never learned how to understand. David Mains writes:

> For a large part of my life I was tuned out emotionally. I wasn't aware of where others were coming from, and I didn't even understand my own feelings.
>
> I was probably extreme in that regard. I didn't know when I was tired. I seldom paid attention to whether I was hot or cold. I wasn't in touch with what I liked or didn't like. If someone would ask me what was wrong, instead of saying, "I feel trapped with no way out of this situation," I'd reply, "I'm OK, why do you ask?"

Most of the time if someone accused me of expressing a negative emotion like anger or pride or frustration, I denied it. Was I stomping mad? No. Did I swear: Had my words stopped making sense because of my intense emotion? Never. What do you mean I was angry? You're accusing me of not acting the way a Christian should!

"You were emoting," my wife would tell me the next day. "It was as if you were sending out waves and waves of high voltage electricity. I don't understand how everybody can sense that except you."

Well, I wasn't in tune with my anger, my pain, my loneliness, my defensiveness, my fears, delights, moods, embarrassment, jealousies, whatever.

I functioned relatively well in the objective world of ideas and facts and words. But the more subjective realm of feeling was atrophying, shriveling up within me.

Thank God that in recent years the Lord has been doing a major healing in me for which I'm extremely grateful. One of the signs of health is that my feelings are coming back into play.[10]

Mains adds that now when he reads the Bible he sees how much the Bible has to say about emotions. When he goes to church he often finds himself filled with inexplicable joy. He is able to shed tears when he is hurt or when he finds he has hurt someone else. He is better able to discern when he has let himself become too busy and needs a rest.

Step 4: Be Aware of Each Boy's Emotional Responses and Unique Patterns

There is a railroad crossing near our home with a sign that all of you have seen before. It says, "Stop, Look, Listen." An essential step in raising emotionally healthy boys is for us to become students of them.

My wife and I have spent untold hours talking about the different emotional responses and patterns of each of our boys. In dealing with the emotion of anger, one of our sons is a hot reactor and can lose his temper in a millisecond. Once he is angry it takes him a long time to get over it. Another one of our sons gets angry quickly, but he also gets over it quickly. Yet another one rarely gets angry, and when he does he gets over it quickly. Three boys with three different anger patterns needing three different kinds of understanding and guidance.

When Nathan was in seventh grade, he came home from school one day, stomped in the house, slammed the front door, stomped up the stairs, and slammed his bedroom door. This wasn't at all like his normal pattern, so I (Gary) knew something was wrong. Because Nathan is more introverted, I gave him some time to be alone in his room and sort through his feelings.

When I finally went into his room, I asked him what had happened at school. While he was slow to open up, he finally told me that a bigger kid had made fun of him and embarrassed him in front of his friends. We were able to talk about how the embarrassment made him feel hurt and how the hurt was able to become anger. If God hadn't allowed me to see this as a teachable moment, I would have stomped right up the stairs and told him in no uncertain terms that he shouldn't slam the doors. That only would have increased his frustration and his anger. The only thing Nathan would have learned was to stay away from certain kids at school and hide your emotions from your parents so that you won't get in trouble.

Instead of that lesson, Nathan learned that it is okay to be angry but that there are better ways to express anger than stomping and slamming. He learned that underneath the secondary emotion of anger are often primary emotions such as fear and/or hurt and/or frustration. He learned that when he is experiencing anger, he is also experiencing one or two other emotions, and by identifying and addressing those emotions, he can resolve the emotional pain he is experiencing. We were able to close our time together in prayer, thanking God for our emotions and for the fact that he can cause all things, even being embarrassed by a kid at school, to work together for good (Rom. 8:28).

Step 5: Listen Emphatically, Validate Feelings, and Help Verbally Label Emotions

One of the things that helped Gary be effective with Nathan in that situation is that he listened carefully to Nathan. He didn't butt in or finish his sentences for him. He also validated his emotion of anger.

He didn't validate the way he chose to express it, but he did validate the fact that anger is a God-given emotion and that there are healthy and unhealthy ways to express it. He helped Nathan identify the emotion of anger and the underlying emotions of hurt and frustration.

When we help our sons verbally label their emotions, it gives them a sense of control over them. Whenever we allow our emotions to control us, we get in trouble. When we are able to verbally label our emotions, we have taken an enormous first step toward being able to deal with them in a healthy way.

Step 6: Set Appropriate Limits While Helping to Discover Healthy Ways to Express and Deal with Emotions

Before Gary left Nathan's room, they talked about the possibility of the same school situation happening again and what it could look like to express his emotions in more constructive ways. Even though he was only in seventh grade, Nathan was able to generate several healthier responses.

So Now What?

Certainly we need to train our boys to have the mind of God and to train their will to make wise choices, but the crying need for boys today is to understand and cultivate their heart. We've written this chapter to help you discover what it means to be a wise and understanding parent of boys. Children who walk with emotionally healthy parents, children who hear and see emotionally healthy parents in action, are more likely to become emotionally healthy themselves with the capacity to develop deep and intimate relationships and model to the world the difference that Christ can make in a life.

We would all agree that good parents are concerned with the behavior of their children. Yet it's easy for us to get distracted by a child's behavior, especially if that child is a boy. Our appropriate concern with their performance can take priority over their person. What they do and how they act can become more important to us than what they are becoming.

Emotionally healthy parents are much more concerned with the condition of their boys' hearts. Emotionally healthy parents are concerned with far more than imparting the correct information or making sure their kids know what kinds of activities they should abstain from. Emotionally healthy parents don't merely discuss and dissect truth; they demonstrate the power, freshness, and relevance of truth manifested in the context of healthy relationships.

Yes, there are many powerful cultural influences that affect and shape our kids. But by God's grace we can still be the most powerful influence in their lives. Parenting is not just providing good input. It is not just creating a constructive home atmosphere and positive interaction between a child and his parent. The ultimate goal of Christian parenting is not kids who merely have a knowledge about God. It is kids who have a personal relationship with God. It is kids who really believe that God's Word is relevant for every aspect of their lives. It involves teaching our children the ways of God, helping them understand the character of God, helping them become sensitive to the darkness of their own hearts, and helping them be aware of the danger of walking alone and trusting in themselves. It involves teaching them the power of the cross and the provision of God's promises.

God has called us to lead, guide, nurture, correct, and discipline our children. God has sovereignly placed us in authority over our children, and we must be willing to assume that responsibility. In Genesis 18:19 God speaks of Abraham when he says, "For I have chosen him, so that he will direct his children and his household after him to keep the way of the LORD by doing what is right and just." In Ephesians 6:4 we are commanded to bring up our children "in the training and instruction of the Lord." Our boys are more likely to become emotionally and relationally healthy young men as they see us modeling and instructing and providing wise direction before them.

Questions to Discuss

1. What was your experience growing up concerning the way boys were taught to deal with the world of emotions? In what ways do you want things to be different with your boys?

2. What have you seen to be the consequences of men not understanding their emotions?
3. Where do you struggle with your own emotions?
4. How can you better cultivate your son's identity as an image bearer?
5. What do you want to do differently the next time your son has an emotional outburst of some kind?

For Further Reading

Dobson, James. *Bringing Up Boys: Practical Advice and Encouragement for Those Shaping the Next Generation of Men.* Wheaton: Tyndale, 2001.

Lee, Steve, and Chap Clark. *Boys to Men: How Fathers Can Help Build Character in Their Sons.* Chicago: Moody, 1995.

Lewis, Robert, and Stu Weber. *Raising a Modern-Day Knight.* Colorado Springs: Focus on the Family, 1999.

Oliver, Gary J., and Carrie E. Oliver. *Raising Sons and Loving It!* Grand Rapids: Zondervan, 2000.

Wright, H. Norman, and Gary J. Oliver. *Raising Kids to Love Jesus: A Biblical Guide for Parents.* Ventura, CA: Regal Books, 1999.

4

RAISING CONFIDENT DAUGHTERS

Lisa Graham McMinn

Apparently Christmas break lasted too long. Sarah, our twenty-one-year-old daughter, felt restless after ten days at home and drove back to her house in Grand Rapids where she lived while attending Calvin College. The next day she called, after having spent a long afternoon and night alone in her apartment. She still had a couple of days before classes started and felt foolish now for thinking she'd rather be in Grand Rapids than at home. Driving the three and a half hours to return felt foolish too—a poor use of miles on her 1998 Ford Escort.

"But cars are intended to be driven," I said.

"Do you think it would be okay for me to come home then?" she asked.

"It sounds like a better idea than spending two more lonely days there," I replied. Our youngest daughter, Megan, had just left for a three-week trip to Indonesia, and our oldest daughter, Rae, had already flown back home to Montana. My husband, Mark, was in California for the week. Sarah's company for two days sounded pretty good to me. About four hours later she coasted into the driveway, and we had two days to nurture a tenderness between us that had been growing throughout the fall, a bonding unique to us in our now adult mother-daughter relationship. We talked about a number of issues that reflected her attempt to live by values Mark and I (and she) had been infusing in her life throughout childhood.

Intentionally or not, parents start instilling values in their daughters in infancy. Some of these mirror the values they teach their sons. We all seek to train our children well so they do not stray when they grow old (Prov. 22:6). Mark and I have three grown daughters (nineteen, twenty-one, and twenty-three years old). Our parenting choices assumed a Christ-centered foundation that recognized each daughter was made in the image of God, gifted to reflect God's image in unique ways, and was being pursued by God into a lifelong love relationship.

We value confidence, contentment, and community, and we have sought to instill these in our daughters as we partnered with God to raise them into godly women. Those three values will be used to illustrate seven general principles of raising daughters during their first dozen years. Confidence, contentment, and community are important to instill in sons as well as daughters, but boys and girls have different cultural expectations for what these look like, which lead to somewhat different approaches in parenting.

Confidence

Rae has a bumper sticker on her car that says, "Speak your mind, even if your voice shakes" (a Maggie Kuhn quote). Confidence emerges out of a strong sense of being somebody who belongs to God. With that comes a sense of giftedness and ability to make a contribution, and the boldness to speak one's heart and mind. When our daughters are confident, they have assurance that they can accomplish meaningful tasks and that they have something valuable to contribute with their words and actions.

Principle One: Stretch Your Daughters

Confidence born out of an understanding that our daughters bear the image of God gives them a powerful motivation to pursue good. When daughters grow up wanting to be artists, lawyers, writers, teachers, or politicians, they seek positions with influence not because it is their *right*, but because they feel obligated to use the gifts God has given them to serve others. Instilling confidence in our daughters is sometimes challenging because we still live in a world that tends to value what boys do and say more than what girls do and say, and that believes boys can do most things better than girls and that girls ought not try to fulfill certain roles at all. Our daughters pick up these biases that undermine confidence from television, in the neighborhood, at school, and sometimes in our churches.

But much of the task of instilling confidence begins long before conversations about what our daughters want to do with their lives as adults. We begin to instill confidence in the first few years of life, by encouraging our daughters, *just as we do our sons*, to stretch toward new challenges.

One summer I took the girls to their grandparents' beach house on the Oregon coast while Mark went out of town. We devoted one day to walking. We walked the four miles along the sandy, quiet beach to Neskowin and had lunch at a beachfront cafe, and then walked the four miles back. We took snacks and stopped when they got tired. Even so, three-year-old Megan wasn't sure she could walk all the way home. At some point she wanted me to carry her, and I would have been glad to do so. Before I could, however, Rae said, "But, Megan, think how proud Papa will be of you when you tell him you walked the whole way by yourself!" Megan walked the rest of the way home and enjoyed telling Mark later that she had done so. The goal is not to push our daughters to the point of failure but to let them stretch themselves, to discover what their bodies and spirits are capable of accomplish-

> **Principle One:** Let your daughters stretch themselves, even beyond what you know they can do. Resist the urge to be overprotective of your daughters from physical, social, and mental tasks you think they are not capable of successfully completing. If we protect our daughters from failure, they will learn to fear failure rather than to gain confidence from having tried.

ing. But even failure is okay. We learn through failure as we learn through success.

Letting our daughters try the impossible allows them to learn from their own testing of possibilities. I certainly didn't expect Megan could walk eight miles. Good parents will attempt to protect their children from experiences that bring harm, but often we can journey with them in their own trial-and-error discovery of what is possible and what is not.

Principle Two: Encourage Your Daughters to Think Well and Speak Up

Another important aspect of developing confidence in our daughters is encouraging them to speak their minds, not just about what they feel, but also about what they think. Informal conversations and dinner table conversations can be used to talk about ideas, to encourage daughters to think through and defend a position they hold. True dialogues between parents and children create a safe place for our daughters to explore their capacity to think, reason, and speak. Parents squelch this opportunity to practice speaking when conversations are primarily monologues in which fathers or mothers instill the correct thoughts, or debates, that daughters are doomed to lose because they are, after all, children. The following conversation could have been one we had over dinner with any one of our daughters during their middle school years:

"We talked in health class about abortion today," one of our daughters said. "I think women should have a right to get abortions if they want to—it's their body—especially if they were raped."

"Rape, and getting pregnant that way, is very sad," I said. "Fortunately, most women who get pregnant were not raped. Let's think about those girls for a minute. Does a growing baby have any right to life once it has been conceived? A lot of people who support abortion say the fetus doesn't have any rights—should someone defend the fetus that cannot defend itself?"

"But the fetus can't even live unless the mother lets it use her body, and it's not fair to make her do that if she doesn't want to," our daughter replied. "We don't force other people to give, say, a kidney, even if it will save someone's life."

"I can see why you think it wouldn't be fair to make her have a baby, and it isn't fair that the boy or man doesn't have to worry about that when he has sex," I said. "But maybe this isn't just about what's fair or not. Is it the baby's fault it was conceived? Is it possible that the right thing for her to do is to give this baby life even if she doesn't want to?"

"But what if she's poor, or still in school, and can't afford to raise the baby?" she asked.

"Girls and women who were not married and didn't think they could take care of their babies used to place them for adoption," I replied.

"But if she *has* the baby, she certainly should get to *keep* it!" our daughter said. "She'd at least have somebody to love who would love her back. Besides, what if the family that adopts the baby abuses it?"

"Nowadays girls do tend to either have an abortion or have their baby and keep it—likely for the reasons you mention," I answered. "Placing babies up for adoption is unpopular these days. I think that's sad. We think more about our rights than what might be right for someone else. I think the most selfless thing she can do is have the baby and then let her baby go to a family that can provide well for it."

"Well, I still think it's bad to force someone to have a baby who doesn't want to," our daughter said.

"Yes, the choices are all bad," I replied. "It's sad that so many girls have to face these hard choices because they get pregnant before they get married."

Throughout the conversation everyone would be contributing thoughts. Mark and I neither squelched the statement or question with a pat answer that ended all debate, nor demanded conformity to a particular position. When we discuss, we articulate our own values. We do not want to stop giving direction, but we want to allow our daughters to learn how to think well and express their thoughts and feelings. We ask questions that make them think deeply, and Christianly, about hard issues.

If we want our daughters to learn to think and speak their minds, they need practice in a safe environment. When questions are squelched, home becomes an unsafe place to ask them. Conversations like this may never arise, and those daughters either silently rebel, coming to their own conclusions, or learn to be passive listeners, sponges that absorb without thinking.

On her way to a wedding in Michigan, Rae passed through Illinois and stopped off at home for dinner and a night's rest. She recently committed to buying only organic food. We told her we were not fully convinced that nonorganic food is that bad for you. She said, "It may not be as bad for you to eat nonorganic food as it is for the environment when we use all the insecticides and herbicides we do. Can I send you something to read?" We said sure, and I told her that an environmental argument could be enough for me if I was compelled by it. At some point along the way, we need to become willing to be changed by our daughters. They are made in the image of God. As confident women they are learning to discern and think well. They sometimes follow issues we ignore, and they know much more about them than we do. We can learn much from our daughters when they're older if we build confidence in their ability to think well as children.

> **Principle Two:** Encourage your daughters to think well and speak up. Girls are often subtly encouraged to take the backseat in rational, theoretical, or political conversations. Encourage your daughters to participate in such conversations, to work through arguments, to develop skills in assessing and understanding various sides of an issue. Do not let sons dominate these conversations, and refrain from dominating them as parents.

Principle Three: Encourage Personal Development Apart from Structured Activities

Confidence also comes from learning a specific skill—playing an instrument or a sport, or picking up a hobby. Knowing our daughters and introducing them to opportunities to which they are drawn allows them to experiment and find some venue in which to develop confidence. However, in our current cultural climate, we tend to think more is better. So we sign our daughters up for soccer, piano lessons, tumbling or ballet, the children's choir at church, and Awana or Pioneer Club.

Being a good parent does not mean introducing them to as many opportunities as can be fitted into a week's schedule. Doing so might undermine confidence because confidence requires being comfortable with one's own company. Children benefit from learning to be alone with their own thoughts. They can connect with God's created world as they play outside, climb trees, look at the clouds, splash in mud puddles, and watch caterpillars and worms make their way across the sidewalk. Overinvolvement can keep this from happening. Overinvolvement also can cause your daughter to become average at many things but good at none of them, or burn out and lose enthusiasm for any particular activity or skill.

> **Principle Three:** Limit the number of activities you sign your daughter up for so that she has time to develop herself apart from activities, in the context of unstructured play alone or with siblings and friends. Limiting the number of activities also encourages her to become strong in one or two areas, rather than causing her to become overstimulated and overwhelmed by many.

Contentment

In a land of plenty, contentment is scarce. Our economy depends on our discontent, so that we always want new clothes (after all, last year's clothes are no longer in style), new toys, and new entertaining activities. Instilling a value of contentment early will serve our children well throughout all of life. It is difficult to live contentedly, yet life is much more satisfying when we do.

Principle Four: Celebrate Simple Pleasures with Your Daughters

Mark and I started married life without much discretionary income and with a commitment to avoid credit card debt. So our children played with simple toys and each other. They wore hand-me-down clothes, went to the local library or school playground for their outings, and took a lot of walks with their parents. They were remarkably creative. They played and performed *The Wizard of Oz*, *Cinderella*, and *Rumplestiltskin*, made up games, created forts out of blankets, and turned caterpillars (and sometimes slugs) into pets.

We used to go on "flip-a-coin walks." We headed out walking and every time we came to a corner, Mark flipped a coin. Heads meant we turned right; tails meant we turned left. He always manipulated it a bit so that we ended up at the corner grocery store where everyone picked out an ice cream bar. Life was simple. We were content.

Rae worked in a coffee shop her first year out of college. She worked twenty-five hours a week, rented a room, and managed to save $1600. She said, "I don't spend much; I don't really need anything." She made her own clothes or bought them at secondhand stores. She picked up an old Royal typewriter for two dollars at a garage sale, and after I showed her a few tricks (like how to put tension on the paper with the front bar and how to use the return and set the margins), she took great pleasure in typing out poetry and letters on her delightful instrument from antiquity. She is still content with little. She enjoys sunsets, hikes in the hillsides, free outdoor concerts, and watching stars. In her contentment, she lives life abundantly.

Contentment also takes on a unique dimension for our daughters regarding how they feel about their bodies. Many girls are weight-conscious by the third and fourth grade, dieting in an effort to become desirable. The pressure to look a certain way begins early, much earlier than it did in my generation. Already in kindergarten many girls are aware of cool and uncool clothes. Our media-saturated culture offers girls pictures of what they should look like if they want to be loved and to belong. Early on our daughters become self-critical for having a body that does not measure up to a standard of beauty manipulated by an industry that camouflages and uses mirrors, surgery, and body doubles to create images of female perfection. Even the cartoon heroines embody an unrealistic standard of beauty with their tiny waists, big breasts, and long, thin legs.

> **Principle Four:** Celebrate simple pleasures—contentment flows from filling our hearts, and our daughters' hearts, with gratitude for what we have and what our bodies are capable of experiencing.

Nurturing contentment in one's body comes from celebrating the terrific things our daughters' bodies allow them to experience. They can taste ice cream and strawberries, inhale the unique fragrance following a summer thunderstorm, or make snow angels after a winter snowstorm. They can climb trees because they have strong arms and legs, and ride bicycles because their bodies can learn how to balance on two wheels. Our daughters can be tickled and touched by the whiskery soft muzzle of a dog; they can climb a ladder and look into a robin's nest and see her little blue eggs. Contentment and gratitude are partners. As we appreciate the natural gifts that come from inhabiting amazing bodies, we experience contentment. Because discontent is necessary to keep us purchasing products, parents need to work hard at countering or moderating pressure to look a certain way with an emphasis on gratitude that leads to a contentment that can be had for free.

Principle Five: Foster Healthy and Realistic Ideas about Relationships

Contentment takes on another unique dimension for our daughters in their relationships, both with other girls and with boys. Historically boys had the initiation power in choosing girls, and girls had the power to reject or accept their offers. This is changing somewhat, as girls are increasingly feeling confident to initiate more in their relationships with boys. Even so, girls know there is an unspoken beauty contest in which they are participating whether or not they want to be. Girls compare themselves mercilessly to each other, wanting to determine their own standing and status. This can create a competition that sometimes betrays the friendships girls long to establish with each other.

Romantic fairy tales and comedies also undermine contentment by developing unrealistic expectations for relationships. Girls learn to hope to be rescued from their boring lives by a gallant, handsome, witty man. Just as boys adopt unrealistic expectations regarding the beauty of women, so girls adopt unrealistic expectations regarding the wit, wonder, and handsomeness of a wooing man.

After watching *How to Lose a Guy in 10 Days*, Sarah said she thought romantic comedies like that were dangerous. "They make you want that kind of man and be discontented with the good man you have because he isn't as handsome and winsome as a Matthew McConaughey." Of course, we are seeing Matthew McConaughey through the lens of a camera, enhanced by cosmetics and lighting and writers who craft witty lines that win the hearts of female viewers, including impressionable preadolescent and adolescent daughters. Even though it isn't explicit, young viewers also get the impression that it would be impossible to stay content with one's spouse after a while. Romantic comedies are always about the excitement of finding a new relationship. We seldom see exciting relationships between people who have been married a number of years.

Perhaps parents should consider that romantic comedies hold the same potential damage for daughters that movies depicting aggressive, violent, and sexualized males hold for sons. One option is to censor such movies, television shows, video games, and books. Perhaps a more realistic option is to talk with daughters about the values and beliefs perpetuated in the plots, why we are drawn to them, and what questions we should ask ourselves after being exposed to them. We need to help our daughters become cultural critics. They cannot escape the culture that influences how they think about themselves and others, but we can help them step away from it and think about it from a slightly more detached perspective. As our daughters become more aware that these taken-for-granted assumptions about life (such as girls have to be beautiful and sexy to be lovable, and the best boys are witty and a little bit bad), they can insert better assumptions (beauty comes from living full, healthy, active lives, and the best boys are kind, faithful, and passionate about life) and thus live with greater contentment.

> **Principle Five:** Contentment spills into all areas of life, including relationships. Fostering healthy and realistic ideas about what it means to be good friends, and to be a good friend, lays a foundation for contentment in relationships and develops insightfulness in choosing friends.

Talking with young daughters about qualities of friendship helps them be a good friend, to both boys and girls, and to discern when others are good friends to them. Ideals we can instill in our daughters include their being present to their friends when they are with them, listening well, and caring well for them. It means being willing to risk honesty for the sake of friendship and not always telling their friends only what they want to hear. Friendship means being loyal to their friends in their absence. Good friends laugh together, play, and talk without putting each other down or criticizing other people who are not present. Good friends are those who make them want to be better people; they accept the faults of the other and recognize that all people fail to love perfectly. As our children mature, the issues and ramifications of relationships change, but fundamental ideals about relationships stay consistent.

Community

Eastern cultures tend to emphasize obligation to family and community more than Western cultures, such as the United States, that emphasize the rights of individuals. The perception in Eastern cultures is that children are naturally inclined to be independent and need to be taught that they belong to something bigger than themselves. Babies are held close, and children are taught about their identity as part of a larger family and community. They learn they have obligations to others and what it means to be a responsible member of the community as adults.

Western cultures tend to believe children, who are born dependent, need to be encouraged to become independent and self-reliant so that they grow up able to take care of themselves as adults. Western cultures tend to believe children must untangle from their mothers' apron strings and ultimately find their unique identity and follow the path of their hearts and talents.

Both cultures express important aspects of being humans made in God's image and made to be in relationships with others. However, Western cultures can learn from Eastern cultures as we seek to raise our children with a strong identification with a community, as well as a strong sense of individual identity and independence.

Principle Six: Strive for Interdependence Rather Than Independence

Even given these general cultural differences, we tend to raise our sons and daughters differently when it comes to independence and community. Many parents tend to emphasize the need for their sons to become independent and self-reliant and their daughters to be caring and mindful of family obligations and relationships. I argue in my book *Growing Strong Daughters* that we need to raise both sons and daughters to be *inter*dependent rather than independent. We need sons and daughters to be taught the value and blessing that emerge from recognizing obligations to family and community. We are made for relationships; no one is intended to have to make it on their own, go their own way, and find their own path without the guidance and help of family, friends, and counselors along the way.

Our daughters often inadvertently end up being dependent because we do not prepare them to take care of themselves in the same way we do our sons. We are more willing to let our sons risk bruises and scrapes from climbing a tree than our daughters, because taking risks and learning limits is important for boys to make it in life. We teach our sons financial responsibility, and we teach them how to drive in bad weather, believing they have a greater need to learn these tasks. We teach our boys how to change a flat tire and negotiate with a car salesperson, assuming they will need these skills throughout life whereas our daughters won't. Yet raising our sons and daughters this way creates dependency in girls and independence in boys.

Principle Six: Interdependence, rather than independence or dependence, is a good goal for our daughters. They learn how to take care of themselves as needed but are also able to work with others to meet their own needs as well as the needs of others.

The basic skills that allow our sons to make their way through life are also important for our daughters. Some of them will not marry, or will marry later in life, or will be taken advantage of by others, or will become insecure in their ability to function well in a world that requires much they do not know. I met with a graduate student who had lived in Chicago a number of years but had never driven in the snow, being too fearful to venture out even once the roads had been plowed. I've had women students tell me they were never taught how to manage money though their brothers were, and the only self-protective preparation they had received so far was a self-defense class that convinced them men were dangerous and resulted in their living in greater fear. Teaching our daughters the same skills we teach our sons helps them negotiate life practically and instills in them a confidence that carries over into the way they approach and see life—less through fear, more through a sense of capability, owner-ship, and a responsibility to contribute meaningfully to the world in which they live.

But the real end goal for both our sons and daughters is to teach them how to be interdependent, to learn to work together with others to accomplish tasks, to learn to ask for help, and to cooperate together to get a thing done. I encourage interdependence in the college classroom by requiring students to work on group projects. We encourage interdependence when we have our children work together to change a tire, to come up with a budget for the family vacation, to wash dishes, to creatively problem solve to work out the best way to accommodate Aunt Kristie and their three cousins coming for a weeklong stay, and to contribute to decisions about where some of the family income will be donated. We are teaching them that they do not have to make their way through life alone. Boys learn it is good not only to help others but to allow others to help them. Our daughters learn they are not helpless and are quite capable of helping others. Part of living in community and valuing community is learning how to live interdependently. We need to stretch beyond our culture's expectations that boys be independent and girls be dependent to create an interdependency that fosters community.

Principle Seven: Instill Respect for Family

We tend to emphasize community more for our daughters than for our sons, encouraging our daughters to be relational, to take care of younger siblings, to baby-sit other children, and to help around the house. Even given that, there is still an underlying belief that successful parenting is to eventually get our daughters out of the house and either married or independently on their own. I ask my students at Wheaton College how many of them intend to move back home after graduation, and while the number of those who say yes is increasing because of decreasing job opportunities, students almost always say yes with a sense of shame, or perhaps failure, and with a disclaimer that it is only temporary. The exception are Asian and Latino students, who have a greater expectation that they will move back home, and without a sense of shame or failure. To move away from home—and in many cases far away from home—has become a sign of independence, particularly in our Western society. But families lose much in the way of family and community rootedness and blessing when they do so.

Developing a sense of community means helping our children respect family members and learn they have obligations to others.

We begin to instill these values in how we raise them to treat each other. We communicate that we honor each other simply because we are all part of the family. So we have our children attend some of their siblings' games, tournaments, recitals, concerts, or plays. We show respect for family members by extending kindness to each other even when we are angry. Developing community means helping our children feel connected to their relatives, which sometimes means visiting with them, whether or not they feel like it, because it is important to foster and honor these relationships.

> **Principle Seven:** Teaching children to respect and honor siblings and other family members helps instill a good sense of obligation toward others that will ultimately help them establish significant communities throughout their lives.

The distance family members live from each other often makes it difficult to help our children know extended family members. In the physical or emotional absence of extended family, friendships in our communities of faith and neighborhoods can become the primary way life is lived out interdependently. Given the realities of our mobile society, encouraging strong friendship and church ties can foster a sense of obligation and community for people who do not live near extended family. Teaching our young children the value of community and relationship builds a foundation for interdependent relationships in their future.

Looking toward the Future

Raising daughters has been a terrific blessing and adventure. We have not parented faultlessly, and God's graciousness has covered many parenting mistakes. Mostly we did not pay enough attention to cultural assumptions that determined some of our parenting choices. We needed to be better cultural critics, examining our parenting choices in light of trends and patterns that were not consistent with our core beliefs. As God's image bearers, our daughters have marvelous traits and abilities to serve humanity well.

We work to instill confidence in them, knowing much in our culture values females more for their sex appeal than for their rational, intuitive, emotional, compassionate, creative, insightful abilities. Introducing our daughters to confident, capable women in Scripture, in history, and in the contemporary culture gives them models to aspire toward.

We fight against the materialism of our affluent country to develop contentment with simple pleasures, and with gratitude for amazing bodies that allow us to enjoy life. So we help them fit in but try to persuade them to stay out of a competition to be the most stylish.

Mark and I came to realize that finding our place in some community larger than ourselves was as important as, if not more important than, finding oneself. Indeed, we cannot find ourselves apart from the relationships that shape and define us. While our daughters can be as capable of caring for themselves as our sons are capable of caring for themselves, the primary aim is interdependence—learning to work in the context of community with others to do the work of living and serving well.

May we think well about raising our daughters and bless the future generation with women capable, confident, content, and mindful of their connections to others.

Questions to Discuss

1. How can we encourage our daughters to speak their minds, even if their voices shake, and to stretch themselves beyond what they think they can do?
2. What is an area of competence your daughter would like to develop? Evaluate her activities—is she involved in so many that she is master of none? Is she so heavily involved that she has little unstructured time alone or with siblings and friends?
3. What simple pleasure do you enjoy with your daughter(s)? Are you modeling and fostering a grateful atmosphere at home?
4. Do you tend to overprotect your daughter? What would it look like to shift from dependency toward interdependency so that she is capable of giving help as well as receiving it?
5. Are you fostering a family environment where appreciation and a sense of loyalty and obligation emerge for other family members?

For Further Reading

Barger, Lilian Calles. *Eve's Revenge: Women and a Spirituality of the Body.* Grand Rapids: Brazos Press, 2003.

Debold, Elizabeth, Marie Wilson, and Idelisse Malave. *Mother Daughter Revolution: From Good Girls to Great Women.* New York: Bantam Books, 1993.

McMinn, Lisa. *Growing Strong Daughters: Encouraging Girls to Become All They're Meant to Be.* Grand Rapids: Baker Books, 2000.

Pipher, Mary. *Reviving Ophelia: Saving the Selves of Adolescent Girls.* New York: Ballantine Books, 1994.

5

THE IMPORTANCE
OF FATHER

Mark E. Crawford, Ph.D.

As a man, I find myself wearing many hats during a typical week. In my career, I often function as a therapist, diagnostician, neuropsychologist, speaker, and author. In my personal life, I am known as a husband, father, son, and friend. Often I must wear several hats simultaneously, and always there is the feeling that if I only had more time, I could be more effective in my attempts to juggle these roles. I am also aware that I live in a time and a culture that send confusing messages regarding the priority of these roles.

Scripture has something to say about each of the roles I listed above. Men are encouraged to worship God (Ps. 95:6); work diligently (Prov. 18:9; 28:19); love our wives sacrificially (Eph. 5:25); honor our parents (Exod. 20:12); be a faithful friend to others (Prov. 27:10); and love and train our children in a godly manner (Eph. 6:4). The world today, however, has a tendency to value certain roles above others. I am particularly concerned that the role of father has been devalued and minimized by popular culture, and I fear that many men fail to appreciate the enormous responsibility and importance, as well as the priceless rewards, of being a father.

The State of Fatherhood in America

It may come as a surprise to learn that an alarming number of children in America today are growing up in homes without their fathers. Consider the following statistics:

- Twenty-four million American children (a staggering 34 percent) live without their biological fathers.
- Thirty-three percent of all births that occurred in 2000 were out-of-wedlock childbirths.
- Approximately 40 percent of children in father-absent homes have not seen their father at all during the past years; 26 percent of absent fathers live in a different state than their children; and 50 percent of children living without their fathers have never set foot in their father's home.
- Forty-three percent of first marriages dissolve within fifteen years; about 60 percent of divorcing couples have children; and approximately one million children each year experience the divorce of their parents.[1]

For today's American child, the experience of growing up in a home with a father is, unfortunately, not a guarantee.

What is responsible for this disturbing trend toward absent and uninvolved fathers? Obviously, there is not just one single reason. Problems such as out-of-wedlock childbirth, the unacceptably high divorce rate, and societal attitudes that contribute to devaluing the role of father certainly must be considered.

Divorce

According to the U.S. Census Bureau, 56 percent of all children living in the United States are living with a divorced or separated parent. I speak with many people, including professional counselors, who believe that it is better for a child to go through the divorce of their parents than to live in a home where the parents are unhappily married. They frequently rationalize this view by saying that "it must be better for the kids to go through a divorce than to live with parents who are unhappy." I was taught this in graduate school. However, my clinical experience and the research of many others suggest that this is untrue. For example, Judith Wallerstein is one of our country's leading researchers in the area of the effects of divorce on children. Her studies are among the most comprehensive available. Unlike much research that relies on survey and questionnaire data, Dr. Wallerstein actually spent time interviewing children about their experiences following divorce. She says the following:

> Children do not dismiss their fathers just because there has been a divorce. . . . The poignancy of their reactions is astounding, especially among the six, seven, and eight year olds. They cry for their daddies—be they good, bad, or indifferent daddies. I have been deeply struck by the distress children of every age suffer at losing their fathers.[2]

Parents also attempt to comfort themselves by observing that their children often voice no complaints or manifest no obvious signs of difficulty following the divorce of their parents. What they often fail to realize, however, is that children are outstanding at hiding their true feelings from their parents. Even at a young age, children often feel protective of parents whom they've seen go through a painful process of divorce. Consequently, children often do not express their sadness to a parent.

According to the book *Divided Families: What Happens When Parents Part*,[3] even when a nonresident father maintains regular contact following a divorce, the nature of the father-child relationship often changes. Fathers often begin to behave more like a relative than a parent, interacting around entertainment activities rather than day-to-day management activities.

A Cultural Shift

During the past several decades, there has been a disturbing trend toward minimizing the importance of the role of father to the well-being of the family and to a child's development. This trend has been seen even among professionals. Perhaps there is no better example of this than the article published in *American Psychologist* in June 1999. This journal is the flagship publication of the American Psychological Association and is sent to every active member of the APA. The following quotes are taken directly from the article "Deconstructing the Essential Father:"

> The authors argue that neither mothers nor fathers are essential to child development and that responsible fathering can occur within a variety of family structures.

> . . . we do not believe that the data support the conclusion that fathers are essential to child well-being and that heterosexual marriage is the social context in which responsible fathering is most likely to occur.

> Our goal is to generate public policy initiatives to support men in their fathering role without discriminating against women and same-sex couples. We are also interested in encouraging public policy that supports the legitimacy of diverse family structures, rather than policy that privileges the two-parent heterosexual, married family.[4]

Support for their claim that fathers are unimportant is based on their claim that "divorce does not *always* have negative consequences for children" (italics mine). Using the same logic, one could assume that because people who smoke cigarettes do not *always* get cancer, smoking must not be risky. They also suggest that families without fathers are more likely to be poor, and that the negative effects of poverty, rather than the absence of a father, are what lead to negative developmental outcomes. The authors also suggest that in the animal kingdom, male animals are involved in the care of the young only when the females can offer specific benefits to the male such as exclusive mating rights or the ability to offer "political assistance" to enhance the male's dominance ranking. These arguments seem to offer weak support for their claim that fathers are not important to the well-being of a child. Furthermore, as I will discuss later, numerous scientific studies indicate the positive effects of father involvement on child development as well as the negative effects of father absence.

While the article I referenced above is overt in devaluing the role of father, other societal messages are subtler. For example, consider how the role of father as portrayed by the media has changed over the last thirty years or so. When I was a child watching prime-time television, most television shows depicting families portrayed intact families with fathers who played essential roles. The typical television father from my youth would include characters such as Charles Ingalls, Andy Griffith, and John Walton. Today, it is much less common to see a prime-time television show that portrays a father as present, involved, and competent.

The National Fatherhood Initiative conducted a study of how fathers are portrayed on prime-time television in the spring of 2000. During the months of March and April 2000, every nonsports entertainment program on the six major television networks with a father and/or mother as a central, recurring character was analyzed by independent raters. The study showed that fathers on television are significantly more likely than mothers to be depicted as poor role models who place less of a priority on the family. Fathers were eight times more likely to be portrayed negatively than mothers. The study indicated that 26 percent of television fathers were portrayed negatively as opposed to 3 percent of television mothers. One fourth of all fathers on television were portrayed negatively.

Without Father Presence and Involvement, Children Suffer

I am concerned that fathers risk being influenced by the subtle and often not-so-subtle message that fathers are not very important to children. I believe this is a dangerous societal message with dire negative consequences for our children. Research in this area is clear and consistent regarding the negative effects of father absence on children. For example:

- Forensic psychologist Shawn Johnston was quoted in the *Pittsburgh Tribune* in March 1998 as saying, "The research is absolutely clear . . . the one human being most capable of curbing the antisocial aggression of a boy is his biological father."

- One study showed that children who exhibited violent misbehavior in school were eleven times as likely not to live with their fathers and six times more likely to have parents who were not married.

- A publication from the National Clearinghouse for Alcohol and Drug Information showed that regardless of gender, age, income, and race, adolescents not living with both parents are 50 to 150 percent more likely to use substances, to be dependent on substances, and to need illicit drug abuse treatment than adolescents living with both parents.

- A study in the *International Journal of the Addictions*[5] showed that children who live apart from their fathers are 4.3 times more likely to smoke cigarettes as teenagers than are children growing up with their fathers in the home.

- Research shows that children whose fathers recently left them exhibit more behavioral problems than their counterparts who live with both biological parents.

- A long-term study of more than one thousand fourth-graders showed greater levels of aggression in boys from mother-only households than in boys from mother-father households.

- A study of over six thousand children between the ages of four and eleven years showed that those children in single-parent homes are more likely to experience emotional problems and use mental health services than children who live with both biological parents.

- A survey of 720 teenage girls showed that 72 percent said that their fathers were very or somewhat influential in their decision to have sex.

- A study in the *Journal of the American Academy of Child and Adolescent Psychiatry*,[6] assessing the effects of marital separation on children, found that those whose parents separated are more likely than their peers to engage in early sexual intercourse.

Father Involvement Directly Benefits Children

The negative consequences of absent and uninvolved fathers are clear. However, there are also significant positive effects of father involvement. Consider the following:

- A study of more than 1200 children showed that children whose fathers share meals, spend leisure time with them, or help them with reading or homework do significantly better academically than those children whose fathers do not.
- A twenty-six-year longitudinal study on 376 individuals found that the single most important childhood factor in developing empathy is paternal involvement.
- The higher a child rated acceptance by his or her father, the higher teachers rated the child on social competence and positive conduct.
- Children whose fathers regularly engage them in physical play are more likely to be socially popular with peers than are children whose fathers do not engage them in this type of play.
- Using a sample of almost one thousand households from the National Survey of Families and Households, researchers found that even after controlling for mothers' involvement, when fathers were highly involved in their children's lives, those children evidenced fewer behavioral problems.
- According to the National Center on Addiction and Substance Abuse at Columbia University, children with hands-on fathers (i.e., those who are involved, set reasonable household rules, monitor TV and Internet use, etc.) are much less likely to use drugs than children with hands-off or absent fathers.
- One study showed that when adolescents rated their fathers high on nurturance, they were less likely to engage in deviant social behavior, including drug use, truancy, and stealing.

The benefits of involved fathers affecting the development and well-being of children have been empirically demonstrated.

Fathers and Mothers Are Not Interchangeable

At the risk of stating the obvious, fathers parent differently than mothers, and each style is important to the overall well-being of a child. Numerous studies show that mothers and fathers vary significantly regarding how they interact with children. They differ in the ways they play, communicate, and discipline, to name a few. Fathers tend to encourage more risk taking, whereas mothers emphasize more caution. The combination results in an encouragement to be independent and take appropriate risks, but to do so carefully and thoughtfully. It is also believed that boys may learn to keep their aggressive impulses in check by playing physically with Dad: When a boy becomes too aggressive, Dad instructs him to calm down or play will stop. This helps a son learn to regulate his activity level and aggressiveness so these things do not get out of hand. Fathers tend to be more results-oriented and less sensitive to the pleadings of children, whereas mothers are more focused on the emotional experience of the child. Therefore, most fathers tend to be more insistent than mothers that children work through their problems, even if doing so causes some emotional upset. Clearly, mothers and fathers contribute something different to the process of raising a child. To raise a balanced, healthy child, both styles are necessary. Fathers should not delegate the role of day-to-day parenting primarily to mothers.

Fathers and the Spiritual Development of Children

Do fathers affect the spiritual development of a child? This question has received less empirical investigation than emotional and behavioral consequences of father absence or father involvement; however, common sense would suggest that the answer is unequivocally yes. For example, many believe that because God is referred to as our heavenly Father (Ps. 2:7; 2 Cor. 6:18), our earliest view of God is influenced by our experience of our biological father. I have spoken with many individuals who have shared that they have trouble with the concept of a loving, gracious, and accepting heavenly Father when their experiences with their biological fathers were of neglectful, rejecting, or abusive individuals. By contrast, I have known individuals who have suggested that because their biological fathers were loving, accepting, and reliable, they had little difficulty picturing God as similar in nature.

In addition to establishing the earliest associations to the role of a father, we dads also have the privilege and responsibility to model for our children the fundamentals of the Christian life. What better place to learn about how to live the Christian life than in the home? Psalm 22:4 states, "Our fathers trusted in You; they trusted in You, and You delivered them" (NKJV). The message from this passage of Scripture is clear: We learn how to trust in God and that God can be trusted often by watching our fathers place their trust in God.

Fatherhood: More Than Just Another Role

The findings are clear: fathers matter. I would encourage every man who has been blessed by God to have children to take his role sacredly. I believe that fatherhood is not just another role for a man; fatherhood is a sacred calling by God. When the angel of the Lord prophesied the birth of John the Baptist, he stated, "And he will go before the Lord, in the spirit and power of Elijah, *to turn the hearts of the fathers to their children*" (Luke 1:17, italics mine). When God blesses a man with a child, he has entrusted that man with a sacred and magnificent responsibility. I believe every father should "live a life worthy of the calling you have received" (Eph. 4:1) with respect to his role as a father. Of all the roles a man fulfills during his years on Earth, I can think of few that will have the eternal significance of the role he plays as a child's father.

Responding to the Call

I would like to encourage all fathers and fathers-to-be to step up to the plate and take their role as a father as a sacred calling from God. In my experience, fathers encounter some common challenges, and all of us fathers need some reassurance, support, and specific advice on how to be the best fathers we can be. While the following is not an exhaustive list of suggestions, I would like to offer a few ideas to help you begin.

Taking your role seriously as a father can be intimidating. Most men are reluctant to take on a challenge unless they are fairly confident they will succeed. Fatherhood is a challenge that can cause even the most confident among us to feel ill-equipped and uncertain at times. Some men are tempted to pull back when they begin to doubt their abilities. Let me strongly encourage you to resist this urge. Children do not need perfect fathers; they need involved ones. If you get involved in your children's lives, you will most certainly make a mistake. Don't let that be a reason to stay on the sidelines.

It can be especially intimidating for new fathers to see a new mother step into the mothering role with ease and confidence. New fathers often feel far inferior to a new mother when it comes to taking care of a newborn. However, this is a most important time to get involved. Much attention has been given recently to the importance of establishing early bonds with infants. Some research has shown that men who are involved early in the caretaking of infants (bathing, feeding, changing diapers, etc.) have better relationships later with their children. However, it is never too late to get involved in your child's life.

I have spoken with many fathers who shared that they felt inadequate to fulfill their calling as a father because they had either a poor role model or no role model from their own father. It is certainly helpful as a father if you have a well of experiences from being raised by a loving, involved, and godly father from which to draw. However, you can be a wonderful father even if you did not have a role model for a father yourself. Draw strength from the brotherhood of men who can mentor, support, and encourage you. Find other men who take their calling seriously and share your struggles and insecurities with them. Find a godly mentor to help you with your desire to be a godly father. Look to God's Word to guide you. And remember, there has been only one perfect father (God), and he's still there to turn to for help and advice. Remember, God himself called you to be a father, and he has promised "that he who began a good work in you will carry it on to completion until the day of Christ Jesus" (Phil. 1:6).

The Five Ts of Fatherhood

I believe that some of the most important ways I can best fulfill my calling as a father can be summed up with what I call the five Ts of fatherhood: time, telling, teaching, training, and together.

Time

Nothing will tell your children that you love them and that they are important to you more than your spending time with them. It has been said that children spell love t-i-m-e. We live in a world today where time is a precious commodity. Most of us complain that we don't have enough time each day. We find ourselves shortcutting where we can to try to steal more time. Unfortunately, many fathers steal time from their children. Our society has come up with a term to assuage our guilt that results from robbing our children of time with us: quality time.

The idea behind quality time is simple: I can't give you as much time as you need, but I will try to make the limited time I can give you very good. I see children emotionally dying from quality time. If we applied the same logic to the physical needs of our children, it would sound preposterous. For example, imagine if I said, "I can't give my children enough food to adequately nourish their young bodies, but I am committed to making sure that the little food they do receive is top quality!" This would surely cause you to question my sanity as a parent. However, when it comes to the emotional, spiritual, and relational needs of our children, we rationalize and come up with euphemisms to justify our unwillingness to give. To father the way God intended, we *must spend time* with our children.

One of the most important reasons for spending time with our children when they are young is to establish a relationship with them. It is our relationship with our children that gives us access to their lives. After working with teenagers for more than fifteen years, I am convinced that more than anything else it is the influence of parents and the quality of the parent-child relationship that determine adolescent choices. Many parents try to rely on their rank to control their teenagers into making good choices and avoiding bad ones. However, as most parents of teenagers know, as your teenagers get older, your

control over them is extremely limited. Most of the teenagers I talk
with who make good choices and successfully resist the most nefari-
ous temptations of adolescence say that they are heavily influenced by
how their choices would affect their relationship with their parents.
I've said many times that one of the best reasons to find time to play
on the floor with your children when they are toddlers is so they
will listen to you when you want to talk with them about substance
abuse and premarital sex when they are teenagers. To have this kind
of relationship, you have to invest time. There is no shortcut and no
substitute for time.

Telling

Fathers need to tell their children clearly and frequently that they
love them and that they are important to them. Many men have a
difficult time with this. They incorrectly reason, "My kids should
know I love them; after all, look at what I do for them." Love is communicated in many ways; however, children need their fathers to look
them in the eyes and tell them, "I love you, and I'm so glad you are
my son/daughter." If you can't remember the last time you did this,
it has been too long. Let me encourage you to put this book down,
go find your child, and tell him or her that you just wanted to make
sure they knew how much you loved them. Proverbs 16:23–24 says,
"A wise man's heart guides his mouth, and his lips promote instruction. Pleasant words are a honeycomb, sweet to the soul and healing
to the bones." Your children need to hear the words.

Teaching

Fathers need to teach their children. Teach them values and manners. Teach them about right and wrong. Teach them about God and
about the world. Teach them how to fish, how to throw a ball, how to
do algebra or cook or balance a checkbook. It is a joy, a blessing, and a
privilege to be the person who gets to teach your child a valuable life
skill. Deuteronomy 6:6–7 says, "And these words which I command
you today shall be in your heart. You shall *teach them diligently to your
children*, and shall talk of them when you sit in your house, when you
walk by the way, when you lie down, and when you rise up" (NKJV,
italics mine). Teaching involves spending time with your children.

Training

Training refers to discipline. Disciplining your child is a necessary part of parenting. When we look at children, discipline is seen
as an indistinguishable part of being a father. Hebrews 12:7–8 says,
"Endure hardship as discipline; God is treating you as sons. *For what
son is not disciplined by his father? If you are not disciplined (and everyone
undergoes discipline), then you are illegitimate children and not true sons*"
(italics mine). Proverbs also refers to discipline as essential: "Discipline your son, for in that there is hope; do not be a willing party
to his death" (Prov. 19:18). Discipline is certainly not the most fun
aspect of being a father; however, it is vital and necessary for those
who take the calling sacredly.

Together

By together I mean that it is important to stay together with your
child's mother. To take your calling as a father seriously, you must
take your calling as a husband seriously as well. Scripture tells us
men to "love your wives, just as Christ loved the church and gave
himself up for her" (Eph. 5:25). Our marriages and the way we treat
our wives are critical to our role as fathers. I am reminded of a study
that showed that self-image in children was dependent on how loving
the children's fathers were toward their wives.

The Best of Intentions

Many men will read this chapter and agree with my encouragement to understand how important a father is to the well-being of a
child. However, they will not immediately change their day-to-day
behavior with their children because they will convince themselves
that today is too busy—but a slower day is around the corner. Rob
Parsons wrote a book called *The Sixty Minute Father*[7] in which he
confronts several myths that prevent men from fulfilling their role as
fathers. He mentions what he refers to as "the greatest illusion of all":
the illusion that "a slower day is coming." Many fathers believe that
it is important for them to be there for their children; however, they
comfort themselves foolishly by telling themselves that today there

are too many important things to accomplish, but a slower day is coming when they can devote the time needed to their children.

Harry Chapin wrote a ballad called "The Cat's in the Cradle" years ago that tells the story of a young father who consistently responded to his son's requests to spend time with him by saying, "I've got a lot to do, but later . . ." At the end of the song, the father calls his now adult son to ask if they can spend some time together. The son responds that he would love to but that there is simply too much to do and he can't find the time. The ballad is haunting, poignant, and tragic. It reminds all of us that each day that passes cannot be regained. Fathering is not something that can be delayed. We are blessed with our children for a few, short, precious years. The time to respond to our calling is *now . . . today.*

It is my prayer that God will turn the hearts of fathers to their children, and that we men who have been blessed with the privilege of being fathers will respond to our sacred calling courageously and faithfully, looking to God to guide us and equip us to fulfill this calling with a new understanding of the eternal significance of our role in the lives of our children, and that we will start *today.*

Questions to Discuss

1. What are some factors that have contributed to a minimization of the role of father?
2. What are some of the negative effects of father absence in the life of a child?
3. What are some of the benefits to the development of children when the father is involved?
4. Explain why mothers and fathers are not interchangeable parents.
5. Why is fatherhood not simply "just one more role"? How should men view fatherhood?
6. What are the five Ts of fatherhood?
7. What are some of the major challenges men face in fulfilling their calling as fathers?

For Further Reading

Horn, W., and T. Sylvester. *Father Facts*, 4th ed. Washington, DC: National Fatherhood Initiative, 2002.

Parsons, Rob. *The Sixty Minute Father.* Nashville: Broadman & Holman Publishers, 1996.

Stoop, David. *Making Peace with Your Father*. Ventura, CA: Regal Books, 2004.

6

How to Empower Your Children

Jack and Judy Balswick

A child is a gift, not a product. God doesn't ask us to make our child into something so we can feel good about ourselves as parents. Viewing children as a gift from God radically changes how we relate to them. God promises to bring forth fruit for our labor beyond our wildest imaginations.

When we hold that precious bundle of joy in our arms, we are in awe and wonderment. God created human beings, unique of all creatures, to develop in and through intimate relationship. Because we are the handiwork of the master Creator, there is something of God's image within us urging us to become the parent God wants us to be. Therefore, it's natural that we feel so strongly about the parent-child relationship. Through this personal relationship, we are being molded into the image of Christ. In this chapter we present Relationship-Empowerment Parenting (REP) as a model that helps parents raise confident, successful children.

In the Beginning

Bonding is the initial attachment between child and parents that establishes the *relationship* as a secure place of belonging. (See Sharon Hart Morris's discussion of this in chapter 9.) The safety of the parent's nurturing arms gives the child confidence. Children need to know they can come back to home base when things get a bit scary in their world. When one-year-old Suzie crawls away from Mommy to discover new places in the house, all of a sudden she may realize Mommy is out of sight. Frightened, she cries out and Mother comes to soothe her. She is comforted by physical contact. She learns that parents can be counted on until she is ready to tackle her world again. Soon she figures out that parents can be counted on even when they are not physically there, giving her the capacity to spend longer periods away from them. Secure attachment (being relationally connected) sets the foundation for empowerment.

To raise confident, successful children, parents must learn how to *empower* through the right amount and kind of support. There is a range within which a child cannot quite accomplish a task without help and yet too much help hinders motivation. The idea is for parents to extend a bit, but not too much, beyond the child's capacity until he or she becomes competent in that area. As with a novice, we must work closely with each child, responding to his or her level of need and capacity for development. Rather than giving too much (overindulging) or not giving enough (underestimating), parents must be flexible and responsive to the child's unique development.

What makes this balance between relationship and empowerment so tricky is that normal oscillation occurs every time our child learns a new task. For example, the time between walking and crawling is accomplished in gradual increments. When baby Jacob takes his first steps, he is cautious, teeters, catches his balance, and falls down more than he walks. He can go faster crawling (no need for support), so he's encouraged to take steps while grasping fingers for support (tighter support). Coaxing and praise are incentives to take steps, but if pushed too hard or if parents are overly invested, little Jacob may refuse and plop himself down. He may even resort to taking steps when parents aren't looking. On the other hand, if parents don't give enough encouragement, he may be content to sit or crawl because he has little incentive to walk.

It is natural for children to explore their world. A new challenge pops up as soon as an old one is achieved. After walking, there is the thrill of learning to run, jump, and skip. Yet differences keep us on our toes because some children crawl on their tummies instead of their knees, some children go backward instead of forward. So it behooves parents to be in tune with each child's unique ways. If you expect too much, too soon, before the child is ready, it sets up unrealistic expectations and failure. At the same time, insufficient stimulation of the child's abilities may result in underfunctioning.

Relationship-Empowerment Parenting

The REP model is based on the two crucial aspects of parenting: *relationship* and *empowerment*. The foundation for the model is based on the biblical analogy of God relating as a parent to the children of Israel and us as believers. The image of God in Scripture is of a parent who loves unconditionally, offers grace when we fail, provides gifts and resources to empower, and desires an intimate relationship with us. This view of human parenting is validated by social science research. It has been shown that sufficient love (relationship) and sufficient discipline (empowerment) are most conducive to optimal growth and development in children.

An age-old debate is one that centers on permissive versus restrictive parenting. Permissive parents recognize the importance of warmth, affection, and emotional security but downplay discipline. Restrictive parents emphasize discipline, responsibility, and self-control but pay less attention to emotional nurture. In her comprehensive research, Diana Baumrind[1] finds that effective parents do both—i.e., develop nurturing relationship and effective guidance.

The strict disciplinarian parent (known as the authoritarian parent) tends to demand compliance through coercive control, such as forcing children to do what the parent says. This parenting style may get results, but children obey out of fear of punishment. Withdrawing love is another tactic used to control children, but in this case children submit out of fear of rejection.

The opposite style—the permissive parent—does more for children than is needed, fostering unnecessary dependence. Failing to provide sufficient guidance leaves children feeling sadly inadequate and floundering. Although permissive parents may give plenty of acceptance and love, they fail to provide sufficient leadership.

In contrast to both of these styles of parenting is the authoritative parent, who is an empowering parent. These parents provide a high degree of guidance (discipline) along with a high degree of relational support (nurture). Children bask in the relationship qualities of love, acceptance, and affirmation. Such parents make a concerted effort to maintain good relationships with their children, communicate well, pay attention to feelings, ask questions, and assist in identifying feelings. These parents also use sufficient structure, wise guidance, and clearly defined rules to empower their children to accomplish goals and master tasks. Children seem to thrive when they are given sufficient discipline, affirmation, and challenge.

REP parents enjoy raising independent, self-directed children. They are good at setting goals, organizing activities, keeping children focused, and teaching children what they must know and how they must behave. They work on relationship skills, explain reasons behind requests, and care about emotional closeness and interaction. The goal is to build and maintain a strong relationship while empowering children toward maturity. Empowerment means always keeping the relationship in the forefront. Guard the relationship dynamics with all your heart. It's the secret to growing competent, self-determined children.

Empowerment Makes a Difference!

The empowering relationship begins the very day our totally dependent babies come into our home and lasts to the day they become mature, independent adults. In the beginning we do a lot of loving, connecting, and nurturing to establish security and basic trust. Our steadfast love shows itself through our words and actions. Children feel secure in our love when they know there is nothing they can do to diminish our commitment to them. Building on relational love and acceptance, empowerment solidifies their progress toward maturity and meaningful existence.

Empowerment requires active involvement, investment, and intentional engagement with our children. It's holding the belief that our children are uniquely gifted by God to make a significant contribution in their world. Whether that child is able-bodied or developmentally challenged, he or she has a sacred meaning that can be achieved only by himself or herself.

Did your parents empower you? Did they believe in you when you lacked confidence? Did they challenge you to go beyond your self-constricted limitations? Did they encourage and equip you to reach your full potential? If you answer yes to these questions, then you know what it means to be empowered by someone. You have been richly blessed and it has made a tremendous impact on your life. If you were not fortunate enough to have empowering parents, you can reverse that generational trend by learning to be a parent who empowers your children. Components of empowerment include:

- Assuring: "I'm on your side and I believe in you."
- Encouraging: "You have strengths, gifts, and talents."
- Challenging: "I invite you to reach your potential."
- Equipping: "Here are the skills necessary to achieve success."
- Trusting: "I know you made a mistake, but I see you've learned from it."

Empowerment is the active process of instilling confidence, teaching, guiding, equipping, challenging, strengthening, and building children up to become all they are meant to be. As children grow and achieve a sense of personal competence, they develop inner strength to carry out the task of living responsibly in relationships and in society. Parenting for empowerment goes beyond developing personal strengths for "self" purposes. It offers the higher vision of developing competence to powerfully serve others. We prepare our children to live as healthy, mature adults, capable of building and maintaining a strong network of meaningful relationships.

To help children reach their potential, we sometimes need to give them a gentle nudge so they can spread their wings and learn to fly.

While spreading their wings may be a fearful idea at first, and they may falter during their first solo flight, unless they take that risk they'll never be empowered to soar. So, like the mother eagle, who pushes her babies over the edge of the nest yet glides beneath to catch them when they falter, we do the same. Empowerment means we step back while urging our children to take age-appropriate responsibility for their lives. Yet we are there to lend a supporting hand if they falter, but only after they've taken flight. Think about yourself as being a "player coach." We empower our children to meet the risky ventures of life by letting them fly, not by refusing to let them try.

Logical Consequences Empower

The promise of Scripture is that good training pays off and children will not "depart from it." The REP model establishes power in children through parents who empower them through word and deed, actions and interaction, love and discipline. All along, strong parents keep the relationship at the heart of parenting, not by yielding to whims or overindulging children, but by guiding them toward responsible interdependence.

We promote the use of logical and natural consequences as a method of discipline that empowers. The Old Testament reveals that God, as a parent, consistently used consequences as a central theme in guiding the children of Israel. God provided manna in the wilderness, with the provision that people were to gather only what they needed. The natural consequence was that uneaten manna would spoil. Then God instructed them to gather a two days' supply of manna before the Sabbath. In this case, the manna gathered would not spoil. Consequences are thoughtful and deliberate plans designed to develop intrinsic motivation in children.

Natural consequences are the unavoidable responses that occur naturally as a result of certain behavior. Take the example of five-year-old Christy rocking back and forth in a rocking chair. The rocking brings her pleasure and joy, but if she becomes too rambunctious, the chair will fall over and she suffers the consequences of rocking too rigorously. Her experience will help her monitor her behavior the next time she rocks in the chair. Children find their limits in these natural ways. Mistakes help them self-correct and set parameters for future actions.

Parents can take advantage of this natural phenomenon by simply staying out of the way and allowing children to learn from their experiences; for example, children throwing sand are bound to get some in their eyes. However, there are times when a natural consequence puts a child in serious danger. A child who runs into the street is likely to get hit by a passing car, and we wouldn't stand by to let nature run its course.

Logical consequences are fair and reasonable rules used by parents to help children learn limits so they can become responsible for their behavior. In this case, parents set the limit until the child learns proper self-limits. Reasonable consequences are devised to help the child learn. For example, before Curtis is old enough to understand that cars are dangerous, he is told he must not go into the street. He must stay in the yard when he plays or else he will have to come inside to play. The consequence for overstepping the limit is clearly understood and to be followed through with consistent firmness: "If you open the gate, you will come inside and can't play in the yard for a time." Precautions of safety are essential in the early learning stage, so Curtis's parents must be vigilant and watch for him to test the limits. When he does, he is immediately taken inside.

Logical Consequence	Child's Response
Consequences related to behavior	Learns to take responsibility for actions
Separate deed from doer	Child feels acceptable/behavior is unacceptable
Presents choice	Learns to make good choices
Respect and goodwill	Self-discipline/self-direction

Once a consequence has been clearly identified and communicated, the parent makes no exceptions, even when the child protests. If your child cries or is angry about the consequence, you still carry through in a firm, calm manner. Consistent, repeated consequence is what makes this approach so effective. Parents are vigilant, taking action in a calm, straightforward way the minute Curtis tries to open the gate. There is no need to be rude or shaming. You simply say, "Curtis, you must come in the house now. The street is dangerous, and if you go into the street, a car could seriously hurt you. You must not open the gate to leave the yard." Notice how the consequence is logically related to the misbehavior and carried out in a clear, matter-of-fact way. The parent lets Curtis know that he has overstepped the limit and therefore must come in the house for a certain amount of time. Be sure that the consequence set (time inside) is appropriate for the particular child and his or her age.

There is no need to get into a relationship hassle such as, "Didn't I tell you that was dangerous! You are a bad boy, and now you must come inside." This puts the parent in an emotional struggle with the child. Such a reprimand focuses on feelings of being bad rather than on the child's responsibility to stay in the yard. It gives the child time to think about what he did and helps him understand limits will be carried out. Consistency of the parent pays off when the child eventually takes ownership of the behavior. Establishing clear consequences ahead of time means you don't have to think on your feet or devise something in the moment. Angry emotion is kept out of the mix when you simply follow through with swift action while remaining calm and loving.

Four Mistaken Ideas

Parents most often view misbehavior from their point of view, but if you can put yourself in your children's shoes, you'll have a better understanding of how to exercise discipline. Misbehavior is often related to a child's mistaken ideas.[2] In turn, parents make four common mistakes in disciplining children. In this section we identify the four mistaken ideas, give the typical responses of child and parent, suggest a strategy for dealing with the mistaken idea, and end with an "extra mile action" that is empowering. We also show how using logical consequences can be helpful.

1. Attention Seeking—"I only count when I'm the center of attention!"

Child's need: To be desired and valued.

Parent's feeling: Annoyance or exasperation. Child can never get enough of me! Tendency is to reprimand and/or pull away. Child gets attention, but it's negative.

Strategy: Ignore your daughter when she demands attention, *but* give her special attention when she's least expecting it. Example: You have friends over for coffee and Alexis constantly interrupts, whining for your attention. After you've told her nicely that you can't be interrupted while you're visiting with friends, ignore her whining. Try to divert her with other activities, but be clear that you won't respond to her demands.

Extra mile action: Look for opportunities to give Alexis your full attention when she isn't demanding it from you. So when she's playing quietly with her dolls, go over to play with her. "I like to see you playing so nicely with your dolls. Can Mommy play too?" Spend quality time really interacting with her. Let her know you enjoy being with her, and do it as frequently as you can. This gives her what she needs without reinforcing her persistent demands at inappropriate times.

Whining example: The thing kids tend to remember about whining is that it works! We can only take so much, and then we've had it and give in. Two-year-old Liam demands to have the pacifier he is only allowed to have in his bed. He fusses and whines and refuses to give up until either parent gives it to him. Then he happily goes off to play, remembering that if he keeps up the whining, parents will give in. If we could be entirely consistent as parents, we would never give in to whining, and as a result, it would cease. This is the key. Don't give your child what he is asking for when he is whining. Walk away and don't give in. Remind him that he gets his pacifier when he's taking a nap, distract him with something else, or put him and the pacifier in bed for a bit. If you give in and change the rules, you reinforce the idea that whining works.

2. Power Struggle—"I only count when I get my way!"

Child's need: To feel important and powerful.

Parent's feeling: Anger and frustration. Child is in control and parents feel they must win. Ends in no-win stance and escalates into emotional outbursts. Even if parents force child into compliance, the child seems to have won the emotional battle.

Strategy: Remove yourself from the power struggle. Refuse to react. Because you are the mature adult, decide to stay out of such no-win struggles. Walk away with dignity. Calmly go about your business without getting caught up in the emotional battle.

Extra mile action: Try to understand why the child needs to feel powerful. Is something frustrating him at school or home where he is feeling powerless or out of control? Has a life change rocked his world? Does he need to have more influence in the family or at school? Check things out at a deeper level. Could you be overcontrolling or overindulging your child? Are your children able to do things for themselves that you still control? Are you impatient when your young children try to do things for themselves, and do you try to hurry them along? Do you let your children take responsibility rather than taking responsibility from them?

During peaceful times, listen to your child and consider what needs to change. Discover positive ways of relating. Focus on harmony and cooperation. Increase your child's influence in appropriate ways. Life will be better for everyone when there is no need to prove who's right.

Defiance example: You ask Kelly, age three, to pick up her toys, and she turns to you and shouts, "No!" in a defiant tone. Here are some things to remember: Kelly is capable of picking up her toys. Apparently, Kelly doesn't want to pick up her toys. Kelly is asserting herself.

Remember that Kelly is learning the parameters of what is in her control and how to express her wishes. She is learning what is allowed and what is not and how relationships work. This helps you reframe Kelly's "defiance" to "Kelly is experimenting." That changes things from "You won't get away with talking to me that way, little girl!" to a more thoughtful "She is testing out her ability to say no and needs to figure out the limits of what is allowed between us." The secret is not to break Kelly's will but to inculcate within her the will to want to do what is right.

As toddlers experiment with their sense of self in these ways, giving choices helps. This affirms their self as separate from you and acknowledges that they have separate desires. Knowing that Kelly is developing a self makes it easier for you to keep your cool and not aggravate the situation or shame her. Positive affirmation is very effective at this age. Take every opportunity to affirm Kelly whenever she picks up her toys. Natural consequences can be applied. When Kelly refuses to pick up her toys, remove yourself from the immediate struggle by walking away.

Later, calmly bag the toys and put them away somewhere, telling Kelly, "These toys will be ready for you later, when you show you can pick up your toys tomorrow."

3. Revenge—"I want to hurt you as I've been hurt by you!"

Child's need: To be healed of hurt, neglect, or a perceived wound.

Parent's feeling: Desire to get back. Hurt. Disillusioned about being a parent. Your child has pushed you to the brink. The pain goes so deep that revenge becomes a way to lick one's wounds. Blaming others is a way to escape self-reproach. You see your child as devious and may even want to get even yourself. This realization signals a deep breach in the relationship.

Strategy: Do not retaliate! Model constraint. Extricate yourself. Maintain order. Refuse to lower yourself to your child's level by showing self-control. Probe the deeper meaning at many levels (family of origin/ traumatic experiences/major changes/complex relationship disappointment, etc.). Your child is badly damaged, and the lack of forgiveness has deepened into revenge. Do whatever you can to get to the bottom of it. Try to understand your child's perspective, even though it may seem distorted or disturbed.

Extra mile action: Try to win the child back. No offense is worth risking the relationship with your child. Do what it takes to restore the breach and be reconciled. Take the needed time and effort to listen with compassion. Go deep enough to make a difference in the long run. Reparation will require confession, forgiveness, and reconciliation for proper healing to take place. Get help from trusted counselors or friends.

Temper tantrum example: Any child can throw a temper tantrum. It is something we all dread, hoping and praying it doesn't happen in public. At this point the child has lost it and is totally out of control. It may be they are angry because they are not allowed to have their way and want to get back at you for constraining them. Whatever the cause and whatever triggers a tantrum may be hard to determine. However, here are some important reminders:

1. Don't try to reason with the child.
2. Don't have a temper tantrum yourself.

3. Keep your cool. Stay calm. Be nonreactive.
4. Decide how and where to deal with the tantrum.

Tantrums rarely happen in isolation; an audience is part of the tantrum package. So remove the audience and decide where this tantrum can take place. It can be in the car away from others, the child's room, or a special place in the house (make sure it's not a scary place). Remove yourself emotionally (don't take it personally) and physically if needed. Stay calm but firm. Extricate yourself from this place and let the child find a way to soothe himself or herself. Usually your presence escalates the situation. Have compassion for the emotional upheaval the child experiences when out of control. When the tantrum is over, welcome the child back graciously by saying something such as, "Oh, I'm glad you're done with that. I missed you!"

While not always necessarily in the revenge category, often there is a striking out at the parent, and the parent may want to strike back. Using few words but taking firm action (consequence) brings a routine way of dealing with tantrums that helps the child reestablish control. Removing yourself keeps the child from hitting or screaming at you. When things have calmed down, try to understand what may have triggered the tantrum; for example, your child was overtired or overtaxed in the situation, or you were too abrupt or harsh. When you can predict situations that bring on tantrums, you can try to avoid these situations or relationship dynamics. Find ways for the child to express himself or herself without throwing a tantrum.

4. Apathy—"I'm unworthy and worthless. I've given up on myself."

Child's need: To believe in self and feel worthwhile.

Parent's feeling: Hopeless, worried, and defeated. Whenever a child gives up, it profoundly affects the parent as well. It is probably the worst, gut-wrenching experience as parents despair in not knowing what to do to help.

Strategy: Do not give up! Believe in possibilities. Refrain from pep talks that fall on deaf ears. Keep from scolding or giving reprimands that get no response.

Extra mile action: Stay connected any way you can. Show interest in your child. Make every effort to understand what's happening for him. If he's unwilling to talk, see if he can express himself in creative ways. Hang in there. He needs you now more than ever. If you give up, things will only get worse. You need to be strong and hopeful during this dark time in his life. You need a place of support to help you be resilient. Therapy and/or medication may help.

Nobody likes me example: Six-year-old Brittany was having a difficult time at school. She felt left out and sad, and it seemed her world was coming apart. All the efforts to encourage her were to no avail. Even though her parents listened with compassion, nothing helped her out of her slump. Because Brittany liked art, Brittany's mother, Sheila, suggested she paint pictures about her feelings. In her expressive pictures, it became evident that a group of girls were taking pleasure in ridiculing her. The meanness and negative impact were real. Her feelings were real. This is when Sheila was able to break through. She shared a similar experience about a time in her life when she too felt isolated and lonely. It opened up a new level of connection for Brittany to hear her mother's story. Everyone wants to be liked, and it's sad when schoolmates reject you. Brittany felt understood.

Over the next several months, the parents were able to solicit the cooperation of the school, and increased connection with a Sunday school friend alleviated some of the problem.

It Takes Two!

It is God's plan that a mother and a father raise children together. The Bible clearly addresses both when it comes to parenting. While there may be differences in how mothers and fathers go about it, each parent brings an essential piece of the puzzle. Children benefit enormously from a "double dose" of parenting.

The balance of relationship and empowerment is not all that counts; children thrive when both parents do parenting. In a well-documented study, Eleanor Maccoby[3] found that coparenting contributed to children's high self-esteem, academic capacity, creativity, honesty and trustworthiness, and competence in life skills.

In another study, Diane Ehrensaft[4] reported that coparented children had a more secure sense of trust, had closer relationships with both their mother and father, displayed greater creativity and moral development, had less animosity toward the other gender, and were better able to develop strong friendship bonds with opposite-gender children. Not surprisingly, it seemed that sons especially benefited when there was a strong bond with both parents. Strong fathering had a positive effect on boys' relational skills. Girls who were coparented had a greater sense of self and personal boundaries. A strong relationship with their father seemed to contribute to the daughters' high achievements and career goals, while self-confident, nurturing mothers contributed to their daughters' ability to set firm boundaries and make emotional connections.

Carolyn Henry and Gary Peterson[5] found that social competence in children also elicited more competent parenting. Isn't this what God intended by creating us as relational beings? In the parenting process, God changes, develops, grows, and empowers us. Parenting is a life-transforming experience. We face things about ourselves, like anger and fear, we never imagined. We become profoundly aware of our limitations. While we grow our children up physically, they grow us up emotionally. And in the process, God changes us.

Most of us find parenting to be one of the hardest things we have ever done. It is not an uncommon thing for parents of young children to be overwhelmed, exhausted, and discouraged. The amount of time it takes to care for babies and toddlers leaves you feeling that there is never time for you. Meeting the constant needs of young children wears you out. Fatigue, lack of sleep, and poor eating habits will burn you out fast.

Taking care of yourselves and your marriage is an investment of a lifetime. Make plans as a couple; do meaningful, loving things for one another; pray together for your children and each other. Doing so will boost not only your marriage but your family life as well.

Questions to Discuss

1. What is it like for you to face your human limitations in parenting young children? Whom do you talk to about your frustrations so you don't take them out on your children?

2. Think about a person in your growing-up years who empowered you. Make a list of the concrete things this person did to empower you. Now make a list of what you can do to empower your children.

3. Identify a concrete misbehavior that is troublesome to you as you parent. Brainstorm three logical consequences you could use in this situation. Now choose the one that is best suited for your children.

4. Take one of the four mistaken ideas held by children and take time to process the responses and feelings behind the responses. Decide on an extra mile strategy and keep to it until you notice a difference.

5. Consider one specific activity you and your spouse can do to enhance your coparenting unity.

For Further Reading

Balswick, J. K., J. O. Balswick, Boni Piper, and Don Piper. *Relationship-Empowerment Parenting: Building Formative and Fulfilling Relationships with Your Children.* Grand Rapids: Baker Books, 2003.

Campbell, Ross. *How to Really Love Your Child.* Colorado Springs: Chariot Victor, 1992.

Karen, Robert. *Becoming Attached: First Relationships and How They Shape Our Capacity to Love.* New York: Oxford University Press, 1998.

MacKenzie, Robert J. *Setting Limits with Your Strong-Willed Child: Eliminating Conflict by Establishing Clear, Firm, and Respectful Boundaries.* Rocklin, CA: Prima Publishing, 2001.

Scott, Buddy. *Relief for Hurting Parents: How to Fight for the Lives of Teenagers: How to Prepare Younger Children for Less Dangerous Journeys through Teenage Years.* Nashville: Thomas Nelson, 1989.

Sears, William, and Martha Sears. *The Attachment Parenting Book: A Commonsense Guide to Understanding and Nurturing Your Baby.* Boston: Little, Brown, 2001.

7

ATTACHMENT DISCIPLINE

Parenting with Sensitivity and Awareness

Tim Clinton

I t is the ultimate parent-child struggle we have all seen too many times. The parent runs after the child, struggling to gain some form of control and doing nothing of the sort, while the child continues to make a fool out of the poor parent, reducing him to the size of a small pea in just a moment. Most likely no one is paying attention, but the poor grappling parent feels as if all eyes are staring at him and judgment is immediately being passed. Those who have no children yet often swear their child will never control them like that, and the force of discipline will emanate from them. You may have been one of those who said that, and today you are struggling with how to get your child under control.

I don't know what parent out there doesn't dread the time and energy it takes to discipline our children. We have all been there. Most of us have learned parenting styles from our own upbringing. We come into our marriages with ideas on exactly how we believe discipline should be handled. It is natural for us to base our decision for discipline on our own experiences. On the other hand, what about those whose experience was very negative? Does their experience cloud judgment when it comes to making the best choice for discipline regarding their child? It is easy for those of us who have been in abusive or negative relationships with our parents to be reactionary as opposed to allowing our past situation to give us insight into how to be more balanced. Any extreme when it comes to discipline is unhealthy, and certainly if we choose to take an opposite extreme, we too could easily become unbalanced in our parenting.

The fact that both parents have come from different discipline styles is challenging in itself. This is why it is so important for you to thoroughly discuss how to approach discipline, preferably even before you have children. Over the years many different theories on discipline have been introduced, but still the decision has always been in the hands of the parents. No matter what parenting style you and your spouse choose to use, one thing is for certain: It must be based on love.

Attachment Parenting

I will never forget the first day my son went to his first hockey lesson; he wanted me right there in the stands cheering him on. I knew he felt overwhelmed. He needed me just to stand there for forty-five minutes as he learned the basics of hockey. I would watch him as he skated by; I could see his little face looking back at me to make sure I was still there. My very presence made him feel secure. Just like any parent, there are moments when my "coaching" is very involved, and then there are moments when just my presence is needed.

The supportive role of a parent is not limited to when children are young. I remember that when Julie had our first son, she needed to know I was there standing by her side, but just as important was her knowing her mom was there with us too. Just her presence gave Julie a peace, helping her know she could get through anything.

Attachment parenting takes place when parents are there for their kids. When parents are there for their kids, they create within their children an important, attachment-based sense about themselves. Children need to grow up knowing they are loved. This gives them a sense of belonging and helps them to believe others are available and trustworthy, not rejecting and unreliable. Of course, most important, they will know that God is loving and is there for them when they are in need. He will never fail them or leave them.

Most important is the value of parents being there on a daily basis for their children. It is this consistency that not only creates a sense of security for the children but gives opportunity for parents to be directly involved in the lives of their children. It is when parents are available that they are able to help their children process the meaning of life, who they are, and what their purpose is. Every child needs goals and direction. Providing these things is an act of love on your part and requires a lot of time and strength. Parenting is one of the hardest jobs around and is not for the faint of heart, but be encouraged, because there is more to come.

The Natural Process of Things

What Julie and I have learned is how natural attachment parenting is. Understanding the basics of this style of parenting will then ready you for attachment discipline (which we will discuss later in the chapter). Your instincts can be your greatest asset. Like a compass is to a person lost in the wilderness, so are our God-given instincts to us in times of wondering what to do. Each of us has faced moments when we didn't know which way to go, and yet something inside of us guided us along the way. Parenting is the same; disciplining is the same. Each of our children is different and therefore requires different methods of discipline. The basic foundations of discipline remain consistent, but overall these principles should be adapted to the situation and your instincts should be a big part of decisions made during the moment of disobedience.

There are four attachment-based parenting guiding principles: vision, training in love, emotional learning, and sensitivity. These principles will help you organize your parenting style and also help you better understand why you do what you do. They will also help lay a foundation for discipline and create a road map to follow.

Vision

Without vision, confusion is inevitable. Scripture tells us, "Where there is no vision, the people perish" (Prov. 29:18 KJV). From the time our kids enter into the world and are able to breathe, they challenge us to be flexible. I heard a pastor once say, "Blessed are the flexible, for they will not be broken." Kids are always changing, and just when you think you have them figured out, they change again. This is why vision is so important. You can always go back to your core ideas when you are frustrated, confused, and downright lost. Understanding the game plan helps bring unity and peace in the midst of chaos. There is no wondering or questioning when little Susie, who is three, talks back to you, yelling, "No, Mommy, I won't sit down in my seat!" while you are in a restaurant full of people. You will know exactly how you are going to handle it, if you have vision. You and your spouse are a team, and just like any other team, you must have a plan of action.

The same goes for the single parent. If you are a single mom or dad, remember that God is your partner, write down your vision for parenting, and pray and ask God to help give you strength to adhere to it. You should look over it often to refresh your memory. You may decide to make changes as you go along and learn more about your child.

Training in Love

You may have heard this before, but here it goes again: rules without relationship are worthless. You can discipline until you are blue in the face, but if there is no relationship, the second your back is turned those rules will go out the window. It is so easy to blame our culture for the way a lot of kids are today, but the problem goes much deeper than that. Not only have many of us been absent in the training, but many of us have trained without the love and acceptance a child needs.

If you want your child to respond to you, then your parenting and discipline styles should stay away from a reactionary way of parenting. If you are just parenting military style, enforcing rules based on principle only and not based on the very foundation Christ teaches us, which is to love beyond all other things, then you are heading down a dangerous path. God in his Word says, "If I speak with the tongues of men and of angels, but do not have love, I have become a noisy gong or a clanging cymbal" (1 Cor. 13:1 NASB). It is important for us not only to display love to our children in training them but to teach them to love and be loved.

The best way to teach these things is through example. We are faced every day with people who wrong us in some way or another. This is the perfect opportunity to display the love of Christ to our kids. When that person who cuts you off in traffic because you are driving too slowly proceeds to roll down his window and yell at you, take the opportunity to smile back and apologize. Then ask the kids to pray with you for that person. If you are consistent in showing your kids how to love unconditionally, you will most likely have children who do the same. Here are seven goals to train your child in the way of love. Help them to

- believe they are worthy of love—God's and yours;
- believe relationships are warm, pleasurable, satisfying, and safe;
- believe they can trust others to respond appropriately and promptly to their needs;
- have the ability to regulate and manage their negative emotions;
- have the ability to live within limits;
- have the ability to deal with frustration, loss, and failures and to actually grow stronger from such experiences; and
- have the ability to solve social problems effectively, using words rather than aggressive behavior or social withdrawal.

Emotional Learning

Julie and I hope that these beliefs will become a key part of your vision and that they will guide you as you continue to deal with your kids. As much as you find it possible, reflect on the seven goals to see if you are accomplishing them. They are key in dealing with the stressful moments involved in parenting. It is so important to remember not to be reactive but to be proactive. Remember, it is in those times of emotional stress that our ability to teach (not just preach) these valuable lessons is so very necessary. It is in the storm of emotional stress where children really find out about themselves and those around them.

Sensitivity

Sensitivity is the mother's milk of attachment parenting. Sensitive parents are attuned or keyed in to their children's needs, which might be quite different from their children's wants. Out of this awareness, parents take the next step by promptly and effectively responding to their children. When they don't respond in a sensitive way, they humble themselves and take the time to listen and understand their children. As best they can, sensitive parents get behind their child's eyes and see the world from their view.

Attachment Discipline

Now that we have concluded the four essentials for attachment parenting, let's move on to some other discipline issues. There are many different styles of discipline, and there are definitely different approaches to different situations. The moment children come into the world, their little personalities are already being formed. Even as tiny babies they express themselves in ways that reveal their true personalities, and they are born with a certain temperament. Early on children can be classified into one of four temperament categories.

Easy kids are pretty even-tempered; they are laid-back. They get into easy feeding and sleeping patterns and adjust well to new situations. Their attention level is good, and they're not too bouncy. Plus, their mood is generally positive and stable.

Difficult kids are often grumpy and fussy; they tend to retreat from new situations, and they are hard to get on a predictable schedule. They are easily distracted, and their activity is often too intense for the situation. Their mood is generally negative.

Slow-to-warm-up kids are less active and have difficulty warming up to new situations and people. Their moods are usually negative, especially in new situations, but when the situation finally becomes familiar, they can blossom into being more pleasant and engaged.

Mixed-temperament kids have a unique blend of each of the above categories, not fitting neatly into any one.[1]

It is important to know the temperament of your child to better understand what discipline is necessary. For example, Mary has four children and each one has a completely different temperament. Her two youngest children are the most like her in personality, and they would be categorized as easygoing. They are both very sensitive and happy most of the time. Because of this type of temperament, Mary very rarely has to discipline them. When these children were between the ages of two and four, she had to exert more effort to train them and therefore more discipline was required, but now that they are six and eight, they are much less likely to get into trouble because of the effort put forth when they were younger. When Mary does discipline them, she keeps in mind their sensitive nature and the fact that minimal consequences will get them back in line.

Her two oldest children are very different in temperament from her, as well as from each other. The oldest child is eleven and can be very stubborn and difficult when he wants his way, challenging her to the limit and therefore frustrating her at times. From the time he was just a little baby, the oldest son was already showing signs of stubbornness. Mary remembers when she took him off the bottle; it was one of the most difficult weeks of his little baby life. He was so mad she wouldn't give him a bottle that when she handed him the cup, he would throw it against the wall. This went on for several days, and eventually her consistency helped him finally to accept the change. He was plenty old enough, but emotionally it was very difficult for him. Now as a preteenager he is still showing signs of his stubbornness and can be grumpy and fussy, but because Mary learned his temperament early on, she knows how to work with him to help him see things for himself. Just recently Mary had an experience when he was frustrated because he had to wait for thirty minutes at a restaurant. He was very angry because he didn't want to wait and wanted to go somewhere else. He complained the whole time they were waiting. Mary knew this wasn't abnormal behavior for him, and she had learned that the best way to deal with him was just to let him complain and not get angry and yell at him. Mary knew he would be happy once they sat down and began to eat. Surprisingly, it took a little longer than that this time.

When they were finally seated, he announced he was not going to eat. Mary knew he was just trying to find a way to disrupt the family and make her angry because she had not given in to him earlier. Again, she responded in love and told him it was fine if he chose not to eat, but she would order him food anyway. Finally the food came and it was definitely worth waiting for. With hamburger in hand, he smiled and admitted he had been acting ridiculous. He even asked her if she was going to say, "I told you so." Mary just smiled and gently told her son, "No, I am not going to tell you that, but I do hope you have learned a lesson on patience and the fact that good things do come to those who wait." Not only did he learn a valuable lesson, but Mary also avoided causing a scene and ruining lunch for everyone else by not getting angry and by not giving in and leaving to go somewhere else.

Mary's second son has more of a mixed temperament. He has such a strong desire to do everything so perfectly and really wants so much to please his mother that when he does do something wrong, Mary really has to evaluate her approach. She has learned to find out about the situation before accusing him of anything. He takes his disobedience seriously and feels very disappointed with himself when he does things wrong. He can think very negatively at times—so much so that his thinking can be very exaggerated. Mary has had to work with him in his thinking and help him to realize when his thoughts are not telling him the truth. For example, there was a time when he was feeling unloved; when he got angry he would say that no one loved him or cared about him. Mary would calmly tell him how much she loved him and remind him of recent examples when her love and caring for him was demonstrated. This immediately would help him feel better, and eventually, after Mary did this over and over again, the problem went away.

If Mary didn't have the understanding of attachment parenting, she wouldn't have the skills to work with each one of her children individually. In each of these situations, Mary was able to use the four guiding principles we discussed earlier in this chapter. Her sensitivity to each one of her children enables her to see into their lives and train them effectively. Mary could have seen her two oldest children in a negative light and rejected them because of their differences; instead, she was able to take the time to respond to them in a way best for their personalities, and in a way that showed the love of Christ. This kind of parenting takes more time, effort, and most important, awareness, but in the long run it will result in healthy, loving children. There are going to be times of deliberate defiance when stronger punishment will be necessary. This is when your intuition and God-given discernment come into the picture.

Tenacity—Sticking to the Vision

Now that we understand the three guiding principles of attachment parenting, let's discuss the importance of tenacity and consistency in parenting.

1. The Importance of a Healthy Belief System

Teach your child to grow from adverse situations by seeing the positive side in negative situations. In a more spiritual light, teach your child to see things with a heavenly perspective, filtering situations through the Word of God. Not only does this approach help children begin to do this themselves as they grow older, but it also plants the Word of God in their hearts.

2. Boundaries and Limits

Remember what we said earlier in the chapter: rules without relationship are meaningless. However, we must not throw the baby out with the bathwater, so to speak. Rules are an important part of life, and boundaries are a necessity in every parenting plan. Every family has a language unto themselves. This language defines the rules and boundaries of the household. Each family varies in their ideas, but just remember that the boundaries you set for your children will also be set for you; therefore, make sure you can follow through on them. If you expect your family to respect one another, yet you turn around and act irrationally, yelling and screaming because little Susie left her shoes in the hallway, this will create inconsistency and confusion for your kids. Kids will not understand why they have to be respectful when you disrespect them.

Remember always to discipline out of love and not anger. This may not be easy when you feel frustrated. If you are angry and know you will act out on this anger when you are disciplining, take some time before you take action. Make sure you calm down and relax; this will also help you use your opportunity to train while disciplining instead of just reacting to the disobedience and therefore losing the opportunity to communicate a truthful lesson to your child.

3. Open Communication

Open communication is vital to your relationship with your children. All members of the family need to feel as if they can speak openly about their feelings. My friend Ray and his family do this by having a weekly family meeting. This is an opportunity for all family members to address their feelings on any topic, as well as share feelings about negative and positive things they are experiencing in the family. This is an open time when both negative and positive can be shared without anyone getting angry or emotional. They all write things down and talk about the progress on a week-to-week basis. Every family is different, just like every child is different, so what works for Ray and his family may not work for yours. Find your own way to encourage open communication in your family, and implement it.

Be Encouraged

God cares about each and every one of us, and he created us to be in relationship with him and with one another. Working through relationships is not easy, but endurance and strength are things that God is good at supplying. Don't forget, there is more to discipline than just the act itself. Take the time to work with your children. They are looking to you to guide them and are hungry for boundaries and guidelines set down by you. These give them a sense of security and peace. Julie and I are not perfect in our parenting, and there are times we fail, but we must always remind ourselves that God makes up for those failures. So be encouraged, my friends, in knowing you are a work in progress just like the rest of us.

Questions to Discuss

1. After reading this chapter, what changes could you make in the ways you discipline your children? What discipline methods have you been using that are an expression of attachment discipline?
2. Discuss together your reactions to the seven goals of training your child in the way of love. Which would be your strength? Which might you need to improve?
3. How would you describe each of your children? Easy? Difficult? Slow to warm up? Or a mixed temperament? How would you discipline each differently?

For Further Reading

Ainsworth, Mary D., M. C. Blehar, E. Waters, and S. Wall. *Patterns of Attachment: A Psychological Study of the Strange Situation.* Hillsdale, NJ: Erlbaum, 1978.

Clinton, Tim, and Gary Sibcy. *Attachments: Why You Love, Feel, and Act the Way You Do.* Brentwood, TN: Integrity, 2003.

Sears, William, and Martha Sears. *The Attachment Parenting Book.* London: Little, Brown, 2002.

Willard, Dallas. *The Spirit of the Disciplines: Understanding How God Changes Lives.* San Francisco: Harper & Row, 1988.

8

THE GOOD ENOUGH PARENT

David and Jan Stoop

J an and I often speak to Mothers of Preschoolers (MOPS) groups about this subject of being a "good enough mom." Where we live in Southern California, every mom seems to think she must be supermom. This is true of those moms who choose not to work outside the home, as well as those moms who do work outside the home. They have to do everything right with their child, or they fear they will somehow ruin the child. As a result, they continually search for answers, for a parenting plan, a comprehensive program that provides the answers for whatever situations may arise in the parenting of their little one(s).

Of course, there are those out there who have responded to this search for specific instruction on what to do and what to avoid doing in every situation. There are parenting programs out there that will tell you exactly what to do in just about every circumstance. Parents who try to follow these instructions—which may make sense on the surface—only end up frustrated because "it didn't work like the book said it would." Bruno Bettelheim, the author of the book *A Good Enough Parent*, highlights the futility of this approach to parenting by comparing it to how one approaches a game of chess. He says,

> Yet banal and oversimplified as chess is as a metaphor for human relations, it can illustrate the fact that in a complex interaction we can never plan much more than a few moves in advance. Each move must depend on the response to the preceding one. . . .
>
> The beginner in chess, who tries to follow his plans irrespective of his partner's countermoves, will soon go down in defeat. And so will the parent who follows a preconceived plan, based on explanations he received or advice given him for dealing with his child.[1]

This may sound discouraging to those who not only seek a plan but also seem to feel more confident when they have a list of instructions. How then does one do parenting? The answer is simply to relax and be "good enough." This may sound simplistic, but research shows that when a parent can relax and just be good enough, the results are far more satisfying for both the parent and the child.

God has made us in such a way that if we are too perfect in our job at parenting, we will create a set of major problems for our child, and if we consistently fail as a parent, we will create a different set of major problems for our child. The goal is simply to be good enough, which is somewhere in the middle, where mistakes are accepted as part of the parenting process and, by God's grace, are not destructive to our child.

Of course, you may think it is easy for us to say such things now that we are grandparents, but the truth is that what we have learned through observation as grandparents is valid for parents. Mistakes are part of parenting, and when we can be honest with our children about those mistakes, we are being good enough.

What makes a parent good enough is the effort on the part of the parent to seek to understand what is going on in the inner world of his or her child. All behavior in a child is purposive. It happens for a reason—a reason that quite often may elude even the child. Perhaps the most important task for a parent is to creatively imagine what things may mean to a particular child, and then to act in such a way as to affirm that what the child is feeling is equally important as what we are feeling. The psalmist puts it this way: "The LORD is like a father to his children, tender and compassionate to those who fear him. For he understands how weak we are; he knows we are only dust" (Ps. 103:13–14 NLT). He knows our hearts, our weaknesses, and our desires.

Recently our two-year-old granddaughter, Robyn, was given a little set of toys that included a plastic ice cream cone. Her mom put the toys in the sink to wash them, and then everyone got busy. A little later, Robyn remembered and asked for her "ice cream cone." It was too close to dinner for her to have ice cream, her mom explained. But that didn't satisfy her need, so she started crying and asking for "ice cream cone." It was only after little Robyn had had a meltdown and was totally upset that Mom remembered the plastic ice cream cone and retrieved it for her. When children are little, it isn't always easy to understand what is going on in their inner world, but that's an important goal of the good enough parent.

How do we better understand the inner world of the infant and toddler? We can do this by looking at the developmental needs of the young child.

Developmental Psychology 101

Entering into the child's inner world isn't as difficult as it sounds, as long as we look at the bigger picture. Understanding the developing world of the child gives us an entrance into their experience. I always like to describe this by beginning prior to birth.

While in the womb, the child's experience is perfect. It's quiet and dark, and every need is met before it is even experienced. It is interesting that if a fetus needs more calcium, for example, and the mother's diet isn't providing enough calcium, the fetus will take what it needs from the mother's body. Only in extreme situations, like when the mother is a drug addict or alcoholic, will the child be deprived of what it needs. I often liken the experience of being in the womb to Adam and Eve's experience of being in the Garden of Eden before they disobeyed God. They were living in the perfect environment!

But then comes the wonderful experience of birth. Now I don't know firsthand about what happens at birth, for when my sons were born, I was relegated to a sterile waiting room for hours where fathers awaited the announcement that their child had been born. And I wasn't there for the birth of my grandchildren. My sons were there, but we were only close by. My grandson Jonathan entered this world through the caesarean section birth method, and my son watched and helped with that whole process. After he and his wife spent some time with their newly born son, Jonathan was taken from the birthing room to the nursery, and we were able to stop the nurse and actually see him about thirty minutes after his birth.

He was, of course, a mess, but he was incredibly beautiful. Then we watched as they took him into the nursery and placed him on a table and turned on some bright lights and a heat lamp. Now remember, he had just spent nine months in darkness, but now he was being flooded with light. It was necessary as the nurses now proceeded to clean him. Of course, they were being very gentle, but remember, prior to birth nothing had ever even touched him except warm fluid.

Once he was cleaned, he was stretched so he could be measured, footprints were taken, some drops were put in his eyes, and he was weighed. Who knows what else went on, but that was what we could see through the window. When they were finished, they wrapped him up tightly in a blanket and placed him in a bassinet, and he fell asleep. I thought they might dim the lights, but no, here came another newborn to be cleaned, pulled, and weighed. What a welcome into this new world!

But the harsh reality of Jonathan's welcome continued. After a couple of hours, he woke up and for the first time experienced a need—he was hungry. So they took him to his mom to be nursed. But neither he nor his mom really knew how to do this, and they had to have a "coach" come in to help his mom learn how to nurse him. I guess that's why a lot of babies lose weight the first couple of days—they have to learn how to eat.

Of course, this tired Jonathan out, so he fell back asleep, only to be awakened by another new experience—he eliminated at the other end of his body what he had eaten several hours earlier. Now diapers needed to be changed, and hunger would soon strike again. Birth is like Adam and Eve being thrown out of the Garden of Eden after they sinned, and now they had to work to survive. It must not have felt very safe for Adam and Eve to be outside the Garden; neither must it have felt very safe for Jonathan to be in this new world outside of the womb.

Figure 1 shows what we have described so far:

Figure 1

Inner World Need #1—To Be Safe

Now we can begin to understand the inner world of Jonathan. At this point, it is really quite simple. All he needs is to be able to eat, eliminate, sleep, and most important, find a way to feel safe again. For the first few months, this is his main agenda. Of course, other things are going on as he begins to explore his body, becomes familiar with voices and faces, and enjoys being held, especially by Mom.

But the primary thing that occupies his attention is to find a way to feel safe, and Mom becomes the primary person to make this happen. If Mom isn't there, someone else must take up the role of mother. Sometimes Dad becomes the mothering figure because Mom is sick or in some way unable to fulfill that role. Mom's primary task is to be a loving center of warmth to Jonathan so that he can begin to feel safe and can learn how to relate to a trustworthy person. She does this by loving him, holding him, comforting him, and so on.

Now let me tell you about my first grandchild, Michelle. We had boys, so when we had a granddaughter, I was thrilled. And she was (and is) very special. I loved to hold her. I would cradle her in my hands and watch her look around and explore the world with her eyes. Then I would put her up by my neck and cuddle with her, hoping she would go to sleep. I wanted to bond with her, to help her feel like I was one of her safe places in the world. She would fall asleep and I would tell her mother, "Just leave her here," and I would sit for several hours holding her as she slept. When she would awaken, she was even cuddlier. Of course, as soon as she became fussy, I was happy to give her back to her mom.

So we can add to our diagram the following as seen in figure 2:

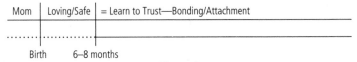

Figure 2

Two very interesting things occur around the sixth or eighth month. Somewhere in these early months, the child makes a terrifying discovery. Obviously, no mother is perfect, so there will be times when she brings her child a bottle when the child really wants a diaper change. Or Mom may change the diaper when her child really needs to be held. And there are those times when the child cries for a while before Mom responds. At first, the child simply attributes this malfunction to someone else out there who has failed. It isn't Mom who has failed. But then around the sixth to eighth month, the child discovers that there is only one Mom, and sometimes she makes mistakes. If the child could think, his or her thoughts might be *How can I learn to trust anyone when Mom fails me at times?* So in order to build that safe place, the child begins what often becomes a lifelong process of blaming himself or herself for Mom's failures. The result is that Mom cannot fail! So Mom can relax and make some mistakes with the knowledge that the infant will not put the blame on her.

Inner World Need #2—To Be Separate

The second interesting thing occurs about the same time. This one I observed firsthand with my grandchildren. For example, the first six to eight months, every chance I got, I would spend time building a loving, safe attachment with my new granddaughter. And this would continue until about the sixth to eighth month when another task began to kick in. Something happened at that point. When I would try to hold Michelle, she would start to squirm. If I put her up on my shoulder and tried to cuddle with her, she would push me away. I wondered how I had offended her and then remembered this second task of life—the first steps toward autonomy.

Erik Erikson, in describing the eight developmental stages of the human person, states that the first task of life is to learn to trust, and the second task of life is to begin the process of developing a sense of autonomy.[2] When Michelle pushed me away, it was like she was saying, "Papa, there's more to the world than your neck, and I want to begin to explore what else is out there." Soon after she pushed me away, she wanted down on the floor, because she was learning to crawl. And then not too long after that, she started to walk. Have you ever noticed that when children begin to crawl, or begin to walk, they always are moving away from Mom? What you will see in the mall are moms chasing their kids. Never do you see a child chasing his or her mom unless they are playing a game.

As Sharon Hart Morris points out in her chapter on attachment, what children need is twofold. They need to explore, but they need a safe haven to which they can return once they have explored. This need for a safe haven is illustrated by the experience of a mom and her eighteen-month-old. Her child is playing in another part of the house and calls out, "Momma!" Mom answers but gets nothing in response. She answers again, and again no response. Finally, she stops what she's doing and goes to see what her child wanted. When asked, the child says, "Nothing." What did the child want? He or she wanted to know that Mom was close by and that everything could feel safe again.

Now Dad is a key figure in this move to autonomy. For one thing, Dad is also part of the safe haven that the child needs for security. He's been there with the child and has built a bonded, attached relationship with him or her. When the child begins to move away from Mom, it is only natural to move toward the other safe people, especially Dad.

And there's another reason for this. The movement toward autonomy is fueled by the energy of the emotion of anger. It isn't that the child is angry; it just takes energy to move out into the unsafe world, and at this early stage, that energy comes from what will later be seen as the emotion of anger. And one of Dad's primary responsibilities as a parent is to help the developing child learn how to properly contain the emotion of anger.

So now our diagram looks something like figure 3:

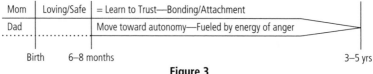

Figure 3

These two tasks continue to interact with each other until the child is around four years of age, and then the two tasks merge, only to resurface during adolescence as the twofold task of attachment and autonomy is dealt with once again. The interaction between the move to autonomy and the need to stay connected to the family intensifies while at the same time, the adolescent seeks to retain the family attachments and the feeling of a safe haven.

The Energy of Anger and Dad

One of the things that may be unclear in the preceding discussion is the role the emotion of anger plays in the move toward autonomy. If you can picture me holding my granddaughter close and then you see her push herself away from me, imagine that she is saying something like, "Out of my face!" She is much gentler than that, and her mind is too young to form that concept, but she is in some way accessing the same energy that might be expressed by one adult to another who is saying, "Out of my face!" That statement would be energized by one person's anger at the other adult. And Dad plays a key role in the infant's ability to safely experience the energy and the emotion of anger.

The reason we put the responsibility for this task with Dad is that he is going to be the one who teaches his children about the emotion of anger. He will do this by example and by behavior, not by his words. For example, let's imagine that three-year-old Johnny has been having a "bad Mommy" day. Those are the days when a little kid's T-shirt that says, "That's it, I've had it, I'm calling Grandma," has special meaning to the little one. And Johnny has been having that kind of day! Nothing has gone right for either Mommy or Jonathan.

Around six o'clock in the evening, Johnny hears Dad pull into the garage, and he heads for the garage door to greet his dad. As Dad comes in, he says, "Daddy, Daddy," as he reaches up, asking to be picked up. As Daddy picks him up, he says, "How was your day?" and Johnny says, "Bad day! Mommy mean! I hate Mommy!"

Now if Dad is wise, he simply holds little Johnny and says, "Oh, that's too bad. What happened?" And out of the corner of his eye, Dad can see Mom sprawled on the couch, her hair not even combed yet. *It's been one of those days,* he thinks to himself. And as Johnny recites all the bad things Mommy did, Dad simply says, "Oh my," and continues to hold Jonathan close and heads for the couch where Mom makes room. Dad sits down and still holds Johnny with his arms firmly around him. Finally, little Johnny has finished his litany of the bad things Mom did, and Dad says something like, "I'm sorry you had such a bad day."

After a few minutes of silence, Johnny's next statement is very predictable. He says, "I want Mommy," and scurries out of Dad's arms into Mom's. What Dad just did was contain little Johnny's anger. He allowed him to express his feelings, but Dad's strong arms around him made it safe to experience his anger and feel like it was kept under control.

What would have happened if Dad had gotten angry with Johnny for being a problem to Mom? Or what would have happened if Dad were absent from the home? Johnny wouldn't have felt safe to express his anger at Mom, in all likelihood. One thing a two- or three-year-old feels is a sense of omnipotence. He has the feeling that he makes the world go around. If it rains on Saturday and spoils the planned picnic, it is because he was a bad boy the day before. He made it rain. It is his fault the picnic is canceled.

Now if Johnny feels omnipotent with his anger, he might feel that if he expresses his anger at his mom without anyone else around, he just might destroy Mom. And then he would be abandoned and alone. That scary thought is usually enough for him to repress his anger and act like it doesn't exist. He learns to suppress or repress his feelings of anger, and those lessons will follow him into adulthood.

On the other hand, in some cases the anger may become so intense that the child acts out his or her anger against other children, or against siblings, or even in overt anger and rebelliousness against

Mom. Dad hasn't shown him how to contain the emotion of anger, so it spills out all over the place.

Whenever we are asked by a mom what to do when their four- or five-year-old is acting out anger against other children or against Mom, we always respond with the question, "Where is Dad?" And invariably, the answer is that Dad is absent from the home all the time or has been extra busy with traveling or something else that has kept him away from his child. Dad has the key role in these early years to help his child learn how to both contain the intensity of anger and properly express anger. One can't say emphatically enough how important it is for Dad to be involved. (Read also chapter 5 about the other aspects of Dad's role in the development of his children.)

So What's the "Good Enough" Program?

As we have described the main tasks of the first years of a child's life, we can draw some solid principles that will help you know more about what your child needs from you. Here are five principles that will guide you in being the good enough parent.

Remember, All Behavior Is Purposive

The good enough parent understands that a child's behavior has a reason behind it. The child may not know the reason, but few behaviors are simply random and meaningless. For example, when a child refuses to do something with a parent, like go to the store, this response isn't simply a desire to frustrate the parent. There is usually a logical reason for the child's behavior. Perhaps the child isn't feeling very secure, and the idea of going to the store, even with the parent, may set off feelings of the fear of getting lost, of not being able to get back home. Or maybe the child is tired or too interested in something he or she is doing and simply doesn't want to stop.

The point isn't that the parent is to cater to all of these reasons, but that the parent should understand that there are reasons. All too often, parents get so absorbed in their own needs that they attribute the wrong motives to their child's behavior. They dismiss the child's behavior as an attempt to frustrate the parent. This may be so in some cases, but if that is true, then there usually has been a long history of frustration in the child and he or she has become so discouraged and feels so unsafe that he or she has resorted to getting even with the parent. If you look early at your child's behavior and seek to respond to the motives and reasons of the behavior, you will be richly rewarded in your parenting.

Don't Ask Your Child Why He or She Did Something

Sometimes parents insist on knowing why their child is acting a certain way, especially if the child has done something to another child or has embarrassed the parents in some way. All they get from the child is "I don't know." And usually the child really doesn't know. They are not introspective enough to know why.

Think about your own behavior when you were a child. What did you feel when you were asked by a parent why you did something? You may still not know, to this day, why you did some things you did as a child. One way to better understand what is going on in your child's inner world is to think back to things you did as a child and try to remember things you felt back then.

Bettelheim makes the point that parenting isn't a science; it's an art. It is a creative activity in which parents are to use their own experiences as children to better understand what is going on within their own child. You may not remember things you felt as a child, but think of a child other than your own and see if you can imagine what he or she might feel in the same situation. And the fact that every child is different calls for more creativity on the part of the parent.

Mom's Focus Is on Attachment and Autonomy

It's interesting that these two tasks—attachment and autonomy—seem to be at odds with each other. But if we think in terms of providing a safe haven for children, from which they can better explore the world at their own pace, we can see the connection between these two major tasks that Mom is to facilitate.

Moms can get caught up in lots of parenting tasks, so much so that they lose sight of what really matters. Many of the things we actively try to teach our children—like showing respect for others, sharing toys, being nice to others—are taught more by example than by active training. So moms need to relax and provide that safe place where children can retreat to, and encourage them to explore the world around them on a gradually widening scope.

Dad's Focus Is on Attachment and Containing Anger

Dad also contributes to the building of a feeling of safety for a child. Like Mom, he builds a relationship of attachment and love with his child. He does this so he can provide the alternate figure to whom the child can turn when Mom becomes too much for the child, or when Mom is at the end of her rope. Like for Johnny on "bad Mommy" days, Dad becomes the alternative to whom the child can turn.

And then Dad fulfills an important role in teaching both sons and daughters how to manage and properly contain their anger. Again, this is done primarily through example. How does Dad handle his own anger? How does Dad respond to the child's anger or to someone else's anger? How does Dad respond when driving? How does Dad respond when one of his children is angry? All of these situations provide the opportunity to teach a child about anger.

Relax!

Perhaps the most important thing the good enough parent can do is relax. When a parent is anxious about his or her parenting, the child becomes anxious. Neither the parent nor the child benefits from anxiety. In fact, "parental anxiety makes life very difficult for parent and child, since the child responds to the anxiety of the parents with even more severe anxiety, and then their anxieties aggravate each other."[3]

You can see this when a child leaves the home to start school. If a parent is anxious in any way, the child will be even more anxious. If the parent approaches that event with excitement and confidence, the child will reflect those feelings. Again, this is a good reason to look into our own childhood experiences to better understand what our child is feeling in his or her inner world.

Conclusion

If we operate on the premise that our children are an extension of us, and therefore we *must* raise the perfect child, we will not do well in our parenting role. But if we can relax as a parent and truly enjoy the process of parenting, knowing that our child is an individual apart from us with reasons and feelings of his or her own, we will be the good enough parent. If you seek to know the inner world of your children, you will raise healthy children.

Questions to Discuss

1. What have been some of your anxieties about parenting?
2. Every child is different, but each child has the same two inner needs. Which of these inner needs—to be safe or to be separate—is strongest in your children?
3. In what ways has Dad been available to help contain your children's anger?
4. If you were to relax more as a parent, what changes might you make?

For Further Reading

Bettelheim, Bruno. *A Good Enough Parent: A Book on Child-Rearing*. New York: Alfred A. Knopf, 1987.

Karen, Robert. *Becoming Attached: First Relationships and How They Shape Our Capacity to Love*. Oxford: Oxford University Press, 1994.

PART 2

THE DEVELOPING CHILD

9

LOVING THE HEART OF YOUR CHILD

Sharon Hart Morris, Ph.D.

I have a newborn baby," I said wide-eyed and full of excitement to my sister the first night my husband and I were new parents. "But now what do I do?" was the next question I asked as I wrapped Vincent like a burrito in a warm blue blanket. "I'm not sure," answered my sister, as this was the first grandchild born into the family. For the days that followed I continued to cry out to the Lord, "What am I to do, Lord, with the gift of a child?" His answer and direction became clear: "Mold his character, and *start by loving him with your full attention!*"

A child is born innocent, helpless, and totally dependent on Mother, Father, and caregiver to be there for him or her. In the loving and caring arms of Dad and Mom, a newborn baby is cared for physically but also nurtured emotionally.

You are everything to your baby. The way you interact with and nurture your baby will guide their discovery of the world, help them make sense of life, and help them know how to act, react, love, and be loved. As a parent, learning to be a safe place, to be sensitive, attuned, emotionally available, and responsive, will be key to building a close bond with your baby and shaping the world, life, and character of your child.

The Impact of Your Relationship on Your Child

As parents, our relationship with our children is of vital importance to the development of our children. Yes, our children need to be fed and kept safe. But more than that, our children's hearts need to be nurtured and loved. Their physical, emotional, spiritual, and even brain development depends on it. The development of a baby's brain is affected by the nurturing interactions between child and parent. During the first three years of life, the brain's growth is vital as neurons become connected and the circuitry of the brain develops. For the brain to develop, it needs and is shaped by interactions between the parent and the child. Amazing what love can do!

Our relationship with our children also prepares our children spiritually, emotionally, and psychologically for life. In relationship with their parents, children learn how to view themselves, how to understand others, and how to be in relationships. They learn how to love, how to deal with their emotions, and how to make sense of and live in the world around them. Studies have shown that children who have a safe and secure attachment bond (relationship) with their parents fare better. These children bounce back from colds more readily, get along with friends better, score higher academically, are more resilient, and are more able to bounce back from distressing situations.

For parents, it is important to realize that feeding, clothing, and keeping your child physically safe are only part of raising healthy, godly, and emotionally mature people. Shaping your child's understanding of life, love, God, and how to make sense of it all happens as you and your child interact in caring and loving ways. In short, your relationship with your child is of vital importance to your child's development.

This chapter will focus on this relationship, or attachment bond, between you and your child. I will outline what an attachment bond is, how it works, how to build and foster a safe, secure bond, and how to maintain this bond as your child grows.

The Relationship: The Attachment Bond

The connection that ties you and your child together is an attachment bond. In the shelter of this attachment bond is where your child will grow, learn about the world, learn about himself or herself, and mature into a godly man or woman. This bond keeps parents caring for their child and a child intricately connected to his or her parents. This bond is powerful; some say it is stronger and thicker than any bond there is.

You probably won't ever have to teach your children to cry when they are hungry, to be sad when you leave, or to be comforted by you when you rock them gently in your arms when they are scared. That is because deep within your child is a biological attachment system designed by God to keep parent and child purposefully connected. It is this attachment system that draws a parent to want to nurture the child, and keeps the child seeking after the parent.

The attachment system is a biological system that sends impulses and hormones rushing through both the child's body and the parent's body and has a corresponding set of behaviors and responses that aim to keep parent and baby close. A baby's cries, kicks, giggles, coos, and fusses are all vocalizations and behaviors that attempt to get the attention of Dad and Mom, either to let Mom know they are hungry, hurting, or scared of a noise or to sound the alarm to Dad that they don't feel safe and close.

A baby acts in a certain way to elicit a particular response from his or her parents, and in return the parents respond in a way that keeps the baby safe, nurtured, and in close proximity. Babies will cry when they have a need, in an attempt to get the mother close, or in protest to the mother's absence. And when the mother hears the baby cry, she becomes alert, poised, ready to meet the needs of the baby. Mother then responds appropriately either by feeding or changing the baby, singing gently, rocking the stroller, or picking up the baby into her arms. These are God-given, innate, biological responses that are good and necessary in order to connect caregiver and baby.

For example, a baby begins to cry when she can't see her dad. The crying is a signal that says, "I would like for you to know that I don't like being away from you for long, and I am hungry. I would like for you to come close and ease this hunger sensation." When the father hears the cry of his baby, his heartstrings are tugged, he is quick about what he is doing, and he returns to the baby. He comes close and comforts his baby by saying, "There, there, here is Daddy. I was just getting your bottle." The sight of Daddy's face is comforting, the familiar voice of Daddy is reassuring, the food in the bottle satisfying. All is well. The baby is soothed, calms down, and enjoys the moment with Dad. This experience is very affirming to the dad, making time with the baby very enjoyable, and so he looks forward to spending time with his new baby.

Attachment Styles

How emotionally available a parent is and how a parent responds to the baby's needs are crucial to the development of the baby. If a mom or dad is able to be consistently attuned to the baby's cries and needs, is able to be emotionally and physically available to the baby, and responds in a caring and nurturing manner, then the bond between the baby and parent is a secure one. But if the parent is not consistent in meeting the needs of the baby, frequently absent, harsh, or neglectful, then the bond becomes unsure and not a safe place for the baby. The bond becomes an insecure bond. The child learns that he or she can't turn toward Mom or Dad or count on them being there when he or she is in need. And so the child learns different ways to deal with this insecurity.

There are four ways babies learn to respond to their parents' nurturing, or lack of it. They are called attachment styles, or ways of being in relationship. They are secure, avoidant, anxious, and fearful-avoidant attachment styles. I will briefly review them here.

Secure Attachment Bond

When a child and parent have a secure attachment bond, it is a result of the parent being emotionally available, accessible to the child when the child is in need of comfort or play. The parent is attuned to the child's needs, pays attention to the child's signals of distress, is able to make sense of what these signals mean, and is able to respond in a timely and effective manner. In turn the child is able to absorb the parent's comfort, is soothed and able to make sense of what is happening. This enables the child to explore the world around him, venturing out with certainty and assurance, all the while knowing that there is a safe place called home to turn to for comfort and love.

For example, Jack begins to fuss in his crib. He has just woken up and finds himself without Mom, hungry and a bit wet. Mom hears Jack beginning to fuss. She recognizes his cry and thinks, *Oh, he is probably hungry and needs to be changed.* Walking into the room to find Jack crying, Mom reaches down and rubs Jack's legs as she whispers, "Morning, my boy, how did you sleep? Did you wake up hungry? Yes, and look at that, you are wet, aren't you? Yeah, that must be uncomfortable. Here, let Mom get a diaper. . . . Your bottle is warming up." As Mom shuffles to get the bottle ready, she hums to Jack, "There, there, yummy food is coming right up." Jack finds this soothing, although he continues to cry until he is changed and fed. In this exchange, he experiences something that will shape his view of the world. He discovers that he is able to get the attention of his mom and that she will respond in a considerate manner. He learns that he is able to get the love he needs and that others are able and willing to love him without him needing to sulk or drum up the dramatics.

As his mother takes in Jack's experience, she gives it back to him in a way that helps him understand what is happening. His pain and cries are not something to be concerned about as Mom is not overwhelmed or rushing in chaos over his cries. She gently mirrors back to him his experience, and he learns that the ache in his tummy is hunger and that his crying while being alone will result in the soothing comfort of someone who cares about him. All is well. Life is manageable. The bond between the two is safe and secure.

Avoiding Closeness and Emotions

Dad is in the family room and Jimmy is taking a nap. Jimmy wakes up and starts to fuss. Dad is busy reading the sports page and does not hear the noise. Jimmy begins to cry. Still Dad does not notice. When the cries become louder, Dad looks up from his newspaper, then looks back down to finish his article, whispering, "It won't hurt the child to cry a bit." Finally, Jimmy is wailing, and Dad, feeling irritated at the interruption, gets up to check on his son. Not sure why Jimmy is crying, Dad is uncertain how to soothe the boy and says, "Stop crying. You have no reason to cry, unless you're a sissy boy." Eventually Dad picks up Jimmy, feels that his diaper is wet, and walks over to the changing table.

Parents like Jimmy's dad do not tolerate emotions, weakness, or signs of neediness. They do not know what to do with such emotions inside themselves. They avoid strong attachment emotions. And so they become firm or have low tolerance for these feelings when exhibited in their children. Often they are self-sufficient and independent and feel that their children should be the same.

Jimmy will, more than likely, grow up rejecting or denying his own attachment needs and emotions. He'll probably feel that those closest to him will be rejecting and unavailable to give him the love he needs. And so he'll come to believe that independence is healthier, emotions can't be trusted, and it's best not to rely on others emotionally.

Anxiously Waiting for Love

Sometimes the parent is caring in meaningful ways, but other times Dad or Mom is intrusive or uncertain how to soothe their child. And so the child learns that he or she can't depend on the parent for a consistent connection, and the child develops a sense of anxiety and uncertainty about whether or not someone will be there. This insecurity causes the child to be a pleaser, or to up the ante in an attempt to get his or her parents' emotional and physical attention.

For example, Mom is busy cooking dinner. She hears Jane cry. Although Mom is a very caring and good mother, she sometimes feels tired herself and does not always have the resource to soothe Jane's crying. But Mom puts down the dishcloth and goes to Jane with a distressed look on her face. Jane is not sure if Mom is mad, and when Mom picks up Jane abruptly, Jane does not get a sense of "Aaah, here is Mom, safe at last." So Jane cries louder and harder, hoping Mom will sense that she is in desperate need of being soothed. Eventually Mom sits on the chair and rocks Jane back and forth. But Jane has learned that crying louder, maybe throwing a toy or two, is the only way to really get Mom's attention. As a result, Jane grows up not sure if others can meet her needs and love her without her attempting to be noticed. And although Jane longs to be seen and loved, she approaches her relationships with anxiety, finding it difficult really to know whether or not she is safe and loved.

Fearfully Avoiding Being Hurt Again

When Jenny is in pain, her natural impulse is to go to her parents for comfort and security. But the paradox Jenny faces is that her parents are the ones inflicting the hurt. Jenny's mom has suffered from depression for many years. Sometimes Mom is the happy mom, and other times she is the mean mom who yells, hits too hard, and has no tolerance for any childish behavior.

Sadly, some children grow up experiencing their parent as the one who is most hurtful, frightening, and chaotic. They face a real paradox: their parent becomes a source of safety and their source of pain. These children adapt and become chaotic in their relationships. They long to be close to and loved by others, so they come close only to fearfully push away. Jennifer, as other children like her, does the best she can to adapt to the world and comes to believe that she is unworthy of being loved and that close relationships are not to be trusted.

The Building Blocks of a Secure Bond

Four keys to fostering a secure bond and a sense of inner security in a child are physical closeness, emotional availability, responsiveness, and trust. Fostering a secure attachment bond with your child does not mean being permissive and spoiling your child. On the contrary, a secure bond is one that is filled with great love and firmly set boundaries. It is a way of being with your child that shapes and molds your child, instilling in them a healthy self-esteem that allows them to venture securely into the world all the while knowing that you are there. It is being there for your child.

Physical Closeness

Being close is of vital importance to a child. As parent and child spend time together, this bond is formed, affirmed, and strengthened. For some parents, the bond begins within the womb, when a mother feels deeply close and connected to her child who kicks and grows within her belly. After birth, the sight, smell, and touch of a child tugs at the parent's heartstrings. As the parent holds, cuddles, feeds, and nurtures the newborn baby, the bond is formed and strengthened. You and your child need to be physically close often to form a secure bond.

Will you be close if your child reaches for you? Cries for you? Giggles or smiles for you? All babies need to know that the answer will be yes. To feel safe and secure, your child needs to feel that Dad and Mom are close by.

Emotional Availability

As for all parents, life gets full. Sometimes it is easier to take care of the immediate and physical needs of your child. You provide them with food and clean clothes; you supervise safe play and entertain them with toys and TV while you do your necessary work. This physical attention, although of great importance, is only part of what children need. They also need you to be emotionally available and attentive. They need to know that when they cry you not only will come and change their diaper but will care enough to ask, "What is the matter?" And in your tone of voice, the look on your face, the love in your eyes, your child will know without a doubt that you are emotionally there. You are not frustrated with their crying and only hoping to stop their noise. Rather, your child knows, "Yes, Mom and Dad are emotionally there for me when I need them." This builds security. They develop a sense that they are worthwhile and that you are willing and able to give them the love they need.

Responsiveness

Responsiveness is being attuned to your baby and then responding in a caring and considerate manner that is in the best interest of the child and family. Attunement helps your baby understand what they are feeling and helps them know how to respond to the sensations and feelings that surge through their body. You are attuned to your child when you gaze into their eyes and consider their experience and attempt to sense what they are going through. After attuning yourself with your child's experience, you can then caringly respond.

How you react and respond to your baby's demands, cries, and displays of joy teaches your baby how to feel about himself or herself and how to make sense of the world. If you are dismissive of their experience, then your children learn not to trust their senses. They will develop a sense of self-doubt. If you are caring but easy-come-easy-go about their experiences, your children will have difficulties knowing what to do with their emotions, dreams, and longings. They may feel loved, but they will feel directionless. If you are overly harsh, your children will learn how to protect their hearts, either by toughening up their hearts or by believing that instead of them being the "bad" person, you are.

Being overwhelmed by your baby's cries, or rushing with great concern, or being irritated by having to get up once again, will teach your baby volumes about his or her emotions and needs and how to deal with them. But when you gently respond with firmness, lovingness, and appropriateness, your baby learns a more secure sense of himself or herself and others.

OVERLY INTRUSIVE

When a parent intrudes on a child, consistently forcing a face-to-face interaction because of their own needs rather than the child's needs, the child becomes overwhelmed, realizing that relief will come only with aloneness. I remember watching a father standing in the checkout line at the grocery store trying to get the attention of his baby in the baby carrier by repeatedly saying, "Here is Daddy; look here; here I am," while tapping on the baby's chest. The baby turned his head from side to side trying to let Dad know, "I am not interested in playing; please let me be right now." But Dad persisted. Maybe Dad took it personally, feeling as though the baby was rejecting him. Nonetheless, he was insensitive to the baby's cues. The baby began to cry, and the repeated intrusion of Dad's face brought no comfort. The baby cried all the way out of the store. Dad muttered to Mom as they walked, "I don't know what you are doing, but you are spoiling this child."

These kinds of babies eventually feel overwhelmed by closeness and learn to value aloneness. Research finds that these individuals become more avoidant in their later interactions.

SELECTIVELY CONTROLLING

"No, don't shake the toy like that." "Here, hold the doll this way." "Use two hands; two hands are better." "This toy is better to play with; here, take this toy." These parents are controlling and steamroll over the natural inclinations of the child. Children of these parents tend to become frustrated as they play or are compliant and emotionally flat. They no longer trust their gut sense and give up their desires for what Mom or Dad says is right.

TO LET THEM CRY OR NOT TO LET THEM CRY?

The question always arises, "Should I let my baby cry?" Remember that the attachment system is triggered when a child has a need or when he or she feels that Dad or Mom is not close by. The attachment behaviors (crying, giggling, whining, fussing, cooing, smiling, etc.) are behaviors a child displays in an attempt to restore the broken bond, get close to Dad or Mom, or have their needs met. A baby is not manipulative, trying to wrap Dad and Mom around his or her finger. You can't spoil a newborn baby. Babies come with their own level of tolerance—some babies can coo while wet; others will cry when even a drop hits their diaper. You can't teach a baby to put up with wetness and to stop crying before being picked up at such a young age. So meet the needs of the baby according to his or her rhythm. Pick up your baby. Be attuned to your baby's needs, and respond by being gentle and sensitive. The touch of Dad's or Mom's arms is soothing, comforting, and necessary.

Trust

There are two kinds of trust for which a child needs to know they can rely on their parents. First is dependability trust. Children gain a sense that their parents will be there for them. The parents will keep them safe, pick them up when they say they will, be truthful, be fair, won't forget what is important to them, and be reliable and trustworthy.

Next is emotional trust. This is when children have a deep sense that their parents will care for them and be there whenever they need them. Despite what is happening, or what they are doing, the parents will consider their view, love them, care for them, and respond to them in a caring and considerate manner. This important building block allows children to know that when they reach for those who love them, those people will be there for them. And that includes their heavenly Father.

Good Enough Parenting

Let's be honest. Parenting is hard work. Not only are we responsible for raising and nurturing a baby into adulthood, we are at the same time trying to mature, grow, and deal with life's struggles ourselves. Because of life's demands and our own dragons we face, we are not always able to be available and responsive to our children. There are times we are sick, working, or just plain too tired. This does not mean that all is lost. We need not be perfect. A child psychologist, David Winnicott, once said the key is to be a good enough parent. This means that a parent need not be perfect for a child to turn out healthy. Just good enough.

Today, as you seek guidance and strength to nurture and care for your child, I pray that you turn your heart toward our heavenly Father and hear his voice gently reminding you that these precious treasures are valuable to him and that our part as parents is to love our children dearly as we shape their characters. Love your child with your full attention. Be comforted to know that God is with us and that he will watch over your children and their hearts all the days of their lives.

Questions to Discuss

1. What is your attachment style? Secure, avoidant, anxious, or fearful?
2. How does your attachment style affect how you respond to your baby/child when he or she cries and makes demands on you?
3. How can you grow to be more emotionally available and responsive to your baby/child?

For Further Reading

Clinton, Tim, and Gary Sibcy. *Attachments: Why You Love, Feel, and Act the Way You Do.* Brentwood, TN: Integrity, 2003.

Siegel, Daniel, and Mary Hartzell. *Parenting from the Inside Out: How a Deeper Self-Understanding Can Help You Raise Children Who Thrive.* New York: J. P. Tarcher-Putnam, 2003.

Stern, Daniel. *The First Relationship: Infant and Mother.* Cambridge: Harvard Press, 2002.

10

Teaching Your
Children to Pray

Cheri Fuller

J ustin, would you pray tonight?" I asked our son when he and his
wife and kids were over for dinner. Sitting in her booster chair, our
granddaughter Caitlin, four, said, "I'll pray, Nandy!" and proceeded
to clasp her hands and cover the bases of everyone in our family who
needed prayer. "Lord, thank you for this food and heal Grandma June,
and protect Uncle Chris on the ship, and bless Mommy, Daddy, Caleb,
Nandy and Papa, Randy [our dog] . . ." She didn't forget to mention
even one of our names before the throne of grace. Her prayers were
simple and concise, but the God of the universe was attuned to her
little voice.

Like Caitlin, kids who are introduced to God early in life during
their spiritual window of opportunity, who have praying parents and
grow up in a home where talking to God is a normal part of life, begin
to understand that the Lord is someone with whom they can share
their needs and thoughts. That's because early childhood is a season

155

of life when talking to God comes naturally and conversations aren't hindered by stilted language or ritual. Kids can learn to pray before they learn to read, ride a bike, or tie their shoes. They don't have to wait until they grow up and go to seminary to become an effective pray-er. Understanding their spiritual capacity is a first step to teaching your children to pray.

Changing Our Minds about Kids

"You fly in after speaking all weekend to pray with *kids*? And why do you have prayer class instead of doing a regular Sunday school lesson?" someone asked me recently. They were referring to the prayer class I lead for children ages six through twelve on Sunday mornings once a month.

"Because the kids are terrific pray-ers," I answered, "and this is how God has provided for them to know him—through talking and listening to him." For example, last Sunday in our church, before the kids were dismissed for children's church before the sermon, they all came up to the front of the sanctuary, and Samuel, nine, was asked to pray at the microphone before they left.

"Lord, help us all to have fun worshiping you and to have a good day. For anyone who has been hurt or who's in pain, please heal them. And, God, make us all holy! In Jesus' name. Amen," he prayed. Samuel's prayer was short but, like that of young Samuel in the Bible, affected many.

Those of us who work, play, and pray with children know there is no junior version of the Holy Spirit. The same Spirit who burdens adult Christians to pray for an unsaved person at home or unreached people in a foreign country also indwells Christian children. God can guide a seven-year-old on what to pray, just as he reveals his will to a twenty-seven- or seventy-year-old person.

One of those times I observed this was a Sunday morning prayer walk when I led kids from our church around a public elementary school nearby. In my small group, one little girl saw the blue disabled parking sign and prayed, "Jesus, help the kids who have trouble learning and who have to be in wheelchairs or have handicaps. Protect them from teasing and let them know you love them."

As we continued walking around the building, another child said, "I was really sad when my parents got a divorce. Let's pray for all those children whose moms and dads are divorced."

"Help their parents, Lord, to be godly and loving. Help their families get back together and please comfort the kids," she prayed.

The children prayed for teachers and the principal to know Jesus, for every student to be saved, and even for the janitor. It took only twenty minutes, but I believe the children's prayers made an eternal difference.

Too often, kids are not brought into the prayer circle, and as adults we underestimate their spiritual capacity. We figure when they grow up, when they have longer attention spans or vocabularies, they can join the prayer meetings, but in the meantime, we have to keep them busy at home and church. But the truth is that kids can be wonderful prayer partners *right now*. They can learn to pray effectively if we tailor prayer times to their present ability to focus and show them how to target their prayers. As we do, God can use their prayers to impact the world. Here are some ways to start.

Modeling Prayer and Encouraging Your Kids to Pray

"The best way for a child to learn to pray is to live with a father and mother who know a life of friendship with God and who truly pray," said eighteenth-century educator Johann Heinrich Pestalozzi. Modeling a lifestyle of prayer for your child will have a powerful effect because kids learn the most from what they see us do in the course of daily life. Children "catch" prayer from parents who regularly talk and listen to God, who are enthusiastic about praying with and for others, and who bring their children into the circle of prayer in both the ordinary time of family life and the crises and problems.

But I'm so busy! you may be thinking. *How can I make time for prayer when I've already got an overloaded schedule?* When my friend Sandy's four children were in first, second, third, and fourth grades in California schools, all were busy with work, school, household, and church responsibilities. But they still didn't want to lose touch with God or one another, so Sandy formed the Breakfast Club, her way of reserving time for God. She gave each child a blank journal for prayer requests and Bible study. She provided crayons, colorful stickers, and markers. Each morning they got up early enough to gather around the dining table with their breakfast and materials. The meeting started with a brief Bible reading by Mom or Dad while the kids ate. Then the parents took time to ask each child their biggest need or burden that day and to pray for their day, for their teachers, and for any possible problems in their classes that day.

The children enjoyed keeping track of answered prayers and having the freedom to draw and decorate their prayer books as they talked and prayed. Breakfast Club lasted only twenty to thirty minutes on busy days, but it gave the family a chance to pray for others' needs: the teacher who hurt her back, the classmate who fought every day on the playground and so on.

Perhaps without realizing it, these parents were passing on to their kids a sense of God's presence and the importance of staying connected with him.

You can also encourage your kids' prayer lives by getting a special night-light for each one's room and calling it a prayer light. Encourage them to put a pillow down on the floor to kneel on and to turn on their prayer light to have a few moments to talk to God before they go to bed.

You can also encourage your kids to pray "popcorn praises and petitions." These are brief, sincere, heartfelt requests and praises like, "What a bright morning, Lord. Thank you!" or "Lord, help me with this test!" Want a biblical model? How about in Matthew 14:30 when Peter began sinking at sea and prayed the powerful prayer, "Lord, save me!" Many of the prayers in the Bible were very short but had a big impact. As your family directs popcorn prayers heavenward from morning till night, staying in communication with God becomes as natural as talking with each other. No matter how busy the day, you can follow Paul's advice to "pray always" (Eph. 6:18).

Teaching Your Kids to Pray Servant Prayers

Sometimes our children's prayers tend to be a bit self-absorbed: "Dear God, help me have a good day at school and a fun time on the field trip, and it would be so great if we could go out for pizza tonight."

"Lord, heal my boo-boo!"

"Jesus, could you send me a puppy . . . and change Dad's mind so he'll let me keep it?"

Do these prayers sound familiar? They do to me. My kids prayed a lot of "help us have a good day" prayers. It's normal for children's prayers to center around their own needs. Kids are born egocentric and the world seems to revolve around them. Preschoolers are in the ME stage; everything is "Mine!" Convincing them to share toys with a neighbor child can be a challenge.

But by school years, their world widens. Prayers for puppies, pizza, and good days continue, but we can begin to gently move kids beyond themselves to develop a concern and compassion for others. We can help them pray servant prayers. It's as simple as noticing people in trouble.

When her boys were young, Patty prayed for their scraped knees and bumps. Grant and Andrew, her preschoolers, usually stopped crying because the prayer took their attention off the boo-boo. This pattern helped the boys develop caring hearts toward others with bumps or problems. When Andrew fell down, Grant would say, "Mommy, let's pray for Andrew." When Mom burned her finger, four-year-old Andrew bowed his head and said, "Please, Jesus, help Mommy's finger and take away the pain."

Patty widened their circle of concern to those outside the family. When they were driving along and heard a medical emergency siren or passed an accident on the road, she prayed aloud and asked her sons to join in. As a result, they grew in compassion for others. When they heard of people who were sick, they reminded her to pray for them. When they passed a homeless person, they asked their mom to buy a sack of food for him. And when Grant went to kindergarten, he took his practice of praying for ambulances to school and shared it with his teacher. Then the whole class of twenty-five kids began to stop and pray whenever they heard a siren. From small seeds like these, God can grow tenderhearted children who care enough to pray for others.

There are lots of opportunities to pray servant prayers. If you're a homeschool parent, you can integrate prayer into academic lessons. For example, when you study American history or government, pray for senators, congressmen, the president, and the vice president. When you study Middle Eastern countries, pray for the people, especially children, in those nations who live in constant conflict and violence.

When an image of a person in a hurricane or other tragedy appears on the TV screen and saddens your kids, turn off the set and pray for the victim whose face you just saw on the screen. Kids hear about disasters, terrorist threats, or national tragedies at school anyway; when they have a chance to pray about them and give their concerns to God, I've found they are actually less burdened and worried about the events. You can also pray through the newspaper. When you see stories that are alarming, turn that concern into prayers for the people involved.

Give Your Kids a Prayer Vocabulary

When asked by parents or Sunday school teachers to pray, kids often say, "I don't know what to pray!" To write well, we need a wide vocabulary. To pray effectively, we need *God's vocabulary!* The Bible is a gold mine of promises and can greatly enlarge children's prayer vocabulary.

As children grow in God's Word, they won't have to struggle for words about who God is and what to say to him. Their vocabulary will grow as they discover that he is their Rock, Shield, and Promise Keeper. They can honestly tell God their feelings as they learn to pray the Psalms, Paul's New Testament prayers, and other prayers throughout the Bible.

How can you help your children pray God's promises?

Model praying the Scriptures. As you read the Bible, look for the promises and plans God has for your kids. Let these verses shape your prayers. For example, I often prayed, "Lord, help Justin, Chris, and Alison trust you with all their hearts instead of leaning on their own understanding of things" (Prov. 3:5–6). When children hear their parents pray God's Word, this becomes a natural way of praying for them too.

Hide God's Word in their hearts. When your kids bring verses home from Sunday school or church, show them how to pray these back to God. For example, if your son has learned Matthew 5:44, and he encounters a difficult child on the playground, help him turn the verse into a prayer: "Lord, help me to love my enemies and forgive this boy who picked on me, and even to pray for him." Here are a few of the wonderful Bible prayers for your children to pray:

Create in me a clean heart (Ps. 51:10).

Come quickly, Lord, and help me (Ps. 70:1).

Fill me with joy from the Holy Spirit (1 Thess. 1:6).

Cause my roots to go down deep into the soil of God's marvelous love (Eph. 3:17).

Flood my heart with light so I can understand the wonderful future you have promised to those you have called (Eph. 1:18).

Praying Creatively

Each of your kids is unique and has different gifts and bents. Maybe one is a quiet, unemotional pray-er. Another is a mercy-minded pray-er. One child might like to draw messages to God, and another prays best in song. When we throw out the cookie cutter and allow kids to approach God according to their natural bents, they enjoy praying more. There are countless ways to help kids express their personal style in prayer.

If you vary the ways you pray as a family, you'll be helping your children connect with the Lord and learn to enjoy prayer. Here are some ways:

Sports-oriented kids can pray for strength and good sportsmanship, thanking God after a win or for the chance to compete.

Musical kids can sing their prayers. They can write original song-prayers or set any of the biblical psalms to a new melody and sing them to God. Playing "musical prayers" appeals to lots of different kids because it involves music and movement. On each chair, write a prayer target on bright paper. Then for a few moments, each child prays (at the same time) for the target taped to the chair before the music starts and they march around the chairs again.

Visual kids can express their prayers through drawings. Suggest they draw someone who needs God's help or something they want to tell God. Or after family prayer, encourage them to draw what God is speaking to them about.

Mover kids love prayer-walking around the neighborhood, praying a blessing on each home. They can rejoice in spontaneous prayers and thanksgivings, sentence prayers aloud in the car, and short "popcorn petitions" aimed toward heaven.

Artistic children enjoy creating prayer tools that help them connect with God. They could make a prayer chain by cutting out seven strips of construction paper in seven different colors. Then with markers, they write on each strip who to pray for each day of the week: Monday (yellow)—family; Tuesday (red)—friends at school; Wednesday (orange)—neighbors; Thursday (blue)—missionaries; Friday (green)—president, senators, leaders; Saturday (purple)—pastor; Sunday (white)—give thanks to God! Decorated with stickers and taped together into a prayer chain, it serves as a visual reminder to pray daily.

Be flexible to your children's changing needs when you pray as a family. There may be some stages when a child is willing to pray aloud with the family and other times when he or she prefers to pray silently. As we approach them with love and acceptance in whatever stage they're in, we can ask, "Would you like to pray with me about this?" and then pray for that one need.

We can give our children a blessing at bedtime or in the morning before school, and at special times like birthdays and graduations. We can speak our blessing or write it in a note. Whatever our children's interest or whatever stage they're in, a blessing assures them of our love and God's care.

Try changing the location where you pray with your kids. In the Bible people prayed on mountaintops, in caves, at sea, in the temple, and on the rooftop. We can encourage praying while they're enjoying nature, walking on a trail, riding in the car, or playing at the park. We can convey to our kids that wherever we are, God is there too. He hears them whether they are in a classroom, in the doctor's office, or at home. They can pray anytime, anywhere!

Impact Others with Your Prayers

Prayer won't only bless your family; God can use you and your children's prayers to impact others outside your four walls. When a Washington family began praying regularly for their neighbors, exciting things started happening. Lewie, the dad, asked everybody, including their five- and three-year-olds, to pick five neighbors to pray five blessings on for five minutes a day for five weeks. At morning breakfast, family devotions, and bedtime prayers, they lifted their neighbors to the throne of grace and blessed them. The parents encouraged the kids, and the kids encouraged their parents to keep praying.

As the kids and Mom and Dad prayed, God started working. Sarah, seven, had been praying for two friends down the street. One day the mom of those girls stopped Sarah's mother at the grocery store and asked if she and her kids could go to church with them. The next Sunday this mother and her two little girls committed their lives to Christ and started praying for her husband. Before long he came to Christ (even though he hadn't gone into a church for years), and the whole family was baptized.

God also touched the policeman on the corner who got a promotion and gave God the credit, and the teen next door who'd terrorized the neighborhood but opened up to Lewie, who gave him new CDs of Christian bands. Two moms of kids being prayed for asked if their children could go to Awana at the family's church. Even their five-year-old, Peter, had a chance to talk with the little boy he was praying for about Christ on the playground.

This family didn't feel they'd "arrived." Like all of us, they struggle with consistency in praying for their neighbors and friends. But the kids have seen their own friends affected by their prayers and the neighborhood families—people who live right by them—touched by God. As they keep praying, they see small miracles and big ones. They see that their parents care enough for their friends' moms and dads to intercede for their needs. And from praying for their neighbors, God has built bridges between this family and their community so they could share his love with them.

Who is praying for your neighborhood? Brainstorm together with your kids about what God could do with a prayed-for community where every person, young and old, is covered in blessings.

Finding Prayer Moments

"Childhood's learning is made up of moments. It isn't steady. It's a pulse," wrote novelist Eudora Welty. Prayer moments are like that too. There are many opportunities to gather our family together in prayer. Most daily hassles and problems are great chances to pray. Yet being a family that prays together doesn't require that we always work through a well-worn list. Nor does it mean we meet at the same time each day or week.

Although regular, structured family prayer times are beneficial and meaningful, as needs arise we can allow both the planned and unexpected events to call us together to pray with our kids.

The Thorpes, an Illinois family, needed new beds for their three kids. They'd outgrown their small beds, so the kids were sleeping on mattresses on the floor. Because the parents were committed to getting out of debt, charging the beds on a credit card was out of the question. So they prayed with their kids that God would provide beds. They didn't know how he'd do this, but the kids kept praying faithfully day after day.

One night the parents went out on a date. While the kids were at home, a furniture store delivery truck pulled up and unloaded three brand-new beds. When the parents returned home, the children asked, "Did you guys go out and buy these beds for us? Who are they from?" Because the deliverymen wouldn't tell them who sent them, they realized the beds were God's provision. The family dropped to their knees in the living room and thanked God together. Instead of watching their parents go into more debt, the kids witnessed God's provision and saw his faithfulness firsthand. It was their very need that drew them to the Lord and helped them see him at work in their lives.

Sometimes a loss or someone else's need creates not only a prayer moment but a prayer project for the family. After Sally and her family moved to Florida, one of their closest friends, the father of six kids, died suddenly back home. They were saddened by the loss and wished they could attend the funeral or help, but they couldn't. Don, the dad, wisely told the children that the only thing they could do was actually the *best thing* they could do—pray. So together the parents and kids committed to rise earlier every day for a week to pray for funeral arrangements, financial needs, comfort for the mom and her children, and other matters. As the week progressed, they sensed that through their prayers God brought not only help to the grieving family but also comfort to the pray-ers themselves. Their sorrow turned to joy as they heard about specific ways God comforted and provided for their friends.

We all carry burdens and worries from time to time, and your children are no different. They may have trouble learning a subject or may be bullied on the playground. These very cares and anxieties can draw them to prayer. First Peter 5:7 tells us to cast all our cares, all our burdens, all our anxieties and worries on the Lord because he cares for us. Teaching this to children is vital, letting them know that God invites them to give him everything they are concerned about. You can have a wonderful prayer time with your child or as a family just by asking, "What are you most burdened or worried about? Let's take it to God."

In uncertain times, instead of wasting our energy in worry or panic over things that are happening in our world or our school, or problems in our own personal lives, we can bring our family together and put our energies into the activity that will bring the most help, the most grace, and the most peace: prayer. Our kids can learn by doing that prayer is our first resource instead of a last resort.

Build a Prayer Heritage

When God answers your prayers, don't forget to thank him. For when you pray together and see the Lord work, you are building a spiritual heritage of great value for your kids.

Most parents want to leave something that would be a blessing to our children. Some leave a big business or great wealth; others leave a house or farm. But leaving a legacy of prayer is a great inheritance for your kids, one that won't rust or be stolen on this Earth.

One way to record this legacy of faith is by using a simple jar and rocks. One dad was trying to find a way to explain the meaning of "Here I raise my Ebenezer" from the hymn they sang in church. When he looked up the words in Joshua 4, he found that they referred to the twelve smooth river stones that Joshua constructed into a memorial. As Joshua and the elders finished the monument of stones dedicated to the Lord, he said, "In the future, when your children ask you, 'What do these stones mean?' tell them that the flow of the Jordan was cut off before the ark of the covenant of the LORD. . . . These stones are to be a memorial to the people of Israel forever" (Josh. 4:6–7).

So the dad took his kids to the river where they picked up flat stones. With permanent markers, they dated each rock and wrote a few key words that reminded them of an event in which they'd seen God at work in their family or an answered prayer. They put these in a clear jar on a shelf by the dinner table. Just as the Israelites' stones served as a concrete reminder of God's intervention on their behalf, so this dad and his kids gathered rocks to make their own remembrance. When they take out the jar to add new stones or look at old ones, they retell the stories of God's provision and rekindle their sense of gratitude toward God.

One rock thanked God for his protective power: *July 4, 1989: God uses Ryan to save Adam from drowning.* Other rocks commemorated God's faithfulness in small things, in a time of job layoff, and in the children's school activities: *September 1989: God helps me to not be afraid of giving presentations in front of the class.*

Your family's rocks might read: *December 1996: God heals Grandma and she gets to come home from the hospital. November 1997: We pray for a family in neighborhood and they come to church and get to know God.*

Whether you make a collection of Ebenezer stones, as this family did, to recall the way God worked when you prayed, or start a prayer journal that records his acts in your family, or create a photo scrapbook of great things God has done, find a way to remember and thank God for what he has done for your family through answered prayer.

As you share prayer times with your children and teach them to pray, it will connect your children's hearts to God and at the same time connect you and your children, heart to heart, and they'll feel cared for and deeply loved. As you pray with your kids, you'll understand their concerns, the things that worry them, and what they care most about. They will begin to see God act and begin to know his faithfulness in their lives. And as you find ways to record answers to prayer, you'll be creating a history of your family's walk with God as well as a wonderful legacy of faith for your children.

Questions to Discuss

1. What are your family's "ruts" of prayer—do you pray the same way at the same time or place? How could you get out of the box?
2. What is something you've learned about prayer that you could teach your kids—like praying Scripture or praying conversationally—or a story about how God worked when you prayed that you could share with them?
3. What's your biggest hindrance in praying as a family? Whether it's busyness or discouragement or different needs and bents, pray together and ask God to show you a way to overcome it.
4. What prayer moments with your children have you missed recently? How can you "catch" these moments more often in the future?

For Further Reading

Fuller, Cheri. *When Children Pray: Teaching Your Kids to Pray With Power*. Portland, OR: Multnomah Press, 1998.

Fuller, Cheri. *When Families Pray: The Power of Praying Together (40 Devotions for Parents and Kids)*. Portland, OR: Multnomah Press, 1999.

Fuller, Cheri. *When Mothers Pray: Bringing God's Power and Blessing to Your Children's Lives*. Portland, OR: Multnomah Press, 2001.

Ilinisky, Esther, Marcus Haggard, and Ted Haggard. *Let the Children Pray: How God's Young Intercessors Are Changing the World*. Ventura, CA: Regal Books, 2000.

Nichols, Fern. *Every Child Needs a Praying Mom*. Grand Rapids: Zondervan, 2003.

11

THE SPIRITUAL DEVELOPMENT OF YOUR CHILD

William and Kristi Gaultiere

Breathe, baby! Breathe!" The desperate pleas of the emergency room doctor echoed in my heart. I (Bill) couldn't believe my ears. That was my two-month-old girl gasping for air, blue-faced, and surrounded by nurses who were frantically hooking her up to oxygen tubes, putting a heart monitor on her, and giving her steroid respiratory treatments.

It seemed like just a few hours ago that I had been holding my precious and healthy Briana Grace, as we smiled and cooed at each other, and now the doctor was asking Kristi and me if anyone in either of our families had cystic fibrosis. "Is she going to be okay? I thought she just had a cold. She isn't going to die, is she?" Cold waves of fear broke through the shock and left me shivering until Kristi pulled me close. "Bill, sing her the special lullaby you wrote for her."

I extended my pinkie to my girl and sang to her just as I had every night since we took her home from the hospital:

> Oh, oh, my Baby Brie, my little cutie, so very cuddly. It's you I like to see, it's you I like to see. Wow, wow, God's gift to me, a blessing that's free, worth more than gold. It's you I like to hold, it's you I like to hold. No, no, let my girl go, oh I must I know, to the Father above. It's you I like to love, it's you I like to love.

Our tears flowed when I got to the part about letting Briana go. But singing and praying her lullaby settled all three of our hearts down. Her life was in God's hands.

Briana was taken by ambulance to the Children's Hospital of Orange County. We later learned that she had whooping cough, which went into pneumonia. And while in the hospital she contracted RSV, a respiratory virus that killed a baby a day that year in 1995. She was in intensive care most of the time from Thanksgiving until New Year's Day. Kristi stayed with her every day, twenty hours a day, to care for her and nurse her, only leaving when I, Kristi's mother, or another family member could stay with Briana to hold her, talk with her, and sing to her.

First the doctors thought she might not survive. Then they thought she'd have permanent lung damage. Then when we brought her home, Kristi and I feared she'd have psychological damage from the trauma and pain. But after two months of prayer, respiratory treatments, and days filled with caresses, smiles, and playful babbling, her breathing cleared up and we could see that she was indeed "hatching"; her self was emerging with eyes sparkling and face smiling and arms reaching out to be held.

Briana Grace means "strong in God's grace." We gave her this name as a prayer for her life. Her name and her lullaby turned out to be prophetic. God knew that she'd need to be strong and that we'd need to care for her with all we had, letting her go into the Father's hands, trusting him to breathe for her and us too.

Breathe God's L.I.F.E. into Your Child

Before Jesus ascended into heaven, he said to his disciples, "Receive the Holy Spirit," and he breathed on them (John 20:22). In Jesus the living God had walked and talked with Peter, James, John, and the other disciples and Christ-followers, but now God's very life entered their souls, and their bodies became temples for the Holy Spirit (1 Cor. 6:19). If there's one thing that our kids need from us, it's the *life of God*.

Do you know what the life of God is? I think maybe not. I know I didn't for many years, but in recent years I'm starting to understand. I'm not just talking about becoming a Christian. That's just the beginning. I'm talking about you and me and our kids having our souls animated by God's Spirit such that we live in the abundant life that Jesus came to bring us (John 10:10), a life that enjoys God moment by moment, a life of faith that overcomes the stresses and dark forces in this world, a life of vitality and purpose that impacts our world with God's Good News. People ripped off the roofs of houses to get this life from Jesus (Mark 2:1–12). Parents fought their way through crowds, with their children in tow, just to have their kids touched by the living God (Matt. 19:1–2, 13–15). It was that important to them. And it is to me. In fact, *nothing* is more important to me than being alive with God's life and imparting this life to others, especially my children. "For in him we live and move and have our being" (Acts 17:28). I believe that the primary purpose of Christian parenting is *discipleship*, inviting my children into my walk with Jesus, investing in them the life of God that I've come to experience so that they grow into being new creatures in Christ (2 Cor. 5:17). This is how it worked for Timothy. The apostle Paul affirmed him and his family saying that his faith first *lived* in his grandmother and then his mother (2 Tim. 1:5).

I think there are four aspects to this living faith that we want to impart to our children (and to experience for ourselves, or else how can we give it to them?). They represent four ways that we need God's L.I.F.E. in our souls, four developmental building blocks for the Christian life: Love, Identity, Forgiveness, and Enthusiasm. Imagine these four spiritual developmental needs as building blocks that stack on top of each other in a certain order, starting with love as the foundation.

Children's Four Developmental Needs for God's L.I.F.E.

Love Your Child as God Loves You

"God is love" is the apostle John's message to us. "Since God so loved us, we also ought to love one another. No one has ever seen God; but if we love one another, God lives in us and his love is made complete in us" (1 John 4:8, 11–12). In parenting our children, I believe that it is our greatest honor and opportunity to be "Christ's ambassadors, as though God were making his appeal through us. . . . Be reconciled to God" (2 Cor. 5:20). Or, as Eugene Peterson puts it in *The Message*, "Become friends with God; he's already a friend with you."

This is our role with our kids: to model and mediate to them the love of God. More than anything else this means developing a caring connection with our children and for our children. The parenting relationship should be focused on the parent providing for the child's needs, not the reverse. "After all, children should not have to save up for their parents, but parents for their children" (2 Cor. 12:14). A loving attachment between a parent and child forms the foundation for the child's psychological and spiritual development. We've got to start here. This is at the very core of who God is. He is a Trinity: Father, Son, and Holy Spirit are one, three persons in one Godhead. In other words, God *is* a community—each person of the Trinity is intimately bonded with the others in a perfect triangle. This is what our children need to experience. They need to belong in God's family by being "rooted and established in love" with God, parents, other family members, and friends so that they receive "glorious riches," "power through his Spirit," "love that surpasses knowledge," and "the fullness of God." (See Ephesians 3:14–21 to read the apostle Paul's beautiful prayer for families.) Children who are part of a family like this learn not only how to receive love but also how to give love to others.

Here's a list of some of the ways that we can establish a loving bond with our children:

- Provide physical care (meet basic needs).
- Offer back rubs.
- Listen.
- Cheer at their activities.
- Verbalize words of affirmation.
- Hug.
- Say, "I love you."
- Play a child's favorite game together.
- Comfort hurt feelings.
- Give gifts.

You could add to this list, I'm sure, but more important is to realize what all these expressions of God's connecting love have in common: time.

Love Takes Time

It takes time with their parent in a warm and caring relationship for children to establish trust in that parent. But in our age of drive-through coffee stores and instant messaging on the Internet, time is not something we have much of. Busy parents like us want to believe that we can cut back on the time we spend with our kids and make up for it by giving them "quality time." But it doesn't work that way!

You probably don't like hearing this. Kristi and I don't. We both are prone to overcommitting and becoming overwhelmed by a multitude of responsibilities, including our kids' activities. Kristi and I have to continually remind each other and discipline ourselves to set limits on our commitments and activities in order to set aside family time and one-on-one time with our three children. Otherwise, we get caught going downstream with the current of our culture, doing what almost everyone else seems to do: sacrificing time at home to advance a career, racing our kids from one activity to the next so they don't miss out on an opportunity, rushing through late dinners with family members missing, or, as I'm doing right this minute, tuning out a child's requests to work on a project. Isn't it easy to let our kids' emotional and spiritual needs take a backseat? We're busy doing our thing and they're busy doing theirs. It's as if we're "human *doings!*" But we're human *beings*, meant to *be* together, loving one another as God first loved us (1 John 4:19).

Show Your Child How to Pray

When I (Kristi) was growing up, my mother always had prayer partners, women she talked with and prayed with on a regular basis. (One of those women was and still is Jan Stoop.) I saw that it was one of the most important things in my mom's life, a priority and a commitment that was not to be interrupted. I remember tiptoeing around the house to be within earshot and listening to her pray in the other room. I saw that the way my mom and her friend prayed was warm and loving and it deepened their friendship. I felt loved by my mom because I heard her pray about her concerns for me. The other thing that meant a lot to me was that I saw her prayer times bring her peace; this was a living example to me of Philippians 4:6–7: "Do not be anxious about anything, but in everything, by prayer and petition, with thanksgiving, present your requests to God. And the peace of God, which transcends all understanding, will guard your hearts and your minds in Christ Jesus." It made me want to pray like that with a friend too!

A few years ago Bill and I took the challenge from Dave and Jan Stoop to pray together every day like they do. It brings back memories for me to see our kids listening to Bill and me pray together or when they listen to me pray with a friend over the phone or ask me about the Moms in Touch prayer group I lead for parents at their school. They're curious. They're watching us and learning from us.

Learning to pray is not something that happens automatically for Christians. I (Bill) have noticed at the New Hope Crisis Counseling Center that I direct that many of the Christians who volunteer to serve as counselors are not comfortable praying out loud with people at first. They need to be shown how to do it, encouraged to try, and given the opportunity. Kristi and I want to give our kids that opportunity right from the start in our home. So when Kristi or I invite them to pray during family devotions, at bedtime, or at the beginning of a long car ride, they know where to start. And we believe that over time learning to pray out loud with our family will deepen their relationships with the Lord and whet their appetites for developing the kind of spiritual friendships (mutually loving relationships that encourage spiritual growth) that are essential to Christian living.

Establish Your Child's Identity in God's Image

The truth that God is holy refers not only to his moral purity but also to the perfection of his being or his wholeness. God is a complete being, which is why he told Moses from the burning bush that his name was "I am who I am" (Exod. 3:14). He was saying in effect, "I am the 'to be' verb; I am the essence of what it means to be." And so throughout the Bible, God shows himself to us, revealing who he is and who he is not, what he loves and what he hates. God's identity is completely established, which is to say that he has complete self-knowledge, has perfect boundaries, and lacks nothing. If this weren't the case, then the Trinity couldn't exist as a loving community. As much as Father, Son, and Holy Spirit are one, they are also three. These boundaries enable the Trinity to be completely separate, even as they're completely intimate.

Just as God offers who he is to help us become who we're meant to be, so also with parents. Our children need us to offer ourselves to them in ways that encourage them to become who they're meant to be: God's image bearers. And we can't do this just by loving our children, at least not according to what we typically mean when we refer to love. Our kids need more than caring connection from us; they also need the structure of discipline and teaching. There are many negative and dark influences (within them and in their environment) that point our kids in the wrong direction. As Solomon said, each of us parents needs to be like a *warrior* pointing his arrow toward the target; we need to stand and fight for our kids, pointing them away from evil and toward God (Ps. 127:4–5). It's a battle for us to "bring them up in the training and instruction of the Lord" (Eph. 6:4). Helping our children to establish a godly identity in which they develop spiritually and grow into God's life represents the second major goal of Christian parenting.

Let's make another list, as we did with our children's love need. Here are some of the ways that we as parents can help our children establish their identity as children of God:

- Establish "house rules."
- Discipline misbehavior.
- Teach God's Word.
- Speak the truth in love.
- Identify unique gifts.
- Challenge them to be considerate of others.
- Label their feelings.
- Respect the Ten Commandments.
- Affirm individual personality.
- Pass on Christian family traditions.

Imprint a Godly Identity for Your Child

As a parent you probably have more power than you realize to develop a godly and glorious (yes, *glorious!* Second Corinthians 3:18 says that we're to "reflect the Lord's glory . . . with ever-increasing glory") identity in your child. Certainly, it often doesn't feel that we can influence our kids like we want. They have minds of their own. But I've found it to be true that most children (and even many adults) are spiritually moldable, but only at critical moments of trust. It's like the way in which a gosling becomes "imprinted." Right after it hatches, and only at that moment, the baby goose attaches itself to the first thing it sees moving nearby. Of course, this is supposed to be the mother goose, but if she is removed, then the gosling will settle for any mother substitute. That could be a mother duck, in which case he'd grow up confused. Or it could be a fox, and in that case he'd be eaten. Researchers have found that goslings imprint readily on blue football bladders being dragged by a string. They follow the blue bladder around wherever it goes!

Time is critical in the imprinting process. The gosling imprints in the few seconds right after it hatches. If the opportunity is lost, it cannot be regained. It's similar for children, but fortunately, we have years to work with, not seconds. But as any parent with older children knows, the time is short and the older they get the harder it is to make a godly imprint. Infants and toddlers will imprint on their mother's relational style and emotional state because their attachment (loving connection) needs are so strong. And preschool- and school-aged children will imprint their parent's affirmations and values to form their identity and conscience. As the proverb says, "Train a child in the way he should go, and when he is old he will not turn from it" (Prov. 22:6). Some Bible teachers say that this verse is better interpreted to say, "Train up a child *according to who he is*, and when he is old he will not turn from it." In other words, discover the God-given personality and gifts of your child and bring those out.

Affirm Your Child's Personality and Gifts

A few months ago I had an imprinting opportunity when my seven-year-old daughter Briana asked me a question I'll never forget. My family was going around the dinner table sharing our "peaks and pits" of the day, and I had just responded to what Briana's sister Jenny shared by affirming her as having a heart of compassion. Jenny is an appreciative girl, so she lapped up my words like a puppy with a bowl of milk. It was at that point that Briana looked at me with her own puppy dog eyes and panted with anticipation, "Daddy, what do I have a heart of?"

I turned to look at her precious face and eager heart. She had caught me unprepared, so I hesitated for a moment, thinking to myself, *What I say right now is crucial. It may be the most important question she ever asks me! Lord, what is Briana's heart made of?* "Little girls are made of sugar and spice and everything nice" wouldn't have met Briana's need. She wanted me to recognize her beautiful uniqueness like I had her sister's. Thank God that all of a sudden he gave me the words, "Briana, you have the heart of a leader. Your name means 'strong in God's grace' and that's what you are. I love to see how you lead people in good ways."

Briana wagged her tail and yelped with excitement, "Mommy! Mommy! I have the heart of a leader!" I was so glad that my little girl brought the question of her heart to me and that God spoke through me to give her the affirmation she needed for her identity. I know that as she grows up there are a lot of other places she could bring that question, like to a fickle friend, a boy with lustful desires, or alcohol at a party. I believe that my affirmation will help her to stand a little taller and smile a little bigger and be better able to pick herself back up when she gets a bad grade, when she feels rejected by a friend, or when I lose my temper at her.

There was also a quiet hound dog at the table who could have been left out, so I affirmed him also by saying, "And, David, you're an engineer and a teacher. I love the way you design and build things and then explain how they work to others." Blessing my children with affirming words is not something that has come naturally for me. I've worked on it because I believe it is so crucial. Our heavenly Father in the Bible models it for us. For instance, he says that children are a "heritage" and a "reward" (Ps. 127:3), a "blessing" (Ps. 127:5), and a "crown" (Prov. 17:6). And in a culture in which children were thought of as possessions and interruptions, Jesus made time for them and repeatedly held them in highest esteem, standing them in front of the crowds to praise them and point out that anyone who wants to enter God's kingdom must become like a child (Matt. 18:1–6; 19:13–15).

A Model for Family Devotions

One of the most helpful things that Kristi and I have done to encourage our children's spiritual development and strengthen their emerging Christian identities was to launch family devotions at dinner. We had tried and failed at this a few times, and I had become quite frustrated, feeling like I was spiritually encouraging my clients, the lay counselors I train, and people who came to my seminars at church, but not getting through to my own kids! We were both sad about this because God's Word is so important to us, and we want it to be important in our family life too. So we tried again and our effort was again met with resistance in the form of protests, complaining, and whining. But this time we persisted, and our kids grew to appreciate this time and only occasionally do they react negatively to it now.

I wish I could show you the three-ring binder notebook with Bible verses that we use. It would demonstrate to you our children's affection for and identification with our family devotions. Each one of them has taken turns personalizing the white cover and pages with messages like, "Bible + Jesus = God," "Hello!" and "Gaultiere's Dinner Devotional." And there are precious pictures of Jesus, a heart, a house, a boy, and a girl reading a Bible in her lap and saying, "Wow!" There's even some good theology represented in a picture of a triangle, labeled "God," with each point of the triangle listing a member of the Trinity: Father, Jesus, Spirit. Our kids have made these devotions a part of their family identity.

Along with the united determination that Kristi and I had, I think what helped us develop our family devotions was that we used a very simple system that fit our family values. We scrapped the idea of the typical family devotional book that has stories and crafts and pictures. Instead, I picked out 365 Bible verses according to thirty-one themes (one theme for each day of the month so that there were twelve verses for each theme). We called our first family devotional book "Essential Christian Beliefs and Values." Its themes include God's love and holiness, the Trinity, Jesus as the way to a relationship with God, confessing our sins, appreciating our incredible worth as God's children, and obeying each of the Ten Commandments. (Our second and current family devotional book is called "The Promises of God" and the next one will be called "Why the Christian Message Is True.")

Because the verses were numbered one to thirty-one and not tied to a specific date, we didn't get behind or feel guilty if we missed a day; we knew we'd catch that verse the next month and it wouldn't matter if it took us longer than a year to get through it (it did!). And we made our devotions very flexible so that if the kids were antsy when we were discussing the importance of telling the truth, for example, then we could read the verse, explain it, and pray in five minutes or less. However, if they were interested because we were discussing what the Bible teaches about sex, to take another example, then we'd let the discussion go on, relating the verse to real situations that were occurring in their lives and answering their questions. As much as possible we got our kids to do the talking, which included having David teach his younger sisters. (If you would like us to email you a free copy of the first devotional we created, contact us through our website, www.ChristianSoulCare.com.)

Encourage Your Child to Do Personal Bible Study

I think I was about ten years old when I received my first Bible. For years I had watched my mother read the Bible and underline verses that were especially important to her. She wrote verses down and put them up on our refrigerator. It was like she was *feeding* off of it every day. I now know that she was! It's just like Jesus said when he quoted Deuteronomy 8:3, "Man does not live on bread alone, but on every word that comes from the mouth of God" (Matt. 4:4). For more than thirty years now, I've been feeding my own soul almost daily on God's Word. I've learned that not only is the Bible soul food, but it's a window and a mirror. It's a window for me to see what God is like, the glorious beauty of his holiness and the wonder of his mercy. And it's a mirror for me to see my need for God's grace and wisdom and to appreciate the astounding truth that he's transforming me to be glorious like him.

Of course, pressuring our kids to read the Bible is not helpful. I've learned that when we do this they either swallow our expectation whole and compliantly read the Bible without digesting it, or they gag over being force-fed and rebel. From birth we've read our kids Bible stories when they were receptive. Then as each one has learned to read, we've provided them with beginner's Bibles. And as we just discussed, once they were all school-aged, we started doing regular family devotions, which we did make nonnegotiable, but we have tried to do them in a way that accommodates their interest level.

Kristi and I were so pleased last summer when Jenny was invited by some of her friends to join a Bible study. She wanted to do this and brought her own Bible to the group. She did her lessons each week, asking Kristi for help when she needed it. Then this year she wanted Kristi to lead the group and to hold it in our home so that she could invite some of her friends in the neighborhood who don't go to church. It's exciting to see her developing her own relationship with God's Word, and it gives us hope that she'll continue this throughout her life.

Forgive Your Child as God Has Forgiven You

The gospel is the most wonderful news there is! Do you ever just stand back and marvel at what God has done by becoming Emanuel, "God with us"? I get choked up just thinking about it. He's made you and me and our children his temple (1 Cor. 6:19). His life—his grace and truth, his perfect love and glorious identity—lives in our souls! Of course, this is only possible because he has forgiven us of our sins. The sin of humanity's first parents, Adam and Eve, has been passed on to us and our children through our genetic code, and we too have eaten the spoiled fruit of sin, choosing to hurt one another, ourselves, and our God who loves us so incredibly.

Our children need to receive God's forgiveness for their sins, and they need to learn it from us. "Forgive as the Lord forgave you" (Col. 3:13), the apostle Paul exhorts us. By forgiving others we're serving as Christ's ambassadors of reconciliation (2 Cor. 5:20), imparting God's forgiveness on his behalf. This is quite astounding. I don't think we grasp the gravity of this responsibility, the possibility of this opportunity! Jesus taught us, "If you forgive anyone his sins, they are forgiven; if you do not forgive them, they are not forgiven" (John 20:23). Indeed, I have observed many times that if a child doesn't learn forgiveness from a parent, then that child will have difficulty understanding God's mercy and grace and will struggle with relationships until he or she gets help.

Let's think about what forgiveness looks like. Here are some examples of how we as parents can share God's forgiveness with our children, how we can teach them to receive it and share it with others:

- Say, "I forgive you," when they sin.
- Don't hold on to their past wrongs.
- Encourage them to forgive a friend.
- Model saying, "I'm sorry."
- Let go of anger.
- Discuss biblical examples of forgiveness.
- Listen to their angry feelings.
- Be warm after disciplining.

Don't Hold On to Anger at Your Child

One of the biggest challenges of parenting is letting go of anger. At times our kids look at us and they disobey, disrespect, frustrate, irritate, overwhelm, deplete, hurt, violate, or betray. Of course, we feel angry! We also feel angry at our kids when it's not their fault, like when we've had a hard day or when they're not meeting our unrealistic expectations. This is where Monique was at. She said to me (Kristi), "I've become the angry mom I don't want to be. I find myself nagging, criticizing, and yelling at my kids." As we talked about different examples, I helped Monique to see that she was react- ing with a hundred volts of anger in situations that called for just twenty-five volts, or maybe only ten volts. She was carrying forward her unresolved anger at her own mother, who had not only yelled at her but hit her. It was as if her abusive mother lived inside her head, criticizing her, demanding that she do more and more, and then when her kids acted up, it tripped a switch and her anger turned on them. This, of course, became a vicious circle: She was stressed and irritable, her kids acted up, she lost her temper, the kids behaved worse, and so on until Monique exploded and then everyone just got quiet and felt bad.

I helped Monique learn how to "be angry, and do not sin" (Eph. 4:26 NKJV). Instead of imploding or exploding (either one leads to the other) with her kids, Monique needed to feel her anger, talk it through with a safe person, take any assertive action that was called for (like calmly discussing the issue with her child, protecting the one being violated, administering a consequence, or making time and space to get her own need met), and then let it go to God. Over time, as Monique learned to talk to a friend or journal about what she was feeling; confess her anger and receive God's forgiveness for losing her temper with her kids; experience the healing process of forgiving her mother; be more active in getting her own needs met; and set better boundaries with her kids, then she became a calmer and more gracious mother.

Model the Need for Forgiveness

For me (Bill), it seems that the most powerful lessons I've given my kids on forgiveness have been the result of my own parental failings. For instance, a few years ago on a rainy Saturday, I was caring for all three of my kids while Kristi was getting a much-needed break from mothering. I was taking David and Jenny to an Awana activity day, and we were late getting back from Jenny's soccer game. We made a quick stop at home, and I told Jenny to take off her cleats and get some tennis shoes on. She took an unreasonably long time, but finally we were in the car. When we got to the church, I went to open the back door of the car, and there was Jenny in her sandals! How was she going to race and jump and play games in the church gym wearing sandals? I lost my temper and slammed the car door and then gave her a scolding. Immediately, I felt terrible about myself. I didn't want to deal with the issue, so I whisked David and Jenny off into the church.

And then Briana, who was five at the time, and I were to begin our "Daddy date," reading books at the bookstore. I wanted to scream or crawl in a hole somewhere. How could I smile, sit Briana in my lap, and patiently read stories with her after what I had just done? Fortunately, like a good golfer (which I am not) who made a bad shot, I made a good recovery shot. As I was driving Briana to the bookstore, I assessed what had happened. I realized that I had been feeling time-pressured and angry, and that I now felt guilty for how I had handled the situation and was starting to feel ashamed as a father. Then I told myself that I wasn't all bad as a father or a person, but I had just made a mistake. I asked for and received forgiveness from God. I reminded myself of my good qualities, like taking that "Daddy date" with Briana. I thought about how Jenny (and her brother and sister) may have felt criticized and scared when I lost my temper. Finally, I asked for forgiveness from each of my kids for slamming the door and being overly harsh, and I asked them how they felt about the incident and listened.

God brought something good out of what was bad. He helped us to recover. He led me out of shame and into feeling sad that I hurt my kids and acted out of character. He gave me the strength to apologize and to offer comfort to each of my kids. They forgave me readily and learned a lesson, not only about forgiving, but also about talking through conflicts and hurt feelings.

Teaching Your Kids to Say, "I'm Sorry," and "I Forgive You"

If you have more than one child in your home, then you've experienced your share of sibling rivalry. Siblings argue and hurt each other. The temptation for most parents is to play referee and try to eliminate the noise and stress by shutting it down. Or you can take the opposite track and just tune it out and detach. Kristi and I have played it both ways, as I imagine you have too. We've learned though to take the role of *coach*. This takes quite a bit of self-restraint and energy (which is why we find it easy to lapse into "fixing" the conflict or ignoring it). But it's more effective to do what a good coach does: Observe the problem and give them a chance to work it out and come to a solution on their own and then step in and guide their process as needed. With sibling conflict this means inviting them to understand one another and soliciting their ideas on how they can work it out. It's unrealistic to try to eliminate your kids' arguments, but it is realistic and very important to teach them to say, "I'm sorry," when they hurt someone and to say, "I forgive you," when they've been wronged. Learning this while they're young will pay dividends in their relationships for the rest of their lives, not only with their future spouse, family, and friends, but also with God.

"I'm sorry" and "I forgive you" are some of the hardest words to say, aren't they? I know how hard they are for me to say sometimes. And I see how hard they are for many of the people who consult me for psychotherapy. I especially see this in the marriage counseling I do. Often husbands and wives don't know how to repair the wounds they give each other. I told a Christian couple just today that their marriage was like a frog that they were boiling to death by turning up the heat one degree at a time. Just like the frog that won't jump out of the increasingly hot water until it's too late, many couples get used to living with unresolved conflicts, hurt feelings, and bitterness. This breaks my heart every time I see it because I know the soul friendship they're missing. Why don't they share their hearts and seek to understand and comfort one another? Because they've buried their hurts and put walls up, probably like they learned to do as children in their families of origin.

I was pleased to hear from Kristi the other day that she overheard a friend say to Jenny, "I'm sorry I was being mean to you yesterday. I don't know why I did that when you're my friend." Jenny replied, "That's okay. I forgive you." It was one of those moments when as a parent you breathe a sigh of relief and say, "Oh, thank God. I think what we're doing is working!" We have to hold on to those moments and remind each other of them often, because, frankly, most days it seems as if what we're trying to teach our kids as parents isn't working!

Invite Your Child to Live with Enthusiasm

You might think it odd for me to suggest that enthusiasm is the fourth need in the spiritual development of a child. Is joy really a need? And what's spiritual about it? Well, if you've ever been depressed to the point of having trouble getting out of bed, smiling, or trusting God, then you know that enjoyment is essential to living. The word *enthusiasm* actually comes from the Greek work *entheos*, which literally means "in God." Enthusiasm is the vitality of God in your soul, energizing you to live with joyful, godly purpose. It's what Nehemiah had as he led the Israelites through the long, hard work of rebuilding the wall around Jerusalem and proclaimed, "The joy of the LORD is your strength" (Neh. 8:10). It's the rejoicing and worshiping faith that David modeled in the Psalms, during times that were happy or painful, peaceful or stressful. It's the proud joy that a wise son or daughter brings to his or her parents (Prov. 15:20). It's even commanded in the Bible: "Rejoice in the Lord always. I will say it again: Rejoice!" (Phil. 4:4). This joy is unrelated to circumstances because it's a fruit of the Spirit (Gal. 5:22); it's the pleasure we feel when our souls are in tune with God (Ps. 16:11).

Enthusiasm is what we experience when God's life is in our souls through faith in Christ and we're living and moving in him (Acts 17:28), keeping in step with his Spirit (Gal. 5:25), and sharing his love with others (Phil. 2:1–2). Jesus said that to live in the Holy Spirit is like having a spring of living water bubbling forth from our souls (John 4:13–14). I want this. And I want it for you and for our children. I desire for my children to discover and then follow the unique and wonderful calling that God has for their lives. I want them to develop their own Christian faith because I know that there's no greater joy in life than to walk hand-in-hand with our loving Lord, bringing him glory through doing his work. Here are some ways we can encourage our children to live out their own, enthusiastic faith in Christ:

- Model an enthusiastic faith.
- Take them to a dynamic church youth group.
- Value their hearts' desires.
- Encourage Christian friendships.
- Explain your own life mission.
- Send them to Christian camps.
- Identify their spiritual gifts.
- Set up spiritual milestones for them.

Rely on the Body of Christ

Each of these ideas for guiding your child into an enthusiastic faith requires depending on the body of Christ in some way. You just can't raise a godly child without Christian community. The first time we sent our oldest child, David, to Christian camp, it was difficult to let go. He was ten at the time, and we worried, *Will he be lonely or get homesick? Might there be some bad influences?* But he came back excited. He wanted a Bible of his own and became interested in reading it with me at night. He got a fish sticker and put it on his bedroom window. And he joined a small group Bible study at our church with other boys his age. Having people other than Mom and Dad encourage Christian living and being around other kids who are enthusiastic Christians is powerful in encouraging children to develop their own dynamic faith in Jesus.

Since I read the book *Spiritual Milestones*, Kristi and I have started planning and celebrating with family and friends our children's spiritual passages. This is an exciting and effective way to encourage the development of your child's faith. The idea is to invite your child to focus on his or her next faith step and then for you and your child to structure a fun and meaningful celebration around that event. You can do this with first communion, catechism class, a preparing for adolescence weekend, a commitment to sexual purity ceremony, or a Christian rite of passage ceremony (like a Jewish bar mitzvah).

For instance, when our daughter Jenny wanted to be baptized at age ten, she and I studied what the Bible teaches about being baptized and she took a class at church on it so she knew what she was doing. She said that she wanted to be baptized to be a witness for Jesus, to show her family and friends (including her non-Christian friends from public school) that she believed in Jesus. So we planned a special service for her. She invited fifty-six people to our house, and amazingly almost everyone came. The invitation that she sent out had her testimony on it, and it was so powerful that her eight-year-old cousin prayed to become a Christian after reading it. Then at the actual baptism service, Kristi and I gathered everyone and gave them a chance to affirm Jenny's faith. The pastor explained the meaning of baptism, people laid hands on her and prayed for her, she said why she wanted to be baptized, and her pastor and I baptized her in our backyard Jacuzzi with these words: "Jenny, because God loves you and you want to follow Jesus, we baptize you in the name of the Father, the Son, and the Holy Spirit." Lastly, we all ate together. Afterward, I asked Jenny what it felt like to be baptized. She said, "Daddy, it was so special. It was like lying back into soft, calming kitten fur!"

Sharing the Joy of Worship

The first time I remember being drawn into worship is when I was twelve years old. My family was visiting at my aunt and uncle's house and my two older cousins had learned to play the guitar and lead worship. That evening we all gathered to sing praise songs. I didn't know what this meant. Even though I was raised in a Christian home, we didn't sing together, and when we prayed it didn't include worship. The church my family attended was a rather formal church, so my association with worship was people singing religious hymns that I didn't understand and praying long, boring prayers. But what I experienced that night was different. It wasn't religious; it was spiritual. I wasn't disinterested; I was excited. I watched my teenage cousins talk and sing to Jesus with such devotion and adoration—and *joy*! My cousins loved praising God and it showed.

The joy I experienced that night was compelling. I knew I needed more of that. As an adolescent I experienced my home and my church as depressing in some ways. But then I had this experience of joyful worship, of being with Christians who were enthusiastic in their love and adoration of Jesus. Since that time I've befriended people who are alive with the joy of the Lord, and I've tried to absorb their spirit and learn from them. I have a ways to go, but I'm learning to "worship the LORD with gladness" (Ps. 100:2) and to share this with my kids.

Perhaps the most obvious ways that we can do this are to take our kids into the church service with us on occasion and let them see us sing praises with enthusiasm to God, or when saying a prayer at dinner or bedtime to include some heartfelt praises to God such as, "Father God, you are so good to us, so kind and generous. We're so blessed to be your children!" But it can also be as simple as to comment while driving, "Hasn't God made a beautiful day for us today!" or to give your child a smile and a hug and a blessing, "I'm so glad that God has given me the chance to be your dad!"

Children Internalizing and Passing on the L.I.F.E. of God

The main point we're emphasizing in this chapter is that Christian parenting is *incarnational*. Think of this as a succession of three triangles, as indicated below. The Trinity Triangle depicts God in loving community with his three distinct identities. The Parenting Triangle shows a parent teaming up with God to care for his or her child and to invite that child into the parent's relationship with God. Finally, the Child's Soul Triangle views three critical psychological constructs that a child internalizes from God and the parent and which can be positive or negative depending mostly on how well the Parenting Triangle transmits the Trinity Triangle to the child.

Helping Your Child to Internalize God

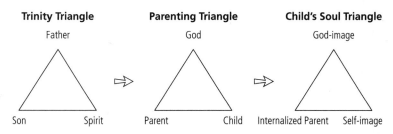

Trinity Triangle	Parenting Triangle	Child's Soul Triangle
Father	God	God-image
Son Spirit	Parent Child	Internalized Parent Self-image

The bottom left corner of each of the three triangles illustrates the incarnational aspect of Christian parenting. God entered human flesh in Jesus, showing us the Father's love and giving us his Holy Spirit to overflow our souls. Then the parent, as Christ's ambassador, is put in position by God to reveal and mediate God's care. Finally, the child internalizes an understanding of the parent (internalized parent) and God (the God-image, along with the conscience) and develops a view of self that's in relationship to the parent, God, and others.

As parents we want to try to pass on the love, identity, forgiveness, and enthusiasm of God to our children so that they internalize the life of God for themselves and then share it with others. If they experience Mom and Dad as caring, affirming, gracious, and inspiring (internalized parent), and this is done in Jesus' name (God-image), then the odds are high that they will see themselves as lovable, significant, made good by God, and joyful (self-image). They'll carry God's glorious image into their lives, blessing other people and honoring their Lord Jesus Christ.

Questions to Discuss

1. What do you think about the view that Christian parenting is about discipling children to be like Jesus?
2. What new idea do you have for imparting more of God's loving connectivity to your child?
3. What things are you doing to teach your child what it means to be a Christ-follower? What is something else you might do to establish your child's Christian identity?
4. Think of a time that you experienced God's mercy or grace and share that with your child.
5. What spiritual milestone would you like to celebrate with your child in the near future?

For Further Reading

Arterburn, Steve, and David Stoop, eds. *Spiritual Renewal Bible, New Living Translation*. Wheaton: Tyndale, 1998.

Cloud, Henry, and John Townsend. *Raising Great Kids*. Grand Rapids: Zondervan, 1999.

Henley, Karyn, and Dennas Davis. *The Beginner's Bible*. Grand Rapids: Zondervan, 1997.

Weidmann, Jim and Janet, and J. Otis and Gail Ledbetter. *Spiritual Milestones*. Colorado Springs: Focus on the Family, 2001.

12

UNDERSTANDING YOUR CHILD'S PERSONALITY

David and Jan Stoop

Remember back to when your child was a tiny newborn. It's an incredible experience to see how your baby's physical makeup is wonderfully knit together by God. The little hands and feet are part of God's beautiful handiwork. Then when we think of what is inside that infant—a heart, stomach, lungs, intestines, a complex brain that will eventually control every aspect of the child's mind and body—we are even more amazed.

We should be equally in awe of the complexity of a baby's personality as it unfolds. It is something that makes every human different from every other human. Yet when God makes something, there is within it a simplicity of design that makes it understandable to us. We have three sons and five grandchildren. They are all part of our gene pool and have similarities in their personalities, yet each one is uniquely different from the other. Let's look at some of these simple yet identifiable traits that develop in our children over the first couple years of their lives.

The Inner-Directed Child versus the Outer-Directed Child

The first personality trait that reveals itself in a child is the preference for what the *Myers-Briggs Type Indicator*[1] calls introversion and extroversion. Children who are more inner-directed are called introverts, and those who are more outer-directed are extroverts. These traits are genetically determined, and if children are not like either Mom or Dad, they are probably like a grandparent, aunt, or uncle.

We can observe this trait early in an infant's life by noticing his or her reactions to other people and to new situations. The natural reserve of the introvert will be seen as a hesitation in approaching the unfamiliar—whether it is a person or a situation. The extroverted infant will be more open to other people and to new situations.

The infant who clings to Mom when guests come to the house is probably an introvert, whereas the child who is curious about the visitor and willing to look at the guest and respond to the guest's baby talk is probably going to be an extrovert. The toddler who holds your eyes with her eyes and then gives you a shy smile is probably a budding extrovert. The one who doesn't even notice you looking at him or her is most likely an introvert. The preschool kids in the van in front of you who are waving at you and everyone else who passes them are all extroverts. The introvert isn't even looking out the window, or if he is, he is not waving; he is looking at people only to try to figure out why the other kids are enjoying waving at you so much. Here is a list that will help you identify which preference your child has.

The Extroverted Child Will More Often	The Introverted Child Will More Often
• relate primarily to an external world	• relate primarily to an internal world
• be comfortable with new places, people, events, and activities	• want to understand or know people, places, events, and activities before experiencing them
• talk while learning—will talk a lot	• think through things silently first
• not be comfortable being alone	• need solitude, or downtime
• need friends to play with	• be content to play alone
• be easily distracted	• be good at concentrating
• find silence frustrating	• find silence comfortable

The Open-Ended Child versus the Child Needing Closure

The second trait we might begin to see is a preference for what the *Myers-Briggs* identifies as the *judging* preference as opposed to the *perceiving* preference when a child is between eighteen to twenty-four months. The judging child prefers and values being prepared for situations. He or she works best when the rules are clear and predictable. He or she has an emerging work ethic about life and loves it when things are settled and finished. Change is uncomfortable to the judging child. They typically like to have their toys in place, and often Mom must put things back where they belong.

The perceiving child is much more comfortable with things being open-ended. Rules are seen as restrictive, and finishing something is very optional. Organization is not important to this child, and this will be seen in the way his or her room is organized, how well the child keeps things in order, and how comfortable he or she is in stopping one activity to do something else. Change is often welcomed, and so are spontaneous activities. The child who prefers closure will be more obvious at a younger age than the child who prefers that things be left open-ended.

The Judging Child Will More Often	The Perceiving Child Will More Often
• prepare for tasks	• give little outward appearance of organization
• work best with clear rules	• find rules to be restrictive
• have a good work ethic	• have more of a play ethic
• be very time-conscious	• find time to be relative, not specific
• have a sense of order in own room	• show no outward sense of order within room
• be uncomfortable with too much change	• be able to handle change well
• work methodically	• work quickly in spurts

The Other Four Traits Come Later

The other four traits—sensing versus intuition and thinking versus feeling—will more likely become clear by the time a child enters school, or soon after. The sensing child prefers concrete things as opposed to abstract ideas. They live in the present and like real things, such as real stories about real people. They need specific, precise instruction and love to deal with facts. The sensing child will start a book on page one and continue reading until the book is finished, or until they get bored with the book and quit. Directions and instructions are important to the sensing child.

The opposite—the intuitive trait—is much more abstract and tends to focus on the future and on the imagination. Having an intuitive child clean his or her room may last only a few minutes, for as the child begins the task of cleaning, he or she discovers some item that sparks the imagination, and an hour later, maybe only three things have been picked up in the room.

In school, the intuitive child will often stop listening to instructions, assuming he or she knows what the teacher is going to say. They love to start with the big picture and then move to the specifics. They love reading but often skim over what seems to be too detailed. Anything that engages their imagination will keep this child busy for hours.

The Sensing Child Will More Often	The Intuitive Child Will More Often
• be very concrete and specific	• be more abstract, live in a world of ideas
• play with toys as designed	• play imaginatively with toys
• love facts	• love to daydream
• memorize easily	• find it hard to focus on specifics
• read more slowly but grasp details	• read quickly—skim material
• want step-by-step instructions	• be impatient with instructions
• start with the specifics and move to the big picture	• start with the big picture and move to the specifics

The thinking child will appear to be detached, logical, and objective about people and situations. They are good at analyzing things, so math and science are natural courses for these children. They are often very competitive, and their need to be right about things can get them into trouble. They can even appear to sacrifice relationship for the sake of rightness. When this trait is found in a daughter, there is often concern that she is not being very feminine, but this is not true. Femininity is not related to the thinking trait except in the minds of some observers. It is important not to attach this value to a daughter who loves to analyze.

The feeling child will make decisions through a subjective personal value system and often looks most at how decisions affect other people. He or she may not be able to give reasons for their decisions or opinions; they just know what is right. People are a primary value to the feeling child, and they are good at understanding what is going on relationally. They know when a teacher is being unfair and are often highly offended by it even though they cannot give exact reasons why they feel that way. It is much easier to "read" the feeling child, for their emotional responses are written all over their faces. They may try to hide feelings but are not very good at it.

Competition is very unimportant to the feeling child. He or she often plays games just to be involved. A son who shows the feeling function as his preference is often misunderstood by others, especially by his father. He may be seen as weak or too sensitive. The *Myers-Briggs* identifies these traits and makes a strong point that they represent a decision process and really are not related to emotions. While the feeling child is much more open about his or her emotions, it is important to recognize as a parent that the thinking child often has the same level of intensity with his or her emotions.

The Thinking Child Will More Often	The Feeling Child Will More Often
• love the *why* questions	• be concerned with others' feelings
• be very objective	• be very subjective
• love competition	• see competition as secondary to relationships
• love to debate with you	• not want to hurt you, so won't debate
• fight to be right	• worry about what others feel
• like individual projects	• like working with a group
• enjoy analyzing things	• show feelings on face
• treat rules as primary in games	• treat people's feelings as primary in games

Examples of How These Traits Work Together

To describe how this simplicity of design helps us understand our child, let's take a look at what happens with some children as they make their choices on the playground during recess. We will identify eight different ways a child's personality can be organized.

The Organizers

One of the first children we meet is Brad. He's hard to miss, for he is right in the middle of a large group of children trying to get a game of kickball started. After all, that was one of the things the teacher had suggested they do, and Brad is up to the task of getting the game started. You can hear his voice above the other children's chatter, and soon he and a friend (whom we will meet later) are choosing sides. Bill (whom we'll also meet later) and several others are quietly waiting for the "leaders" to finish organizing so that the game can get under way.

Brad's female counterpart is Margaret. She's over on the cement with a bunch of girls getting a game of hopscotch organized—another game suggested by one of the teachers. Margaret has enlisted several of the quieter ones to go and find some chalk so they can begin drawing the squares. Soon Margaret has everyone organized; the girls are lined up, and the game begins.

Both Brad and Margaret are "out there" children. They are quick to speak, often thinking as they talk. Their sense of order and need for closure make them junior administrators. Each took a suggestion from the teacher and organized a group of children to make it happen. They didn't start the game just because the teacher suggested it; they did it because it made sense to them and because they wanted to. Their young personalities have equipped them already to enjoy the task of getting everyone organized so the fun can begin. They are both examples of children who combine the extroversion, sensing, and judging traits.

The Monitors

Bill and Miriam are similar to Brad and Margaret, except they are quieter and more inside themselves. They want to play the game, and they could probably organize it as well. But the thought of organizing the game would only occur to them a little later on. They appear to be less aware of what is going on around them because they are more preoccupied with their own private internal worlds.

While Brad and Margaret are enthusiastically directing the other children to get organized for the game, Bill and Miriam are each clustered around two or three other friends, talking and patiently waiting.

Even though they also have an internal sense of structure and like things to get started, you would see these traits in Miriam and Bill only if there were no Brads or Margarets around to press ahead.

Bill and Miriam could also be called the *cooperators*. They cooperate with the teacher as well as with the other students. They can become easily frustrated with peers who are not as cooperative as they are, especially when it comes to cooperating with teachers or other authority figures. Whereas Brad and Margaret will organize the game because the job is there to be done and they want to play, Bill and Miriam might organize the game more out of a sense of duty, because the teacher said they should and because no one else is present who can. They are both examples of children who combine the introversion, sensing, and judging traits.

The Relaters

Now that the games of kickball and hopscotch are under way, we notice Julie in another part of the playground. She and a group of girls are sitting at the lunch tables talking a mile a minute. It seems that this group of girls is often together, and they love to talk. If you stand nearby and listen, you will notice that they often interrupt each other, and no one seems to mind. You will also notice that their conversation wanders all over the place, and no one seems to mind that either. Their goal is to be together and talk. Sometimes Julie and her friends join in the games around the playground, but even then, their focus will be on friends and talking together.

Daren is very much like Julie. But because he is a boy, his friendliness will be more task-oriented. He may be playing kickball with Brad's team, but he makes sure that most of his friends are also on his team. They are always chattering with each other on the field, and when they are on the bench, they seem to be having a party. Brad often has to interrupt Daren to let him know it's his turn to be at bat.

One of the fun things about Daren is that he usually has something he's willing to trade. It may be a pocketful of baseball cards, a baseball glove, or even one of the new puppies at home. He is a natural salesman, even on the playground. Both Daren and Julie are curious about the world of ideas and about getting to know other people. Both of them are enthusiastic about life, and they are usually very idealistic about their friends. Both Julie and Daren are examples of children who combine the extroversion, intuitive, and feeling traits.

The Dreamers

Jennifer is much like Julie, the relater, except that she is more reserved. She has the same idealism and enthusiasm, but hers is more hidden. Rather than sit and talk with a group of girlfriends, Jennifer can be seen walking the perimeter of the playground with her one best friend—Sally—deep in conversation. Sally is fairly new at the school, and when she was introduced to Jennifer's class, she seemed uncomfortable and somewhat sad to be there. Jennifer felt her discomfort and immediately reached out to her. Jennifer is always concerned about how others are feeling, especially those who seem to be being treated unfairly by their peers or by a teacher.

Dan is very much like Jennifer in that he is also quieter and more reserved than some of the other personalities. But rather than wander around the perimeter of the playground with a friend, he's sitting off by himself, watching what everyone else is doing. At least it appears that he is watching. But if we were to speak to him, we would probably find that he started out watching the others but ended up lost in a daydream. In his mind he has escaped to some exotic place in space or time. Perhaps he's fighting with the Native Americans they read about in class that morning. Or maybe he is thinking how he would have kicked in the winning run if he had chosen to play kickball. Dan has several close friends who are interested in the same things he's interested in, but they aren't in school today.

What's interesting about both Jennifer and Dan is that they are very content with their small circle of friends. In their minds, a whole other world is available through their imagination, and it seems senseless to crowd life with too many people. Even though they are usually the only ones in a classroom with their particular personality, they often find a kindred-spirit friend with whom they can relax and be themselves. Jennifer and Dan are examples of children who combine the introversion, intuitive, and feeling traits.

The Competitors

Calvin is the boy who chose teams with Brad. While Brad organized the other kids who were going to play, Calvin was strategizing as to whom he would pick and whom he thought Brad would pick and whom he was going to pick first. Once the game starts, Brad has a great time playing kickball. But on the other side of the field, Calvin is much more intense with his team. To him the fun is in winning. So he is always trying to figure out what the opponents will be doing and then getting his team set up in some way that will neutralize the play. This intensity is missing in Brad, but Calvin's intensity seems to limit the fun he could have at whatever he is doing. For Calvin, play is serious business, and whenever it is competitive, he is up to the challenge. Unfortunately, Calvin's seriousness doesn't always carry over into his classroom work. If he's challenged by a subject, he can excel, but if he's bored with a subject, Calvin's mind is off somewhere else and he'll miss what's going on in the classroom.

Abbey is very much like Calvin. She is playing hopscotch and is very careful about how she plays, and she also is determined to win. As the others take their turns, Abbey's strong sense of justice kicks in quickly if someone complains about a landing. Abbey can out-argue any of them; she can even out-argue most of the boys. Sometimes her logical abilities are a source of both joy and embarrassment to her. She doesn't mind being smarter than most of the other girls, but there are times she does mind being smarter and more logical than most of the boys.

Abbey has to work hard at fitting in with the other girls. That's why she plays every game she can. She is good at almost everything she tries, but she is never satisfied with her performance. To her, she always could have done better. Both Calvin and Abbey can be very self-critical, and Abbey's critical spirit seldom spills over onto others. They are self-critical because they are always bent on improving whatever they are doing. Calvin and Abbey are examples of children who combine the extroversion, intuitive, and thinking traits.

The Explorers

Carl is different from Calvin only in that he is quieter and more inner-directed. That little shift makes a big difference in how each of these boys lives his life. Rather than joining in with what the others are doing, Carl is usually off by himself exploring. He has found an old piece of concrete and moved it, revealing a whole new world of bugs. For most of the time on the playground, Carl is lost in this bug world. He watches them scurry around to find the safety they lost when the rock was moved. He picks up one that he's never seen before and examines it carefully. He even has a magnifying glass in his pocket that helps him see what happens as he manipulates and dissects the bug by hand.

Annie is a lot like Carl. When she noticed that Carl was preoc-cupied off in a corner of the playground, she was curious and went to check on what was so interesting. At first, she couldn't have cared less about the bug population under the rock, but when Carl pulled out his magnifying glass, she was interested in seeing this strange new bug as well. When Carl pulled off a leg and tossed it at her, she simply gave him a disgusted look instead of the typical female reaction. As a result, they were soon having their own private science class, oblivious to the other kids on the playground. They were so engrossed in their microscopic world that they missed the bell signaling the end of recess. It took a teacher calling them by name to get them back into the classroom. Annie and Carl are both examples of children who combine the introversion, intuitive, and feeling traits.

The Players

Rick is always in motion. He often struggles just to stay in his seat in the classroom, so the playground is a welcomed break for him. He was ready to play kickball as soon as Brad started gathering the troops, but while Brad and Calvin were working out the details and choosing their teams, Rick had the ball and was already playing with a couple of friends. When Calvin chose him on the second pick, he acknowledged it but then went on kicking the ball back and forth with his two buddies. He is usually picked early, for he seems to be a natural athlete. He never practices much; he simply plays a lot, and he plays well. He is a player because he loves to play. All of life is a game to him, and it matters little who wins or loses, just as long as he gets to play.

Sandy loves to play also, but for her, playing is performing. She's often the center of attention because she is such a great entertainer. She loves an audience and knows how to keep them laughing. She joined in the hopscotch game not so much because she wanted to play the game but because that was where most of the girls were gathered. She's usually able to keep the boys laughing as well.

As the girls play hopscotch, Sandy is watching everyone and is quick to imitate anyone who does something unusual. If there's a lull in the action during the game, she may imitate the teacher who gets on everyone's nerves. There's always something to laugh about when kids are around Sandy. She's also the one who, during a tense time in class, whispers some funny remark at just the right time to break the tension. Of course, she's often in trouble for what she says, but that's a small price to pay for being able to grab the spotlight and be on stage. Rick and Sandy are examples of children who combine the extroversion, sensing, and perceiving traits.

The Individualists

Ryan and Sarah are the quiet, inner-directed versions of Rick and Sandy, the players. On the inside, they love fun and action just as much as Rick and Sandy do. They have a very different sense of humor, but that humor is an important part of their behavior.

Ryan joined Rick in playing on the sidelines while waiting for the teams to be chosen. But Ryan would have been content to stand by and wait for the game to begin, at least for a short time. His attention span is somewhat longer than Rick's, but he can remain inactive only so long.

Sarah may have tried to participate in Jennifer's group conversation but soon would have left because she couldn't understand what the wandering conversation was all about. She also would have left because just sitting around talking isn't quite enough action for her. Sarah also has a real appreciation for color and texture. This is expressed in the clothes she chooses to wear. Not one to follow the crowd, Sarah often will dress in a way that is all her own. She may wear a hat to school or to the mall. Her sense of style can be seen in the splashes of color or variety of textures in her clothes. Her mom often can't quite understand her taste but has to admit, "It's Sarah!" Sarah is the epitome of the individualist.

Both Ryan and Sarah are often misunderstood by their teachers, by their parents, and even by their peers. Their active side, though not fully seen until late adolescence or adulthood, gives them a restlessness that is unique to their personality style. It can also be interpreted as ADD, especially if what they are studying seems to be irrelevant to what life is really about. And, of course, in elementary school they really know what life's about—at least they think they do. Ryan and Sarah are examples of children who combine the introversion, sensing, and perceiving traits.

My Child's Personality

So did you see your child in one of these eight portraits? You will get hints at these styles in the younger years, but by the time your child is in the third or fourth grade, you will begin to see a pattern that is similar to one of these eight types.

Raising Your Child "According to Their Bent"

The proverb about training our children is sometimes translated "Train up a child in the way he should go [and in keeping with his individual gift or bent]" (Prov. 22:6 AMP). Understanding our child's personality helps us do this. But what do we do when one of our children just rubs us the wrong way? We love him or her, but it is a real chore to live with that child. Not everything in a child that rubs us the wrong way can be explained by personality. Sometimes a child drives us crazy because he or she reminds us of someone else in our family who drove us crazy when we were younger. Karen's son Tom, who is eight years old, is just like his father—Karen's ex-husband. He looks like his father and sounds like his father. And because Karen and Tom are still angry over the divorce, little Tom triggers all kinds of negative feelings inside Karen, his mom. Obviously, Karen needs to find some way to make peace with her ex, or if that is impossible, she needs to look at ways little Tom is uniquely himself, and stop focusing so much on the similarities with his father.

But perhaps more often a particular child will drive us crazy because we see too much of ourselves, and our weaknesses, in that child. We struggle with facets of our own personality and then see our child do the same thing. Sometimes our focus on our child's struggles takes the spotlight off our own failures, but at some level, they are still painful reminders of our own issues.

A beautiful example of this appeared in the comic strip *Sally Forth*. Sally is the mother confronting her daughter Hillary. She says, "This bedroom is a disaster. There is absolutely no excuse for it." Hillary comes back with a great excuse in the next box as she reminds her mother, "But, Mom, this is your room!" Talking with this particular child about your own struggles will often defuse the internal battle and give you both the freedom to be yourselves.

Sometimes the child who is a problem to get along with is one whose personality is very different from his or her parents. The problem is compounded by the fact that parents often interpret these differences in some personal way. Sometimes a parent, who might be an organizer, interprets the behavior of the dreamer child as a defiant act of irresponsibility aimed at the parent. That's why it's so helpful to understand our own personality as well as the personality of our children; we see behaviors for what they are—an expression of a unique and wonderful personality.

It is our responsibility as parents—the ones who are more mature—to teach our children the importance of accepting our differences and for all of us to learn how to work together. We begin to do this by accepting the differences we see in our children and learning how to understand and affirm them in these areas. There really is little that is more important in our family life, except learning how to use their personality to help them build their faith in God.

Building Their Faith through Their Personality

As adults, our personalities color our appreciation of different forms of worship, different ways of praying, and different ways of organizing our faith-walk with the Lord. For example, an introvert will approach the whole area of prayer differently than an extrovert will. An intuitive will see different things in the nature and character of God than the sensing person will. Feeling people will pray for different things than thinking people will. And the person who seeks closure—the judging person—will structure his or her devotion times quite differently than the person who is more open-ended—the perceiving person.

It's fun to have your children talk about the different personality types of people in the Bible. For example, Paul was probably a dreamer—he was a visionary who saw the whole world as his mission field. James and Matthew were probably either organizers or monitors, both of whom leaned heavily on their Jewish traditions, were concerned with proper behavior, and were very practical in what they wrote. Peter was probably an impulsive player, not only in what he said but also in what he did. So was Mark, who wrote the shortest Gospel and whose favorite word seemed to be *immediately*.

As you "people watch," both in the Bible and in real life, you will become more familiar with the characteristics of personality and God's creative design, and over time you will be better able to understand not only your children but also what works and what doesn't work in human interactions.

Conclusion

It's important never to see these personality differences as excuses for decisions, actions, or emotions. We teach our children this by example, by our taking responsibility for our own decisions and behaviors. Nor should we allow our children to be irresponsible simply because of their personality. To understand is one thing, and it can be very helpful and freeing, but personality difference can never be an excuse. These differences give us insights and help us better understand each other. As we better understand, we can begin to celebrate our differences—both within us and within our children.

Questions to Discuss

1. Look at these traits as to how they relate to each of you as parents. Which are your personality preferences?

2. How are your children different from each of you? How are they similar?
3. If you have a child who is different from both parents, which close relative is he or she most like?

For Further Reading

Kroeger, Otto, and Janet Thuesen. *Type Talk: The 16 Personality Types That Determine How We Live, Love, and Work.* New York: Delacorte Press, 1988.

Murphy, Elizabeth. *The Developing Child: Using Jungian Types to Understand Children.* Palo Alto, CA: Consulting Psychologists Press, 1992.

Myers, Isabel B., and Peter B. Myers. *Gifts Differing: Understanding Personality Type.* Palo Alto, CA: Consulting Psychologists Press, 1990.

Neff, LaVonne. *One of a Kind: Making the Most of Your Child's Uniqueness.* Portland, OR: Multnomah Press, 1988.

13

THE IMPORTANCE OF PLAY

Daniel S. Sweeney, Ph.D.

Consider the play of the child, and the nature of the Kingdom will be revealed. Christ is that fiddler who plays so
sweetly that all who hear him begin to dance.

Robert E. Neale

hildren need to play! Play is the most important and the
most natural activity of childhood. Children need to play to
develop physically, emotionally, socially, and spiritually. While this
is promoted and understood by child development experts, child
psychotherapists, and teachers, too few of us parents recognize the
absolute necessity of play for children of all ages.

Play, something that too many adults have forgotten about, is a
blissful and fulfilling pursuit. Play should be considered as vital to a
child's life as the basic needs of shelter, food, health, and education.
Play is the business and occupation of children. This isn't to say that

play is child's work, as some have stated. True play, which will be discussed later, is characterized by a spontaneous and voluntary nature as opposed to a work activity.

Children have played throughout history, both for the pleasure of it and sometimes to make sense of their tragic world. As an example, in the Nazi concentration camp in Auschwitz during the Holocaust of World War II, children played while preparing to die and while witnessing the horrors of war. From the Black Plague of the Middle Ages, we get the child's game "Ring around the Rosie"—the "rosie" refers to the red blotches and lesions from contracting the plague; the "pocket full of posies" refers to the flowers for the dead and the practice of putting flowers into the pockets of plague victims to ward off the smell of death; and "ashes, ashes, we all fall down" alludes to the imminent death of the plague-stricken and the practice of burning the bodies of plague victims. Children not only use play to comfort themselves but also need play to make sense of and bring some order to a nonsensical and out-of-control world.

Even Scripture recognizes the importance of play in Zechariah 8:5: "The city streets will be filled with boys and girls playing there." This picture of the restoration of Israel prophesied in the Old Testament points to play as a primary and expected enterprise of children.

What's Become of Play?

Play has become a four-letter word in our society. According to a study by University of Michigan researchers, in 1981 the average child had 40 percent of the day for free time—this includes the hours left over after sleeping, eating, studying, and engaging in organized activity. By 1997, this figure had declined to 25 percent.

Most parents at least verbally acknowledge that play is important for children. A survey conducted by the American Toy Institute showed that 91 percent of parents believe that play is important for the overall well-being of their children. Forty-three percent said that their own play opportunities contributed to their success as adults. Additionally, 47 percent believe that the educational system places far too much emphasis on grades.

A paradox, however, exists as well. Some 72 percent of parents believe that it is important for their children to begin academic learning early. Also, 66 percent believe strongly that it is important for their children to perform well academically. Within the school setting, 54 percent believe that there is already enough play time in the academic arena.

In interviews of teachers, many said that parents did not understand the importance of play, as well as what was actually occurring in the classroom. These teachers said that this has led to decreased opportunities for play, both in the classroom and out. Teachers are concerned that the pressure to be academically competitive (including high grades and test scores) from parents, school boards, and politicians has been a significant factor in a decreasing emphasis on play in schools. The firm that conducted this survey said, "This survey clearly demonstrates that play and academics are on a collision course and play is losing."[1]

Many parents want their children to be Einsteins. If our children spend too much time playing, how will they get into Stanford? It is interesting to note that this very rush might have thwarted the real Einstein. Albert was a well-known (to his teachers) daydreamer, who had fairly poor grades in school as a youngster. Within the depths of his playful mind, however, he managed to define the formula for the theory of relativity ($E=mc^2$). Play, arguably, stimulates and refreshes the mind. Einstein himself said, "The imagination is more important than knowledge."

What Is Play?

While this may seem to be a question with a simple and obvious answer, it is not always clear to adults. We have, in many ways, forgotten how to play. We tend to think of play in terms of events, or even specific activities. However, play is more than activity; it is a state of mind, body, and soul. Additionally, with our busy lives and overscheduled days, adults take far too little time to play.

Play is certainly not limited to childhood; it is, nevertheless, largely the domain of children. The play of adults is quite often characterized by seriousness and competition. The play of children, which is internally and intrinsically motivated, is normally void of the burdens that adults place on leisure and recreation (what we mistakenly call play).

It is difficult to arrive at a concise definition of play. What adults define as play may be very different from how children see it. Rather than a definition, I will list some basic characteristics of *true* play:

1. *Intrinsic motivation*: True play is not motivated by external rewards, physical drives such as hunger, or goals like power or success. Rather, the motivation for play comes from within the person (of any age). Play activities are pursued for their own sake.

2. *Intrinsic completeness*: Without these goals and rules, true play is complete in and of itself. While it can be diminished by interference, it does not need to be supplemented by adults.

3. *Voluntary*: Free choice is crucial to true play. The ability to choose to play (or not) is a crucial aspect of true play. In a world filled with rules, requirements, and structure, free play is refreshing. It offers a respite from the everyday world. A study of kindergartners once showed that they considered a building block activity to be play if it were freely chosen, but considered it work if it were assigned by a teacher.

4. *Evaluation-free*: When play occurs apart from the evaluation of adults (which often comes through criticism and judgment), it is true play. Children (or people of any age) are then free to play without the fear of making mistakes and risking the ridicule and criticism of adults.

5. *Pleasure*: True play is naturally fun and pleasurable for children. Regardless of the nature of the activity, apart from the elements of enjoyment and satisfaction, true play cannot occur.

6. *Process versus product*: When children are truly allowed to play, the play activity itself is more important than the goal of the activity. Play may then become a matter of choice as opposed to goal-directed or goal-oriented behavior.

7. *Person-dominated versus object-dominated*: Similarly, true play is about the player himself, not the play materials. The focus is not on the objects used in play, but on the person(s) playing.

8. *Freedom from externally imposed rules*: This freedom encourages fantasy and imagination. Without externally imposed rules (which often foster competition), children can exercise their own autonomy and control.

9. *Freedom from reality or literal perspectives*: With true play, internal realities are more important than external realities. The meanings of play media (toys) and play behavior can be ignored, invented, or substituted. Children are then able to escape reality, which has so many constraints, and experiment with new perspectives and possibilities.

10. *Interest and involvement*: A child's level of interest and involvement is increased in true play. Play that is restricted by the absence of some of the above qualities is less interesting and attractive to children. The naturally short attention spans of children are freed through play that carries the above qualities.

Dr. Garry Landreth, founder of the Center for Play Therapy at the University of North Texas, makes the following comments about children and play:

> Children's play can be more fully appreciated when recognized as their natural medium of communication. Children express themselves more fully and more directly through self-initiated spontaneous play than they do verbally because they are more comfortable with play. For children to "play out" their experiences and feelings is the most natural dynamic and self-healing process in which children can engage.[2]

There are various social levels within which children play, all of which have beneficial elements. Children can engage in *solitary play*, which is simply playing without others, or with materials and activity different from those of other children or adults. Playing alone can stimulate creativity and the imagination. There is also *parallel play*, which involves playing with materials or engaging in activities similar to those of other children or adults nearby. This may also stimulate the imagination and lead to interactional play with those in close proximity. Additionally, there is *group play*, which involves playing with other children or adults. Play roles and specific goals may or may not be a part of group play.

Play is also sometimes categorized by type as well as social level. Although it is not crucial for parents to categorize the various types of play, it is helpful to consider these so that we can promote a variety of play activities for young children. Four general categories include the following:

1. *Functional play*: Involves repetitive muscle movements, with or without objects. Examples include running and jumping, gathering and dumping, manipulating objects, and games.
2. *Constructive play*: Using objects (e.g., blocks or Legos) or materials (e.g., sand, paint, Play-Doh) to make something.
3. *Dramatic play*: Involves role-playing (e.g., pretending to be a superhero, parent, person in an occupation, etc.) and make-believe transformations (e.g., pretending to drive a car or using a pencil to give an injection).
4. *Games with rules*: Includes the recognition and acceptance of pre-established rules. Examples include tag, marbles, or kickball.[3]

Play has many benefits and functions for children. There are physiological benefits as children learn about movement (for example, hand-eye coordination and balance), the expenditure of energy and vitality, and kinesthetic arousal. There are interpersonal benefits as children learn to separate from caregivers, practice relationships (both pretend and reality), and acquire social skills. There are intrapersonal benefits as children learn about self-mastery, self-control, and dealing with internal and external conflict. And there are sociocultural benefits as children learn about rules, roles, and authority, as well as the culture in which they live. These are only some of the benefits of play. The learning and developmental importance of play bears further discussion.

Play for Learning and Development

Play affects all areas of a child's development. When children are playing, they are learning about life. Playing teaches children some basic life lessons that we adults have long taken for granted. Children learn about cause and effect as they discover that a wooden block can make a ball of Play-Doh as flat as a pancake. They learn about problem solving as they share limited play resources or try to piece together a jigsaw puzzle. Children learn about their own bodies as they discover that their fingers can manipulate a pencil or scissors and their legs can run and kick. Children learn cooperation when they create play dramas with friends, such as a trip to the moon in an appliance crate.

Gross-motor skills are developed and reinforced through play behavior. When a toddler pushes a toy lawnmower or even a laundry clothes basket or a kindergartner jumps rope or plays hopscotch, gross-motor abilities such as walking are strengthened. A child learns coordination and balance through kicking a ball, when one foot kicks the ball and the other remains standing balanced.

The same play benefits are seen in the development of fine-motor skills as well. This happens when a child grasps drawing implements and makes a picture or makes a sign for her lemonade stand. Hand-eye coordination is developed when a child plays catch, which involves both visually following the ball and grasping it to throw and catch.

Through play with other children, social skills are learned and practiced. Children are compelled to communicate and cooperate. In play groups, children learn about sharing and caring, and they begin to develop empathy and understanding beyond their immediate family.

Play helps children practice and develop language and communication skills. As toddlers move into language acquisition, they play with words just as they play with toys. Games of jump rope, hopscotch, and tag are often accompanied by songs and rhyme. Through this, children practice and begin to master articulation and language skills. Word play becomes a part of daily play activities.

Along with language development, play broadens and enhances cognitive capabilities. Through play activities and games, children develop problem-solving skills, often simply through trial and error. Children are compelled to make decisions and evaluate the results of these decisions in play. They must direct play activities, which involves planning and strategizing.

Psychologist Charles Schaefer, cofounder of the Association for Play Therapy, asserts that "one of the most firmly established principles of psychology is that play is a process of development for the child."[4] According to developmental psychology pioneer Jean Piaget, play provides an "emotional laboratory" for children and is crucial to their development. Play is where children learn about themselves, others, and the world around them. While developmental stages may vary according to both theory and culture, the importance and inclusion of play as an element of developmental growth are universal.

Play for Therapy

In the discussion of the importance of play, it is valuable to consider the therapeutic value of play. As much as we would like to protect children, they may experience such things as abuse, trauma, or family dysfunction. These circumstances often result in acting-out behaviors (for example, disruptive behavior problems) or acting-in behaviors (for example, depression or anxiety). There may be a need to consider professional intervention in some of these cases.

Some mental health counselors would say that children need to talk about these negative experiences. Focusing on verbalization, however, ignores the developmental truth that children do not communicate in the same way that adults do. Adult communication requires both verbal abilities and abstract thinking skills. Children do not communicate this way; they communicate through play. Counseling interventions with children should be play therapy–based, which honors children through entering their world of communication rather than forcing them to enter our adult world of verbalization.

Don't people need to talk about their issues in order to process them? Yes, people need to. Children, however, *talk* through the play—the toys become their words. Is this the same as verbalization? No. To emphasize this point when I am conducting trainings on play therapy, I often ask the audience for a volunteer to stand up and share with us his or her most embarrassing and traumatizing sexual experience. After the nervous laughter has subsided, I point out, "Isn't this what we do to children who have been molested when we say, 'Tell me what happened to you'?" This is unfair at the least, and potentially retraumatizing.

As we discussed already, for children, play is not just what they do but an expression of *who they are*. Because play is the natural medium of communication for children, children are more comfortable expressing themselves through play as opposed to verbalization. Playing out negative experiences and feelings is a natural dynamic and a self-healing process for children in therapy.

Dr. Garry Landreth defines play therapy as a

dynamic interpersonal relationship between a child (or person of any age) and a therapist trained in play therapy procedures who provides selected play materials and facilitates the development of a safe relationship for the child (or person of any age) to fully express and explore self (feelings, thoughts, experiences, and behaviors) through the child's natural medium of communication, play.[5]

There are crucial elements contained within this definition. Play therapy involves a dynamic interpersonal *relationship*. Relationship is the basis for any therapeutic healing. It should also be without question that therapeutic relationships be dynamic and interpersonal. The play therapist should be *trained in play therapy procedures*. Providing toys and using talk therapy do not make the process into play therapy. Attending a brief workshop or reading a book about play therapy does not make a play therapist. Training is essential. *Selected play materials* should be provided, not a random collection of toys. The *development of a safe relationship is facilitated* by the play therapist. This does not involve following the agenda of the expert therapist. Children in need of therapy already feel disempowered and out of control. Children need to be given the opportunity to *fully express and explore self*. Healthy self-exploration enables children to discover a healthy self-image. And, as already noted, play therapy allows children to use their natural medium of communication, play.

Denise Weston and Mark Weston, in their book about play and parenting, summarize the importance of play, which speaks to what happens in the play therapy process:

The instinctive method children use for solving problems and mastering conflicts is play. Play is the all-encompassing business of childhood—in it, children take charge of their world, sort out misconceptions, and re-create life experiences. For example, consider the child who is terrified

of monsters he believes are lurking at night in the shadows of his bedroom. During the day, this same child draws monsters, pretends he is
slaying them and even makes believe he is a monster. Without realizing
it he is using various modalities of play to explore, to problem-solve, and
eventually to overcome his terrors. He can do the same thing with his
behavior problems.[6]

There is strong research backing up the effectiveness of play
therapy.[7] When children are in need of counseling, parents should
remember that child counseling and play therapy should be interchangeable terms. Finding a qualified play therapist may be crucial
for a child to overcome obstacles and move forward with life.

Play as Relationship

If children really do communicate through play and the way to
develop relationships is to foster communication, then parents must
be willing to enter their children's worlds as well. This involves spending time and playing with children.

We start making connections with children from the moment
they are infants. We engage them with eye contact, smiles, touch,
and words. Often adults speak to infants in higher-pitched singsong
voices. There is a dance of connection when infants are gurgling and
adults are cooing.

One typical and wonderful example of this dance with very young
children is the game of peekaboo. Across age, gender, and culture,
parents play this hide-and-seek game with their infants. It is a delightful way to make connection and develop relationship. When I see
parents and infants connect with each other, it really does seem like
a choreographed dance.

This dance—this *play*—is core to the attachment process. Infants
and children who are securely attached are those who do well emotionally, mentally, and physically. There are many theories of attachment, but perhaps there is a simpler way of looking at the process.
Consider attachment as a drinking well that is initially filled by an
external source. In this case, the infant or child is the well, and the
parent is the external source. It is the parent's responsibility to fill the

well, and he or she does so by providing love, care, nourishment, protection, etc. The securely attached child has his or her well filled regularly, whereas the unattached child is left with very inconsistent fillings or perhaps an empty well. Play is one primary ingredient for filling the well.

Insecure attachment can lead to problem behaviors, among other challenges. Consider the challenge of parenting the difficult child. Many child therapy and parent-training programs focus on behavior management or control. Arguably, behavioral interventions for children who act out can be useful. However, most often a child's misbehavior is a fundamental reflection of emotional turmoil and unmet needs; thus, behavior controls will not really have a lasting impact. It therefore becomes necessary to provide a parenting or therapeutic experience that touches the child at emotional and relational levels.

As parents look to Christian therapists and to Christian parenting literature, however, they often are met with a focus on the child's behavior and the need to provide appropriate discipline. Discipline, while biblically and psychologically appropriate, is incomplete. There is potential to equate discipline with behavioral control or punishment. The concept of discipline as a relational or teaching process can easily get lost. Labeling a child as strong-willed or a problem may in fact be an accurate interpretation. Nevertheless, such labeling may result in the justification of the use of force to bring about compliance. This leads to adversarial parent-child interactions, not relationships noted for understanding, valuing, and honoring one another.

This is where parent-child play can have a great impact. Play promotes relationship. When I conduct parent training, my fundamental argument is that *rules without relationship equals rebellion*.[8] Parents can employ the most researched, effective, and developmentally appropriate rules of parenting and behavior management; but if the parent-child relationship is poor, the result will involve minimal compliance and potential rebellion. It is relationship that creates the environment for emotional expression and problem solving. Play fosters this relationship. My approach to parent training is based on promoting the parent-child relationship through training parents in the use of basic play therapy skills.

Tools of Play

The basic tools of play are *toys* and *time*. When we provide children with toys and the time to play, we are providing more than a simple play experience. It is important to remember that play is a means of learning to live, not a mere passing of time. It is the responsibility of adults to make these tools available.

Children in school benefit from having the appropriate tools—paper, pencils, rulers, etc.—as well as having classrooms, desks, adequate lighting, freedom from distractions, and reasonable calm and quiet. Children at play benefit from the appropriate tools as well—toys. These need not be fancy or expensive. They do not even need to be typical store-bought toys. Cardboard boxes can be used for forts or puppet theaters. The puppets themselves can be paper bags, socks, or oven mitts. Paper, scissors, crayons, and tape work marvelously. There is nothing wrong with a trip to the toy store, but it is important simply to provide toys, not to make them the focus.

Children in all cultures play, as do children from all socioeconomic levels. The toys and games may differ, but the activity of play occurs worldwide. I have pondered what a truly cross-cultural set of toys might look like. My conclusion is a couple of rocks and sticks might do just fine. All children can have fun with these.

In counseling children with play therapy, I try to provide a wide selection of play materials. I look for toys that will facilitate relationship—competitive games and video games do not do this! Toys in play therapy should provide children with the opportunity to express a wide range of feelings and explore both real-life and fantasy experiences.

The second and perhaps more important tool needed for play is time. Having the finest toys that money can buy is useless if there is no time to use them. As mentioned earlier, the average child has moved from 40 percent free time in 1981 to 25 percent in 1997. Time for play has been reduced for many children and eliminated for others. Remember that structured physical activity and competitive sports do not fit into the play category. Just as adults need to schedule important engagements, children should have scheduled time to engage in free play. We cannot increase the rate of children's physical growth, and we cannot hurry along developmental growth. By reducing or limiting play time, however, we can slow down emotional and intellectual growth. Play simply takes time.

Enemies of Play

Play has its enemies. It is important that parents fight for the right for their children—all children—to play. Scripture tells us that "the thief comes only to steal and kill and destroy" (John 10:10). I believe that it is the enemy's plan to rob children of their right and need to play. When this basic activity of children is stolen, the enemy is also stealing from their adulthood and thus weakening the effectiveness of the church. This should not come as a surprise. Scripture shows us that throughout history, children have been targeted for murder: In Moses' time newborn boys were ordered by the pharaoh to be slain, and in Jesus' time Herod gave the same directive.

As we take a brief look at the enemies of play, there are two that quickly come to mind. The first one is adults. We are the ones with the control and the ones who make the rules. Just as we are overscheduled and exhausted, so are our children. It is not unusual for children to be awakened at dawn and then scheduled well into the night. With school, before-school activities and after-school programs, music lessons, sports programs, homework, etc., children have precious little time to relax, much less time to engage in unstructured and free play.

Adults, specifically parents, are also sometimes paralyzed by fear—the fear of child molesters, disease, reckless drivers, and guns, to name just a few. This fear can prevent parents from allowing their children to play freely without structure and supervision. While it is necessary and appropriate to ensure children's safety, we may end up overscheduling or limiting play opportunities out of paranoia. Safety first, but not at the expense of play.

The second major enemy of play is the television. Television is probably the nation's leading baby-sitter. It is an easy and convenient diversion but arguably has great potential for destruction. It destroys family time as well as child play time. It is a passive, nonrelational, noncreative, and time-consuming activity. On average, children watch twenty-eight hours of television each week (not to mention the some 100,000 murders and attempted murders the average child will see on television by age eighteen). This number of twenty-eight hours also jumps considerably if we add video and computer games to the mix. Television and similar media rob children from family and social interactions and creative and abstract thinking and activity—and play.

When children are not overscheduled and not watching television, they are not only free to play but also to engage their natural creativity and imagination. Of course, if parents do limit television and don't overschedule, they run the risk of hearing an age-old childhood complaint: "I'm bored—there's nothing to do." This may be irritating to parents but may be valuable for children. Children often seek structure, direction, and entertainment from parents. However, it may be a mistake to quickly look to solve the child's boredom. When we refrain from providing external stimulation and structure, creativity and imagination are facilitated. When children are forced into a void of external stimulation, their internal world is given the chance to flourish.

Conclusion

Play is the language of childhood. It is how children express their joys, sorrows, wants, and needs. Without play, children experience developmental challenges across physical, emotional, and spiritual realms. Stuart Brown, founder of the Institute for Play, has coined the term *play deprivation*. He says that this can lead to depression, hostility, and the loss of "the things that make us human beings."[9]

Parents must actively work against a society and educational system that do not value play. Two hundred years ago, when the church still sponsored the education of children, the following rule was created: "We prohibit play in the strongest terms. . . . The students shall rise at five o'clock in the morning, summer and winter. . . . The student shall be indulged with nothing which the world calls play. Let this rule be observed with strictest nicety; for those who play when they are young will play when they are old."[10]

Beyond its outlandish wording, this policy sounds obviously antiquated and inappropriate. Yet hundreds of schools have reduced or eliminated recess in the pursuit of academic endeavors. While there is no evidence that doing this improves test scores, several studies show that when recess is delayed, school-age children get increasingly agitated and inattentive. Children *need* to play.

The apostle Paul tells us, "When I was a child, I talked like a child, I thought like a child, I reasoned like a child. When I became a man, I put childish ways behind me" (1 Cor. 13:11). As adults, we may have "put away childish things." Our children, however, have not. Children still talk, think, and reason as children, and play. Let's let them, encourage them, and join them.

Questions to Discuss

1. Do you allow your children enough free time to express themselves, cultivate their imaginations, and experience development through play?
2. Are your children overscheduled (or are you as parents overscheduled) so that play time is squeezed or perhaps almost eliminated?
3. How often do you play with your children? When you play with your children, how often do they get to lead and direct the process?

For Further Reading

Cohen, Lawrence J. *Playful Parenting*. New York: Ballantine Books, 2002.

Sweeney, Daniel. *Counseling Children through the World of Play*. Eugene, OR: Wipf and Stock Publishers, 1997.

Weston, Denise Chapman, and Mark S. Weston. *Playful Parenting: Turning the Dilemma of Discipline into Fun and Games*. New York: J. P. Tarcher/Putnam, 1993.

14

PREPARING YOUR CHILDREN FOR SCHOOL

Cynthia Ulrich Tobias, M.Ed.

I remember the first day of my first year of teaching. I was so excited to teach because I just knew those students would be very excited to learn. But they weren't. It didn't take me long to discover that many of the students over the next few years would consider their time in the classroom with the same enthusiasm they would have toward spending nine months in a jail cell. Perhaps it has a lot to do with the fact that these children's parents hadn't prepared them for the experience of learning, or for the whole of what school is all about.

Whether your child is starting kindergarten for the first time or is about to enter the last year of high school, you can help make sure the school year will be successful. Awareness is half the battle, and if you can help your children recognize their unique learning styles, you

223

can help them adapt and accommodate those strengths in classroom situations that are frustrating or uncomfortable.

What If They Talk Too Much?

Highly auditory children learn best by hearing, but not by hearing others talk to them. They learn best by hearing *themselves* talk. They are often highly verbal, talking about almost anything they can think of and chattering to pretty much anyone who will listen. These are the children who are often doomed to frequently get in trouble for talking in class. Auditory learners, as soon as an idea or an answer occurs to them, tend to blurt it out. They know they were supposed to raise their hand. They know they will probably get in trouble yet again, but the information just bubbles up to the top. If they can't talk to the teacher, they'll talk to the student sitting next to them or behind them. The fact is their auditory nature doesn't mean they can never be quiet; it means if they need to remember something important, they will need to talk about it soon after they learn it.

If your child has a teacher who is very strict about being quiet during class, encourage him not to talk during class. However, he should make sure he finds a classmate he can talk to immediately after class in order to verify what was discussed or assigned. Sometimes just talking about it is enough to make the information stick. If the class is longer than an hour, suggest your auditory student jot down a word or phrase that she needs more information about during the time the teacher is talking. After class, she can quickly glance at her list and check with the teacher or a fellow student to clarify or discuss what she noted.

What If They Won't Sit Still?

Many children were simply born to move. Of course, restless movement or changes in position or frequent trips to the bathroom and drinking fountain can result in these highly kinesthetic children becoming behavior problems in the eyes of their teachers. As a parent, you have already dealt with a highly active child for several years, and you know how exhausting it can be. In most classrooms, students do not have the freedom of movement these restless children yearn to have. Fidgeting, squirming, getting up and down several times—all of this can get a child in trouble very quickly in most traditional classrooms.

But you can help your child learn to move without becoming distracting. Think about yourself as an adult. You rarely ever sit completely still either. But you have learned to move in subtler ways that don't distract others. Challenge your kinesthetic child to do the same. Practice with her when you're sitting in church or other group situations. Can she learn to tap her foot without making any noise or being noticed? Can he use a highlighter when he's reading or perhaps draw or doodle while he's listening without seeming to be inattentive? What about a Koosh ball or worry stone? Could your child hold on to something she can handle while she's focusing on the teacher? Many teachers are willing to be flexible as long as a student can prove he was listening while he was moving. If your child is fortunate to have one of these teachers, you may be able to bring in a rocking chair or an exercise ball so your child can move in his or her seat while listening. If your child ends up with a teacher who simply won't tolerate movement, help your son or daughter practice sitting still for longer periods of time and make it a game by seeing if they can beat their own best record for no movement. Remember, though, the whole point is being able to remember what they learned!

What If They Can't Remember What They Learn?

For many highly analytic learners, remembering specific details comes quite naturally. The bigger picture, however, can be a little more difficult to grasp. On the other hand, there are children who naturally get the gist of things right away but struggle later to remember exactly what was said. Both kinds of learners can struggle in school, usually when they encounter an assignment that calls for a strength opposite of their own. If your child focuses naturally on details and seems stressed when not enough details are given, you may need to help her practice asking the teacher for more information. For example, "Mrs.

Baker, I'm a little confused about what my assignment is supposed to look like. Could you show me an example?"

If your child tends to naturally be more global or big-picture, he can easily skim over the details while he's trying to figure out where the whole assignment is headed. Help him practice identifying which details are going to be important in an upcoming assignment or test. Encourage him to ask the teacher for more information without seeming to be asking just for a personal repetition of the instructions. For example, "Mr. Ryan, can you tell me what I should be looking for when I read this chapter?"

It's important that your child and his teachers both understand why some tasks may be more frustrating than others. The chances are good that if anyone is going to be asked to stretch outside their comfort zone, it's probably going to be your child. After all, there is a classroom full of different learners, and only one teacher to try to be effective with everyone. Just remember that awareness is half the battle, and be on hand to reinforce your child's learning style while nudging him or her into unfamiliar territory.

What If They Don't Get Along with the Teacher?

Believe it or not, some students will do well in almost any class, regardless of their relationship with the teacher. Most students, however, are significantly impacted by the match or mismatch between the teacher's style and their own. We sometimes forget that our own personal learning style greatly influences our evaluation of someone else's style. I've worked in dozens of classrooms over the years, and in all the times I've asked a class to tell me what they think their teacher's learning style is, I've never gotten a unanimous response. Each child's personal filter dictates how he or she views the teacher, and what he or she sees as being important. By far, most teachers care about the kids they teach and are dedicated to giving students the best education possible. But there are bound to be personality conflicts and misunderstandings at times, and it's important to help your child recognize that it's almost never a personal or deliberate insult.

At the beginning of every school year, talk to your child about each of his teachers. Discuss what the teacher is like, what's going to be expected, and how your child feels about spending time in that teacher's classroom. Encourage your child to identify what traits or characteristics of a particular teacher have the potential to get frustrating, especially in stressful circumstances. Encourage your child to write a brief note to each teacher, explaining his individual learning-style strengths and pledging to do his best to accommodate the teacher's style. In the end, positive communication will be the key for both you and your child, so establish that connection with the teachers as early as possible in the school year.

Where Is the Best Place to Study?

It's a great temptation to insist your child study at a clean desk with a bright light for at least an hour at a time. It's a time-honored tradition, and most parents are under the impression that to study anywhere else would be a violation of academic standards. The bottom line, though, is that your child needs to be able to complete homework assignments in an accurate and timely manner, and needs to be able to review for tests in such a way that she can remember the information and perform well on the exam. For some students, the traditional study area will be the very best environment for accomplishing these goals. For others, however, it could actually work against them. Always keep in mind that all-important question: What's the point? If the point is getting the work done, be prepared to be somewhat flexible in providing the physical environment for doing the tasks. Challenge your child to propose a design for the space at home where she will be doing her homework. Perhaps you could even give her a budget to work with and help her experiment with aspects of time, snacks, noise, etc., all the while reminding her that she must be able to prove that having a study area personalized to her specifications will result in the work being done according to the highest standards.

How Will We Keep Them Motivated?

As parents, we often worry about making sure our children are living up to their potential. After all, we see so many possibilities for them! It's hard to step back and remember that no amount of desire on our part can *force* our child to want the same thing. We can inspire, provide incentives, and hold them accountable, but we can't *make* them accomplish a goal. Only they can decide to do that.

The key to motivating any child is almost always getting them to motivate themselves. The first step in doing that is to establish what goal it is they are committed to achieving. For example, if you want your daughter to get an A in science but she has decided she would be just as happy with a C, you do not have a common goal, and motivating her to raise her grade may be pretty hopeless. If, however, you can establish that *she* is not happy with a C and she wants to get a better grade, now you have something positive to work toward. You can ask her, "What do you think it will take to get an A in science?" If she's not sure, ask if she will find out from her teacher, or ask if she would like a suggestion or two from you. If she agrees, give her the suggestions. If not, resist the temptation to give her advice anyway. Until she is ready to hear it, no amount of good advice will motivate her to follow it.

When she has established what will be required to achieve an A (a grade *she* decided she wanted), ask the next important question: "What will it take to motivate you to do that?" Again, if she has no immediate ideas and wants some of yours, feel free to share. If she doesn't ask for input from you, tell her to think about it, and promise to ask her again in a couple days. When she comes up with a solution or two she thinks might work, you can ask yet another question: "How do you want to be held accountable for doing that?" The answers to each of these questions help your child assume the responsibility for identifying the means for and the results of motivating herself to do something that may not come easily for her. That's not only a good idea while she is in school, but a great idea when she is out on her own.

Not all preparation for school is done at the beginning of the year. It's important for you as a parent to do a sort of status check at the midpoint. Halfway through the academic year, sit down with your child and assess how the year is going so far. What's working? What's still frustrating? What does he need your help with, and where does he need more motivation? If you'd like a guideline for helping both your child and you to get a handle on progress in school, try using the survey below.

Preparing for Parent-Teacher Conferences

Before you talk to your child's teacher about progress in school, take a few minutes to review the year so far from both your and your child's point of view. The following are two sets of suggested questions for you—one to work through on your own as a parent, and another for you to discuss with each of your children. Remember, if you believe your child is struggling at school, the most important person to talk to first is your child. We suggest you briefly summarize your child's response to the following questions and give it in writing to the teacher. You and your child may prefer to actually tape record the responses and submit the tape.

The following questions should be discussed in the most positive surroundings possible. Everything is designed to bring out your child's strengths and the positive aspects of his or her school experience so far. Resist the temptation to focus on what needs to be improved; instead, emphasize what is already going well!

Parent Survey

Student Name_____Date_____

Please answer the following questions based on your own observations of your child. You will have an opportunity to ask similar questions directly to your child later.

1. **When does your child feel smart? How do you know?**

2. **What kind of positive comments have you heard your child make about school lately?**

3. **What seems to be your child's favorite aspect of school?**

4. How do you know your child is learning so far this year?

5. What could your child's teacher do for you that would be most helpful?

Student Survey

Student Name_____Date_____

For younger children, you may want to write or record the answers. Encourage older children to write their own responses and then discuss them with you before you turn a copy of the survey in to their teacher(s).

1. What makes you feel smart?

2. Talk about your favorite teachers—what do they do that you like the most?

3. What are the three things you enjoy most about school?

4. If we could wave a magic wand over you at school and make everything perfect, what would change?

5. If you could choose only one thing to improve on in school, what would it be? Why?

For Further Reading

Tobias, Cynthia Ulrich. *I Hate School: How to Help Your Children Love Learning*. Grand Rapids: Zondervan, 2004.

Tobias, Cynthia Ulrich. *Bringing Out the Best in Your Child: 80 Ways to Focus on Every Kid's Strength*. Ann Arbor, MI: Servant Publications, 1997.

Tobias, Cynthia Ulrich. *Every Child Can Succeed: Making the Most of Your Child's Learning Style*. Colorado Springs: Focus on the Family, 1996.

You can contact Cynthia Ulrich Tobias at AppLe St. (Applied Learning Styles), P.O. Box 1450, Sumner, WA 98390; (253) 862-6200; Fax (253) 891–8611; email Applest@aol.com; websites: www.applest .com; www.cantmakeme.com; www.amatterofstyle.com.

15

BALANCING GRACE AND TRUTH IN PARENTING

William and Kristi Gaultiere

Jeff and Rhonda (names and identifying information changed in this and all cases) were arguing before they even got into my counseling office. I (William) smiled anyway, motioned for them to have a seat, and shut the door on potential eavesdroppers in the waiting room. They were fighting about how to parent their two boys, Kyle and Kramer, ages nine and five.

"You're being too soft on them, Rhonda," Jeff complained. "You're doing Kyle's homework for him. He has to learn to do it himself. When he gets out in the real world, his boss won't do his work for him, that's for sure! And neither of the boys does any chores around the house. When I was Kyle's age, I had to empty the garbage every day and shovel the snow off the sidewalk."

"I know. I know," Rhonda interrupted. "And you had to walk to school in the rain! You just don't understand. It's a lot of work caring for the boys. It seems that I'm always cooking for them and cleaning up after them and helping them to treat each other nicely. I just don't have the energy to be getting them to do chores in this stage. Besides, they're growing up so fast. Kramer will be starting school this fall, and I want to enjoy him. My days with them are so busy. I feel good if I get through the day without falling apart and am able to make time for us to play a game or go to the park. Maybe if you helped out more around the house and spent more time with the boys—"

Jeff shot back before Rhonda could finish, "Whenever I try to get involved, you shoot me down! I can't even correct the kids without you stepping in because you don't want their feelings hurt. You—"

It was my turn to interrupt in order to turn down the heat and refocus things. "Jeff, it sounds like you have some good ideas for teaching your kids to be responsible. And, Rhonda, I can see that you're connecting well with your boys, showing concern for their feelings and playing with them. The problem I see is that the two of you are on opposite extremes. Instead of attacking one another's approach, you need to learn from each other. Jeff, you need more of Rhonda's compassion in your parenting, and, Rhonda, you need more of Jeff's discipline."

I showed Jeff and Rhonda that they were confusing their boys with their approaches that split apart God's grace and truth. Children need caring *and* responsibility, connectivity *and* structure from each parent.

What's Your Approach to Parenting?

If I could sit down and talk to you right now, I'd ask you, Why are you reading this book? What is it about Christian parenting that you're eager to learn? And I'd try to get to know you as a parent. You'd probably identify somewhat with either Jeff or Rhonda. Most parents who seek help have, in some way, a problem balancing the tender and tough issues of relating to their kids. I'd ask you some questions about your parenting to see how you're balancing God's grace and truth in the way you parent your child. So let's do that in the form of a survey that I developed for parents like you. Once we understand your position, I can better help you to understand more of what God has for you and your family.

Parenting Style Map Survey

Use the scale below to answer each question about your relationship with your child or children. For each question write the number that corresponds to your answer in the blank. Both parents should take the survey.

1	2	3	4	5
Almost never	Once in a while	Sometimes	Frequently	Almost always

1. When my child is struggling, I worry about how he or she feels. ____

2. I like to tell my child what to do. ____
3. I try hard to make my child happy. ____
4. When I discipline my child, his or her feelings have little influence on me. ____
5. I spend my free time with my child. ____
6. I give little weight to my child's suggestions in decisions. ____
7. I like for only our immediate family to do things together. ____
8. I make sure that the rules stay the same in our family. ____
9. When my child hurts my feelings, it has a lasting effect on my mood. ____
10. Even on stressful days I insist that my child do his or her daily chores. ____
11. When I'm with my child, it's hard for me to be happy if he or she is not happy. ____
12. I enjoy structuring my child's activities. ____

Scoring Your Parenting Style Survey

First, obtain your Relationship Scale score by adding up the point values you've written in the blanks after each *odd*-numbered question in the survey. You should get a total of between zero and thirty. Mark an *x* on the bottom horizontal axis of the Parenting Style Map according to your score. Then obtain your Structure Scale score by adding up the point values for each *even*-numbered question. The total on this should also be between zero and thirty. Using that score mark a *y* on the left vertical axis of the map. Finally, plot your *x* and *y* scores on the map and identify your relationship and structure styles as a parent. Then have your spouse enter his or her score on the map. (In locating where you fit on the Parenting Style Map, you may need to adjust where you plot your score if the descriptions below suggest to you that you belong on a different spot on the map than your survey score indicates.)

Parenting Style Map

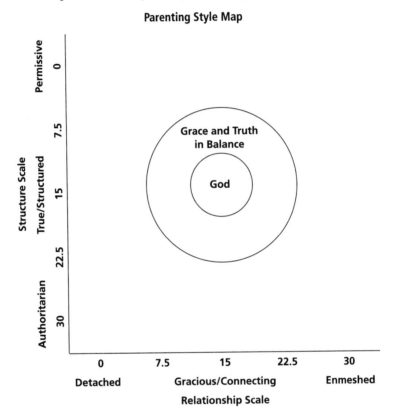

On the Parenting Style Map above, you want to be somewhere in the circle of "grace and truth in balance." The horizontal axis is assessing the quality of your relationship with your child. You want to relate to your child with kindness and compassion to promote a caring bond between the two of you that meets your child's needs for both intimacy and separateness. A grace-giving relationship like this avoids the extremes of being disconnected (too busy or emotionally detached) or enmeshed (emotionally intertwined or lacking in clear boundaries of separation). The vertical axis looks at the direction or structure in your relationship with your child. You want to structure your relationship with your child in a way that promotes responsibility and wisdom, harmonizing your child's needs for clear direction and flexibility. This kind of truth-honoring relationship avoids the extremes of authoritarianism (rigidity or harshness) and permissiveness (chaos or laxness).

A word of caution is in order in understanding your score. Don't expect perfection. That's what God's for! But if you do find that you're not where you want to be, don't get discouraged. Just getting a picture of where God is and where you are and asking God for help will get you started in becoming a parent who is more like God in using both grace and truth in your parenting.

Parenting the Way God Parents Us

My understanding of Christian parenting begins with the model that God is the perfect parent to us. To parent our children well, we first need to be parented by God. He is the Father from whom all fatherhood derives its name (Eph. 3:15). When we connect with God's love through prayer and our relationships in the body of Christ, then we have love to give. "We love because he first loved us" (1 John 4:19) is the succinct way the apostle John described it. It's the same with God's truth. When we structure our lives according to God's Word, identifying ourselves with him, obeying him, and practicing spiritual disciplines, then we have wisdom to share with others. Through Moses God has told us, "These commandments that I give you today are to be upon your hearts. Impress them on your children. Talk about them when you sit at home and when you walk along the road" (Deut. 6:6–7).

The amazing thing about God's grace and truth is that they're completely *integrated*. The psalmist gives us an unforgettable, poetic picture of this by announcing that with God "unfailing love and truth have met together. Righteousness and peace have kissed!" (Ps. 85:10 NLT). In God, you can't have the connection of love without the structure of truth, and you can't have the structure of truth without the connection of love. The psalmist emphasizes this by reversing the order of the pairing in the second half of the verse from love and truth to righteousness (truth) and peace (love).

Throughout Scripture we see the interplay between and integration of these two wonderful sides of God's character. This is best seen in Jesus Christ, who, the apostle John tells us, came to us to bring us the fullness of God's grace and truth (John 1:17). Jesus showed us that God is wholly gracious and wholly truthful, completely loving and completely holy. In other words, there's a *tender* and a *tough* side to God's character. And so in the Bible we see in the way God parents Israel and in the way Jesus ministers to people that not only does God offer himself to care for our needs, but he also disciplines us to produce in us a harvest of righteousness and peace (Heb. 12:4–11).

When Grace and Truth Are Out of Balance

Eugene Peterson's translation of the apostle Paul's instructions to fathers brings out the fact that children need to be trained in a tender way: "Take them by the hand and lead them in the way of the Master" (Eph. 6:4 Message). The diagram below, "Grace and Truth in Parenting," illustrates how difficult it is for parents to integrate grace and truth. God keeps grace and truth in perfect balance in the way that he parents us, but we tend to give greater weight to one or the other. We may try so hard to be caring that we don't provide the structure and discipline of truth, and then we become parents who are enmeshed and permissive. And if we err too far on the other side, disconnecting emotionally from our kids to pressure or punish them into doing what we think is right, then we become detached and authoritarian parents. Both extremes are hurtful divisions of God's grace and truth.

Grace and Truth in Parenting

| Enmeshed and Permissive | Detached and Authoritarian | Loving and Structured |

Love without Limits

Of course, love without limits isn't really love at all. "If you refuse to discipline your children, it proves you don't love them; if you love your children, you will be prompt to discipline them" (Prov. 13:24 NLT). Rhonda's gentle way with her kids and the priority she put on being available to them and playing with them were certainly loving expressions. But her love went sour when it was split off from limits. She was living by the motto "I have to fix your problems no matter what you do." She was *enmeshed* with her boys' feelings and took responsibility for them. When Kyle had a hard day at school and came home grumpy and irritable, then Rhonda became depressed and pressured him to get over it so that she could feel better. Kyle learned that getting too close to Mom felt intrusive or overwhelming. He felt responsible for her well-being and so he became emotionally detached.

With Kramer things were different on the surface. Because Kramer was scared to go to prekindergarten, Rhonda felt insecure and anxious for him and "protected" him by keeping him home another year. In time Kramer developed a pattern of seeking attention for his problems and getting his mom to fix things for him. So because truth (discipline and structure) was being de-emphasized, the boys weren't learning to take responsibility for their feelings, problems, or (as Jeff pointed out) contributions to the household.

Many people today don't see a problem with this love-without-limits approach. They want to be their child's friend. Maybe when they were children they were beat up by criticism and controlled by rules and so they don't want to do that to their children. I saw a shocking example of this coming from a Christian home a number of years ago when a teenage boy (I'll call him Ricky) was referred to me for help with depression and compulsive masturbation. But his problems were much more serious than that. He lied. He stole. He violated girls sexually. And yet he went to church and youth group every week. He was raised in a Christian home and identified himself as a Christian, but he had *no* conscience. He felt no conviction for his sins, no empathy for the troubles he caused his parents, and no sadness for the girls he violated. He had no self-control. And it's no wonder, because at home he received no discipline or consequences for his irresponsible and abusive behaviors, just futile attempts to "love" him with niceness and "help" him by doing things like getting an attorney to keep him out of juvenile detention—efforts that were interspersed with criticism and nagging from his enmeshing mother and withdrawal from his permissive father.

Ricky's parents' approach wasn't loving or helpful. His deviant behavior needed to be confronted and reformed through painful consequences (in the context of an understanding and caring relationship). So that's what I did, and it's what I taught his parents to do. Thank God he started to feel some empathy and conviction and gradually became more responsible, appropriate, and considerate. I think we got to him just in time!

Just the Cold, Hard Truth!

In our permissive society today, it's obvious to most people that truth without grace is not right. Nonetheless, I see some parents, like Jeff, who slide into this extreme. Their hard line with other people, even their own kids, is "You have to fix your problems without my support." It's not that Jeff wasn't trying to love his kids. In fact, he justified his cold confrontations by saying, "It's only because I love my boys." He was right that his boys needed to be doing chores around the house and to learn to behave responsibly. And they needed firm parental discipline to learn to respect authority and to develop self-control. But to receive these truths from their father, they needed to trust him and sense that he had compassion for them. It wasn't enough for him to direct or discipline his boys *because* he loved them; he needed to first *show* them his love (as Rhonda kept saying) and then provide accountability in a loving way.

The children of authoritarian parents like Jeff are likely to rebel. This is why the apostle Paul advises, "Fathers, do not provoke your children to anger, but bring them up in the discipline and instruction of the Lord" (Eph. 6:4 NASB). Other children of authoritarian parents become compliant, trying to please for fear of the parent's anger. Still other children become passive-aggressive, which is a combination of pleasing and rebelling, being compliant to the parent's face to avoid conflict or criticism and then quietly resisting. When these hard-nosed parents communicate an expectation, they shut down any protest from their kids, calling it defiance. But not only do kids need to learn to submit to authority and obey, they also need to learn to stand up to authority by *respectfully* disagreeing.

Jesus makes this point in his "parable of the two sons" (Matt. 21:28–32). A father who owns a vineyard tells both of his sons to go work in the vineyard. The first son stands up to his dad and refuses to work in the vineyard, but later he changes his mind and goes. The second son says, "Sure, Dad, I'll go!" But he doesn't. Jesus praises the protesting son who later obeys and condemns the passive-aggressive son.

Teeter-Tottering between Grace and Truth

You may see that at times you're like Jeff *and* Rhonda, going up and down, up and down on the grace teeter-totter. This is perhaps the most common problem that we parents have in trying to balance grace and truth. We try to be compassionate and caring with our children. We feel bad when they complain, "C'mon, Dad. It's not fair. I've got all this homework and you're telling me that I still have to empty the garbage." So we "cut 'em some slack." Or instead of punishing disobedience, we give more chances and nag them until they obey. Or when our kids beg for more dessert, to stay up later, or to have some extra spending money, we give in, thinking that we're showing our love. But all the while, anger is building inside us and eventually it bursts out; we come down hard on them with harsh words, sudden high expectations, or severe punishments.

Does your parenting ever look like this? I have to admit that mine does at times. It's hard to be consistent. Of course, this flip-flopping is quite confusing for our children. They like the pushover parent better than the drill sergeant and will likely ride out the storm until the niceness returns. But regardless of what they want, what they need are limits in the context of love, grace along with the structure of discipline.

Children who live with grace and truth split apart will also do their own flip-flopping. You probably remember hearing about the story of John Walker, a young man who became an Islamic extremist. His reversal was extreme and tragic. According to the *Boston Globe*[1] his "'oh-so-progressive parents' had answered 'Yes' to his every whim, indulged his every fancy, permitted—even praised—his every passion." His mother said that "it was good for a child to find a passion" and his father was "proud of John for pursuing an alternative course" that progressed from hip-hop CDs with very nasty lyrics at fourteen, dropping out of high school at sixteen, dressing in white robes and a skullcap along with other Muslim followers of Malcom X, moving to Yemen and befriending gunmen who'd been to Chechnya to fight the Russians, and joining an Islamic extremist group in Pakistan.

Even when it was clear that their son, who then called himself Abdul Hamid, was deep into Islamic fanaticism (he told them he philosophically supported Osama bin Laden's terrorist bombings of the USS *Cole* that killed seventeen American servicemen), his liberal, permissive parents wouldn't pull in the reins but continued to enable him by wiring him more money. Without limits or guidance from his parents, he developed a disdain for authority and a lust to be free to do as he pleased with no accountability, leaving him in a vacuum, desperate for love, standards, discipline, truth, and God. Finally, his antiauthoritarianism took him full circle, and he joined an ultraauthoritarian, extremist sect of Islam: the Taliban in Afghanistan. He flip-flopped from wanting permissiveness to wanting authoritarianism, from pushing his parents away to attaching himself to Osama bin Laden's Al Qaida terrorist training organization.

When Two Parents Are on Opposite Extremes

Maybe you and your spouse split apart grace and truth in your relationship. One of you gives love without limits and the other plays out just the cold, hard truth. For the kids, not only do these separate approaches divide caring connection and structured guidance, they also create anxiety and confusion because of the conflict between their parents.

This was the case with Jeff and Rhonda's family. They "triangled" Kyle and Kramer into their unresolved conflicts, which forced them to choose one parent to align with. So if either of the boys wanted understanding and help, then he went to Mom, and if he wanted space and competence, then he went to Dad. Each could align with only one parent because of all their unresolved conflicts. Being the oldest, Kyle was identifying with his father's approach and was becoming an independent achiever who was quick to criticize himself and others. Kramer was internalizing his mother's approach by becoming a sensitive and caring boy who tried to make other people happy and expected them to do the same for him. To avoid these alliances that divided their boys' needs for God's grace and truth, Jeff and Rhonda each needed to work on their own issues and learn to respect each other.

Getting Grace and Truth in Balance

I helped Jeff and Rhonda learn to stop reacting and criticizing each other and instead take ownership of their feelings and weaknesses and work on them. Jeff needed to worry less about his standards for his boys and learn to relate with them more, connecting with their interests and considering their feelings. This meant spending more time with his boys and developing his compassion for them. And Rhonda needed to realize that two of the most caring things she could do for Kyle and Kramer were to teach them to be responsible by giving them chores to do and to set limits for them by disciplining them when their behavior was out of line. Rhonda needed to develop more structure in her parenting. Jeff and Rhonda needed to integrate grace and truth individually and as a couple. Like King David who prayed, "Do not withhold your mercy from me, O LORD; may your love and your truth always protect me" (Ps. 40:11), they and their boys needed both sides of God.

Become More Gracious

Grace is a theological word, first used by the apostle Paul in the New Testament to describe the favor (unconditional love and acceptance) that God extends to sinners. Grace is a gift that originates with God and can't be earned. So to be a grace-giving parent, you need to first receive it from God by admitting your need for it and depending on him in faith. We do this through prayer and the sacraments, of course, but the primary way that we internalize God's grace in our souls is through relationships with people in the body of Christ. This is because "no one has ever seen God; but if we love one another, God lives in us and his love is made complete in us" (1 John 4:12). This means that the bonding relationship that parents provide for their children is essential, not only for their psychological development, but also for their faith.

I'll never forget when our first child, David, was only a few months old, and my wife, Kristi, was talking to a friend from church who also had an infant son. She worked outside the home long hours every day and commented to Kristi, "It doesn't matter to Jason that I'm not home with him. He can't tell the difference who is caring for him." Kristi gently suggested otherwise, but this friend wouldn't see it because she wasn't emotionally connective. Consequently, baby Jason's capacity to bond and to connect with God's grace didn't develop as fully as it could have.

Let's get really practical now by thinking of some specific ways to give our kids more grace. Here's a list of examples of what you can do to be a more grace-giving parent.

- Be kind, even to a grumpy child.
- Show compassion for hurt feelings.
- Take your child on a special outing.
- Accept your child's weaknesses.
- Occasionally give a gift for no reason.
- Listen patiently when your child is upset.
- Give lots of TLC when your child is sick.
- Affirm your child's good qualities.
- Be quick to forgive your child.
- Consider your child's explanations in discipline.

For you to work more of God's grace into your parenting in ways like these, you need to absorb more of it into your own being. In your personal life you need to reach out to Christ's ambassadors for grace by asking for what you need, taking it inside you through trust, and making use of it by relying on it continually. Then your eyes and heart will be opened and you can become a cheerful giver, giving from God's fullness instead of just trying harder to do what you should and getting frustrated with yourself (2 Cor. 9:7). For instance, when you know what it feels like to be listened to with compassion, then you can become more sensitive to and caring toward your children's feelings. Or when you've asked someone to accept you in your struggles, then you're better able to embrace your kids when they fall down. And if you've learned to rely on comfort from your spouse or friend when you're hurt, you'll be more likely to be patient and tender with your children's tears and fears.

Provide "Optimal Frustration"

There's another aspect to connecting with our kids and giving grace that most people I talk to in counseling or parenting seminars don't think of because it seems contradictory. If you give your child unconditional love, compassion, acceptance, affection, comfort, and the like *all the time*, then they won't feel loved *inside*. It's true! He or she will feel loved only when physically in your presence. Internalizing love requires something else, something painful: *separation*. Psychologists call this "optimal frustration." It's frustrating for children when they want their mother's (or father's) attention and can't have it. This is actually a good thing if they usually are able to get the connection they need from him or her. Then the pain of separation forces children to take Mom or Dad inside while they're away. This is the way children develop the capacity to soothe themselves when they're hurt and to talk to themselves in kind ways.

God does the same thing with us. You may not have thought of this as being something that was good for you, but I'm quite sure that you've experienced times when God wasn't immediately available to you with the comfort you needed or with the answer to your prayer. As long as you have experienced his love and provision in the past, the distance and deprivation that you experienced at that moment actually could have had a good effect on you. The apostle Paul explains this good effect, encouraging us that suffering develops perseverance, character, and hope in us and teaches us to rely on God's love that is in our hearts (Rom. 5:3–5).

Jesus told the apostle John and the other disciples that his leaving would be the opportunity for them to internalize him: "It is for your good that I am going away. Unless I go away, the Counselor will not come to you . . . But when he, the Spirit of truth, comes, he will guide you into all truth" (John 16:7, 13). Often I wish that I could lean up against Jesus' breast and talk with him as my best friend like John did, don't you? But what we have instead is his Spirit, the Paraclete (the word used in the original Greek language that John wrote in), as our Counselor, Comforter, Encourager, or Advocate (John 14:16, 28; 15:26; 16:7).

We want our kids to have God's comforting and encouraging love in their hearts too. The foundation for them to develop a faith relationship with our loving Lord is built when we connect with them in gracious and loving ways and provide them with "optimal frustration" so that they learn to internalize our love.

Honor Truth More

Truth is about reality, the structure of the way life is meant to be. It's the way God set up the universe and it's exhibited in his laws and creation. We learn the truth by studying God's creation and the Bible, his Word to us. We live in truth by being honest and moral, by doing what is right and good, by being holy and whole as God is. When we study and meditate on God's truth in the Scriptures and live it out, we are in a good position as parents to train our children in godliness. God's wisdom guides us in how to structure our home, gives us godly values to teach our children, and encourages us to discipline them in love when they get off track. But truth by itself is like oat flake cereal without milk. It's healthy, but too hard to swallow! So we need to speak the truth in love to our kids (Eph. 4:15). Let's think about some of the ways that we can do this. How do we provide godly structure for our children?

- Give them standards to live by.
- Read the Bible together.
- Assign them chores to do.

- Reinforce positive behavior.
- Discipline disobedience and disrespect.
- Teach them godly values.
- Establish house rules.
- Set protective limits on their behavior.
- Let negative consequences of choices teach them.
- Reward honesty.

Even if our children protest when we provide structure in a godly way, they still crave those boundaries. Have you heard about the study in which researchers took the fences off a preschool playground to see what the kids would do? It's fascinating. The kids all huddled in the center, scared to venture out! Just yesterday I heard an example of this. A mother said to me that her twelve-year-old daughter had been playing at a friend's house and they went into a chat room and pretended to be eighteen-year-olds and flirted with men. In the age of the Internet, that's like a parent's worst nightmare. This mother handled it well though. Instead of reacting with immediate panic or anger, she considered that her daughter was confessing this all on her own, and so she calmly listened to her daughter describe what she had done and then asked her about it. The daughter said, "I know we shouldn't have done it, Mom. I don't want to do it again. Just tell me not to do it and I'll tell her that I'm not going into chat rooms with her again." She knew that she needed fences up to play safely, and she went to her mom for help in erecting those boundaries.

Discipline Your Child to Be Responsible

You've probably had the experience of being around irresponsible teenagers. They leave the dinner table without saying thank you or cleaning their dishes, do few if any chores in the home, spend most of their free time watching television or playing video games, talk back to their parents, and expect their parents to pay for whatever they want. Kids like this aren't likely to have good relationships or successful careers as adults. Nor are they likely to develop a mature

Christian faith. Being responsible—respecting authority, exercising self-discipline, working hard, developing good values, being eager to help others—makes up the structure of a godly identity. The wise parent knows this. For thousands of years God's wisdom for parents has been, "Discipline your children while you still have the chance; indulging them destroys them" (Prov. 19:18 Message).

A couple of years ago Kristi and I realized that our first two kids (ages five and ten at the time) were heading toward looking like that in a few years when they entered adolescence. Maybe what woke us up to this danger was when Jenny wasn't getting what she wanted from Kristi and declared, "You don't even care! You shouldn't be a counselor for other people!" Or the time when Kristi was scolding David, and Jenny pronounced, "Mommy, you committed adultery! I mean child abusion!" In any case, we knew that time was running out to train them to be responsible. How could two hardworking, highly disciplined, and conscientious parents raise lazy and selfish children? Actually, it happens all the time. We're both good at nurturing and comforting and affirming our kids, but not so good at disciplining them. It takes a lot of energy to train kids to obey, pick up after themselves, use good manners, and work until a job is done. It's easier to avoid the stress and conflict, let issues go, and do it for them.

Thankfully, we gathered ourselves, joined together, and steeled our wills in training them to respect authority, to do their share of work around the house, and to be more considerate of others. We worked hard to be consistent in rewarding them for good behavior and punishing them for bad behavior. We developed systems for rotating daily and weekly chores among our three kids and required that they do these things on top of their homework. We also made a job list of extra jobs that they could do (like washing a car, cleaning the baseboards, or fertilizing plants) to earn money for the things they wanted. And when they disobeyed or disrespected our authority, we administered a consequence. It's been almost three years now, and we're encouraged by the results we're seeing, but at times we still struggle to provide the discipline our children need. Sometimes we slip into the old, easier, softer ways and have to regather ourselves.

A Gracious and Truthful Conscience Is Your Child's Best Friend

An essential part of a child's character is a conscience that guides him or her in the world of relationships and decision making. Some people say that the conscience is the voice of God, but that's not true. In reality it's the part of the self that is meant to hear God; it's an imperfect vehicle that God wants to use to convict us of sin and lead us to what is good. The value of a good conscience is portrayed in the story of *Pinocchio*. *Pinocchio* is a story about a wooden boy puppet with a talking cricket named Jiminy for a conscience. When his father, Geppetto, sends him off to school for the first time, Pinocchio is followed by his wise and caring friend, Jiminy Cricket. But eventually Pinocchio spurns Jiminy and follows two other boys who entice him to Pleasure Island, where the fun is short-lived and he finds himself enslaved by a vicious master who begins to turn him into a donkey. Finally, Jiminy finds Pinocchio and helps him to escape the hellish island. Pinocchio then realizes that Jiminy Cricket is his true friend, and because he learns to listen to his conscience, the Blue Fairy turns him into a *real boy.*

Parents must take a proactive role in helping their children develop a loving and holy conscience so that they too can become real, living souls that bear God's image. By giving grace and honoring truth with your child in the ways that we just discussed, you can shape your child's conscience according to biblical values. This is because over time they will internalize what and how you communicate to them. They will learn to talk to themselves with the same words and tone that you've used with them. Recall that Jeff was quick to point out things that were wrong and his kids picked up on this. Because Kyle identified with his father, he became self-critical and had what the apostle Paul calls a weak or legalistic conscience that caused him guilt even when he did nothing wrong (1 Cor. 8:7–12).

On the other hand, Kramer was scared by his dad's intensity and so he connected with his mother. But Rhonda was on the other extreme, trying to soften things all the time because she didn't like how hard Jeff was on the kids. She was continually looking to cut them some more slack. So Kramer was having trouble learning responsibility. It was hard for Rhonda to see that there was a problem, because Kramer was such a "good little boy." He was nice and well behaved, but only because he wanted to please his mother, not because he was developing a good conscience of his own.

Think of a conscience as being like a compass. My son David is a Boy Scout, and he's learned how to find his way out in the wilderness with a map and a compass. It's called orienteering. It's a mystery to me how he does this, but all by himself he can find where he is on a map and which direction according to his compass he needs to go to get to camp and then back home again. To find his way in life, he needs to read his Bible like a map. But the Bible alone isn't enough, because he needs to be able to understand and apply it. That's where his conscience comes in; it's the compass that enables him to find where he is on the map and which direction he's heading spiritually.

A good conscience is oriented to God's grace and truth, and it guides a person according to biblical morality even when he or she is without direction from a parent or a godly friend. We know a conscience is good if it sounds like God does in the Bible, a God who is for his people, not against them (Rom. 8:31). As kids get older they need their conscience more because they become increasingly independent of their parent's influence. So it's crucial for our children to develop consciences that are sensitive to the compassionate and wise voice of the indwelling Holy Spirit. Remember, as we discussed earlier, he is our Counselor, Comforter, Encourager, and Advocate.

So, like a compass, our conscience is only as good as our ability to discern God's voice. The apostle Paul in his second letter to the Corinthians gives us some very important instruction about the conscience. He says that we want our consciences to prompt us to feel "godly sorrow," not "worldly sorrow." "Godly sorrow brings repentance that leads to salvation and leaves no regret, but worldly sorrow brings death" (2 Cor. 7:10). An angry and condemning conscience is worldly sorrow at work. It drives a person to self-criticism, guilt, shame, and isolation. That's depressing, isn't it? (I've experienced it at times, as I'm sure you have too.) It's because this worldly sorrow is so painful that most people become legalistic in an attempt to avoid guilt (this is the "weak conscience" that is referred to in 1 Corinthians 8:7–12) or make light of sin, "suppressing the truth" and disregarding their conscience altogether (this is the "senseless conscience" that is described in Romans 1:18–32). God's way of convicting us is different. He speaks the truth to us in a gracious way; he comes to us in love and shows us how our sin has hurt ourselves, others, and him, which motivates us to feel sad instead of bad, sorry instead of guilty. We miss being connected with him, and we don't want to hurt someone we love, so we turn back to God and his ways; we return to putting our trust in the God of grace and truth.

If you help your child develop a conscience like that, one that is sensitive and responsive to God's grace and truth, then you've done a great job as a parent!

Questions to Discuss

1. Do you put more emphasis on grace or truth in your parenting? Discuss where you are and where you'd like to be on the Parenting Style Map with your spouse or a friend.
2. How are you at giving grace to your child? Do you tend toward detachment (not enough caring) or enmeshment (caring so much that you get overinvolved)? What's something that you'd like to do to be more gracious with your kids?
3. How are you at providing God's truth for your children? Do you slide more toward permissiveness (letting standards and rules slip) or authoritarianism (being rigid or harsh in how you train your children)? What's something that you'd like to do to honor truth more as a parent?
4. What does your child's conscience look like? What can you do to help him or her integrate God's grace and truth?

For Further Reading

Cloud, Henry. *Changes That Heal*. Grand Rapids: Zondervan, 1990, 1992.

Cloud, Henry, and John Townsend. *Raising Great Kids*. Grand Rapids: Zondervan, 1999.

Dobson, James. *The New Dare to Discipline*. Wheaton: Tyndale, 1970, 1992.

16

Teaching Values and Building Character in Your Child

Lynda Hunter Bjorklund, Ed.D.

I turned on the evening news: Another priest is accused of child molestation, a well-known CEO is tried for illegal insider trading, and a professional sports figure is charged with rape. The priest, CEO, and the sports figure all deny the allegations. Attorneys sat on both sides and argued, "Yes, he did!" "No, she didn't!"

As I watched these arguments in the public arena, my head spun. *Which is it?* I wondered. Someone is telling the truth, and someone else is lying. I grew up in a more black-and-white world, where wrong was wrong and right was right. But these three examples and countless others tell us that the lines in the sand of values have been swept away with the waves of political correctness, moral relevancy, a valueless society, and a postmodern view of "old-fashioned" Christian ethics.

Then I remembered my work as a state university professor more than a decade before. One semester I taught a class of 120 students on current issues, such as pro-life versus pro-choice, creationism versus evolutionism, heterosexuality versus homosexuality, abstinence versus safe sex. I chose my guest speakers carefully, each of them Christians who upheld godly principles. Following one of those presentations, a student stood up and made a comment I will never forget: "We've been told we *shouldn't* cheat, but no one ever told us why. As a result, our challenge is to go ahead and cheat but not get caught."

This unnamed girl echoed the challenges and frustrations of this modern generation. In his book *The Seven Laws of the Learner*, Dr. Bruce Wilkinson relates these startling statistics:

- 75 percent of all high school students cheat regularly and think it is okay.
- 65 percent of all Christian high school students are sexually active.
- 30 percent of all high school seniors have shoplifted during the past thirty days.
- 40 to 50 percent of teenage pregnancies are aborted.
- One in every nine teenagers (3.3 million) is an alcoholic.
- One thousand teenagers try to commit suicide every day.
- Up to 10 percent of high school students either have experimented with homosexual behavior or are living in a homosexual lifestyle.[1]

And things are getting worse, not better. Dr. Wilkinson goes on to list the seven major school problems in 1940 contrasted with today. In 1940, the seven greatest challenges in school were seen as talking, chewing gum, making noise, running in the halls, getting out of line, wearing improper clothing, and not putting paper in the wastepaper basket. Today, however, dominating the list of most common problems are drug abuse, alcohol dependency, pregnancy, suicide, rape, robbery, and assault.

So what do we do as parents? Do we despair, wring our hands, and accept failure on behalf of our children? No way. We as parents get proactive, deliberate, and on-the-ball when it comes to teaching and preparing our kids with godly principles.

One of my favorite *Focus on the Family* radio broadcasts hosted a man who talked of his fears when he sent his son off to kindergarten. To that point, he had been able to protect his young boy and structure his environment toward godly things. But now much of the boy's day was out of his dad's control. That night, as the anxious dad walked outside, he looked up in the sky and watched a giant airplane move confidently through the clouds. Again, an overwhelming feeling of helplessness engulfed him as he saw the lights flash on the giant monster in the sky. Then a firefly flew in front of his face, and the light from that tiny insect obliterated the huge lights of the mechanical genius above. Suddenly the man knew what to do for his son: he would keep him close; close enough to let him recognize the false lights from the true ones; close enough to keep him focused on the right things and not on the wrong ones that worked everywhere in every way to distract and destroy him.

I became a single mom when I was pregnant with my third child and my girls were three and one. When their dad left, my children, whom I would have given my life for, had joined the ranks of the more than 30 percent of families in America with children under eighteen living in a broken home. I assessed my children's chances of turning out okay, and I grew fearful. To that point I had not surrendered my life to the Christ my parents had taught me about. But then I was afraid to go forward without God leading me, so in September 1985, I walked in the field behind my home and turned over my life to Christ. "I give you not just this situation," I prayed, "I give you my whole life."

That prayer changed my life, and it certainly changed the way I raised my children on my own for more than fourteen years. With help from lots of others in my family and my church and through books and radio, I kept my children close. I taught them the eternal truths of God so they would always recognize the lie. Josh McDowell conducted a study comparing kids who are taught such a solid, biblical belief system with young people who lack basic biblical values.

He cites these statistics about those from all types of homes who are not taught Christian values early:

- They are 225 percent more likely to be angry with life.
- They are 216 percent more likely to be resentful.
- They are 210 percent more likely to lack purpose in life.
- They are 200 percent more likely to be disappointed in life.

In addition, McDowell gives the following report about children from good families but who are raised without a biblical belief system:

- 36 percent are more likely to lie to a friend.
- 48 percent are more likely to cheat on an exam.
- 200 percent are more likely to steal.
- 200 percent are more likely to physically hurt someone.
- 300 percent are more likely to use illegal drugs.
- 600 percent are more likely to attempt suicide.[2]

It's time to get serious about instilling the timeless and eternal truths of God. Once I told my daughter when I drew a biblical boundary, "I didn't create these rules. They were truths long before I was a mom, and they will endure for every mom to come."

My children are now twenty-two, twenty, and eighteen, and I'm still instilling values, though my opportunities have lessened. One way I stay motivated to keep showing them the biblical way is to ask myself the question in Matthew 12:29: "How can one enter a strong man's house and plunder his goods, unless he first binds the strong man? And then he will plunder his house" (NKJV).

I picture myself, along with my husband, Dave, sitting at the door of our home, guarding our family from the intrusions of the enemy. We sit, not with a gun across our laps, but with an open Bible, learning its truths and passing on those values to our now-grown children—all the while resisting Satan's attempts to steal their souls and destroy their lives. When I taught my children to color, I showed them how to draw with a crayon and outline around the object they would color. This outline helped them stay in the lines.

Values do too. By learning what the Bible says and reinforcing these boundaries, our children learn to stay in the lines and to do life God's way. When the Pharisees questioned Jesus about the Jewish rules for the Sabbath, he answered them, "The Sabbath was made for man, not man for the Sabbath" (Mark 2:27). The same could be said for all God's rules or values. He didn't make us for the rules; he made the rules for us because the One who made us also knows us and what we need. To make values-teaching and boundary-drawing a natural and deliberate part of *your* parenting, consider the following ten beatitudes:

Be about Relationship

Teaching values can naturally lend itself to nurturing relationships. If done well, it begins in natural, loving settings between you and your child, and it ends in natural, loving settings between your child and God. I picture the girl in my university class, who spoke of having no one in her life to tell her why she shouldn't cheat. With little human example for conducting life the right way, chances of finding a relationship with God diminish. We must teach our children that their ultimate goal for obeying biblical truths is to please God, not us.

One day as I drove my daughter Courtney to school, I spoke to her about something someone had told me she had said that damaged her Christian testimony. "I don't want you to tell me whether or not you said this. I wasn't there, and I didn't hear, but God was and he did."

In early Jewish days, the center of education was the home. But even in the schools, teachers were called "school fathers," indicating a close, filial relationship. My hope is that as I lovingly nurture my relationship with my child while I teach her in a Christ-centered way, she will broaden her love and her obedience to God. Once that relationship with God is forged, living out his values will follow.

Be Fun

Proverbs 22:6 tells us, "Train a child in the way he should go, and when he is old, he will not turn from it." *Train* in this verse means "to begin, initiate, inaugurate." Early Jewish midwives rubbed the palates or gums of newborns with honey with the hope that this experience would cultivate a taste for sweet things as that child grew. Once the children attended school, teachers wrote on primitive chalkboards such things as vowels and consonants, the alphabet, and Scriptures. Then the board was coated with honey, and when the child recited the information, he or she could lick the honey off the board. This obvious Jewish connection between the use of *hekh* (palate, gums) and *hanakh* (to educate) is conveyed in verses like these:

> Eat honey, my son, for it is good; honey from the comb is sweet to your taste. Know also that wisdom is sweet to your soul. (Prov. 24:13–14)

> How sweet are your words to my taste [*hekh*], sweeter than honey to my mouth! (Ps. 119:103)

Thankfulness is something my children have learned in a fun way. We prayed every day while driving to school. Often that prayer would consist not of asking God for anything but of going from one to another thanking God for his blessings.

One day Clint and I went to a nearby park and ran around the lake. Then we sat down on a log lying on the ground amid the pine trees. I put my arm around my son, and in familiar fashion I said, "Let's send up thank-you prayers to God."

Clint smiled and began with thanking God for his tennis shoes. I thanked God for where we lived and the beauty of the scenery we saw. Thank-yous continued, and thankfulness was once again instilled in a sweet and fun way, just before we raced back to the car.

Be Consistent

Children notice inconsistencies. Whether those inconsistencies come through how often you teach values or how faithfully you uphold them yourself, inconsistencies will come to light. Our kids realize that what is truly important to you will come out not only in what you say and do but in how you spend your time and make your priorities. If you announce you will be starting a Bible study after dinner on Monday nights, believe me, they'll be watching to see if you really carry it out. And if they see it's not all that important to you, it won't become that important to them either.

One of the slogans all of my children can recite from much use is that they are to be "100 percent respectful to 100 percent of adults 100 percent of the time." I told this to them often and also taught them to forgive wrongs that had been done to them. But the difficult circumstances of divorce caused my children to see conflicts I wish they had never seen. Though I reminded them that we are to forgive as Jesus did, my actions told them I hadn't done that completely. I walked with God and served in ministry around the world through my work as editor of Focus on the Family's *Single-Parent Family* magazine, but it wasn't until 1998 that a mentor of mine, Bruce Wilkinson, sat me down and made me face the fact that I held on to unforgiveness toward my ex-husband. Based on Matthew 18:34, he showed me that when we don't forgive, God turns us over to the tormentor, and Bruce Wilkinson helped me take care of forgiveness business that day, once and for all. Before this event, my children saw inconsistency in what I said and what I did. But they have seen a marked difference in me since July 1998, as I not only do what I say but follow through regularly.

Be Natural and Honest

Classrooms for teaching your children values happen at unexpected and unplanned-for times and places. As parents we need to watch for those teachable moments. The well-known passage in Deuteronomy 11:19 tells us, "Teach them to your children, talking about them when you sit at home and when you walk along the road, when you lie down and when you get up." I have enjoyed passing on to my children lessons God teaches me. This reveals many of the vulnerabilities in myself, but it also models for my kids where I go to find help.

The book of Joshua, in the Old Testament, became a significant and prolonged study on my journey through single-parenting. I remember once telling my children about how I struggled with going to God about everything in our lives, and then finding the "urim and thummim"—God's way of telling Joshua and his "kids" the way they should go. I sat on my bed and taught my kids about these truths from Scripture. When I finished, Ashley said, "I can't believe how relevant the stuff in the Bible is today."

After his sisters had left the room, Clint looked up at me with tears in his eyes and his Bible clutched to his chest. "I love this," he said. "I love this." Then he was off, busy doing his own thing.

I cannot stress enough the importance of letting our children see our own honesty, vulnerabilities, and even failures of not upholding biblical values. If we keep our eyes open, God will create classrooms for our teaching in the simplest and most ordinary places. But through the ordinary, God accomplishes extraordinary things in the lives of our children. Be honest. Be natural.

Be Responsive

You couldn't make a list of every topic you will cover with your kids for the next year. Current events and issues your kids are facing create the most appropriate subjects you can cover.

One day while in elementary school, Ashley came home disheartened about the way a certain friend was treating her. We talked about it a little, but I sensed more needed to be done, so I prepared a value lesson on finding and being a friend God's way. I gave each child pieces of paper with different verses on friendship, such as a friend loves at all times (Prov. 17:17) and a friend sticks close (Prov. 18:24). Then I drew a line down the middle of a marker board. I labeled one column "Friends to Find" and the other "Friends to Be." After we read the verses, we made lists of qualities that we needed to find in friends as well as those we needed to become. Then I had Ashley summarize based on the challenge she faced.

We can decide on all kinds of lessons we want to teach, but if you will keep your eyes and ears open, God will make you responsive to what your children need.

Be an Example

Another way you can determine a value you want to teach is to look at what your children are seeing, then exemplify the qualities you want them to learn.

Take the quality of generosity. I had saved a little money to take my kids on a daylong trip. We drove to the bank to get the money, then we planned to head out for our excursion. The bank was situated at the edge of a mall complex, and as we pulled back out onto the street, a woman stood toting a baby in a pouch and holding a sign asking for money. I drove on by as I talked to my family, and suddenly I knew I had to retrace my steps. I circled around the block and had the children hand them some of the money we had planned to spend that day.

As we pulled away, Ashley asked, "What if she's a fake? What if she spends that money on drugs or alcohol? What if that baby isn't even hers?"

I answered confidently, "All those things could be true, but that is between her and God. What is between us and God is that we keep our hearts tender, that we practice generosity and mercy just as Jesus would." It was easy to follow up on more information about generosity once my children saw it lived out in their own lives and demonstrated by their mom.

This event happened about ten years ago. Recently I was driving with my daughter, who is not completely where she needs to be with God today as she is busy pursuing her own interests and plans. But as we were driving, we encountered another person asking for money at a street corner. My child stopped our conversation and asked what we should give to the beggar. "I'll never forget when you told us to keep our own hearts tender."

Wow! I'm trusting every day that God continues to bring back the truths they learned as children, not because their mom was perfect or handled every situation well, but because we serve a perfect God.

Be Biblical

I'm a big proponent of children's books and poetry when teaching values to my kids. I read them *The Evergreen Wood* when I taught them to live a life of purity. I've also read many poems and even Dr. Seuss books that emphasize certain truths. But foundational to it all is the Bible. Show your kids the connection between what the Bible says and how it plays out in real life.

When Clint turned thirteen, God gave me wisdom to do something really special for him. He had grown up without his dad, so I began thirty-one days before his birthday, and together he and I read one proverb each night. I gave him intermittent "boy gifts" through that month (flashlight, alarm clock, thank-you notes and stamps), and I taught him one stanza from Rudyard Kipling's poem "If":

> If you can talk with crowds and keep your virtue,
> Or walk with kings—nor lose the common touch;
> If neither foes nor loving friends can hurt you;
> If all men count with you, but none too much;
> If you can fill the unforgiving minute
> With sixty seconds' worth of distance run—
> Yours is the earth and everything that's in it,
> And—which is more—you'll be a Man my son![3]

To celebrate Clint's actual birthday, I invited several men who had been involved in his life in some way. I asked them to come to a lasagna dinner and bring an old or new tool and a letter passing on a life lesson. His pastor came with a tool belt and talked about the importance of always telling the truth (Eph. 6:14). An Air Force football player brought a level and talked about the importance of balance. His principal and coach gave him a compass and talked about seeking godly guidance (Ps. 37:23).

Be creative, but always be biblical, and always draw your child's attention back to the scriptural truth involved.

Be Resourceful

If all this sounds overwhelming, remember, you don't have to reinvent the wheel. Here are several books that have already been written to help you teach values to your children:

- *You Hold the Keys to Your Child's Character* by Lynda Hunter. In this book, I show you as parents how to structure your prayers to ask for specific things regarding values in your kids. This book is available on my website at www.lyndahunter .org.
- *The Book of Virtues* by William Bennett. This book offers popular literature to reinforce different character qualities.
- *Lord, Bless My Child* by William and Nancie Carmichael. This excellent book combines verses, quotes, stories, activity suggestions, and prayers to help you teach different values, such as compassion, contentment, gentleness, and purity.

Many other resources are available. Go to your Christian bookstore and have them run a topic search for you. This will help you customize your value-teaching efforts for your unique child.

Be Discerning

My oldest daughter, Ashley, was placed in gifted classes in public elementary school, so topics such as evolution arose often. I tried to listen well, and I watched for newspaper and magazine articles that could spark spiritual discovery.

One day I clipped a newspaper headline that espoused the big bang theory. I gathered my kids around the kitchen table to enjoy a yummy snack, and I read the article aloud to them. Then I pulled my Bible to me and began to read the Genesis account of creation. What fun we had laughing, comparing, eating, and discerning the truth from the lie. I hope I stimulated their inquisitive minds instead of squelching them.

As the years went by and issues deepened for my growing children, I kept my eyes open for other truth-teaching tools. Any way I found people or resources to reinforce the things I had taught them, I pulled them in. My work at Focus on the Family helped me keep abreast of all kinds of resources and ideas for creatively passing on timeless biblical values.

Be Releasing

In her book *Give Them Wings*, author Carol Kuykendall reminds us that we as parents should not prepare the road for the kids, but we should prepare the kids for the road. Every value we teach them, from avoiding the pitfalls of sexual immorality through purity to learning to work hard through diligence and perseverance, we should instruct them today in preparation for tomorrow. Whether I'm teaching my son about generosity or showing him how to sew on a button or sort laundry, my responsibility is to get him ready to leave. I know we as parents don't like to think of empty nesting, but it's God's design. I once heard a professor who specialized in working with special-needs children say, "Time stands still for no one but the handicapped child." Parents I know whose child is handicapped would love nothing more than to be able to send him or her off competently into the world.

As you have probably realized, I like picture words. God knows this, so he has tended to teach me lessons through ordinary things. One such "classroom" happened on a ski slope. We had moved to Colorado in May, and our first chance to ski didn't come until January. My children had taken lessons when we lived in Ohio, but the mountains there were more like bumps where it took thirty minutes to stand in chairlift lines and thirty seconds to ski down the small slope.

Clint, Ashley, and I rode the chairlift to the top of one of the truly high mountains in Colorado, at Copper, while Courtney remained behind with a cold. As we made our way off the chairlift, eight-year-old Clint began to cry. "This isn't like the mountains we skied at home," he said. Ashley grew impatient with her brother's fear, so we agreed to meet her at the bottom. That's when "skiing lessons" began for Clint—and for me.

As we moved down the mountain, I realized my role was sixfold:

- I *taught* him the right techniques to navigate the turns.
- I *guided* him into the safe paths.
- I *encouraged* him that he had what it took to succeed.
- I *protected* him from out-of-control skiers and unforeseen dangers.
- I *modeled* how to put the techniques all together.

Clint started to get the hang of skiing as the bottom of the mountain drew near. My lesson, however, continued. I had taught, guided, encouraged, protected, and modeled for my son to the best of my ability. But then Clint moved past me yelling, "Come on, Mom, can't you go any faster?" Then as I watched him ski on ahead making tracks of his own, I realized my role was also to *release* him. I needed to let him make his own way.

Every day as you are faithful and deliberate about instilling values in your kids, remember they are only yours for a short time. God has lent this wonderful, fearfully made, unique being to you for you to help God fulfill his plans for that child's life. And don't think God gives that assignment without providing for you the wherewithal to do it. Teach, guide, encourage, protect, and model biblical values and character development every day in everything you see—when they lie down and when they rise up. But always, always keep in mind that they belong to God and your job is to release them back to him well prepared.

Conclusion

One more thought before I let you go. Because I didn't surrender my life completely to God until I was in my early thirties, I made mistakes I never had to make. As a result, I feel passionate about helping kids turn their lives over early to God.

I once set out to wallpaper the basement family room of our home. I decided I could hang straight pieces by just eyeballing the wall and without the benefit of a plumb line. So I hung the first piece, and the second, and it was looking pretty good—good, that is, until I arrived at the finish. When the last piece met the first piece, I cringed as I saw the six-inch difference between the top and bottom of the strip of paper. My problem could have been avoided if I'd bothered from the beginning to use a plumb line.

Amos 7:7 talks about a plumb line too—God's plumb line—and that plumb line is his Word. Teach your children the importance of holding it up from the first piece on in their lives, and show them others who have failed to do so. Hold the plumb line up for them in the beginning, but allow them to do it for themselves as soon as they can. Most of all, teach them that the plumb line was made for them, not them for the plumb line, by the One who made them, loves them, and knows them best. "I love them that love me; and those that seek me early shall find me" (Prov. 8:17 KJV).

Teach your kids to seek him early through the values you instill. Then not only will God love your child, but your child will learn to love and honor God too.

Questions to Discuss

1. How do you keep your children close enough for them to be able to recognize the false lights from the true ones?
2. How do you handle your children's "why" questions?
3. Talk about the ways you have fun with your children. What do you think you are teaching them through the fun?
4. What do you think might be keeping you from being as consistent as you want to be?
5. When you look ahead to releasing your children, what can you do now to prepare them for that point in their life?

For Further Reading

Bennett, William. *The Book of Virtues*. New York: Simon & Schuster, 1995.

Carmichael, Nancie. *Lord, Bless My Child*. Wheaton: Tyndale, 1995.

Hunter, Lynda. *You Hold the Keys to Your Child's Character*. Ann Arbor, MI: Servant Publications, 1998. (Available from the author at www.lynda hunter.org.)

17

UNDERSTANDING AND REINFORCING YOUR CHILD'S LEARNING STYLE

Cynthia Ulrich Tobias, M.Ed.

I was speaking at a homeschool conference in North Carolina a few years ago. One rather tired-looking mom came up to speak to me after the session. "I have sixteen children," she said. I quickly offered her a chair and asked if she had adopted some of them. She shook her head. "No," she replied, "believe it or not, they are all biologically mine. But I just wanted to tell you that it's true—no two children are alike." I thought, *Wow—I could have told her that long before the sixteenth child!*

When it comes to identifying learning styles, temperaments, or personality traits, you'll never be able to simply give your children a test or fill out a survey and figure out "what they are." Each child is fearfully, wonderfully, and complexly made, and no two will *ever* be exactly alike. It's really like pieces of a puzzle, and each person has every piece. Not all are the same size, but no one has just one big puzzle piece either. As you focus on discovering what brings out the very best in each of your children, you need to remember there will never be just one simple explanation for why he or she thinks or acts a certain way. There are so many pieces to this puzzle that we will never fully discover all the dimensions and possibilities.

You don't need to hire an expensive consultant or take a lot of education courses before you begin to discover your child's individual learning-style strengths. As a parent you are usually the most qualified expert of all when it comes to truly knowing your child. There are, however, five basic steps you can take to get a clearer picture of the learning-style strengths for each of your children.

Observe

Even the youngest child will be able to show you how his or her mind works, often without uttering a word. Start to deliberately notice your child when she is happiest or most successful, even if it's just playing or interacting with other children. When she is at her best, what are the circumstances and environments that seem to consistently be a part of that happiness? It's best if you have a notebook or journal and jot down casual notes as you begin to observe her behaviors and surroundings. What time of day is it? Who is with her? How does she organize her work or play space, and how particular is she about keeping it a certain way? Does she move around a lot? Does she talk to herself or hum or sing? Does she like to write or draw? Give yourself at least two weeks of keeping notes before you sit down and try to figure out what the consistent factors seem to be. If your child is old enough, discuss your observations with her and get more input. You'll be surprised how eager she'll be to share her likes and dislikes with you when you seem genuinely interested.

Listen

It's easy as a busy parent to start tuning your child out when you hear the same things over and over again. But what your child says, and—more important—how he says it, can give you valuable insight into how his mind works. For example, is he usually asking for more details? Does he need to know specific plans and times and reasons? He may be an analytic thinker who gets frustrated when information is too general or directions are too vague. On the other hand, he may tend to explain himself more than he needs to or ask you to repeat instructions. If he is a more global, big-picture thinker, he usually will become frustrated by details if he doesn't know what you're trying to tell him in the first place. He also may try to explain himself when he is forced to give yes or no answers.

For highly auditory learners, listening can quickly become tedious because they tend to talk almost constantly. They don't usually need you to hear every word they say; it's just that they won't know what they're thinking until they hear themselves say it. Sometimes it helps to have a code word that you and your child can agree on. Then you don't really have to tune in and listen until your child says that magic word. That way, you won't be frustrated listening to unnecessary chatter, and your child will know he can have your undivided attention when it's really important to him.

Experiment

Keep an open mind when it comes to finding what works for your child. As parents, of course, we usually want our children to do it our way; after all, we are living proof that our way works! The fact is, of course, that there are often several ways that work, and the bottom line is accountability. An important question to ask and answer is always What's the point? If you can define what it is you are trying to accomplish or measure, you can help your child find a way to do that without unnecessary frustration and misunderstanding. For example, many parents get a little uptight when they walk into their daughter's room where she is supposed to be doing homework. She is lying on the floor, textbook and notebook in front of her, headphones on, TV on in the background, with Diet Coke and chips beside her. A parent's first response is often, "You can't possibly do your homework like this!" But what if she can? If the point is getting the homework done and at the end of the evening it is done legibly and correctly, wouldn't it be worth letting her keep doing it her way? I'm not suggesting she use her style as an excuse, but as long as accountability stays intact, the goal is being met in the most effective way for her. If you are careful to define and agree on the goal for your child, you and she can both experiment with what works best to accomplish it.

Focus

When that report card comes home, it's easy to focus on what needs to be improved. Those average and below average grades leap off the paper, and our first inclination as parents is to insist that those grades come up. But the fact is you can't build on weakness; you can only build on strengths. When you first of all focus on what your child's strengths are, you can then use those positive characteristics to improve areas of weakness or limitation. For example, if your son loves and excels in PE but is really struggling in math, you can suggest he try practicing his math facts on the basketball court or reviewing basic concepts while running the track. If your daughter is highly social but can't seem to settle down and study for tests or do her homework, suggest she start a study group. (This should be closely monitored by you, of course, to make sure they stay on task!) Begin with what you know your child is good at and truly enjoys, and try to figure out how many ways you can incorporate that into the areas that need improvement.

Learn

Let your children know you are always willing to keep on learning. Set the example for being a lifelong learner by encouraging them to discover more about themselves and what they do best. Read books together—a chapter a night or a quick paragraph or two after dinner a couple times a week. For children old enough to read, share a copy of *The Way They Learn* (my first book about the basics of learning styles). Give each person in the family a different colored highlighter or colored pencil and ask them to go through the book, marking everything that really describes them as a learner. It sure makes for some interesting family discussions.

You as a parent understand and appreciate your children as unique and wonderful individuals with strengths and gifts. But the reality is that you may find that the teachers they have during their years in school aren't usually able to take the time and energy necessary to find out every single student's learning-style strengths when there is a classroom full of kids. One of the best ways to help your child's teacher get a jump start on gaining insight is to fill out a short, nontechnical survey with your child and briefly summarize what the teacher needs to know to better understand your child's learning style. The following survey is designed to help you get started. Remember, awareness is at least half the battle. The more you know about how your child learns, the better you can become at helping each of your children succeed.

Communicating with Your Child's Teacher: A Student Profile

The following is based on information in *The Way They Learn* by Cynthia Ulrich Tobias. It is designed to be a guide for parents in describing each individual child's strengths and preferences to a teacher. As you share this information with your child's teacher, remember, you are sharing what you know about your child and asking the teacher for insights that may aid you in helping your child understand, appreciate, and cope with demands in the classroom that may or may not match his or her natural learning style. Whenever possible, fill out the following with your child together.

Child's Name_____**Date**_____

*Each line represents a continuum—place a mark somewhere
between the extremes.*

I. How Does Child Best Concentrate?

Seems most alert during which time(s) of day?

Early morning   Late evening   Almost never

When doing his or her best work, needs or doesn't need some sort
of intake (food or drink).

Needs to eat or drink   Distracted by eating or drinking

Seems to be able to concentrate best in bright or dim light?

Bright light   Dim light

Is almost always most comfortable doing homework in a formal or
informal setting?

Formal (desk, table)   Informal (floor, bed, sofa)

II. How Does Child Best Remember?

*When trying to remember or review, child is successful most often
when he or she can:*

Repeat the words aloud, drill verbally, or turn the information into
a song or rhyme.

Almost always   Almost never

See a picture of what is meant, sketch out an idea, use colorful folders to organize.

Almost always   Almost never

Keep on the move, take frequent breaks, work in spurts of great
energy, shift positions.

Almost always   Almost never

III. How Does Child Process and Interact with Information?

When listening to information or directions, child usually seems to:
Get the gist of things, understand the main idea.

Almost always	Almost never

Remember specific details, can repeat things word for word.

Almost always	Almost never

When reading, child often:
Reads quickly, skipping unfamiliar words; tends to choose fiction or personal interest.

Almost always	Almost never

Reads slowly and deliberately; reads every word, stopping when there is an unfamiliar word; tends to choose subjects that can further knowledge, not much light reading.

Almost always	Almost never

When organizing, child usually:
Works with piles instead of files; may spread materials out over several work areas; tends to procrastinate.

Almost always	Almost never

Works best with a structured schedule; needs a clear and efficient work space; needs to break larger projects into manageable parts.

Almost always	Almost never

IV. How Does Child Understand and Communicate What He or She Knows?

When learning, child is:
More interested in obvious facts than in hidden meanings.

Almost always	Almost never

Often interested in where a person got the facts.

Almost always	Almost never

Most interested in the background of the person giving the facts.

Almost always   Almost never

Mostly just interested in how much of the facts are really necessary.

Almost always   Almost never

On a day-to-day basis, child prefers:

Having a parent or teacher provide predictable plans and routines.

Almost always   Almost never

Designing his or her own schedules or routines.

Almost always   Almost never

Knowing what will make everyone else happy.

Almost always   Almost never

Doing whatever the inspiration of the moment dictates.

Almost always   Almost never

When it comes to responding to authority figures, child seems to especially need:

Clear and specific rules and expectations.

Almost always   Almost never

Logical reasons for procedures and guidelines.

Almost always   Almost never

Reassurance of personal worth despite making a mistake.

Almost always   Almost never

To feel the mutual respect of the person in authority and input on the issues.

Almost always   Almost never

Summary

Child's Name_____**Date**_____

Here is what we feel is most important for you as a teacher to know about_____ (child's name):

_____

_____

_____

_____

©Apple St., LLC, P.O. Box 1450, Sumner, WA 98390 (253) 862-6200; Fax (253) 891-8611; www.applest.com

Talking to the Teacher

When talking to your child's teacher, keep the following in mind:

1. Treat the teacher as the expert. Assume the best, and approach the teacher in a positive, upbeat way.
2. Let the teacher know what you have read, and ask for his or her opinion. (Perhaps even loan the teacher a copy of *The Way They Learn*.) Ask the teacher to give you some ideas for further reading.
3. When discussing your child, start many of your questions with the same four words: "What can I do?" For example, "Jane's learning style is very different from your teaching style. I think it's great that she is learning how to deal with lots of different approaches. I'm wondering, though, what could I do to help her understand the way you teach? What could I do at home that might help her succeed better in your classroom?" Let the teacher know you and your child are taking the responsibility for learning and coping with the classroom demands.
4. Recognize that there are very practical limitations on what the teacher can do for your child. Try to make it as easy as possible for the teacher to accommodate your child's learning

style while still meeting bottom-line outcomes. For example, if you have discovered that your child needs to follow a certain system for recording and keeping track of homework, you go ahead and make up the necessary assignment sheets so that the teacher would only need to fill in a couple blanks and sign the bottom.

5. Remember, every teacher is a lesson in learning for your child. The more variety your child experiences in the classroom, the more opportunities he or she will have to discover and develop natural style strengths and to use them to cope with uncomfortable style demands. Instead of resenting a different teaching approach, do your best to help your child understand and value a variety of methods. By helping children discover and appreciate their teachers' unique styles, you can be preparing them to face a world of differences with the confidence of knowing they can use their strengths to cope with almost anything![1]

Communicating with Your Child's Teacher: An Early Childhood Profile

The following is based on information in *The Way They Learn* by Cynthia Ulrich Tobias. It is designed to be a guide for parents in describing each individual child's strengths and preferences to a teacher. As you share this information with your child's teacher, remember, you are sharing what you know about your child and asking the teacher for insights that may aid you in helping your child understand, appreciate, and cope with demands in the classroom that may or may not match his or her natural learning style. The following should be filled out by you as you carefully observe and talk with your child.

Child's Name_____**Date**_____

*Each line represents a continuum—place a mark somewhere
between the extremes.*

I. How Does Child Best Concentrate?

Seems most alert during which time(s) of day?

_____

Early morning   Late evening   Almost never

When concentrating, even at play, needs or doesn't need some sort
of intake (food or drink).

_____

Needs to eat or drink   Distracted by eating or drinking

Seems to be able to concentrate and play best in bright or dim
light?

_____

Bright light   Dim light

II. How Does Child Best Remember?

*When trying to remember or review, child is successful most often
when he or she can:*

Repeat the words aloud, or turn the information into a song or
rhyme.

_____

Almost always   Almost never

See a picture of what is meant, draw or cut out pictures, or use colorful folders, stickers, etc. to organize toys or materials.

_____

Almost always   Almost never

Keep on the move, take frequent breaks, work in spurts of great
energy, shift positions.

_____

Almost always   Almost never

III. How Does Child Process and Interact with Information?

When listening to information or directions, child usually seems to:

Get the gist of things, understand the main idea.

Almost always   Almost never

Remember specific details, can repeat things word for word.

Almost always   Almost never

When being read to, child often:

Doesn't mind if story is abbreviated or paraphrased; prefers stories of personal interest.

Almost always   Almost never

Wants to hear every word, no variation from printed story; prefers nonfiction subjects.

Almost always   Almost never

When playing or creating, child usually:

Prefers a variety of projects all at once; may spread materials out over several work areas.

Almost always   Almost never

Prefers one project at a time; works best with a schedule; needs efficient work space.

Almost always   Almost never

IV. How Does Child Understand and Communicate What He or She Knows?

On a day-to-day basis, child prefers:

Having a parent or teacher provide predictable plans and routines.

Almost always   Almost never

Understanding the purpose for and having time to complete the schedule and routines.

Almost always — Almost never

Knowing and doing what will make everyone else happy.

Almost always — Almost never

Doing what the inspiration of the moment dictates.

Almost always — Almost never

When it comes to responding to authority figures, child seems to especially need:

Clear and specific rules and expectations.

Almost always — Almost never

Confidence in the ability and position of the authority figure.

Almost always — Almost never

Reassurance of love and personal worth despite making a mistake.

Almost always — Almost never

To feel that the person in authority respects and seeks input on the issues.

Almost always — Almost never

V. Strengths and Preferences

Which of the following are your child's favorite types of free time activities?

☐ Blocks
☐ Legos/other construction materials
☐ Puzzles
☐ Computer
☐ Books
☐ Alphabet blocks/manipulative letters
☐ Sandbox
☐ Nature/science activities
☐ Drawing, coloring, creating with art materials
☐ Outdoor play
☐ Sports

☐ Lacing/sewing cards, stringing beads, pegboards
☐ Role-playing or play-acting
☐ Playing with dolls
☐ Other:

My child's favorite toys

Most often, my child prefers to play:
☐ alone
☐ with other children
☐ with adults

Summary

Child's Name_____**Date**_____

I would consider the following to be among my child's greatest strengths:

I feel my child needs encouragement in the following areas:

My goals for my child's school year include:

Here is what I feel is most important for you as a teacher to know about my child:

©Apple St., LLC, P.O. Box 1450, Sumner, WA 98390 (253) 862-6200; Fax (253) 891-8611; www.applest.com

Communicating with Your Colleagues: An Individual Profile

The following is based on information in *The Way We Work* by Cynthia Ulrich Tobias. It is designed to be a guide for describing your individual strengths and preferences to those with whom you live and work.

Remember, you are *not* using this to provide an excuse for not doing what is difficult or unpleasant. You are simply providing insights that can help your family and colleagues understand and communicate with you more effectively. After you have filled out one of these profiles for yourself, try asking another person who knows you well to fill out one on your behalf. It will be interesting to see if the two match.

Name_____**Date**_____

Each line represents a continuum—place a mark somewhere between the extremes.

I. How Do I Concentrate?

I am most alert during which time(s) of day?

_____
Early morning   Late evening

When doing my best work, I need or do not need some sort of intake (food or drink).

_____
Need to eat or drink   Distracted by eating or drinking

I normally concentrate best in bright or dim light.

_____
Bright light   Dim light

I am almost always most comfortable doing work in a formal or informal setting.

_____
Formal (desk, table)   Informal (floor, bed, sofa)

II. How Do I Remember?

I am successful most often when I can:

Use others as a sounding board to talk through issues or plans.

Almost always   Almost never

See a picture of what is meant, sketch out an idea, use colorful folders to organize materials.

Almost always   Almost never

Keep on the move, take frequent breaks, work in spurts of great energy, shift position often.

Almost always   Almost never

III. How Do I Interact with Information?

When listening to information or directions, I usually seem to:

Get the gist of things, understand the main idea.

Almost always   Almost never

Remember specific details, can repeat things word for word.

Almost always   Almost never

When reading, I often:

Read quickly, skipping unfamiliar words or substituting words; tend to choose subjects of personal interest and fiction.

Almost always   Almost never

Read slowly and deliberately; read every word, stopping when there is an unfamiliar word; tend to choose subjects that can further knowledge, not much light reading.

Almost always   Almost never

When organizing, I usually:

Work with piles instead of files; may spread materials out over several work areas; tend to procrastinate.

Almost always   Almost never

Work best with a structured schedule; need a clear and efficient work space; need to break larger projects into manageable parts.

Almost always   Almost never

IV. How Do I Communicate What I Know?

When learning, I am:

More interested in obvious facts than in hidden meanings.

Almost always   Almost never

Often interested in where a person got the facts.

Almost always   Almost never

Most interested in the background of the person giving the facts.

Almost always   Almost never

Mostly just interested in how much of the facts are really necessary.

Almost always   Almost never

On a day-to-day basis, I prefer:

Being provided with predictable plans and routines, specific expectations.

Almost always   Almost never

Designing my own schedules or routines, grasping an overall design or structure.

Almost always   Almost never

Knowing what will keep everyone happy, what will bring harmony and understanding.

Almost always   Almost never

Doing whatever the inspiration of the moment dictates, keeping lots of action in my day.

Almost always   Almost never

When it comes to responding to authority figures, I especially need:

Clear and specific rules and expectations.

Almost always   Almost never

Logical reasons for procedures and guidelines.

Almost always   Almost never

Reassurance of personal worth despite making a mistake.

Almost always   Almost never

To feel the mutual respect of the person in authority and input on the issues.

Almost always   Almost never

Summary

Name_____**Date**_____

Here is what I believe is most important for you to know about me in order to understand and work with me:

_____
_____
_____
_____
_____
_____
_____
_____
_____
_____
_____
_____
_____

©Apple St., LLC, P.O. Box 1450, Sumner, WA 98390 (253) 862-6200; Fax (253) 891-8611; www.applest.com

All of this may seem like a lot of work, but if you work through each of these worksheets and share the information with your child's teachers, you are laying an important foundation for the relationship between your child and his or her teacher that will lead to successful learning and growth for your child.

For Further Reading

Tobias, Cynthia Ulrich. *The Way They Learn*. Colorado Springs: Focus on the Family, 1998.

Tobias, Cynthia Ulrich. *Every Child Can Succeed: Making the Most of Your Child's Learning Style*. Colorado Springs: Focus on the Family, 1999.

Willis, M. S. Mariaemma, and Victoria Kindle Hodson. *Discover Your Child's Learning Style: Children Learn in Unique Ways—Here's the Key to Every Child's Learning Success*. Rocklin, CA: Prima Lifestyles, 1999.

18

Teaching Your Child about Money

Mike and Terri Stoop

> Whoever can be trusted with very little can also be trusted with much, and whoever is dishonest with very little will also be dishonest with much. So if you have not been trustworthy in handling worldly wealth, who will trust you with true riches?
>
> Luke 16:10–12

Teaching our kids about money is no easy task. We all come from varied backgrounds that taught us different ways of thinking about money. It is difficult enough just to agree on how we manage our household funds, let alone agree on how we are going to teach our kids to manage it.

When it comes to learning money skills, both Terri and I grew up in very similar homes. I don't think I would classify us as coming from poor families, but we were not wealthy either. We seemed always to have enough just to get by, but nothing more. For our parents, the answer to us kids about buying something excessive was easy—we couldn't afford it. We had the necessities and that was that. I don't remember ever talking about money growing up. Most of what we know about money was discovered as adults, or came from watching what our parents did. Unfortunately, financial mistakes as adults are much more painful and long lasting than those as children. We wanted our kids to learn from their own mistakes as kids when the consequences are much easier to deal with.

Colleen is our social butterfly and loves to hang out with the large group of girls her age on our block. Several years ago, the girls decided to start a club called the Lava Lava Club (named after the Lava Lava she wore once on a mission trip to Samoa—more about that later). It seems the club is always coming up with a new harebrained scheme about one thing or another. Recently, they all decided it was time to raise some money—for what, nobody knew. The fundraising activities ranged from lemonade stands to pet-walking services to washed cars. It was a flurry of activity for a couple weeks while the funds poured in. Finally, it was time to decide what to do with the money.

As parents, we watched the process wondering what the girls would do with the money. If a large sum of money were dropped in my lap at that age, what would I have done? Could we trust Colleen to be a good steward and make a good decision? The next Sunday would tell. There was an announcement in our church bulletin talking about a giving project called Boxes for Bosnia. The project allowed you to pick a male or female from Bosnia in a specific age group and put together a box of goodies to meet the specific needs of whomever you picked. Colleen saw this and knew this was the reason for the fundraiser. She presented it to the rest of the club, and it was a done deal. They were off to the store to fill up the boxes. As parents, our egos were glowing; Colleen might turn out all right after all. In reality though, God deserves the credit, because all we had done was follow his plan by teaching her little by little to be trustworthy in the small things.

So is it really important that we teach our kids about money? Should we really be focusing our kids on this subject in our materialistic society? Surely, there are more important things we should be teaching our kids, and then, if we have time, we'll teach them a thing or two about money. The answer may seem obvious to some of us, but let's look at what God has to say. Jesus obviously thought it was a key topic; almost half of his parables deal with the topic of money. According to Crown Ministries, an organization dedicated to biblical principles regarding money, the Bible contains approximately five hundred verses on prayer; fewer than five hundred speak about faith, while more than two thousand verses speak about how to handle money! How we handle our money is extremely important to God.

To complicate the task, though, each of our kids has a completely different perspective on money and how to use it. Michelle, our oldest, was our squirrel. I think she may still be living off birthday earnings she received when she was eight. Because she was so frugal, it may seem that Michelle would have been the easy one to teach. But if she didn't spend it, how were we going to teach her to manage it? Colleen was completely opposite of Michelle. If she had any change left over after a purchase, the shopping spree was deemed a failure. It became clear that all of the money lessons we had used with Michelle were going to need to be revamped for Colleen. Then there is our youngest, David. David is still new on his journey into money management, but so far he seems to be completely different from Michelle and Colleen. Clearly, whatever plan we came up with was going to have to be different for each of our kids.

Terri and I decided we needed to settle on some basic principles that would teach our kids the basics about managing money. The principles we chose were not intended to be all-encompassing or to make our kids into expert financial planners. Our purpose was to ground them with basic biblical principles they could build on later in life.

Earning Money

So how do we begin the daunting task of teaching our kids about money? To learn how to manage money, our children need to have money to manage. There are several ways we as parents can accomplish this. One way is to give them an allowance, not tied to chores, not tied to behavior, but just given to them. Or we could give them wages for chores they complete around the house. Of course, we could incorporate both and have their allowance loosely tied to their chores around the home. One way or another, we needed to figure out how to give our kids an income before we could start teaching them how to manage their money.

I believe there are two issues we need to balance as parents. Paul wrote to the Thessalonians, "If a man will not work, he shall not eat" (2 Thess. 3:10). The point here is that we need to teach our children a good work ethic. If they are not willing to work for what they need or want, they are not entitled to it. Unfortunately, many kids today feel that they are entitled to whatever they want regardless of whether they work for it. Actually, if we are completely honest, many of us probably had some of that sense of entitlement when we were growing up too.

The other side to balance is caring for your family. Paul writes to Timothy, "Anyone who won't care for his own relatives when they need help, especially those living in his own family, has no right to say he is a Christian" (1 Tim. 5:8 TLB). It is equally important to teach our children about family commitment and caring for each other, even without material rewards. We decided we needed to strike a balance between these two issues, which brings us to our first principle.

We decided that our kids would be given a set amount based on their age and then they would be rewarded with extra money for things they did above and beyond their weekly responsibilities. This can begin at a very early age. Replacing the toilet-paper roll was traditionally our first assigned job. It's great fun and easy for them to learn, and even a two- or three-year-old can handle it. Our kids were to check daily and make sure there was a supply. It's important for the job to be a necessary chore and for us to make sure we let them do it. Many times in our home, a bathroom would go unused until the job was done.

Principle One
An Honest Day's Work for an Honest Day's Pay
Whatever you do, work at it with all your heart, as working for the Lord, not for men, since you know that you will receive an inheritance from the Lord as a reward. It is the Lord Christ you are serving (Col. 3:23–24).

So the question always arises, "How much do we pay them?" When you are determining how much to pay your kids, realize that it must be an amount that is significant to the child. They must give value to it. At the same time it should not be so much that they can go out and buy everything they want.

Over the years we have varied the amount depending on what seemed to be a significant amount to our kids. It has also varied from child to child. Spend some time watching what your child sees as a lot of money. At Christmastime, we always seem to receive lots and lots of catalogs in the mail. Our kids loved to look through them and circle what they wanted for Christmas. We often looked at what the kids had circled and talked about it with them to gauge what they thought was a lot of money.

Talk about chores: Sit down with your kids and come up with a list of jobs that need to be done around the house. Make sure you include any chores the kids think are important no matter how insignificant.

Offerings to God

Probably one of the most difficult lessons for us in our immediate satisfaction–driven society is to pay God before we pay anyone else. So here we are at our second principle.

In reality, we are not "paying" God; we are returning the firstfruits. As adults we can easily get into the habit of giving to the Lord out of what we have left over after paying our bills each month instead of the firstfruits. Our kids easily get into the same trap when they first realize, *If I don't tithe [give to the Lord] this month, I can get that new action figure now instead of next month.* But Jesus wants a sacrificial giver.

> **Principle Two**
> **Pay God First**
> Honor the LORD with your wealth, with the firstfruits of all your crops (Prov. 3:9).

In the Gospel of Mark, we read the story of the widow who came and dropped two pennies in the collection box at the temple after all the rich men had put in their large amounts. Jesus said, "This poor widow has put more into the treasury than all the others" (Mark 12:43). Our kids need to learn that it's not the amount that is important but the attitude of the heart. When a child is giving a part of their weekly allowance, it may not seem like a lot of money to us, but what is important is the sacrifice, not the amount.

We decided to teach our children to give a tithe, which is 10 percent. When our kids first learned to count, we showed them how to take their money and divide it into ten equal piles. We had them take the first pile and put it into a paper cup labeled with a picture of a church. Every Sunday it was their responsibility to take it to their Sunday school class and put it in the offering plate. If they forgot, it would sit and accumulate until the next Sunday. The important thing was that they experienced giving money that they earned back to God. If your child feels that they want to give more than 10 percent, encourage them but don't "guilt" them into it. God also wants us to be a cheerful giver: "Each man should give what he has decided in his heart to give, not reluctantly or under compulsion, for God loves a cheerful giver" (2 Cor. 9:7).

We feel it is important to teach our kids that the money is not just thrown into an offering plate on Sunday morning. We need to help them understand where the money is going. When I was growing up, my elementary school gave us "mite boxes," named after the widow's mite. Each student was to collect money and turn it in at the end of the school year. The money was to be used to help orphan children. Unfortunately, I had no idea what that meant. Where was the money going? Who were these children? Did it really help? As a child I didn't make the connection between the giving and the impact on lives that it probably had.

We wanted our children to see how God used the money to make a difference. We found there are several great ministries out there that can help us do this. The first one is World Vision. When our kids were very young, each of them sponsored a child who was about their same age. Over the years as the kids have written letters back and forth, they have begun to see the impact that World Vision is having on these kids' lives.

Another great ministry we have found is Samaritan's Purse. This organization takes shoe boxes that are filled with everything from toys to toiletries and distributes them to needy children all over the world. Our kids would take part of their tithe and go shopping for items to fill the shoe boxes. Here, our kids get to see real stuff, not just money, being shipped off to needy children. In fact, there are probably a few toys in those shoe boxes they would like to keep, so we get to help them experience the sacrifice also.

Colleen was fortunate enough to experience the other side of giving. Several years ago, Terri and I decided to go on a mission trip to

Samoa. Terri and I led children's worship at our church at the time, and we were given the opportunity to lead the music for a vacation Bible school. Colleen was our hand motion leader, so of course she had to go and help teach the kids how to do the hand motions. Part of preparing for the trip was for the team to raise money to cover the costs of the trip. We wrote letters to friends, held bake sales at school, and started saving. Colleen was involved every step of the way. She helped write the letters and staffed the bake sale booth. We also included her in how much was collected and how much we had left to go. Colleen got to experience firsthand God's supplying what seemed at first to be an overwhelming amount of money. When the mission trip happened, she got to see firsthand the fruits of what that money was used for.

If we look around us, there are many opportunities to help our kids experience God's money at work. It's important that we remember to involve our kids in the process and let them make their own decisions with our guidance. When we went shopping for the items in the Samaritan's Purse shoe boxes, there were many items that we probably wouldn't have picked, but this was their opportunity to serve, not ours. We just needed to guide them, not make the choices for them.

Learning to Be Content

I can't count the number of times walking through the store when one of the kids would run up and say, "Can I buy this?" My first reaction is usually, "No, I'm not buying that now." Unfortunately, this response doesn't really resolve anything, except my child now sees me as a mean, stingy parent—after all, Johnny's dad bought him one. The issue is not whether or not we can afford to purchase the item, but teaching our kids to be content with what we have and to be good stewards of our resources. Terri and I wanted to teach our kids to make their own decisions about what they could buy in the store. So on to the third principle.

How do we teach our kids to be content in a materialistic world where they are hammered with TV ads telling them they need more stuff? My simple answer to the problem was to get rid of the television and move to a remote area where the kids would be isolated from any form of materialism. Fortunately, Terri provided some sanity and reminded me that was not a practical solution. What we decided to do was allow them to learn the same way Terri and I did as adults, through trial and error. Only this time it would be as children, when they could be provided boundaries and support by us. Each of the kids already had an allowance, and they were already tithing. We decided the rest of their allowance was free to spend on whatever they wanted. If they wanted to spend all of their allowance immediately when they got it, it was their choice.

Principle Three
Get Control of the "I Want It Now"
For I have learned to be content in whatever circumstances I am. I know how to get along with humble means, and I also know how to live in prosperity (Phil. 4:11–12 NASB).

Now we have placed the decision to buy something back with our children. Colleen was our spender, so the real test would be when she found something she wanted during our next shopping expedition. Sure enough, "Can I buy this?" came up as expected. Only this time my response was, "Sure, you have your own money. Do you have enough?" Now, an interesting thing happened. She had enough money to buy it, but now that it was her choice and her money, the item didn't seem as desirable. Her final response was, "Oh, I have to use my money? Then I don't want it." What was amazing is that we not only avoided the argument of "Can I buy it?" but Colleen realized she really was content to be without it. I can't say it always went that easily. We progressed to the "I don't have enough—can I borrow from next week's allowance?" and the "I shouldn't have to pay for that; you should buy it for me." But we can look at these as new teaching opportunities and use them to teach about credit (and its consequences) and about the attitude of entitlement.

We as parents did struggle at times with this principle because sometimes we had a strong opinion about what the kids should buy and what they shouldn't. I'm not talking about items that they are not allowed to buy; I'm talking about situations in which we as parents need to step back and let them reap the consequences of their actions. It's difficult sometimes not to jump in and rescue our kids, but sometimes the results of a bad financial decision are the best teachers.

David loves his skateboard. He uses it pretty much every day. Some of the boys on our block have what David calls a "longboard." David decided one day he had to have a longboard. So we gave our new response, "Sure, save up and you can buy it." David saved for quite a while, and when we thought he had enough, we were off to the sporting goods store. Well, my estimate of what a longboard costs was way off. The longboard was a lot more than what David had saved. Here's where Dad's opinion tried to creep in: "It won't take long just to save up for what you really want; let's just go home and save up a while longer." But David decided that because he couldn't get the longboard now and his old skateboard was getting pretty beat up, he would just buy a new regular skateboard. My opinion interjected again, and I said, "Don't spend all your money on the regular board; you'll have to start saving all over again." Fortunately, I realized before it was too late that the lesson here was much more important than which skateboard David ended up with. David did buy the regular skateboard and never did get his longboard. It was more important for David to experience the consequences of an impulse buy than for him to have the joy of getting his longboard.

We need to remind ourselves constantly that the purpose of letting our kids spend money is for them to learn what works and what doesn't. We need to let them make mistakes while they are young when the consequences are not as painful.

Planning Ahead

Colleen is a dancer. With dance lessons come dance shoes. And of course there is the dance leotard and tights. And certainly you need to have two pairs so that if one is in the wash, the other is available to wear to class. The bottom line was that this dance thing was getting out of hand. When we started the dance lessons, I thought once we paid the tuition and bought a pair of shoes, we were done. Wrong. We decided that this was a great learning opportunity for Colleen. Instead of us deciding if the dance shoes could go another month, Colleen was going to decide. After a little thought, I sat down with Colleen and asked her to come up with a list of what she thought she needed through the year for her class. The list was to include everything except the tuition.

Colleen took the challenge and spent several nights figuring out how long her shoes should last and how often she got a run in her tights. After the list was complete, we sat down and attached amounts to each of the items and came up with a total amount required to get through the year. I tried not to gasp too loudly and continued on with our plan. Next, we divided the total amount by the number of months she was in class and came up with what we could expect to spend on a monthly basis. We instructed Colleen that this amount would be added into her allowance and it was now her responsibility to buy all of her dance supplies.

The money accumulated rapidly because she didn't need anything at first; everything was still new. I cautioned her to plan ahead; new shoes cost more than what she received every month. Along came the temptation to get that snazzy leotard that she could afford now. She knew that would sacrifice her ability to buy new shoes when her current ones wore out. I held my tongue, repeating to myself that the lesson was more important than my ego when the other parents would see Colleen in worn-out dance shoes.

Colleen didn't always make the decisions that I would have made when buying her dance supplies. But she was learning what worked and what didn't. Colleen was learning how to manage a budget and to plan ahead for large expenses. This brings us to our fourth principle.

We found teaching this principle very different with each of our children. Michelle, our saver, had no problem saving and accumulating cash. But she still needed to know how to plan. She was very content with what she had, and if she wanted something, she usually had plenty of money saved to get it. Well, the teenage years arrived, and all that was about to change.

Michelle was driving and I was starting to recover from the driver's training phase. I have often argued that there is no greater fear than the first time a parent sits in the passenger seat of the car for the child's first driving lesson. Michelle's dream car was one of the midsized two-seat trucks that she could fix up like a lot of kids do today. Michelle had saved several thousand dollars toward her

Principle Four
Plan for the Future
The wise have wealth and luxury, but fools spend whatever they get (Prov. 21:20 NLT).

truck. Unfortunately, the trucks that were in reasonable condition (and ones I felt comfortable letting her drive) were a little more than what she had saved. Michelle asked me if I would loan her the rest of the money and said that she would pay me back out of her paycheck.

Debt is much more a part of our lives today than it was when we were growing up. We felt it was important for our kids to understand the impact debt can have on our budget and the pitfalls we can get into. Michelle had been working as a restaurant hostess for a while now and was demonstrating good responsibility. We decided this would be a good time to teach her about debt and planning. Michelle was already responsible for her own insurance (actually, it was the difference we had to pay for her to drive our car). I challenged Michelle to come up with a plan to show how she would pay for her insurance, gas, and entertainment and still pay back Dad in a reasonable period of time. We sat down several times and went through the numbers before she came up with what I thought was a reasonable plan. I told Michelle we were going to handle this like a bank (well, kind of like a bank). If she missed a payment, I would impound the car until the payment was made. Because the insurance was paid along with mine, the insurance payment would be handled the same way. Michelle learned what it was like to have a monthly payment that took a substantial portion of her pay. She never caused the car to be impounded, but the pressure to make that payment on time served its purpose.

If we get creative, we can find many ways to let our kids plan their own budgets. When we decided to do some renovation in our home, we gave the kids a budget and allowed them to decide what they wanted to do to their rooms (with approval from our chief decorator—Mom). We also allow our kids to use their own money when buying family Christmas presents. Deciding what to buy each family member without spending a lot of money is no small task, but it's a great lesson in planning.

Giving to Others

When Terri and I talked about the number one money skill we wanted to send our kids out into the world with, it was a spirit of generosity. This brings us to our last principle.

Principle Five
Be Generous
Remember the words of the Lord Jesus, that He Himself said, "It is more blessed to give than to receive" (Acts 20:35 NASB).

We can teach our kids the mechanics of giving, but our prayer should be that God would produce in their hearts the spirit of generosity. We wanted our kids to learn the lesson that it is more fun to give money away. It brought me such joy to watch the neighborhood girls join with Colleen and have such a great spirit of generosity. They were genuinely concerned about what they were buying and kept wondering what the recipients of the boxes would be like. Not once during our trip to the store to buy our supplies did the girls ask for anything for themselves. They gave from their hearts and were extremely cheerful givers. We should always look for opportunities for our children to show generosity. When you see them exhibiting this, praise them. Let them see you opening your home or giving to others. Involve them in decisions regarding your family giving. Allow them to see you make giving a priority.

Most of what we have talked about involves real-life experiences that teach our kids why it's important to give. We can't forget that we as parents provide the most important experience of all, acting as the role model. If our kids see us show a spirit of generosity and compassion, they will emulate it.

One day while I was driving into a mall parking lot, we came upon a homeless man. Colleen asked if we could give him money. I had often had this struggle within myself before. Do I give him money? What will he do with it? What would Jesus do? I was so happy that my children wanted to give money, and it was difficult for me to explain why I hesitated to give so willingly. We decided that we needed to do something—but what? Recently, a friend of mine suggested an idea that helped. We filled gallon-sized sealable plastic bags with articles that a homeless person might need (antibacterial wipes, nonperishable food, soap, a gift certificate for fast food, etc.). We also decided to include a number for a nearby shelter, a booklet that would tell them about Jesus, and the address of and directions to a local church. Now when we come across a homeless person, we are prepared.

Another passion we have wanted to instill in our kids is a passion for missions. We look for every opportunity to involve our children in missions work. It is important that they realize that we have been blessed in many ways. For several years now, we have worked at an inner-city church helping to serve Thanksgiving dinner. Last Thanksgiving was one of the first times David realized that some people don't have enough to eat every day. Our involvement with World Vision is also teaching our kids to have a heart for others. Because we receive mail from the children we sponsor, they are very real to our kids. Our kids now realize that not everyone can go to school and that in many instances children need to work to help support their family.

Opening your home to missionaries is another great opportunity for your children to see the spirit of generosity. You can get the names of missionaries who are serving in local or foreign countries and put their names on your prayer list. Invite them to your home for dinner or have them spend the night when they are traveling through your town. Our kids have come to know one of our missionary friends as Uncle Ray because he has become a part of our family. He has traveled to many places including South Africa and Russia, and when he stays with us or calls us, our children get to be a part of his journey.

Conclusion

Of course, we can't really teach our children something unless it is part of our lives as well. Each of these principles needs to be incorporated in our own lives, because children learn a lot by what they see us doing with our money.

Questions to Discuss

1. Discuss several options with your children about where you might give money and let them help decide.
2. How did you and your spouse learn to handle money? What are the differences in how your families of origin handled money?
3. Sit down as a family and ask each other what you would do if you had $1000, $10,000, or $1,000,000. Spend some time talking about why your decision is important to you.

4. Locate some areas through your church where you can get involved, and let your children see you exhibiting the spirit of generosity.

For Further Reading

Burkett, Larry. *Money Matters for Kids*. Chicago: Moody Press, 2000.

Kay, Ellie. *Money Doesn't Grow on Trees: Teaching Your Kids the Value of a Buck*. Minneapolis: Bethany House, 2002.

Lucas, Daryl, David R. Vreemar, and Richard Olson. *105 Questions Children Ask about Money Matters*. Wheaton: Tyndale, 1997.

19

GUARDING YOUR
CHILDREN'S FAITH
AS THEY MOVE INTO
ADOLESCENCE

Jim Burns

We were *never* their age. Sure, we were six, eight, twelve, and even sixteen once, but never their age. Our children today are experiencing so much so early in their lives. When our youngest daughter was ten years old, she innocently asked my wife and me a question about sexuality that we had not discussed until we were married. I asked her where she had heard about this issue, and she told me it was in the headline of the newspaper about the president of the United States. The average young person will have the opportunity to watch more than 14,000 acts of sexual intercourse or innuendos to on prime-time TV this year. It is truly a different world than when we were growing up.

Because it doesn't appear as if the world is going to move backward, parents today have to ask the question, "How do we guard our children's faith as they move into adolescence?" Kids today are rapidly moving from dependence on you toward independence. A weaning process takes place that is not always easy for the child or the parent. Both have to make adjustments, and sometimes the adjustments don't go as smoothly as we had hoped.

Cathy and I have three daughters, and one of the shocks that came my way as they entered the teen years was that I lost some of my "Dad's cool" status. I can tell you the exact time and place it happened. Christy, my oldest, and I had treated ourselves to generous portions at Golden Spoon Yogurt for the past twelve years. It was one of our special connection times. On a beautiful spring evening, I asked if she wanted to stop for a yogurt. As we pulled up to our spot, Christy panicked and said, "Dad, we can't be here." Dumbfounded, I asked, "Why?" The answer was polite but firm: "There are some boys I know over there and I don't want them to see me with you." Ouch! I acted like it didn't hurt, but her verbal punch really hit me hard. Cathy wasn't much help when I complained to her. She reminded me it was a normal part of Christy's development. I quickly reminded Cathy that this kind of thing might be the way it is for many kids and their parents, but not for Christy and me. The next week I was humbled again.

Believe it or not, my next oldest daughter, Rebecca, and I had the same experience two years later at the same yogurt store. Then, with our youngest, Heidi, it happened again, and I was just as shocked. Only this time it wasn't at the yogurt place—it was at the movie theater! The moral of the story is simply that we parents have to get ready for the inevitable changes that will occur rapidly in the lives of our children as they move into adolescence. Their bodies change, their worldview changes, their faith changes, and their relationship with their parents changes. At the same time we have the responsibility and privilege to guard our children's faith and life throughout their preadolescent and adolescent years.

Because change is inevitable, parents must take a proactive role in the changing spiritual climate of their child's life. There are no easy answers and there are no magic formulas, but there are five biblical principles that can make the transition a bit smoother. Remember that our children are on loan to us from God and that the ultimate goal is to raise responsible adults. We can't be too shortsighted that we miss this objective of parenting. With this thought in mind, let's look at five principles that make the transition a bit smoother while we help guard our children's faith and prepare them for their next developmental stage.

Guard Your Child's Faith by Being a Good Role Model

Excitement and enthusiasm are caught, not taught. Influential parents and churches have smothered excitement for God by treating him like a great killjoy or a boring, distant relative. Recently, I had the privilege to spend time with a roomful of deeply committed Christian teenagers. Their faith was ablaze with energy. I asked them, "What brought you to this point in your faith?" One young man mentioned prayer, a few mentioned friends or youth workers, but the vast majority told of their parents' influence.

From childhood we learn best from role models. Principles and methods mean little to a child, but example means everything. What do Mom and/or Dad teach when they leave their children at church, go to brunch or sit and read the paper, and then pick up the children after church? How about the parent who knows all the right doctrines, never misses a church meeting, but is a tyrant at home? Martin Luther once said, "I have difficulty praying the Lord's Prayer because whenever I say 'Our Father' I think of my father who was hard, unyielding and relentless. I cannot help but think of God that way."

Parents set the pace. As children, our earliest concepts of God usually come not from a book or church, but from our parents. "The Bible is the most important book in the world," we say, but if our children never see or hear us read it, how can they relate to what we say and do? One of the great proverbs says, "The man of integrity walks securely" (10:9). Let's take it a step further: the man or woman of integrity walks securely and will have children who also will feel secure in their parent's integrity. Deuteronomy 6:4–9 is central to the Jewish faith. It is no doubt one of the first Scriptures Jesus memorized as a young person. When he was asked, "What is the greatest commandment?" he immediately responded by quoting Deuteronomy 6:4–9:

> Hear, O Israel: The LORD our God, the LORD is one. Love the LORD your God with all your heart and with all your soul and with all your strength. These commandments that I give you today are to be upon your hearts. Impress them on your children. Talk about them when you sit at home and when you walk along the road, when you lie down and when you get up. Tie them as symbols on your hands and bind them on your foreheads. Write them on the doorframes of your houses and on your gates.

Central to this passage is that parents are to impress their faith on the next generation. The Hebrews in the days of Jesus knew exactly what their spiritual role was with their children. Not only were they to impress their faith on their children, but their faith was to be throughout their home through traditions, rituals, family worship, lifestyle, and teaching according to the Scriptures.

Today parents who care about a spiritual legacy for their children must be proactive in their passing the torch of faith to their children. They will have to set the pace. The job is not just that of the church or the school; the leadership must come from the home. Adolescence is truly a rite of passage. Parents who set the pace and are proactive in their parenting will have much better results at guarding their children's faith.

Guard Your Child's Faith by Understanding Their Culture

Today's parent must take an active role in studying the culture in which their child is growing up. Today's kids are called "millennials." They look at life differently from their baby boomer parents or the group who preceded them, generation X. Some parents will assume their kids think like they do or even like the previous generation, but this is simply not the case. As a baby boomer parent, I prefer black-and-white moral values. A millennial is comfortable with paradox. This generation is more tied in to communication and information from the Internet than any other form of media. It has been said that people twenty-four years and older use the

World Wide Web, but people under twenty-four will live by the Web. With the rapidly changing culture, parents simply must keep up with the changes and become students of today's influences and culture.

Christian parents have not done very well when dealing with popular culture. We tend to fluctuate between pulling ourselves completely out of the world and blending into the culture as if there were very little difference between our faith and our society. But there's no question that the way we parent is affected by the world we live in. And what a world it is!

Instead of Ozzie and Harriet, we've got Ozzy Osbourne. We have to help our children deal with AIDS, the drug Ecstasy, and terrorism. Movies, music, television, video games, and the Internet offer thousands of ways for our children to get into trouble. It can feel overwhelming to try to give our teenagers the tools they need to make godly decisions in an ungodly world. Jesus knew we would always live in a delicate balance with culture. He commanded us to go out into the world for his sake (Mark 16:15), but the Bible also reminds us to step carefully (1 John 2:15–16). As parents, we need to teach our children to do just that. Thankfully, Paul's letter to the Ephesians can serve as our guide.

Know What You're Up Against (Ephesians 6:10–12)

In any battle, it's essential to understand your opponent. As I mentioned, parents must become students of today's culture and have a sense of reverence for its power and influence. Become familiar with the music your teenager listens to, even if you can't stand the sound of it. Know what Internet sites they visit, what movies they watch, what books they read. Read teen magazines and check out MTV once in a while to learn more about the voices that are influencing today's teens. Do this before your kids are teenagers. But even if your kids are older, it is never too late to begin.

Keep Your Eyes Open (Ephesians 6:13–17)

Just because your children are growing up in a Christian home or are part of a church group doesn't mean they won't face the same temptations and influences as their peers. As your preteens or teens begin to make more of their own decisions, help them stay grounded in their Christian values and the Word. Talk with them about the gifts God has given them and how they might use them in the world. Ask them about ways their faith can help them deal with the challenges they face. Encourage their devotional life and help them apply God's Word to their daily life.

Use the Power of Prayer (Ephesians 6:18)

I often wake up in the middle of the night and go into each of my daughters' rooms and pray over them. I lean toward my daughter, place my hands above her head, and pray for spiritual protection for her. I do this not because I'm a spiritual giant but because I am desperate! The Bible is clear; it is our duty as parents to pray regularly and often for and with our children. In the end, it will be God at work in your teen's heart that helps him or her be a light in our dark world.

Guard Your Child's Faith by Teaching a Biblical View of Sexuality

When it comes to teenage sexuality and preparing preteens, there's good news and bad news. The good news is even though they are in the minority, thousands of teenagers are taking seriously the biblical mandate to refrain from sexual intercourse until marriage. The bad news is that far too few parents are stepping up as the primary influence in their children's sex education. Studies tell us that only 10 to 15 percent of junior high and high school students receive positive, healthy, value-centered sex education at home. I recently spoke to four hundred parents on the subject of teaching our children about sex. I asked the parents, "How many of you received positive, healthy sex education at home?" Eight people raised their hands! The vast majority had not received sex education from their parents, and they were passing that silence on to the next generation.

Most young people base their decisions about sexual activity on three factors. The first is good old *peer pressure*. When a teenager lacks a strong moral and spiritual base, the pressure to conform to the world's standards is just too strong. Few of us have strong moral fiber innately built into us. Someone has to take the time—sometimes lots of time—to instill a child with a sense of morality.

The second factor is *emotional neediness*. Show me a young person with a low view of themselves and an extreme desire to be accepted by their peers, and you have a young person who can be fooled into instant intimacy and easily seduced sexually.

Studies on both the liberal and conservative side of sex education tell us that kids often make sexual decisions based on a *lack of information*. Today's young people are bombarded with hundreds of sexual images a day. Yet Christian parents often spend too much time telling their kids that sex can lead to AIDS or pregnancy and far too little time helping their teens understand their sexuality from a healthy, biblical perspective.

Our best defense against these three factors is God's Word. Lay a spiritual foundation for sexual purity early and reinforce it often. Teach a biblical view of sexuality that helps your kids understand that God created our sexuality and sees it as very good (Gen. 1:26–27; 2:18–25). Help them understand that the reason God gives strong instruction on the sins of adultery and fornication is because he wants the best for his children and their future marriages (Exod. 20:14; 1 Thess. 4:3).

Don't be afraid to challenge your kids with the powerful words of Paul in 1 Corinthians 6:18–20, which teaches us that we are to refrain from sexual immorality because our body is the temple of the Holy Spirit and we are to honor God with our bodies. Parents must talk about all of the issues of sexuality with their children, but they can't miss providing the spiritual foundation that will ultimately produce the fruit of purity in their children's lives.

Too many parents wait until the teen years to start the sex education teaching and training of their children. Age-appropriate sex education must begin as soon as our children can understand that God created our bodies. We want to teach our children not only that our sexuality is created by God but that it is precious and good in his sight. As they get to an age of understanding, we teach them that the Bible sees sex as beautiful in the context of marriage. Silence from parents is the worst way to guard our children's faith when it comes to sexuality and all morals and values.

Guard Your Child's Faith by Encouraging a Healthy Relationship with the Church

As most young people approach the teen years, there is a time when they move from owning your faith toward owning their own. Sometimes that means a time of rebellion. As your child moves from dependence to independence, there are some practical steps you can take to guard their faith by encouraging a healthy relationship with the church. Our children have all had their "moments" with church, but we just have to hold to our purpose and hang on. I remember when our daughter said these words to me: "Dad, I hate our church. I think it is boring and I don't want to go there again." Even though I had heard similar words from my older daughter a few years before, I was absolutely not ready to hear the negativity and passion of this statement from our second daughter at age sixteen. My first reaction was to get angry with her. Then I felt myself moving into preaching mode. But before I said something I knew I'd regret, I took a good look at my daughter. Something was causing this most-of-the-time wonderful kid who sings in the worship band and helps lead a Fellowship of Christian Athletes huddle to react so strongly.

After taking a few deep breaths, I simply said, "It sounds like something might have happened to make you hate something you liked so much just a few weeks ago." She blurted out, "Josh and Justin are spreading rumors about me. Plus, I'm bored with the worship." After separating the statements, I realized Rebecca wasn't rejecting the idea of church but rather looking for new ways to deepen her developing faith.

As teens grow more independent, it's natural for them to want to separate from the family and find their own expressions of faith. At the same time, I believe it's vitally important for families to worship together. This is an area where I encourage parents to make their own desires clear. We've told our daughters that church is not an option; it's a part of our family's life. We eat, sleep, go to school, work, and attend church. Like every other American family, we've missed a Sunday or two because of gymnastics championships, soccer tournaments, and other events, but our commitment to participate in the life of the church is nonnegotiable.

Still, we want to give our daughters the chance to find additional ways of practicing their faith that are meaningful to them. We expect the girls to participate in one worship service a week and one other faith-based activity. For the most part, this keeps arguments about church attendance to a minimum. If your child is adamant about not attending your church or youth group, encourage them to invite a friend to the worship service or to youth retreats and special events.

For teens, relationships supercede just about everything else. When I was a youth pastor, I never once had a student ask, "I'm considering going on the retreat, but I was wondering what Scripture passages you will be using." Instead, they'd ask, "Who else is going?" When one of our daughters was feeling left out in her youth group, we helped pay for a friend to join her on one of the group's outings. They went for the fun but ended up being drawn into the spiritual atmosphere of the group as well.

Of course, youth group isn't the only option for helping your teen stay involved in faith-based activities. Find out if their school has Young Life, Campus Life, Fellowship of Christian Athletes, or any other parachurch ministry. Look for service projects they can do with a group of friends. We've told our children that they can join us for a one-on-one Bible study in lieu of another activity. Our girls have never taken us up on it (smile), but we know a family in which a wayward daughter came back to the Lord through a weekly coffee date and Bible study with her mom.

No matter what other activities your teen or preteen finds for strengthening his or her faith, make church attendance nonnegotiable. Let them know this decision from an early age. That way when your child becomes a teen, he or she will be more likely to join your family for the worship service without too much grumbling.

Guard Your Child's Faith by Being Consistent with Discipline

"It's just not fair." "You are sooo old fashioned." "Everyone in my entire school has seen that movie but me." Here's the answer to all those accusations: "If I were your age, I would feel the same way."

Providing consistent discipline, setting boundaries, and guiding our children to become responsible adults are simply not easy. With today's cultural influences, clothes, curfew, friends, movies, music, magazines, lifestyle choices, and the list goes on, parents are bombarded with the opportunity to easily become the "bad cop" in the parenting relationship. The biblical proverb says, "Spare the rod and spoil the child." This doesn't mean we beat our kids into obedience, but rather we guide our children toward becoming responsible adults. The root for the word *discipline* is the same root as that for *discipleship*. Christian parents are called to disciple their children often through consistent discipline.

"If I were your age, I would feel the same way" is my way of saying to my children, it's okay to be frustrated, but we still are going to live by our established boundaries. Far too many parents dream of being their child's best friend through the teenage years, but if we are doing a good job providing consistent discipline and setting boundaries, it is almost impossible. You can't usually be best friend and chief disciplinarian.

In biblical days, the "rod" was a staff to help guide the way. Here are four practical rods of guidance as we move our teens from dependence toward independence.

1. *Quit fighting and arguing.* You can't effectively guide, disciple, or mentor your teenager if you are fighting and arguing with him or her all the time. Use whatever technique you can to walk away until things have calmed down. Don't expect them always to like you or your rules. Some parents don't enjoy me saying this, but whether the parent-child relationship is tension-filled or relatively relaxed during the teen years primarily rests on the parent. Constant negativity, nagging, fighting, and yelling can be stopped if you don't allow it or engage in it.
2. *Clearly express your expectations.* Children, regardless of their age, feel more secure with parents who are perfectly clear on where they stand and where they want their kids to stand. Proactive parenting takes more time but is much more effective than reactive parenting.
3. *Be consistent with consequences.* Our job is not always to prevent our children from making mistakes but rather to make certain they learn from their mistakes. We so badly want and sometimes feel the need to be liked by our kids that we bend the

consequences, which tends to produce confusion and mixed messages. Take a deep breath and follow through.

4. *Don't expect to be thanked for your discipline.* I recently asked a group of parents, "How many of you really liked your parents when you were a teenager?" Only a few hands went up. Parents are the most influential force in a child's life. Your kids will thank you after they have had their own kids, but rarely will they thank you in the heat of the battle.

Morgan came home from a party, and she had been drinking. Morgan's parents had been quite clear with her: If she ever drank and then drove, they would immediately sell her car. That night there was very little discussion. The next day the car had a "for sale" sign on it, and Morgan is now saving up enough money to buy her own car. Morgan wasn't very happy with her parents, and not having a car inconvenienced her folks. However, her parents did the absolute right thing. She protested. Her parents commented: "If we were your age, we would feel the same way."

There is absolutely no guarantee that our children will be free from the problems that face this generation. Most likely they will struggle with their faith, their friends, their moral compasses, and even their relationship with you. However, when parents take an active role in guarding their children's faith and help them develop a positive relationship with God, the opportunity for much healthier results are very possible.

Questions to Discuss

1. What are the most difficult issues to deal with as your child moves from dependence on you toward independence?
2. How can you practically energize your family's spiritual growth?
3. Keeping in mind the Scripture, "Where there is no counsel the people fall but in the multitude of counselors there is safety" (Prov. 11:14 NKJV), what areas of your family life would be helpful to discuss with your pastor, counselor, or youth worker?

For Further Reading

Arterburn, Stephen, and Jim Burns. *Parents Guide to Top 10 Dangers Teens Face*. Wheaton: Tyndale, 1995.

Burns, Jim. *The 10 Building Blocks to a Happy Family*. Ventura, CA: Regal Books, 2003.

McDowell, Josh, and Bob Hostetler. *Beyond Belief to Conviction*. Wheaton: Tyndale, 2002.

St. Claire, Barry. *Ignite the Fire: Kindling a Passion for Christ in Your Kids*. Colorado Springs: Victor, 1999.

PART 3

SPECIAL ISSUES FOR PARENTS

20

Defusing Anger

When Counting to Ten Isn't Enough

Kathy Collard Miller

nger. Anger! ANGER! Why did God give humans this strong emotion anyway? Didn't he know it would get us into a lot of trouble?

The primary reason we have the ability to get angry is that God made us in his image, and he gets angry!

What is anger? Christian psychologist and author Dr. H. Norman Wright says in his book *The Christian Use of Emotional Power* that anger is a "strong emotion of displeasure."[1] In my workshops about anger, parents have defined it as rage, a blazing flame, intense frustration, violent wrath, and other anguished feelings. Although anger has many basic causes, such as being misunderstood and having one's feelings hurt, over 95 percent of these parents attributed theirs to frustration. Such frustration may stem from having a goal or desire

315

blocked, not getting enough done, facing deadlines, or a host of other problems.

Sometimes, rather than honestly admitting our anger, we hide it behind other reactions and don't recognize it for what it is. We might say we're aggravated, upset, cross, or annoyed. Somehow those words don't sound as bad as angry. We try to disguise it because many people, especially Christians, mistakenly believe that anger is always sinful. Those people usually equate anger with losing control, and thus brand all anger as wrong.

But the Bible is clear in its attitude about anger: not only did Jesus get angry (and he never sinned!), Ephesians 4:26–27 instructs us, "Be angry, and yet do not sin; do not let the sun go down on your anger, and do not give the devil an opportunity" (NASB). Those verses indicate that the initial feeling of anger is neither right nor wrong, but the way we handle it can be right or wrong. And thankfully, it is possible for parents to get angry and not react destructively.

When my children were young, it was hard for me to believe that was possible. I felt like my anger was always out of control and inappropriate. I was so very often angry at our two-year-old daughter, Darcy, that I finally had to admit that I was physically and verbally abusing her. I feared that my next angry reaction would actually take her life, because there were times I kicked her, hit her in the head, and even choked her. In the depth of depression and hopelessness, I even seriously considered taking my own life, believing God had given up on me since he didn't answer my prayers for an instantaneous deliverance.

But then God worked—but differently than I had anticipated: I learned through a process of growth over a period of about a year how to identify the causes of my anger. I also learned how to control myself and become the patient, loving mom I really wanted to be.

Whether or not you feel out of control, know that every parent loses their temper at one time or another. Here are some practical ideas for preventing anger from becoming destructive to your family. We'll also find some tools for helping our children cope with their anger. First, we must identify two important causes of anger: displacement and unrealistic expectations.

Displacement

Elizabeth and her two-year-old daughter are in Judy's home, visiting with Judy and her three-year-old son. Elizabeth and Judy are talking as the children play on the floor. Elizabeth's daughter continually yanks Judy's son's toys away and makes him cry. Elizabeth tells her to share. Again and again the little girl yanks the toys away, and Elizabeth becomes more and more embarrassed.

She speculates, "I bet Judy thinks I'm a terrible mother." Elizabeth continues to try to help her daughter play cooperatively, but nothing works. As she worries about Judy's possible critical thoughts, she becomes more and more upset. Finally, in a burst of exasperation, Elizabeth grabs her daughter by the arm, slaps her bottom hard, and reprimands her, saying, "You start sharing right now or we're going home." Looking away from Judy's startled glance, she blushes in embarrassment and tries to distract her crying daughter with a toy.

This scene is an example of displacement. Displacement is the transference of an emotion to an object which is logically inappropriate. Did you notice how Elizabeth transferred her embarrassment into anger at her daughter?

As I reflect back to how I reacted uncontrollably toward Darcy, I can see how I displaced my feelings. I usually was irritated or angry with my husband, Larry, or myself, but because I couldn't manage that situation, I leveled my frustration against an innocent bystander, Darcy. She usually had not done anything to deserve my blowup; she was just the nearest object that couldn't strike back.

I usually blamed Darcy for my outbursts, thinking her disobedience caused my anger. Now I know it was only the straw that broke the back of my patience. Other situations and relationships were at play, but I didn't see their influence or significance.

If we can begin to see when we displace our anger from the real cause to our children, we'll be on our way to learning godly reactions to their disobedience. The best way to prevent displacement is to deal with each situation or problem as it occurs, instead of storing them up. Also, by recognizing when we are about to displace anger, we can stop ourselves from spilling out frustrations over other problems onto our children's misbehavior.

Now let's go back to Elizabeth and revise that scene. As Elizabeth and Judy talk, the children play on the floor. Elizabeth's daughter continually yanks the little boy's toys away, making him cry. Disconcerted with her daughter's behavior, Elizabeth comments to Judy, "I feel so embarrassed when my little girl doesn't share. I just don't know what to do about it."

"Oh, don't worry about it," Judy responds. "It's perfectly normal for a two-year-old not to share. My son has learned to share only in the last couple of weeks."

"Oh, really? Well, I guess she'll learn someday too!" Elizabeth breathes a sigh of relief and settles into the sofa to enjoy the visit.

Of course, not every situation will turn out perfect just because we share our feelings. But by recognizing those feelings and trying to deal with them, we can prevent displacement. Even if we cannot change our situation, we still will release the pressure that is building inside us.

We can also release that anger within our children by teaching them about displacement. We can ask them, "Are you really angry about this situation, or is there something else that's bothering you?" Help them to get in touch with the real reason behind their reaction.

Unrealistic Expectations

One of the main reasons our children make us angry is that we have unrealistic expectations of their behavior. We believe they can do or understand something, but they can't. Then when they disobey or misbehave, we get angry.

That's what happened to a young mother I recently observed in a department store. Her six- or seven-year-old daughter had begged to push the stroller that held her one-year-old brother. The mother finally relented, and as the little girl followed her mother, trying to maneuver the stroller between the racks of clothes, the stroller tipped over. Her mother turned and saw her daughter straining with all her might to stand it back up again. The woman immediately righted the stroller and, with a fierce scowl, yelled at the little girl, "Now look what you've done!" She instantly smacked her daughter's bottom. Tears sprang into the little girl's eyes, and she hung her head in fear and humiliation.

Similar circumstances happen many times a day anywhere there are parents dealing with their children. The situations are different, but the underlying cause is the same: An overstressed mother expects too much from her child. When the child fails or doesn't meet the parent's expectations, the parent becomes angry and overreacts.

Please don't think I'm condemning that mother. I've been in her shoes. She most likely had a to-do list a mile long, wanted to get a gift quickly in the store, and had listened all day to her daughter's constant chattering. When the stroller tipped over, it was just too much. She had gone beyond her frustration level, and she probably believed that her daughter had pushed the stroller over on purpose.

In situations like this, we expect a child to do something that he or she is not physically or emotionally ready to handle. That mother in the store wasn't wrong to allow her daughter to push the stroller, but when it tipped over, she could have thought, *Well, that stroller was a lot for her to handle. My getting upset is not going to help make her stronger.*

Sometimes we don't know what to expect or we are uninformed about the developmental patterns of our children. If you think you might be expecting too much from your child and are getting angry as a result, refer to a child development book and make a list of the things you can expect from your child at his age. Put the list on your refrigerator. Then when your child does something that is listed, before dealing with the child, walk to the refrigerator, make a check mark by that action, and realize that your child is only doing what is normal for his age level. Does he spill his milk at every meal? Check it off. Does he scribble on the walls? Check it off. Does he mess up his room with toys and have difficulty putting them away? Check it off. After you've checked off his behavior and you realize that it can be expected, you can go back to the child and discipline him calmly and effectively.

I love to tell the story about the father and his toddler daughter who were walking through a national forest. The father instructed his daughter, "Stay on the path, honey." But she continually ran back and forth, hither and yon, noticing every tree, bird, and flower. Several times he told her to stay on the path, and each time he became increasingly irritated. Finally, he grabbed her arm and said through gritted teeth, "I said stay on the path." She looked up at him in wide-eyed amazement and asked, "What's a path, Daddy?"

Our expectations of our children must take into account that they don't have the same knowledge we do. Sometimes they don't know what a path is, or how to make the bed, or what is involved in cleaning the bathroom.

Consider for a moment what it must be like to be a child and have adults telling you what to do, but you don't understand what a word means or how to do what they want. They must feel as I would if a computer expert set a personal computer in front of me and said, "Load this disk into the computer's memory."

Having never seen a computer before, I ask, "How do you do it?"

"Well, it's very simple," he replies. "You just do it." In the computer expert's brain, a procedure as simple as loading a disk is a one-step process. But for me, it's a multifaceted procedure, because I don't know where to start.

Sometimes your child doesn't know where to start. You may tell him to make the bed, something you've done for many years. Obviously, it's a simple task. But not for him. Therefore, you have to break it down into steps: "First, you take off the pillow. Then pull back the sheet and blanket. Now smooth the bottom sheet . . . ," and so on.

If we could look at our interaction with our child through his eyes, we quickly would see when our expectations are too high and become overwhelming for him.

Let's be realistic in what we want and not be like the mother who gazed down at her child, who was screaming and kicking on the grocery store floor. She angrily muttered to another woman passing by, "Look at him. It's disgusting. He's acting just like a two-year-old!"

The woman whispered, "How old is he?"

The mother looked amazed at first. Then her face relaxed and she started to grin. "I forgot. He *is* two years old!"

That mother had unrealistic expectations that fueled her anger. Believe it or not, expectations can also fuel our children's behavior. Maybe they are reacting in anger because they thought we had promised them something when we meant we *might* do it. Try to open communication to discover the source of the child's anger by asking, "Did Mommy (or Daddy) do something to make you feel your anger?" It's a humble parent who can risk the possibility that they are the cause of their child's anger.

I saw the possibility of that one day as I visited some friends. A six-year-old son came up to his father, who was looking adoringly at his newborn son, and said, "Dad, when are we going to play ball like you said?" The father continued to stare at his baby's eyes and never responded to his older son. The boy eventually wandered off to do something else, but his expectations were unmet. I couldn't help wonder whether some form of anger could have been fueled in those moments. We must be careful not to stimulate our children's anger through creating expectations we can't meet.

A Constructive Method of Defusing Anger

Now that we've examined anger and two of its causes, let's look at a constructive method of defusing our anger. By going through the following five-step process every time we get angry, we can have healthy reactions. Healthy means being fully aware of and possessing our feelings (as opposed to our feelings possessing and controlling us). You can also use these steps to assist your child to cope with his anger.

The five-step process is

1. realize you feel angry by noticing your red-flag warnings;
2. magnetize your mind away from your anger with a distractor;
3. recognize the real, underlying cause of your anger;
4. analyze your thinking for incorrect assumptions about life; and
5. verbalize your anger appropriately.

Let's look at each one in more depth.

1. Realize You Feel Angry by Noticing Your Red-Flag Warnings

Elaine has been a Christian for four years and condemns herself for the way she reacts toward her five-year-old son. When I asked her to describe her anger, she used strong terms, such as rage, heat, out of control. Then I asked her how she feels before she loses her temper. She replied, "I feel calm, and then I suddenly blow up."

I explained to her that she had repressed and ignored her first feelings of anger for so long that she no longer believed they existed. I instructed her to begin paying attention to early warning signals before she blew up and to realize she feels angry.

Recognizing early warning signs of anger—your red-flag warnings—gives you time to deal with your feelings before they become destructive. To discover these signals, write down facts about the last three times you blew up. Then recall how you felt fifteen minutes, ten minutes, and five minutes before the flare-ups. If you can't remember those details, then monitor the next three times it happens.

Chances are you'll see a pattern of warnings in the three incidents. For instance, fifteen minutes before I blow up, I usually am worried about a time schedule or some other pressure. At the ten-minute warning, I feel tense and hurried. Even though, on the outside, I may not look hassled, inside I feel like the wheels are turning faster than normal. My five-minute signal is that I'm gritting and grinding my teeth and raising my voice in quick, terse commands.

As I teach this material and ask people to share their red-flag warnings, they have said things like they feel hot or cold, their neck muscles tighten, they clench their fists. They also report they get a headache and their chest muscles tighten. There is a big variety of responses that people describe.

When you become aware of your own unique red-flag warnings, you can realize that your fifteen-minute countdown has started. Then you can break the cycle by using a distractor, which is part of the second step.

Help your children recognize their own unique red-flag warnings by asking them how they felt in the minutes before they blew up. Of course, you'll have to wait until they've calmed down, but even if they can't identify those feelings in the first incidents, in time they'll begin to pay attention to them.

2. Magnetize Your Mind Away from Your Anger with a Distractor

The second step is to draw your mind away from your anger by using what is called a distractor. A distractor is anything you can use to take your mind off your anger, if only for a few minutes. This gives you a break to cool down. Anger always causes physical tension and energy, but a distractor helps to relieve that tension before you blow up at another person.

Being distracted for a few minutes allows us to come back to the situation with an improved, calmer perspective. Like the whistling kettle, the steam of our anger is released. The cause of the anger is still there (that will be taken care of in step 3), but at least the energy that makes us want to lash out is gone.

Here are a few possible distractors:

Take a vigorous walk.

Run in place.

Hit a pillow or a punching bag.

Take a shower (with or without screaming).

Sing loudly.

Take ten slow, deep breaths; count them out loud.

Play a musical instrument.

Recite an uplifting Bible verse.

Telephone a friend, a hotline, or a professional counselor.

The important part of this exercise is to determine our distracting action beforehand (while we are calm) and then practice it, asking God to remind us to use it when we start the fifteen-minute countdown.

For instance, during a peaceful period, I tell myself that the next time I feel angry, I'll take three steps backward and walk away from the irritating or frustrating situation. I continue to remind myself and rehearse it in my mind. I may even take three steps backward once in a while to practice. Then when I notice I'm getting within that fifteen- or ten-minute countdown range, I remember, "Aha! It's time for me to take three steps backward and walk away!" That gives me time to think through what's causing my anger and how I can resolve it.

Deep breathing is another simple distractor that I have found helpful. It is especially effective because intense emotions inhibit breathing. As I get angry my chest muscles seem to tighten and tense up, but slow, deep breathing eliminates that pressure.

For our children, we can determine beforehand what their distractors will be. Then you can use a nonsensical, humorous word to remind them to take advantage of this step. You might decide with them that their distractor will be jogging in place and the humorous word is *monkey*. When their anger starts to rise, call out to them, "Monkey!" and begin jogging in place to remind them. Their anger may be quickly dissipated because they'll be laughing too hard at you! But if not, you can have them put the second step into place by having them jog in place next to you.

3. Recognize the Real, Underlying Cause of Your Anger

The third step is to recognize the underlying cause of your anger. In most cases, the immediate circumstances are not the cause of anger. Instead, we displace our anger from the real cause. Remember displacement? That's the transference of an emotion to a logically inappropriate object.

I find it helpful to keep a mental checklist of possible causes, which I quickly go through to try to determine the actual cause. Here are some questions for you to consider:

- Physical: Am I tired? Do I need some exercise? Have I been eating too much sugar or caffeine? Am I in a premenstrual depression?
- Psychological: Am I thinking negatively about something? Am I worried? Is a relationship troubling me? Are my expectations for myself unrealistic? Am I feeling embarrassed, frustrated, or insecure about something? Is my self-esteem low? Have my goals or desires been blocked? Has my child mirrored a bad habit of mine?
- Spiritual: Am I not trusting God? Do I have some unconfessed sin? Is there someone I need to forgive? Am I bitter toward someone or God?

It is important to dig up the underlying cause and expose it. Then we can recognize that whatever is going wrong probably doesn't warrant the kind of intense reaction and behavior that are building within us. For our children, we can help them ask the same questions to reveal the real cause.

Once you identify the true cause, you can move on to the fourth step.

4. Analyze Your Thinking for Incorrect Assumptions about Life

All of us make assumptions about life and people that we assume are correct; it's our belief that life operates in a certain way. In our way of thinking, we can't imagine that there is another way of thinking. But we may not be correct, and those incorrect assumptions can cause us to respond with anger and frustration. God's Word is the most accurate way to filter our thinking to see if we hold wrong ideas. Second Timothy 3:16–17 tells us, "All Scripture is inspired by God and profitable for teaching, for reproof, for correction, for training in righteousness; so that the man of God may be adequate, equipped for every good work" (NASB).

With God's help, we can also evaluate our thought patterns as we hear others share correct assumptions, because the Bible doesn't cover specifically every single issue we'll face. This doesn't mean we accept everything other Christians say, but we can use discernment before we accept new ideas and verify them with mature Christians we respect.

Here are some wrong assumptions that I've had to change and some of which others have shared with me:

It's my right to be happy. Happiness and joy are different. Happiness is a response to circumstances going the way we want them to; joy is an inward response of trusting God regardless of the circumstances. God has promised us joy, but not happiness.

My spouse (or someone else) should meet my needs. Although God uses people as instruments to meet our needs, ultimately he wants us to look to him. We cannot make someone else fully responsible for meeting our needs.

If I don't say yes to everyone's request, I'm not God's servant. Even Jesus said no to other people's requests. According to Luke 5:15–16: "The news about Him was spreading even farther, and large crowds were gathering to hear Him and to be healed of their sicknesses. But Jesus Himself would often slip away to the wilderness and pray" (NASB).

The crowds wanted Jesus to meet their needs. But Jesus also had needs, and one of them was to spend time alone with the Father. Jesus made sure his own needs were met so that he had the energy and power to minister to others.

There are a variety of incorrect assumptions we can believe, but Romans 12:2 tells us, "Do not be conformed to this world, but be transformed by the renewing of your mind, so that you may prove what the will of God is, that which is good and acceptable and perfect" (NASB). If we don't, incorrect assumptions can cause us to get angry and irritated easily.

What incorrect assumptions are you or your child believing? Evaluate your and your child's thinking based on the Bible and the godly input of others.

5. Verbalize Your Anger Appropriately

The last step is to verbalize your anger appropriately. This means using "I messages" instead of "you messages." "You messages" express blame, as in, "You make me angry," "You shouldn't do that," and so on.

In contrast, "I messages" express how you feel or what your opinion is, without telling the other person what to do about it (unless he or she asks). "I messages" express your needs. A child can also learn to use "I messages."

In addition to watching the wording, we need to monitor our motives. We should not use "I messages" to try to subtly change the other person. Instead, we should honestly share our feelings while trusting God to control our circumstances.

We also can verbalize our anger by calling a friend who will keep a confidence and not put us down for our emotions. Another possibility is to call a hotline, a professional counselor, or a pastor.

It is most effective to express our feelings at the time of the misunderstanding. If we can't seem to talk about them at that moment, though, we can prepare ourselves for verbalizing them later by writing them out in a speech or letter. A woman shared this insight with me and says it works for her. When she realizes that she is angry with someone, whether it is her husband, a neighbor, or a friend, she first determines what really is bothering her and then writes it down. By doing so, she can ensure that she expresses her feelings in a way the other person can accept. Then she reads it to someone else who can help her critique it. Finally, she practices it before she actually calls or visits the person involved—or sends the letter.

This process gives her the courage she needs to confront the person, because she knows she's expressing herself in the best possible way. If the other person rejects her feelings, she doesn't experience guilt, because she did the best she could. She tells herself that if that person won't accept her opinions, maybe he or she is not a true friend after all.

In expressing feelings, we should be "speaking the truth in a spirit of love" (Eph. 4:15 GNT). That begins with being responsible for our reactions. No one *makes* us angry; it is *our* choice.

Because I am accountable for my own response, I need to express my feelings appropriately and ask forgiveness for my part of the problem. Whether or not the other person accepts my apology or changes his or her mind or actions, I can choose healthy reactions and not try to control the other person. I can trust God to work in both of our lives.

Recently, I applied these principles when a woman broke a promise to me and I felt deeply hurt. After the hurt came the anger, and I knew I would have to travel through my five-step process so that I wouldn't take my anger out on my children.

I realized I was indeed angry. Even after I tried to understand my friend's viewpoint, I still believed she had treated me inappropriately. Then I played the piano for a while to pound out some of the energy that my anger was creating. That was my distractor.

The third step, finding the real cause of my anger, was obvious. Yet when I thought more about the situation, I discovered even more reasons I was angry. For instance, her broken promise prevented me from completing a project I'd promised for someone else. Therefore, not only was I angry because of how she had treated me, but I was angry because it influenced my reputation before others.

Then I analyzed my thinking and realized that what she had intended to be a *possibility*, I had believed was a *promise*. I'd thought we had communicated clearly, but I realized I had only assumed she knew what I was requesting.

Finally, I verbalized my anger in a letter to her. I really let my fury fly; then I edited it to make my sharing appropriate and acceptable. In the letter, I asked her to forgive me for my reactions and I shared how she had hurt me. Larry read my edited letter and approved it.

As I typed the final letter, I decided to wait one week before I mailed it, to make sure the Lord wanted me to send it. The next day, my anger was gone. I knew I wouldn't mail that letter. Verbalizing my anger, even on paper, had dissolved it, and I was able to forgive her. Today I have no bitterness toward her.

After battling with anger, even abusive anger, I've learned that we can keep anger under control. Years ago, I thought there was no hope for a healthy relationship between me and my daughter, whom I abused. But today our family is a happy one, and my daughter is a well-adjusted, married woman and we have a wonderful relationship. With God there is always hope, even for coping with parental anger.

Questions to Discuss

1. What have you been taught about the emotion of anger? Was it always wrong?
2. How did each of your parents handle their anger as you were growing up?
3. Can you describe a time when you displaced your anger? What made it hard for you to be direct with your anger?
4. What are your red-flag warnings that anger is building inside of you?

For Further Reading

Barnhill, Julie. *She's Gonna Blow! Real Help for Moms Dealing with Anger.* Eugene: Harvest House Publishers, 2001.

Chapman, Gary. *The Other Side of Love: Handling Anger in a Godly Way.* Chicago: Moody, 1999.

Miller, Kathy Collard. *Why Do I Put So Much Pressure on Myself and Others?* Ann Arbor, MI: Servant, 2000.

Miller, Kathy Collard. *When Counting to Ten Isn't Enough*. Longwood, FL: Xulon Press, 2003.

Priolo, Lou. *The Heart of Anger: Practical Help for the Prevention and Cure of Anger in Children*. Amityville, NY: Calvary Press, 1998.

Warren, Neil Clark. *Make Anger Your Ally*. Wheaton: Tyndale, 1999.

Wright, H. Norman. *The Christian Use of Emotional Power*. Grand Rapids: Revell, 1986.

21

Educational Options— Homeschool, Private School, or Public School

Rachel and Christopher McCluskey

"Would you tell me, please, which way I ought to go from
here?"
"That depends a good deal on where you want to get to,"
said the Cat.
"I don't much care where—" said Alice.
"Then it doesn't matter which way you go," said the Cat.
"—so long as I get somewhere," Alice added as an
explanation.

"Oh, you're sure to do that," said the Cat, "if you only walk
long enough."

Lewis Carroll, *Alice in Wonderland*

As soon as the heat of summer wanes and the leaves prepare for
their autumn display, the sight and sound of the big yellow
school bus trigger a wave of childhood nostalgia for most of us—the
first day of school. We recall shopping for new clothes, getting our
hair cut, picking out notebooks, pencils, and crayons, and if we were
lucky, even a new lunchbox. The school bus meant a new year with
a new teacher and perhaps a new school, a new room full of kids,
and a chance to make new friends. There would be new things to
learn, new challenges to face, new skills to master. For most of us,
the start of the school year was met with excited anticipation mixed
with disappointment that the summer was over, and always a bit of
anxiety about how the year would go.

For parents of young children, the start of the school year is also
met with a mixture of emotions—relief, perhaps, that life will return
to a more structured routine, excitement over all that the children will
learn and experience, and often considerable anxiety about whether or
not they've made the right decision for their children's education.

Deciding on a schooling approach is one of the most important decisions you'll make as a parent because of the character-shaping influence
of the educational environment. Many parents feel as lost as Alice in
her conversation with the Cheshire Cat, knowing the importance of
choosing a direction but lacking a clear sense of the desired destination.
It's easy to be swayed by the opinions of mothers in the neighborhood
play group or the advice of the latest parenting magazine or talk show
guest, but doing the hard work of exploring school options and choosing the approach that's best for you and your child is no easy task. Public school, private school, parochial school, magnet school, Montessori
school, multicultural school, gifted school, career prep school, umbrella
school, classical school, homeschool, even an "unschooling" approach!
Which is right for your child? It's our hope that this chapter helps you
think through your options as you try to answer that question.

We live on the farm where Chris's mother was raised in the foot-
hills of the Ozark Mountains. On one corner of the property, nestled

into a meadow at the base of a hill, stands the one-room schoolhouse she attended through the eighth grade. Looking like an abandoned set from *Little House on the Prairie*, it sits as a reminder that, not so long ago, parents didn't have many choices about schooling. Children either went to the public school within walking distance or the parochial school within their parish, or they were schooled at home. Only the very wealthy could afford other options.

Options are wonderful and it's a blessing to have so many, but parents often express frustration in evaluating them. The decision is complex because the schooling approach chosen becomes a central piece of the overall plan and vision parents have for raising their children. To make a wise decision about education, they need a clear vision of God's call to raise up children for him.

The Importance of Vision

We believe parenting is the most important role to which any human can be called. There is no higher ministry and no responsibility for which we will be held more accountable before God's throne. This is surely why Scripture insists on evidence of effective parenting as one of the criteria for selecting leaders within the church. We must prove ourselves able to lead first at home. If we are faithful with a little, *then* we can be placed over much. God can call any number of people to preach or teach or head up various outreaches and ministries, but he can't get anyone else to be the parents of our children. That slot is filled, whether we carry it out well or poorly. Our children were entrusted to us, and we will answer for them one day to him.

Having been called to so great a task, we need to ask, "What is my vision for parenting? What is my vision for educating these children God has entrusted to me?" Without a vision, our parenting style and education choices are not intentional and purposeful. Without a vision we become reactionary, tossed around through the parenting years, always in a defensive posture, never on the offense.

Without a vision, we perish. We default to the vision put forth by our culture and gauge our success by comparing our kids to those around us. We define success as merely *surviving*; if our kids don't get themselves killed or end up on drugs or alcohol or pregnant or dropping out before graduation, we can breathe a sigh of relief and say, "We made it." It's a pathetic vision, but it's all we have if we don't do the hard work of catching a clearer vision from God. If our vision is only for survival, our children will actually perish spiritually. Our vision must be for *thriving*.

A Vision for Education

For our children to thrive, we must recognize that education is about much more than academics. To be sure, academics are a huge consideration, but we must also address their *character* education, their *social* education, their *sex* education, and their *spiritual and religious* education. Each of these will become a critical gauge of their maturity and of their fitness for kingdom work. We all know people who received excellent academic training and even hold postgraduate degrees, but who are sorely lacking in character or social skills or morality or spiritual maturity. They may have great careers, but they've often lost their marriages, their children, their health, and/or their faith. Attending the best academic schools is not enough. We must educate the whole person.

Educating the whole person means *preparing them for life*. It's about teaching responsibility and self-discipline, communication and relationship skills, problem solving, time management, self-control, leadership, cultural sensitivity, artistic appreciation, a Christian worldview, and even good parenting skills. It's about teaching the Word and how to study it, practicing the disciplines of our faith, dying to self, yielding to the Spirit, persevering through trials, growing in intimacy, and allowing God to mold us into his image. A godly vision for educating our children must incorporate all of these things. None of them is superfluous or excessive, and none of them is trivial.

Searching for the Perfect Solution

By now you may be thinking, *What schooling approach does all that?* The answer is none of them—not in isolation. Any approach to education needs to incorporate elements from several different sources, with parents always serving as the center, the hub, the education directors. Every school teacher, public or private, will tell you that the children who do best and are most well rounded are those whose parents are very involved in their education, helping them with homework and exposing them to many life experiences outside of the classroom. And any homeschooling parent whose children are healthy and balanced will tell you they expose their children to structured group activities and programs in the community to augment the work they are doing at home.

Whatever primary schooling approach you choose, you should view it as only one of many tools used in your child's education. For example, if you choose a public school or a non-Christian private or specialized school, you will probably need to augment that with other resources to address your child's spiritual and sex education. If you choose a Christian school or homeschooling, you will probably need to find additional resources to round out his or her social education, such as group sports and special activities. No single schooling choice will address all of your child's educational needs, nor should it. As parents, we need to be constantly evaluating and directing their education using whatever tools may be best for a particular season of their lives. We do not have to provide the education ourselves, but we must always be supervising and directing it.

We can't emphasize this enough. In our Christian coaching practice, we find that many parents have unwittingly abdicated their role as education directors for their children. They've become so concerned about what the so-called experts say that they don't trust their own judgment about what's best for their children. They have farmed out the responsibility to those with advanced degrees, and they don't realize how important their role is in constantly assessing each child's development and making changes as necessary to their educational plans based on their overall vision for each child.

It's helpful to think of our children as coming to us like wet clay. Each day provides an opportunity to let God guide our hands as we intentionally shape the clay into the vessel he desires. If our hands are not there guiding the process, they will be shaped by the views and opinions of other hands—their peers, the media, teachers, coaches, the government. There will come a day when the clay begins to harden into the shape in which it has been molded. If we have shaped them well through their education, God will be able to use the vessel of their life in his kingdom work. If we have failed, they will not be fit for service and the Master will have to break and rework the clay. This is often horribly painful and is largely preventable if parents take an active and ongoing role in directing their children's education.

The Way Children Learn

To wisely direct our children's education, we need to understand a bit about how children learn and grow. Children learn very differently from adults. Adults are able to work with abstract concepts such as ideas. We can easily take in new information by reading, listening, or observing. We can compare the information to what we already know or have experienced and form new conclusions—all in our heads. This is why most adults enjoy picking up a book, listening to a lecture, or dialoguing with another person to learn something new.

Children, in contrast, cannot work well with abstract concepts. They work primarily with the concrete, things you can see, touch, and experience. While adults can process new information inside their heads, children must move new information around outside of their heads, with their hands, their senses, and language. Learning comes by doing, through experience.

This is why reading or lecture is so boring for most children; they do very little real learning this way. It's often all they can do just to sit still through it. True, they may be able to memorize information, answer questions, and study for a test, but this does not necessarily mean they are learning. Many children quickly forget what has been taught in this manner.

The famous child psychologist Jean Piaget was fascinated by the ways in which children learn. He identified four stages of cognitive development, or ways of learning, that children pass through as they mature. A brief understanding of these is helpful when assessing the ideal schooling choice for your children at various stages of their lives.

Sensorimotor Stage (Ages 0–2)

In the sensorimotor stage, the child has not yet developed language. Without language, the child explores and learns about the world through the senses, through what he or she sees, smells, hears, touches, and tastes. This is why parents of crawlers and toddlers find themselves constantly repeating, "No, no, don't touch that." "Get out of there." "Don't put that in your mouth." The child is learning! Sensory exploration is critical for healthy cognitive development.

This obviously requires that parents closely supervise the learning environment so the child doesn't get hurt. (As this was being written, our twenty-two-month-old got into Rachel's makeup and emptied a brand-new bottle of Clinique foundation all over herself and the carpet!) Most parents are the primary caregivers at this stage, and we strongly advise against placing a child this young in the care of any other educational environment. Much of what they are learning is about whether or not they are loved and if the world is a safe place in which to get their needs met. No one else can teach your children the answers you want them to have to those questions. Don't put your children in anyone else's care at this stage if you can possibly avoid it.

Preoperational Stage (Ages 2–7)

At the preoperational stage, children begin using language as an additional means of exploring the world and learning. These are the years of the "why" questions. "Why do we do that?" "Why can't I go?" "Why does it rain?" "Why did that happen?" A child at this stage needs people with whom to converse and asks lots and lots of questions. This is one of the many shortcomings of day care programs and the use of television to pacify little ones—they don't accommodate this kind of interaction. Many parents worry that they may not be starting their children in preschool programs early enough, when in fact the student-teacher ratio makes it impossible for children to ask the questions they need to at this stage to learn best.

The preoperational stage requires a great deal of adult intervention. Children are just beginning to use language and when frustrated will fall back to what they know—the sensorimotor stage—screaming, whining, hitting, and biting. They need to be shown how to use language in these frustrating situations. Be sure the educational environment you choose accommodates that kind of learning. When children are left to play on their own or fight it out without adult intervention (as many "experts" suggest), they will naturally resort to more immature ways of dealing with problems. These eventually become habits and patterns they'll take with them into adulthood. Many of the couples Chris saw in his counseling practice were still using unhealthy patterns learned in childhood to work out problems in their marriages. That's a sign of a poor education for life.

Play and learning go hand-in-hand at this age. While some play is discovery, much of it is pretending and imitation. Pretending allows children to practice what they see modeled. We've often watched our little ones playing with dollhouse figures, saying, "Please stop." "Oh, I'm sorry. Will you forgive me?" "Okay. I forgive you." This is valuable learning, and it's very important that the educational environment provide plenty of opportunity for pretending.

Imitation reinforces what children have learned. It's how boys learn to be masculine and girls learn to be feminine. Imitation is one of the primary ways they pick up manners, organizational skills, ways of interacting with others, and the ability to get along. Children in the preoperational stage love using new words and expressions and imitating nuances and voice tones. What they see and hear, they imitate—the good and the bad. This requires that parents supervise and constantly evaluate the peers, adults, TV shows, movies, and music to which their children are exposed. They will develop the habits and attitudes of those with whom they spend the most time.

Concrete Operational Stage (Ages 7–12)

During this stage of development, children begin to retain what they have learned much better. It is only after children enter this stage that they can be counted on to become truly responsible for a chore like remembering to feed the dog. They simply will not remember well before reaching the concrete operational stage.

Children in this stage continue to learn through concrete (hands-on) experiences. Their development of language allows them to articulate more difficult questions: "Why do people get a divorce?"

"Do you think we will be children or adults when we get to heaven?" "How do I know God really exists?"

Imitation continues, with children desiring to wear their hair like everyone else or to use the same verbal expressions. Girls become more drawn to imitating their mothers or other images of femininity they see. Boys practice being tough to win the approval of Dad or other males in their learning environment. Media, obviously, is extremely important to monitor from this stage forward.

Children at this age have difficulty making cause-and-effect or if-then connections, lacking the discernment of a more mature teenager who has reached the formal operational stage. They may do things with no apparent forethought and no real understanding of the potential consequences. In some learning environments, this can result in their being ridiculed and ostracized, which is horribly damaging to their developing self-esteem. Watch for signs of this and address them proactively.

Children typically grow out of this stage and into formal operational thinking around twelve years of age, but there is growing concern that this stage is becoming prolonged—even past age eighteen—in a surprising number of children. Much of this may be a consequence of family instability and poor parental involvement resulting in children having to learn everything by trial and error—the "school of hard knocks." Many researchers are concerned that rushing children through the earlier stages of cognitive development is limiting their experiential learning and contributing to this problem.

Formal Operational Stage (Age 12+)

As children reach the formal operational stage of thinking, their desire to dialogue increases as they learn to mentally take in ideas, think them through, and draw new conclusions. Teenagers at this stage really enjoy talking with adults who are available. If the adults are too busy or are not involved, they will dialogue with peers instead. Although the peer group is important during this developmental season, it is imperative that parents stay actively involved in every aspect of their teenagers' education. Remember, you are educating them for life, not just for academic achievement.

Be intentional about deepening your relationship with them. You can't afford to take a passive or backseat role in these years. The cultural wisdom says parents should dread the teenage years and that kids have to rebel to discover who they are. Nothing could be further from the truth. If you have been actively involved in your child's education up to this point, these can be some of the richest years you'll have! After-school snack time, attendance at extracurricular activities, regularly scheduled "dates" with your child, and special group activities that you supervise can all create a tremendous atmosphere for dialogue, connecting, and learning.

These are the years your child will begin thinking about big concepts like careers, sexuality, spirituality, the future, marriage, and raising children. It is during these talks that you will help your child develop a vision for the kind of marriage they want and how they will recognize the person who will be a good mate. You will have the opportunity to help them investigate vocations and consider college and career paths. You can have some of the deepest conversations about God you've ever had (*before* they go off to college and have their theological underpinnings challenged as never before).

Whatever schooling choice you make, your child will need you through this stage as much as at any previous stage. Don't lose your vision in the teenage years! Your child will be making decisions that will impact his life more than any others he will make in his entire life.

Clarifying Your Vision for Each Child

It is our position that there is no single best way to educate your child. What works well with one child may fail miserably with another, even within the same family. We are all unique, endowed with different temperamental qualities and learning styles, and constantly affected by a wide variety of internal and external influences. Parents must be tuned in to the uniqueness of each child and seek to discern which schooling approaches will work best for them at each stage of their lives. Not only do the needs of a child change at various developmental stages, but many other factors affecting the family can change as well and affect the choice of a schooling approach. A death in the family, divorce, a move, a job change, unemployment, serious illness, and many other family stressors can trigger a need to reevaluate a previous schooling choice.

As you step into the role of education director for your children, begin clarifying the vision you see for each child as they mature. Take notes, make lists, and do some journaling to put this vision in black-and-white. Consider each child separately, because each is unique. Note the natural strengths and weaknesses of each. Consider how various schooling approaches might play to those strengths and address those weaknesses. Try to discern each child's natural leanings. Are they artistic? Gifted in math? Fascinated with science and nature? Good with spatial skills? Musical? Athletic? Are they social, or more quiet and reserved? Energetic, or ponderous and thoughtful? Foster an ongoing dialogue about these things with your spouse and key people in your children's lives. Consider hiring a parenting coach to develop your vision. Always remain open to new insights as you seek to discern their changing needs and how your schooling approaches can meet them.

In clarifying your vision, factor in other things such as the character you want them to develop, the spiritual walk you want them to have, social skills you want them to develop (such as confidence, patience, self-control, leadership), extracurricular skills you'd like them to explore, life experiences you want them to have, and how you will handle the dating years. All of these will significantly affect the choices you make.

Matching the Options to Your Vision

Once you have done this kind of thoughtful analysis, you are finally ready to match the schooling resources in your community with the vision you have for your children. If you were to start researching schooling options before clarifying your vision, you would find yourself like Alice in Wonderland, asking advice without knowing where you want to go.

Talk with other parents, check the phone book, and find out what schooling choices your community offers. Get information on the philosophy and outcome research behind each approach in which you are interested. Attend informational meetings and check out some books from the library on different approaches to schooling. It's impossible to make an informed decision if you don't have good information.

Schedule interviews to meet with those in charge and spend time in the classroom getting a feel for the environment and teaching style. Find out about the student-teacher ratio and about the education requirements for the teachers. Ask to see the evaluation reports from accrediting boards or governmental agencies that review the school. Find out what creative learning approaches they take to accommodate your child's developmental stage and any special needs he or she may have. Read their discipline policy and make certain you feel it is appropriate. Find out about structured social activities, clubs, sports, music programs, and the like. Try also to get a sense of how much unstructured socialization your child will have with peers. Be sure to ask key curriculum questions like what sex education program they follow, what they teach about creationism verses evolution, what they will be taught about spirituality and various religions, and how closely they adhere to the values you want your child to have regarding definitions of marriage and the family, acceptance of sinful lifestyles, and the like.

If you're considering homeschooling, visit some local support groups and attend a state or regional conference. Go to a curriculum fair and get an overview of the numerous approaches to homeschooling. Interview homeschooling parents and find out how they structure their days. Ask how they ensure a well-rounded social education and how homeschooling has impacted their lifestyle. Find out how they school children of different ages and how they handle subjects in which the parent may not have much knowledge. Inquire about how they accommodate learning disabilities and how they provide for specialized learning such as computers, advanced science and math, art, and music. Read some books and visit websites that look at the research and outcome measures of homeschooled students. Learn what laws govern homeschooling in your state and what kinds of testing, periodic evaluation, and record keeping are required.

Like most other things in life, the choice of a schooling approach will, at some point, come down to considerations of time and money.

We purposely saved these for last because they are many times the first (and often the only) factors parents consider. We hope by now you realize that the greatest consideration in choosing a schooling approach is the vision you have for each of your children. Once that vision is clear and you are committed to it, *then* it is time to look at the time and money required to make it happen. Parents can make dramatic shifts in priorities to free up time and/or money when they're passionate about a vision for their children's lives. First catch the vision and then count the cost.

Educating your child for life requires time no matter what schooling approach you choose. Public- and private-schooling parents face the challenges of finding quality time for connecting with their children outside of school, being on top of homework, getting everyone up and out the door at very early hours, flexing their work schedule when children are sick, and driving their children to and from school and activities. Homeschooling parents face the challenges of having little time alone, researching curriculum, preparing lesson plans, documenting for the state, and driving the kids to outside activities. It's impossible to argue that one approach is more difficult than the other—they're perceived differently by different parents. One type of time pressure is traded for another.

Financial cost is another matter. Public schooling is generally the least expensive option, although before-school and after-school care can drive that cost up if a parent's work schedule doesn't allow him or her to be home during nonschool hours. Private and specialized schools of all kinds can run anywhere from a few hundred to a few thousand dollars a month. Homeschooling parents need to invest several hundred to a few thousand dollars each year in curriculum and outside learning opportunities.

Money will often be the final decision maker when parents have narrowed down their schooling choices to the few that are most in line with their vision, but money should never be the first nor the most important factor. God is a God of possibilities, and what may seem impossible to us is nothing for him. Don't allow money or time to prematurely shut down your creative thinking and praying about any specific schooling choice. Once again, catch the vision first and then count the cost.

The Toughest Job You'll Ever Love

As we said earlier, it is our belief that there is no single best way to school your child, and we are blessed to have so many options available. It is our responsibility as parents to study our children and seek to discern their unique gifts and calling. We are to accept the awesome responsibility God has placed on us to catch a vision for our children's education for life and become their education directors throughout all of their years in our care. After catching that vision we must do the hard work of researching our options and making whatever accommodations can be made to provide our children with what we believe is the best approach for their learning style and needs. We must then constantly evaluate how they are doing in that environment and ensure that they thrive as God shapes them into the vessel he desires for his service.

Parenting isn't easy, and choosing a schooling approach may be one of the hardest but most important decisions you will make as a parent. Remember that this is your highest calling and that you will answer for your parenting before God's throne. Embrace your role, invest in your vision, commit to the work, and glorify the Lord by raising your children for him.

Questions to Discuss

1. What is your vision for each of your children by the time they leave home?
2. What does it mean for you to be your children's educational director?
3. What schooling approaches do you need to investigate?

22

AD/HD:
Myth or Reality?

Glen Havens, M.D., with Diana M. O'Neill

True or False:

- AD/HD is overdiagnosed and overtreated.
- AD/HD is not a real diagnosis. It is an excuse for bad parenting or lack of personal discipline.
- Medications should be used as a last resort.
- There is little scientific evidence to support the existence of AD/HD.
- Individuals with this disorder are unable to be successful academically or professionally.
- AD/HD is a learning disability.

The diagnosis and treatment of attention deficit/hyperactivity disorder is still a controversial subject among Christians and within the community at large. I have often had the fantasy of putting the skeptics in a locked room with a seven-year-old hyperactive little boy for a week.

Of course, that would be grossly unfair to the child. For the families and individuals with this disorder, there is no myth. The reality is all too discouraging and profound. They feel misunderstood and alienated. A significant part of the problem is misconceptions and misinformation regarding this complex brain disorder. For starters, the terms "attention deficit disorder" and "attention deficit/hyperactivity disorder" don't capture the true essence of the disorder. It isn't really a deficit of attention but rather a problem in regulating attention. It isn't that children, adolescents, and adults with this disorder can't pay attention. They just can't regulate the process. It controls them. As a result, they can actually overattend as well as underattend. If the diagnosis could be renamed "attention regulation/hyperactivity disorder," it would likely make better intuitive sense to everyone.

It is very common for parents to say that their child could pay attention if he or she wanted to. They will use the example of video games or television, saying that they can't get him or her to stop doing these activities. Several years ago, I placed a Nintendo game in the reception room. I then waited to hear what decibel level parents escalated to in an attempt to get their child away from the game and used this as an indirect measure of distractibility. What parents and observers frequently don't understand is that the child really can't stop attending. For these children, attending is much like trying to control a fire hose. For people without this disorder, attending is like using a garden hose. For the most part, the direction and force of a garden hose can be adjusted as needed. You can lose control, but it is easily regained and redirected. With a fire hose, you dig in with both heels and hold on for dear life. Even with help, it still goes where it wants to half the time. To disengage a child from a video game or television, sometimes the parent needs to walk over, tell the child they understand that he or she can't stop, and tell him or her they are going to help by turning off the game. Sometimes taking direct action is the only way to go.

What Exactly Is AD/HD?

Attention deficit/hyperactivity disorder is primarily a neurobiological disorder. Until fairly recently, only the structure of the brain could be documented on film. Now it is possible to actually create visual images of the brain as it performs ordinary tasks. It is clear that the frontal part of the brain expends energy differently and is actually underactive in individuals with attention deficit/hyperactivity disorder. Advanced technology also shows that other parts of the brain are also either underactive or overactive in related disorders such as depression, obsessive-compulsive disorder, bipolar disorder, and anxiety.

A good deal of the problem with understanding mental health disorders is the inadequacy of our current language. Words like *depression* and *anxiety* have different meanings depending on how they are used and in what context they are used. In psychiatry and psychology, depression generally means a malfunction at a neurological junction box (something that cannot be seen with the naked eye) that results in observable changes in mood, behavior, or functioning. Actually, it is a good deal more complicated. We are only now on the cutting edge of understanding how the living brain functions. The challenge is first to increase our knowledge of the brain and second to develop the words to communicate what research uncovers.

Personally, I find the phrase "chemical imbalance" troublesome. From my experience, it is often an attempt to convey that people can be both responsible for and unable to control their behavior at the same time. Parents of children with AD/HD frequently know there is something different about them. The children themselves also know they are different. There is a common fear of affecting a child's self-esteem by giving them a label. Parents fear that their child will be treated differently or that they will think of themselves as flawed. Truth be known, they already know something is not right. The real risk is that the child will silently mislabel it as something far more damaging. Over and over again, I hear a child say he or she is lazy or stupid. He or she will get up, determined to have a good day, and yet not make it to the school bus without already getting in trouble.

Children, teens, and adults with AD/HD are looking for nonjudgmental language to describe their struggles, and it is crucial that we give it to them. I hope and pray that ten years down the road, we will have a different medical language for this disorder and for other psychiatric/psychological conditions. Perhaps they will be described in neurological terms. Depression may be called something like "serotonin receptor down-regulation syndrome." Attention deficit/hyperactivity disorder may be described as "hypoactive frontal-lobe syndrome, primarily dopaminergic subtype." My point is not to throw out fancy terms but to underscore this disorder's bioneurological basis. It is not a character flaw. It is not a blatant disregard of God's will or appropriate authority. Nonetheless, it does not mean that AD/HD does not affect character or that character flaws may not develop. What it does mean is that to reduce the possibilities of other difficulties developing, the neurological part of the disorder has to be understood, accepted, and managed. I would like to say uncategorically that it is not caused by bad parenting. Unfortunately, that does not mean it cannot result in bad parenting. Parents of children with this and other related disorders often do things they would never do under normal circumstances. These same parents would be the first in line to tell other parents not to follow their example.

What Causes AD/HD?

According to the National Institutes of Health, the surgeon general of the United States, and an international community of clinical researchers and physicians, there is compelling evidence that AD/HD is a neurobiological disorder with significant, lifelong consequences. Extensive studies indicate by far the major cause is genetic. It appears to be inherited in the kind of mode that gives a 75 percent (more or less) chance that a child inherits a neurological predisposition from one or both parents. I use the term *predisposition* because it does not always present in the same manner or severity, and it can skip generations. There is a great deal of research in the area of genetic inheritance. Recent studies at the University of California, Irvine, have provided pieces of the molecular genetic puzzle of AD/HD that may someday help to identify subtypes of AD/HD and direct the development of new treatments for this disorder.

What can be safely stated at present is that many genes are inherited in a grouping of some sort. Depending on how these genes are expressed or "turned on," the outside picture can look very different. It is possible that only some of the genes are passed on to one child, while another child may get a full dose from both parents. Environment has a significant impact as well. Depending on the exact genetic complex a child inherits, how the genes express themselves, and the impact of the environment on the disorder, one child may be much more severely affected than another. This may be true even in the same family. The reverse also may be true in that one parent may be more affected than any of his or her children. This is an important consideration in the management of the disorder.

The other closely associated problem in terms of genetic inheritance is that the gene complex and its expression may result in overlapping and/or concurrent diagnoses. Consequently, AD/HD is best conceptualized as a component of a spectrum disorder. Even if the criteria for other diagnoses in the spectrum are not fully met, there may be symptoms in several areas other than those specifically required for a diagnosis of AD/HD. Related disorders include obsessive-compulsive disorder, Tourette's syndrome, anxiety, depression, bipolar disorder, autism, and Asperger's syndrome. These occur together much more frequently than can be expected in the general population. More and more studies are beginning to suggest that disorders in this spectrum are part of the same overall gene complex. External symptoms among family members can look very different, depending on whether the child inherits all the genes or only part of them and on factors related to how the genes express themselves. That is why it is not at all uncommon for a child or parent to have two or three of these disorders simultaneously. Accurate diagnosis of all disorders is essential to effective treatment. Rather than being frightened or discouraged if you recognize this in yourself and/or your child or spouse, you should realize that it can be the key to successful symptom management. What it does mean is that this is not a one-dimensional problem and that you have to be careful not to reduce children and adults with this disorder to a single label or category.

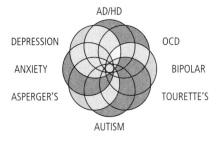

SPECTRUM DISORDER

AD/HD

DEPRESSION   OCD

ANXIETY   BIPOLAR

ASPERGER'S   TOURETTE'S

AUTISM

In addition to genetics, situations such as oxygen deprivation at birth, head trauma, strep infections, toxic exposure, extremely high fever (greater than 105 degrees for twenty-four hours), and others can result in the symptoms of this disorder. A thorough clinical history is therefore a critical assessment tool. Regardless of origin, symptoms are treated in the same manner.

What Are the Core Symptoms of AD/HD?

The core symptoms of attention deficit/hyperactivity disorder as it is currently understood are distractibility, impulsivity, and hyperactivity. Distractibility is a complicated concept. Inattentiveness is probably better understood as a function of distractibility. Many factors are involved in the act of attending. Ironically, it is easier to say what is happening when you are not attending than what is happening when you are. To attend, you must filter incoming stimuli from the environment. This is a selective process. There are times when you need to shift attention from what you are doing to something else, and then shift back. On some level, you must ignore much of what is going on around you, yet be aware of it at the same time. You must sustain an appropriate effort level, coordinate thoughts, and hold them in your mind over a period of time. You must evaluate incoming information, discarding some, retaining some.

Even if information is properly attended to, it must be organized and eventually transferred to long-term memory. Unfortunately, short-term memory and long-term memory live in different parts of the brain. One of the most frustrating aspects of attention difficulties is that short-term memory doesn't work well, but long-term memory is often excellent. It is somewhat similar to temporary memory on a computer. Once everything is entered into the computer, it must be saved to the hard drive or the information will be lost when the computer is turned off. Individuals with attention problems can't predict what information will make it to the hard drive. They can look at or hear information and think they know it. This is particularly evident for students who study for a test and know the material then, but when they try to retrieve it from long-term memory during a test, it isn't there. This makes it very difficult to predict success. For students, each test becomes a new opportunity to fail.

As a result of distractibility, important facts or information may be displaced by irrelevant input. Distractibility can be internal or external. Many children, particularly girls, are distracted internally by their own thoughts. External distractibility refers to shifts in attention due to movement, sound, visual information, physical sensations, or other changes in the outside environment that pull the mind away from its current focus. Interestingly, the percentage of adult men and women diagnosed with AD/HD is about equal. In children the preponderance is clearly in boys over girls. This is because girls and women tend to have the inattentive form of the disorder. And, as we all know, little girls and their mothers usually behave in more socially appropriate ways. The saddest part of this is that unless a child is starting fires in the hallway and failing in school, he or she is not likely to be identified or receive assistance. Distractibility appears to remain a constant problem throughout life and may even seem to worsen with age.

Impulsivity is a component of many different diagnoses. Impulsivity is like putting the ball in motion in a football game before looking to see which end of the field your team is trying to reach for a touchdown. Impulsivity has many facets and tends to change with age in terms of intensity and obviousness. It can be behavioral, such as shifting from one activity to another, spending money, changing activities, getting into fistfights, touching or picking up things, and so on. It can be verbal, such as "shooting off your mouth" or simply saying things that don't make much sense. It can be emotional, such as launching into a rage, a tirade, or exaggerated ecstasy over something trivial. Feelings surge internally without any buffer between experience and expression. Parents often cannot understand that the reason a child with AD/HD says what he or she does is that the thought crossed his or her mind while his or her mouth was open! Regardless of whether the overreaction is positive or negative, the result is still considered inappropriate behavior.

Hyperactivity is the stereotypical hallmark of AD/HD. This characteristic is primarily associated with boys and often thought of as the target for treatment. If it is not present, the diagnosis may not even be considered. This part of the disorder is not a constant and often appears to transmute with age. It can be present in boys, girls, or adults of either gender. I remember one husband who described his wife as always standing up even when she was sitting down. From my standpoint, there are several forms in which hyperactivity expresses itself. As a person ages, what is observed is more an internal restlessness. I call it "itch and wiggle." There is a buildup of neurological tension that has to be expressed. After ten to fifteen minutes in the office, it usually shows up as the gradual shifting of positions on the sofa, foot tapping, subtle or not-so-subtle bouncing, and so on. Overt movement clearly decreases with age. If the individual is also dealing with depression, what may be seen is actually a lack of energy accompanying the distractibility.

How Is AD/HD Diagnosed?

The major controversy surrounding diagnosis seems to be that the core symptoms can be present at different times and to different degrees in everyone. These symptoms also can be seen in other conditions such as depression, anxiety, medication side effects, illicit drug use, diabetes, thyroid disorders, and many other medical conditions. Ultimately, just as it is with all mental health diagnoses, it is the job of the clinician to sort all of this out. The intensity, duration, and impact of the symptoms are what distinguish this disorder as a separate entity. If there is no appreciable impact, regardless of the duration or intensity, it is not a disorder.

When making the diagnosis, it is important to gather information from several sources, such as parents, relatives, school personnel, and adults who observe the child in social settings. Parents need to remember that teachers may have their own bias and may over-report or underreport symptoms. One parent may be unable to recognize significant problems because he or she is experiencing the same struggles. There is no substitute for a careful clinical history and interview. A full battery of psychological testing is very useful for several reasons. First, it gives the school something to work from. Most psychologists will provide a list of reasonable accommodations for teachers to reference. It is also important to identify any learning disorders that may be present. Technically, AD/HD is not a learning disorder. Learning disabilities must be addressed separately. Medication does not change a learning disability. Second, testing assesses general intellectual potential (also known as IQ), as well as determining the knowledge base a child has relative to his or her peer group. What may look like a learning problem can be secondary to a lack of sufficient training in a particular area. Common specific learning disabilities in children with AD/HD are expressive writing, mathematics, and auditory processing. These are more comprehensively addressed in some of the references at the end of the chapter. Testing alone does not prove or disprove the diagnosis. However, when administered properly by an examiner who is well versed in this area, testing is invaluable.

Psychological testing is recommended through the college level. Any academic institution that receives government funding is obligated to provide accommodations to individuals with AD/HD under Section 504 of the Rehabilitation Act of 1973. This civil rights law prohibits discrimination against people with disabilities that substantially limit one or more major life functions. Because learning is typically considered to be a major life activity, many post–high school institutions have excellent disability assistance programs.

What Is the Impact of AD/HD?

The impact of attention deficit/hyperactivity disorder can be profound. Current estimates indicate that 3 to 10 percent of children have AD/HD. An estimated 8 to 9 million adults have the disorder, although less than 25 percent are diagnosed. The personal and societal costs are immeasurable because AD/HD affects all areas of an individual's functioning. It impacts academics, career, relationships, spiritual development, and self-esteem. What we now know is that there is tremendous variability in the expression of this genetic complex. Many children and adults have a mild form of the disorder. Others have a more severe expression. There is much in between. Some areas may be affected more than others, and the severity of the impact is related to the degree of understanding of the disorder and willingness of the child, adolescent, adult, or parent to seek and accept diagnosis. If a child or adolescent is bright, he or she may compensate by working harder to function well in school. Adults often intuitively seek out AD/HD-friendly professions such as sales.

Even if success as defined by others is achieved, the impact of AD/HD is present on an internal level.

Probably the most common struggle in children and adults with AD/HD other than the core symptoms is a form of learning problem called executive dysfunction. This is a disorder of organization. If you think of what an executive secretary (or a mom) does—organize, plan ahead, sequence, schedule, prioritize, manage time, and so on—you can begin to understand the complexity of skills required to perform tasks efficiently. For many of you, this is already an all too familiar experience. You know what it feels like to pick up the slack for your child, watch him or her miss important social cues, struggle to chain together a series of events in a cause-and-effect sequence, or deny involvement in a problem.

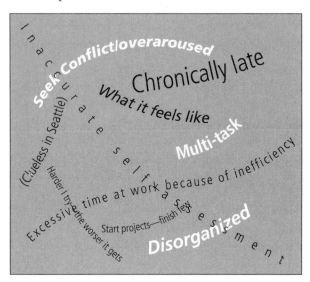

Many experts think executive dysfunction is actually a more generalized form of learning disability. In many ways, it is similar to a specific learning disability in terms of lack of response to medication. Medication improves focus and decreases distractibility, impulsivity, and restlessness. It does not change the fact or experience of being an organizational disaster area! A common parenting mistake is picking up the slack to get a child through high school only to find that he or she cannot transition to college and succeed. Learning disabilities of all kinds are agonizing. The concept can be mastered, but not the execution. Organizational plans are established, often meticulously, only to fail and have to be restarted over and over again. To make it worse, individuals with executive dysfunction can organize someone else and even follow someone else's progress but not be able to do it for themselves. What is also frustrating for children is seeing that a parent isn't any better than they are at organization or execution, but miraculously they are expected to improve. Recognition and resentment of the double standard are understandable. Please do not be too discouraged if you recognize yourself or your child here. Once they are identified, learning disabilities can be overcome or circumvented.

Why Is the Treatment of AD/HD So Complicated?

It is very common in my practice to see children and adults with more than one diagnosis. The problem with not recognizing that there is more than one diagnostic entity is that it often leads to overtreatment of one diagnosis. Obsessive-compulsive symptoms such as counting, rituals, avoidance of certain textures in clothing or food, the need for balance and symmetry, excessive fears of injury to family members, inability to make decisions because the decision has to be just right, and getting stuck on certain thoughts or behaviors are almost always present. That does not mean they need to be treated. However, at times, treating the attention component means the obsessive-compulsive symptoms get worse and have to be addressed separately. It is as though the distractibility part holds the obsessive-compulsive component in check. Once the person is better able to focus, his or her anxiety becomes more apparent, which triggers obsessive-compulsive symptoms.

Although not nearly as great a problem as once believed, a previously unnoticed tic disorder can be aggravated by the stimulant medication used to treat the AD/HD. Suddenly, treatment of vocal, motor, or combination tics is necessary. Severe mood instability actually may be a variant of bipolar disorder, which many times does not have a clear presentation in childhood. More pervasive presentations such as Asperger's (a higher functioning variant of autism) are easier to determine, but it is not unusual for it to be confused with severe AD/HD. If it is, it usually means both are present. If other diagnostic entities are not addressed, what generally happens is that treatment failure is blamed on the child or the parents.

Anxiety and depression often coexist with AD/HD. This is certainly understandable given years of feeling inadequate or stupid compared to peers. Depression in children often presents as anger and rage. Emotional storms are a common experience. This is much more than just low frustration tolerance or your garden-variety temper tantrum. It is a neurological overarousal that comes from an overload of sensory input. Many of these children (and adults) seem to have an endpoint beyond which they are no longer able to manage their emotional response to internal as well as external stimuli. Parents often intensify their attempts to regain control by escalating themselves, resulting in extending the episode. The duration and frequency of these meltdowns can leave everyone exhausted and feeling bad. The parents feel like bad parents. The kids feel like bad kids. The school, church, and neighbors aren't quite sure it isn't both.

Where Is the Hope in Treating AD/HD?

So what is the good news in the bad news? The good news is that by and large AD/HD is a treatable disorder in children and adults. The most important components are proper diagnosis, education, and medication. There is still a tremendous bias against medication within the Christian community as well as the non-Christian community. Because AD/HD is fundamentally a neurological flaw, it cannot be overcome by sheer willpower or discipline. In that regard, it is similar to other medical disorders. Until the necessary level of insulin is present in the bloodstream of someone with diabetes, the disease cannot be managed. That is not to say that exercise, diet, stress reduction, education, and so on are not important. They are vital. But the first step is insulin.

In most AD/HD presentations, there is a deficit in the functioning of a neurotransmitter called dopamine. It is not present in sufficient amounts for the brain to function normally. Medication increases the amount of dopamine available to the brain. There may actually be more than one neurotransmitter involved in AD/HD, which would help explain the variation seen in the disorder and the effectiveness of medication. Just as insulin has to be adjusted, the medication regimen for AD/HD has to be tailored to the individual. Medication is very successful in many, somewhat successful in others, and useless in a few. For reasons that are unclear, one medication may work well in one person and not at all in another. Although many people expect too much from medication, it cannot be stressed enough how important it is to use medication as a fundamental building block in treatment.

Medications from the category called stimulants are the most widely used for the treatment of AD/HD. These medications are marketed under a variety of brand names. While they differ in terms of strength and length of time of effectiveness, all are formulated from either methylphenidate or dextroamphetamine. All target the neurotransmitter dopamine. As of January 2003, the Federal Drug Administration approved the first nonstimulant medication for the treatment of AD/HD. There are a few older antidepressants that sometimes help with attention problems. Other categories of medication may also be used for hyperactivity, impulsivity, and significant mood instability; however, this is a detailed discussion that is beyond the scope of this book.

Education is equally important to successful management of AD/HD. The more the family and the child understand, the more they will be able to develop coping strategies. This includes trying to decide what is a neurological symptom and what is a normal childhood behavior. The concept of normal is a curious one. Everyone seems to have a different "normal." What is normal for me may not be normal for you. What is normal for someone with AD/HD would not be normal for someone who doesn't have the disorder. Knowing the common patterns helps to predict behavior and avoid common roadblocks. Parents need to ask themselves if their child's behavior stands out from his or her peers. Often a hyperactive child is fairly easy to pick out when put in a group of children the same age.

A recurring problem in children with this disorder is an inability to read social cues. Social rules that are intuitively learned by most children often need to be explained over and over. Social skills groups are an excellent resource, especially for teenagers. They are able to share common social difficulties and compare problem-solving strategies. Group settings seem to be less frequently available for parents but can be extremely helpful to avoid feelings of failure or isolation.

In the same spirit, it is important for all members of the family unit to be evaluated and supported. The issues faced by both family members with AD/HD as well as those without deserve consideration. Individual, family, and marital counseling can all help to lessen the impact of this chronic, lifelong disorder.

Are We Ready for the Challenge?

For some reason, support in the church setting has been a troublesome area. Parents and children with AD/HD have trouble fitting in. They miss social cues, fail to follow through, and are erratic in attendance and general support. Many churches have support programs for grief, divorce, alcohol/drug abuse, and even eating disorders. Sadly, I have yet to learn of a program organized around AD/HD, although this disorder affects almost 10 percent of any population in some form or fashion.

An extension of this problem is found in Christian schools. Children with AD/HD need a smaller class size and lots of structure. As a result, the small Christian school seems very attractive to parents. Unfortunately, Christian schools often do not have the resources or expertise to deal with these children. Structure and rigidity are sometimes difficult to tell apart. As a result, children with AD/HD (and their parents) end up failing in yet another system. Isn't it time to offer hope and support within the Christian community? Isn't it time to face the reality of AD/HD?

For Further Reading

Dornbush, Marilyn P., and Sheryl K. Pruitt. *Teaching the Tiger.*Duarte, CA: Hope Press, 1995

Fowler, Rick, and Jerilyn Fowler. *Honey, Are You Listening? Attention Deficit/Hyperactive Disorder and Your Marriage.* Gainesville, TX: Fair Havens Publications, 2002.

Greene, Ross. *The Explosive Child: A New Approach for Understanding and Parenting Easily Frustrated, Chronically Inflexible Children.*New York: Quill, 2001.

Hallowell, Edward M., and John J. Ratey. *Driven to Distraction: Recognizing and Coping with Attention Deficit Disorder from Childhood to Adulthood.* New York: Simon and Schuster, 1995.

Hallowell, Edward M., and John J. Ratey. *Answers to Distraction.* New York: Bantam Books, 1996.

Novotni, Michele. *What Does Everybody Else Know That I Don't?* North Branch, MN: Specialty Press, 2000.

23

ANSWERING THE CRIES OF THE SPIRITED CHILD

David and Claudia Arp

What is it that frustrates you most about your spirited child? When we asked parents this question, we got these answers:

> "My son bounds out of bed each morning and races through the day like a ten-ton truck. He's only eight years old. I shudder to think what he will be like as a teenager!"

> "I feel as if I'm always bribing my child or giving in because I just don't want to fight the battle. It takes too much energy to try to reason with her."

> "I don't know what to do when my child looks me right in the eye and says, 'No!'"

"My child is so intent on having things go his way—and when they don't, he explodes!"

"When I discipline my son, he just looks at me and says, 'So?'"

Sound familiar? The interesting thing we've discovered from more than two decades of work in parent education is that spirited, difficult children have common needs, but they rarely verbalize them in a calm, direct way. Instead, they cry out in angry words or forceful actions, and it's up to their parents to hear what they're really saying. Behind each cry is a deeper meaning, one that your child doesn't quite know how to express but one that needs to be met. What does your child *really* mean when he or she cries out, "I hate you!" or "You can't make me!"?

In our book *Answering the 8 Cries of the Spirited Child*, we present the eight most common cries of the spirited child and give practical strategies for meeting each need. In this chapter we will take a quick look at each, but first let's deal with the "Why me?" question that parents ask.

Why Me, God?

If you are the parent of a spirited child, you may be asking, "Why did I get this spirited child?" The answer is that God chose you because you are the parent your child needs. And he didn't make a mistake. *You have what it takes.* God will give you whatever you need to see this job through. Your challenge is to help your child channel his or her surplus energy, spirit, and determination in a positive way. Who knows, you may be parenting the future scientist who will discover the cure for cancer!

This being said, you may still feel frustrated and inadequate, and you may experience three emotions that are common to parents of spirited children: guilt, shame, and anger. When we have a child who is not happy and who constantly causes discord in the family, we naturally assume that we're not good parents and we feel guilty. It's easy to feel shame, because spirited kids are good at embarrassing their parents.

Strong-willed kids are also good at generating angry feelings. But your kids might not be the only ones you are angry with. You might also be angry with God. Contrary to what you might think, God is not punishing you by giving you a difficult child. While you probably wouldn't have volunteered for this job, you can be certain that this is the right child for you. Now let's look at the eight cries of the spirited child and what each cry really means.

The Eight Cries of the Spirited Child

Cry #1: "Look at Me!"

What it really means: "Please understand me."

Spirited kids do not set out deliberately to vex us. When they cry out, "Look at me!" (although rarely in such direct terms), what these children really need is understanding. We need to make every effort to understand our child's God-given uniqueness, even when that uniqueness includes a strong will and a spirit that's hard to keep in check some days.

We also need to understand the basics of child development. One excellent resource we recommend is *Child Behavior: The Classic Child-care Manual from the Gesell Institute of Human Development.* Physical development in children tends to follow a predictable order, although the timetable can vary from child to child. Emotional growth tends to occur in cycles, with periods of balance followed by periods that are more out of balance. Times of pleasant, agreeable behavior are followed by times of insecurity and disorder. These periods are evident whether a child is spirited or compliant; but with a spirited or difficult child, the cycles tend to swing from high to low with very little in between. Many psychologists say that these normal emotional cycles are punctuated by two key periods of independence. The first comes between babyhood and childhood (the so-called terrible twos), and the second between childhood and adulthood (the onset of the teen years).

As our children develop, the cycles of their lives are bound to include periods of rebellion, stress, and even obnoxious behavior. The good news is that if we know these times are coming, we can better accept them and handle them when they arrive. By being aware of developmental trends, we can recognize that the undesirable behavior we're witnessing is not true disobedience or a sign of parental incompetence. Instead, it is behavior necessary to growth—an important step for our kids in developing independence physically, mentally, emotionally, socially, and spiritually.

Don't get frazzled about the stage your child is in right now. By the time you've worked yourself into a total frenzy, your child will have done a flip-flop anyway! The good news is that each stage marks progress; each stage is leading to maturity. And each stage is *temporary*.

In addition to understanding the typical stages of child development, it's important to understand your child's unique temperament. Can you identify your child's basic personality? Is your child the one who likes to take charge? Or is he more laid-back or more like an emotional roller coaster? Or perhaps she is outgoing, sparkles, and flits around like a butterfly. Actually, most children are a combination of types, with one type that is dominant. For example, one child might be 60 percent take-charge and 40 percent roller-coaster; another child might be 70 percent sparkle and 30 percent laid-back. Of course, every personality has its positives and negatives. When we know our children's basic personality traits, we can be realistic in our expectations of them, concentrating on playing up their strengths and encouraging them to overcome their weaknesses.

Cry #2: "Did I Do Good?"

What it really means: "Encourage me. Look for the positive."

If you consistently refer to your strong-willed child as "the difficult one," he or she will only become more difficult! But even kids who tend to be defiant or explosive have positive traits. Like other children, they want to know that *someone* can see past their smoke screens to something good in them.

Granted, for most of us, maintaining a positive focus is not an easy task. Our children's negative behaviors tend to cast a long shadow over the positive ones. And unfortunately, many well-meaning relatives and friends only make matters worse.

Sandra always dreads her mother's visits. One of Sandra's daughters, Tabitha, is strong-willed, and from the moment Grandma walks in the door until she leaves, she nags Sandra incessantly about the way Tabitha is (or isn't) disciplined. She lavishes attention and praise on Tabitha's younger, more compliant sister; but toward Tabitha, she is cool and distant. Tabitha senses her grandmother's disapproval, of course, and is stiff and unfriendly in return. She then acts out to get her mother's attention, fueling her grandmother's negative view of her even more. Poor Sandra feels caught in the middle. Plus, at times when her daughter acts up, Sandra, for the moment, really doesn't like her! The truth is that we would have to be angels to enjoy children when they're hurting us and draining us emotionally by their words or behavior.

How can we turn negatives into positives? Self-fulfilling prophesies work both ways, you know. When we begin to see our children in terms of their positive traits rather than their negative ones, they start to become what we see.

If your child's extreme behavior was modified somewhat, could it have a positive side? Can you look at your child's up-and-down, melancholy personality as sensitivity? Can the term *whininess* be reframed to *very expressive*? In a University of Nebraska study of three thousand families, the following extreme behaviors were "reframed" and given more positive terms:

Extreme	Reframed
wastes money	generous
talks too much	likes to share with others
bossy	a leader
messy, into things	curious
won't follow rules	creative, innovative
too picky	attends to details
interfering, nosey	interested, concerned
domineering	has strong opinions
stubborn	determined
gossipy	articulate[1]

When we look at our children through a positive filter, we give more positive feedback, we smile more, we're more pleasant to be around, we listen more attentively, and we're more encouraging. We expect more from them, and they expect more from themselves. It's that simple. By becoming an encourager, you help to draw out the very best in your child.

Cry #3: "You're Not Listening!"

What it really means: "Listen to me; talk to me."

Sometimes when our children talk to us, they just need to be heard. As the parent, you need to identify with their feelings (not necessarily agree with them). Spirited children, in particular, can be very sensitive; they feel things deeply and get their feelings hurt more easily than children who are easygoing. For them, the tears that always seem to be near the surface aren't a put-on. And if they're defiant as well as sensitive, they are likely to express their hurt feelings with anger. Listening to them can be difficult, but it's imperative that we understand the real meaning of what they're trying to express. If we immediately jump in, criticize, and try to solve all their problems, we haven't really listened.

When parents listen with interest, children feel that their ideas are valued, and their sense of self-esteem and confidence is built up. They reason, "If my parents believe I'm worth listening to, I must be a person of value and importance." When our children feel good about who they are, they are much more willing to open up and talk to Mom or Dad.

Here are a few keys to getting your child to talk—*really talk*—to you:

1. *Be attentive when your child wants to talk with you.* Stop what you're doing and give full attention. Put down the paper or the dishes, turn off the television, and focus on your child.

2. *Encourage talk.* Smile, nod, and give short, one-word responses to indicate your interest. Keep questions brief, open, and friendly. Try to avoid "you" statements and "why" questions, which tend to be attacking. Instead, use "I" statements, which are much safer.

3. *Empathize with your child.* Try to put yourself into your son or daughter's shoes. Think back to your own childhood. Chances are you were a spirited child too! Try to remember some of your own strong feelings and how you dealt with them.

4. *Avoid knee-jerk reactions.* It's so easy to respond to a spirited child in a knee-jerk sort of way. The problem is that those kind of immedi-

ate reactions are almost always ineffective. The last thing you want to become is a drill sergeant, shouting out orders to your child that simply don't work. Consider the following typical knee-jerk reaction—and a better response:

Situation: Your child won't get out of bed in the morning.

Knee-jerk response: "Get up, you lazy head! This is the last time I'm going to call you!"

Instead, say: "Good morning. It's seven in the morning. What should you be doing now?"

5. *Realize that every moment is not a great time to talk*. Regardless of how clever you are or what good communication skills you use, at times your child will clam up and be uncommunicative. Other times your child will be talking (perhaps very loudly), and you will need to say, "Time out." You can't reason with a child who has gone over the top emotionally or who is clearly trying to manipulate the situation. You'll end up with a prolonged argument. At such times it's best to take a break and return to the issue later when everyone can deal with it more constructively.

To improve communication with your spirited child, you need to look for good times to talk such as during a car ride or at bedtime. Think creatively, and you'll find those perfect opportunities to talk alone with and listen to your child.

Cry #4: "Let Me Do It My Way!"

What it really means: "Teach me how to cooperate."

Spirited kids love challenges and hate ultimatums. One of their favorite phrases is "I want to do it my way!" Because of their inflexible nature, they often lack the cooperation skills of negotiation and compromise.

It will help if you can develop a team spirit. Studies show that a child's compliance rate varies based on how well parents connect with their child and how consistently they apply discipline. We know from experience, however, that it's hard to connect with your child—or even to *want* to connect—when he or she is throwing one tantrum after another. And we know how hard it is to be consistent with discipline when you're being worn down and worn out day after day by your child's refusal to cooperate with even the simplest of requests.

Not every battle needs to be fought, and you only have so much emotional energy anyway. That's why you need to pick your battles carefully—very, very carefully. What are the major issues you battle over with your child? What are the minor ones? Over the years in our seminars and Pep Groups for Parents, we've used two key questions to help parents determine whether a matter is major or minor, and whether or not it's worth a fight:

1. Is it a moral issue? (If the answer is yes, it's always major.)
2. What difference will it make in light of eternity?

These two questions can be invaluable, especially as children head into adolescence. As one youth pastor put it, "If it can be taken off, washed out, or cut off, don't worry about it." You don't want to use up all of your emotional energy fighting over minor issues; when a major issue comes up, you won't have enough left in reserve to take a strong stand. Asking these two questions can help you keep things in perspective.

Cry #5: "You Can't Make Me!"

What it really means: "Give me boundaries; discipline me."

Despite protests to the contrary, when spirited children cry, "You can't make me!" they are really pleading for the clear boundaries and consistent discipline they desperately need to bring balance and order to their lives.

Next to love, discipline is a parent's second most important gift to a child, says child development authority T. Berry Brazelton.[2]

And while most parents know that it's important to set boundaries for their kids, enforcing them in a consistent and effective way is one of the most difficult tasks of parenting.

Essentially, discipline is about *teaching*, not punishment. As parents, our job is to teach our children how to become mature, responsible adults who honor God and consider the needs and feelings of others. The most effective forms of discipline take into account the ages, stages, and personalities of the children involved. There is no one size fits all. And with spirited or difficult children in particular, discipline needs to be geared toward helping them develop self-discipline and self-control—two very important qualities necessary for their future success.

Think about the way God disciplines us. His discipline is always in our best interest, as Hebrews 12:10 says: "God disciplines us for our good, that we may share in his holiness." God's discipline is designed to help us grow and develop and prepare for life at its best. The discipline we apply to our own children should have that same goal. We should respect them enough to discipline them with their best interest in mind.

That means we should never punish a child out of anger or frustration. A big emotional blowup may feel good to us, but the child can be devastated in the process. It also means that we should attack the problem, not the person. There's a big difference between "Lance, you're so clumsy! You spilled your milk again" and "Oops! The milk is spilled. What's the best way to clean it up?"

We need to distinguish between defiant and childish behavior. For instance, did Lance spill his milk deliberately out of anger, or was it merely an accident? Here are some tips:

Establish reasonable boundaries. Even though spirited children may try to push against them, boundaries will help them learn to be responsible.

Say what you want. Sometimes we get so good at telling our children what we *don't* want them to do that we forget to tell them what we *do* want. We shouldn't assume that our children automatically know what our expectations are in any given situation. And even if they do know, many spirited, strong-willed kids will be looking for the loophole. If you say, "Stop kicking the table leg," your child may start tapping on the floor, the chair leg, or the sibling sitting in the next seat. It would be better to state exactly what you want: "Keep your feet and legs still and quiet."

Use positive reinforcement. Instead of always chiding them for bad behavior, we should compliment our children on their *good* behavior whenever possible. For example, praise them when they remember to feed the cat, practice the piano without a reminder, or put away their toys.

Use "reality discipline." Whenever practical, we tried to let our children experience the natural consequences of their actions. Dr. Kevin Leman and Randy Carlson, authors of *Parent Talk*, call this concept "reality discipline." Using reality discipline, they say, keeps parents from having to punish their children and trains kids to be accountable and responsible. "Instead of having to play the heavy," Leman and Carlson tell parents, "you simply depend on reality to do the admonishing and disciplining."[3]

For reality discipline to work, rules and agreements must be set up ahead of time with the understanding that if the child fails to comply or meet the agreements, he or she will have to face certain consequences, many of which are natural consequences. Say you have a fifth-grade daughter who calls home to ask you to bring her forgotten gym clothes to school—for the fourth time in two weeks. You may have to tell her to face the gym teacher without them this time. (You might also help her become more organized by adding a hook or shelf next to the front door to hold items needed for school the next day.)

Make the discipline fit the offense. Withholding a privilege can be a useful form of reality discipline. The length of time that privilege is withheld, however, should fit the offense and the child's age. A four-year-old who colors on the wall, for example, may lose the use of the crayons for a few days; a thirteen-year-old who abuses his or her phone privileges may have calls restricted for a week. For the most part, the limitation of privileges should be reasonably brief; otherwise, kids can become overly discouraged. A month of no phone calls, for example, would seem like an eternity for a teenager, and probably for the rest of the household too!

Keep a future focus. When it comes to disciplining spirited children, our main focus should not be "How should I punish my child for this offense?" but rather "How can we avoid this situation in the future?"

Take a timeout. We all—parents and children alike—sometimes need a cooling-off period to get control of our emotions and regain a proper perspective so we can deal with a situation rationally.

What's the best way to do a timeout? Let's say your five-year-old son has just hit his little sister. Keeping your volume low and taking deep breaths to help you stay calm (the exercises learned in Lamaze class are wonderful for this!), calmly explain to your son that he must have a timeout. Place him in a chair away from family activity, perhaps in another room; don't send him to his bedroom, where he would get distracted. Once he is sitting quietly and not trying to get up, set a timer for a predetermined amount of time. One minute for each year of age is a good guideline.

Then there are those times when a timeout is necessary—and *we're* the ones who need it! One mother told us, "I once left my son wet and naked in his room while I put myself in timeout. I needed a break! He wasn't toilet trained yet, but I figured if he wet the carpet, cleaning up the mess was better than venting my anger—which I was tempted to do because I was at the end of my rope." This wise mom recognized her limits and knew the value of a good timeout.

Cry #6: "I Hate You!"

What it really means: "Help me deal with my anger and frustration."

Parenting a spirited child can be like an avalanche. Everything seems to be going along quite smoothly, then suddenly he or she explodes and dumps on you. Maybe your child stomps, hits, or throws things. Maybe he or she screams angry words, including the ones that always stab a loving parent in the heart: "I hate you!" The truth is these words reflect the heat of the moment; they're not the real message. What your child is really saying, pleading, is this: "Help me deal with my anger and frustration."

Remember, the spirited child is wound tighter than more compliant kids and can be set off by the smallest thing. He or she can go ballistic when we least expect it. And once the avalanche starts rolling, it's almost impossible to turn it back.

Anger, because of its intensity, is easily mishandled by the unsuspecting parent who is hit by it. After all, we're not exempt from angry feelings. Sometimes when our kid explodes, we explode. Think back to the last time your child got really angry. How did you feel? Were you angry too? It's so easy to react to your child—and before you know it, you're both angry!

If your son or daughter is struggling with anger, think about the past several weeks and months. How often does he or she act out? What happens in those outbursts? What behaviors do you see over and over? Does your child get angry when he or she is tired, hungry, stressed? When things aren't going well at school? Is there something in particular that's frustrating your child?

Consider the family schedule. Is your child booked every day of the week? How many out-of-school activities does he or she participate in? One boy told us he hates Tuesdays because he has soccer practice and a piano lesson after school, and when he finally gets home at seven o'clock, he still has homework to do. That's a lot for anyone to be saddled with. No wonder this little guy is frustrated!

Sometimes when children are angry, they just need a little space. Closed doors are okay. We used to feel, when one of our boys went in his room and closed the door, that he was closing us out of his life. We took it personally. But then we realized that everyone needs space occasionally, even the little people in our lives. The *where* isn't important. When the daughter of one of our friends needed space, she'd go outside and sit in her dog's house!

After an episode in which you get angry, record it in an "anger notebook." Write down what made you angry, how you felt, and what you did. If you're not happy with the way you handled your anger, include what you wish you had done and what you would like to do the next time a similar situation comes up.

Teaching children to process their anger in a mature, responsible way takes lots of time and patience on our part. We have to learn how to process our own anger and then set a good example. And it takes all of us, parents and children alike, looking to our ultimate example, God, who is always slow to anger and abounding in amazing love.

Cry #7: "I Don't Want To!"

What it really means: "Give me the opportunity to develop responsibility."

Is your child crying out for someone to teach him or her responsibility and self-discipline? Probably not in so many words. You are much more likely to hear "I don't want to!" than "Help me be responsible!" But *we* know what they really mean.

Take a trip into the future for a moment and picture yourself with your spirited child as an adult. (Yes, even your spirited child will eventually grow up.) What kind of relationship would you like to have with your adult son or daughter? Can you imagine having good times together, talking, laughing, appreciating one another? Wouldn't it feel good to enjoy your adult child without feeling responsible for his or her life?

Now back to the present. What does your child need to know by the time he or she leaves home? What will your child be personally responsible for when he or she is an independent young adult? Take a few moments to make a list.

Now think about how that list can be broken down and fleshed out at different age levels or stages. Starting at your child's age, you might want to complete the following sentences:

- When my son (or daughter) is two, he should be able to . . .
- When he enters preschool, he should be able to . . .
- When he's a first-grader, he should be able to . . .
- When he starts middle school, he should be able to . . .
- When he becomes a teenager, he should be able to . . .
- When he leaves home, he should be able to . . .

Research shows that children who help at home with specific chores learn responsibility, gain self-esteem, and develop valuable work habits for their adult life. So how can you motivate your spirited child to accept responsibility? You might want to make a chore chart. Charts help children know what is expected of them, and parents have a tool to gauge the follow-through. We've found that the secret to using charts effectively is to change them often. Consider making weekly charts, one-time charts, or checklists for different times of day.

Teaching responsibility and self-discipline—especially to a strong-willed or spirited child—is not easy, but it's worth all the effort we put into it. The result is what we all want: children who grow into responsible young adults, equipped with all the tools necessary to navigate life.

Cry #8: "I'm a Big Kid Already!"

What it really means: "Guide me to maturity."

Because spirited children are more difficult, we need more of everything to guide them to maturity: more patience, more energy, more unconditional love, more trust, more humor. We need more faith that God has a plan for our children's lives, especially as we give up increasing degrees of control and responsibility as our kids approach adulthood.

When one of our spirited sons was twelve years old, he told us, "Mom, Dad, I don't want to learn from the *experienced*. I want to learn by *experience!*" Those are scary words for a parent to hear. But the fact is that "by experience" is often the way spirited children learn best.

If your spirited child is determined to learn by experience, how can you provide the framework he or she needs to learn positive life lessons in the process? One way is to teach your child good decision-making skills.

Being able to make wise, independent decisions is a key to successful adult living. That's why it's so important for us to involve our children in the decision-making process as often as possible. Here are four tips that helped us teach decision making to our sons:

1. *Allow your child to participate in family decisions.* Whether it's deciding what television program you are going to watch as a family, what game you are going to play, or where you're going on a family vacation, let your children take part. This builds their confidence in their own decision-making abilities.

2. *Let your child choose between options.* Even young children can make simple decisions like these: "Do you want the red apple or the green one?" "Do you want to brush your teeth with the green toothpaste or the striped toothpaste?" "Do you want to take your nap in your bed or on the couch in the playroom?" Giving choices on simple matters helps your child develop his or her ability to analyze options. If your child asks, "Why do I have to wear a coat?" you can turn the question into a decision-making opportunity. Say, "What is the weather like outside today? Is it hot or cold? Do you think the light red coat would be warm enough, or would the heavy blue coat feel better?"

3. *Encourage your child to negotiate.* This tip may not excite you, because your spirited son or daughter is probably a natural born debater. But when you have an issue to work through with your child, it's a good idea to walk through the four steps of negotiation:

- Let your child summarize what he or she wants.
- Summarize what you want.
- Propose alternatives.
- Work out a compromise.

Negotiating with a strong-willed kid can take lots of time and effort. It's so much simpler to say, "Do this," or "Don't do that." But when you take the easy route, you are not training your child to become a competent decision maker.

4. *Expect your child to make mistakes.* The hardest part of teaching decision making is watching your child make mistakes. Sometimes we just have to bite our tongues and resist the tendency to want to be in control. As one parent said, "You hope and pray that when your child makes a mistake, he or she will have an excellent learning opportunity, and your tendency to nag will be stifled."

The more we help our children develop confidence and competence in making decisions on minor issues like hairstyles, clothes, and so on, the less likely they'll be to rebel and make bad choices when it comes to major things like drugs, alcohol, and sex. If we do the hard work now, by the time they are selecting colleges and mates and making their own moral choices, we'll be able to breathe a little easier knowing their decision-making skills are well developed.

Spirited children have a natural desire to control their own lives. Yet precisely because they can be difficult, we tend to strip them of control just when they yearn for it the most, such as when they move into adolescence. The summer before each of our sons turned thirteen, we gave them a teenage challenge to help them prepare for the adolescent years. We challenged them in four areas: physical, intellectual, spiritual, and practical. The physical challenge was to run a mile in under eight minutes. The intellectual challenge was to read a book about someone they admired and give a book report to the whole family. The spiritual challenge was to complete a Bible study teaching a biblical code of conduct and to commit to abide by that code through their teen years. For the practical challenge, they planned a campout with me (Dave) and did all the work involved, including cooking all the meals. (Yes, I ate some very interesting things!)

A teenage challenge is a great initiation into the teen years. It will help to ensure that your new teenager will enter this turbulent phase of life with increased confidence and self-assurance. Check out our book *Suddenly They're 13, or The Art of Hugging a Cactus* for information and suggestions on planning and carrying out a teenage challenge.

Challenges can be a motivation to greater maturity at any age. For example, your preschooler can be challenged to learn his phone number and address and how to tie his shoes before entering kindergarten. Your fifth-grader can be challenged to set the alarm clock and get up in the morning without your assistance before starting middle school.

As your children get older, your role in their lives needs to change from that of *director* to *facilitator* and then *observer*. Scary as it seems, your children must make the jump from living by your family rules and standards to living by their own personal convictions. They must move from dependence on you, the parent, to dependence on God. And it's your job to help them.

Unfortunately, this transition is not a science. There are no ten easy steps to helping kids grow spiritually. When they're young, we can read them Bible stories and teach simple Bible verses. Later, we can encourage quiet-time notebooks and check-up charts. We can pray with and for our children. We can involve them in sending supplies to missionaries and giving assistance to the needy. We can teach by example. But as much as we'd like to legislate spiritual growth and maturity, we can't.

Ultimately, their faith must be internalized and their convictions must be their own. We can only do what we can do and put the rest in God's hands. We encourage you to start planning and working *now* to shift the responsibility for your child's spiritual life from your shoulders to your child's.

Humorist Erma Bombeck gave us a great word picture of what it means to let go as we lead our children to maturity when she compared children to kites. Think about it. We spend a lifetime trying to get them off the ground. You run with them until you're both breathless. They crash and then you add a longer tail. They hit the rooftop. You pluck them out of the spout. You patch and comfort, adjust and teach. You watch them being lifted by the wind and hope that someday they'll fly. At last they are airborne, but they need more string and you keep letting it out. And each time you release more string, the kite becomes more distant, and somehow you know that it won't be long before the lifeline that bound you together will snap and the kite will soar as it was meant to soar—free and alone.

Yes, letting out more string is risky. Finally releasing that string is riskier still. But that's the ultimate goal of parenting: to guide our spirited children to become godly kites that can soar successfully on their own.

Are you afraid that when you finally let go, you'll be empty-handed? You won't! What you'll have left is the relationship you've built with your child through the active parenting years. As two parents who managed to release three soaring sons, let us encourage you: the joy of seeing your precious kite rise on the wind, full of purpose and grace, is worth all the risks. And your relationship with your adult child, not to mention any grandchildren he or she may produce, will have its own rewards. Did we mention that we have an abundance of spirited grandchildren? It's payback time.

Questions to Discuss

1. Which of the cries described in this chapter can you relate to your children's inner need?
2. How might you have contributed to your children's limited ability to talk with you? How can you help each other improve in your ability to better respond to your child's inner cry?
3. What are some issues you have with your spirited child that indicate that you need to be more careful in picking your battles?
4. What can you do as parents to better help your kids make decisions?

For Further Reading

Arp, David, and Claudia Arp. *Answering the 8 Cries of the Spirited Child*. West Monroe, LA: Howard Publishing Co., 2003.

Arp, David, and Claudia Arp. *Suddenly They're 13, or The Art of Hugging a Cactus*. Grand Rapids: Zondervan, 1999.

Ilg, Frances L., Louise Bates Ames, and Sidney M. Baker. *Child Behavior: The Classic Childcare Manual from the Gesell Institute of Human Development*. New York: HarperCollins, 1991.

Leman, Kevin, and Randy Carlson. *Parent Talk: Straight Answers to the Questions That Rattle Moms and Dads*. Nashville: Thomas Nelson, 1993.

For information about the Arps' Marriage Alive seminars or other Marriage Alive resources, visit www.marriagealive.com or call 1-888-690-6667.

This chapter is adapted from the book *Answering the 8 Cries of the Spirited Child* (West Monroe, LA: Howard Publishing Company, 2003) and used with permission.

24

Helping Your Child with Grief and Loss

Lauren Littauer Briggs

By the time I was eight, my first brother had died and my second was diagnosed with the same fatal condition. My great-grandmother had died, but I wasn't allowed at the funeral. Instead, I peeked through the heating ducts to watch what was going on. My dog was given away with little explanation and my second brother was placed in a children's home where he could receive the medical attention he needed. I never saw him again. My loss experience was more extreme than many and remained a dominant theme in my childhood.

The usual way children learn about loss and death begins at an early age in a benign sort of way. A toy gets broken and can't be repaired. A favorite stuffed animal or blanket is taken away and put in a safe place. As time goes on, a pet such as a bird, fish, or hamster may die. The pet is lovingly wrapped in a cloth, placed in a box, and may be buried in the backyard. The child begins to understand that death is final. A friend from school moves away. Letters are written and cards are sent. As time goes on, new friendships are made, and old ones become fond memories. Later, a long-time family pet like a dog or cat dies. Again, that death is handled with compassion and tenderness. The child feels sadness and misses his or her treasured pet. A distant relative dies, and once again loss is explained. At some point in a child's life, a precious grandparent or aunt or uncle dies. This loss is experienced more intimately, the absence more noticeable. As each loss takes place, a new lesson is learned, a new understanding of loss is gained, and a new sensitivity is developed.

Other children have devastating loss thrust upon them at a very early age, which is out of the natural order of life. They may watch a classmate die of a lengthy illness, Mommy may be killed by a drunk driver, a sister might be murdered, the brand-new baby sister might die from SIDS or a birth defect, a parent might be killed in a car accident or plane crash, they may lose an uncle to suicide, or they may learn that their older brother was killed at war. When devastating loss comes early in a child's life, the emotional needs and responses will be much greater.

There is a young family in our church whose Daddy died recently at the age of thirty-three from stomach cancer, leaving a loving wife and four young children. I've had the privilege of spending time with them, sharing my heart and home as they walk this most difficult path.

Who would have thought that their outdoor play would include trips to the cemetery, placing birthday cards at their daddy's headstone, sending balloons off with birthday greetings, bringing spinners and flowers to spend Father's Day at his grave, and blowing bubbles as if they were kisses to be carried to heaven for Daddy?

Who would have thought their collection of children's books would include *What on Earth Do You Do When Someone Dies?*; *When Someone Very Special Dies*; *Saying Goodbye to Daddy*; *When Dinosaurs Die—A Guide to Understanding Death*; and *What's Heaven?* When a child's life is touched by the death of someone precious, their life is never the same. They need to learn the definitions of words such as *grave*, *funeral*, *autopsy*, *hearse*, *coffin*, and *cremation*, words we wish even we didn't need to know—never mind having to teach to our children.

Whatever situation you find yourself in at this moment, it is vitally important that you are aware of what your children need from you and how to help them face the losses in their lives. We may overlook children's emotional needs because we think that they are too young to understand and that they don't grieve. Most counselors believe that if a child is old enough to love, they are old enough to grieve.

As I recall my childhood, I realize now that I had feelings of loss over my brothers' illness and resultant death when I was seven years old. My sister, who was four years younger, and who had a totally different personality than me, remembers little of the trauma surrounding my brothers' problems. As parents, we need to realize that different children respond differently to loss and that children move in and out of the grieving process. A child can be sad and tearful one minute and tossing the football in the backyard or playing with her dolls the next. Children are more prone to compartmentalize their grief than adults.

Explain Death Clearly and Truthfully

Children need honest, open communication about death. Keep in mind that what may be comforting words to an adult may terrify a child. Don't say, "Uncle Bob passed away." Or "Grandmother just went to sleep." A child doesn't know what the term *passed away* means. The child needs to hear that Uncle Bob died. Using the words *die*, *death*, and *dead* may seem harsh, but they are much more helpful for children. Children are literal thinkers. If you use the words "went to sleep," the child may think the person will eventually wake up, or the child may be fearful of falling asleep because they know the person who died never woke up.

Use the correct words and terms and accurate explanations. That's what we did with six-year-old Randy Jr. when Grammy Chapman was taken to the hospital. I went to school early to pick him up. As we sat on the lawn outside our house, my husband and I explained that Grammy had been taken to the hospital that morning and she was very sick. We went on to say that she had a bad disease in her body, the doctors were taking care of her, but it didn't look like she would get better. She was unconscious (*unconscious* was a new word and we taught him its meaning), and we said that she was probably going to die.

I asked Randy Jr. if he wanted to go see Grammy even though she wouldn't be able to talk to him. He said, "No, I was with her yesterday and we had a good talk." He was content with his positive memories of yesterday and didn't feel a need to see her in an unconscious state. He was not left out of anything, yet he was not forced to do something he didn't need or want to do. Depending on a child's maturity, he'll need to know what happened to the body.

Age Makes a Difference

Infants

While infants and toddlers will not understand what death is, they will sense the distress of the parents, the emotional atmosphere at home, and a disruption in regular schedules. Try to keep the baby's usual sleeping and eating schedule whenever possible. Your baby will need extra holding and touching. It is important to stay close physically to provide security and stability.

Preschoolers

The preschool child may have a beginning concept of death; however, they often think it is reversible or not permanent. They may ask when the dead person is coming back. The child also might feel they did something that caused the death. Reassure your child that their thoughts, feelings, wishes, or actions did not cause the death. Children ask a lot of questions and are quite open about what has happened. A child this age moves from sadness to play quite quickly and may even seem unfazed by the loss.

Elementary Years

Children in their early elementary years usually understand that death is final and will want more details about how the person died. The child may feel vulnerable and worry if other loved ones will die. The child needs reassurance that he will not be left alone but that there will always be people to love and care for him. A child this age may want to hear stories about their loved one and to recount their loss experience often.

Preteens and Teens

Emotions and feelings become a major focus for preteens and teens when facing a loss. Children in this age group often feel anger and guilt, but don't really understand why or where it is coming from. In an effort to avoid the sadness or not add more trouble to their parents, they often hide their feelings. They may prefer and seek solitude, withdrawing from their friends and support systems. When the opportunity arises, encourage your child to talk about his or her feelings, thoughts, and memories.

Helping Children with Their Grief

Prepare your children for what will come. The more open you can be about what is ahead, the less uncomfortable your children will be. Explain what the funeral will be like, what they will see, and what feelings they may experience. I tell children and adults alike that we hurt so much because we love so much. I feel it is very important to honor the sadness and hurt as a tribute to how much we love. If we didn't care, it wouldn't hurt. Each moment of sadness and every teardrop shed represents our love for that person. We must never be ashamed of that love.

Encourage your children to ask questions and answer them clearly and accurately. Tell them, "Anytime you have a question or don't understand what is happening, please ask me. I will tell you anything you want to know." Children have a great need to talk about what has happened, but they will only do so when the environment and time are right and they are ready.

Spend one-on-one time with each child. Sit on the floor or ground so that you are on their level. Play with them or color with them. Then when the timing is right, ask questions about their feelings, memories, and understanding. Have you had any dreams about _____? Do you feel sad some of the time? Would you tell me what you've been feeling? Could we draw a picture of _____? You will probably be amazed how easily the conversation flows when your children know you are available and want to be a part of their feelings. Ask, "Do you know how Grandpa died?" A question like this encourages the children to gather information and enables you to clarify misconceptions they might have.

Don't overspiritualize the death with comments like, "Grandma is in heaven now"; "Jesus came to take your sister to heaven"; "God is in control"; or "God just needed another angel in heaven." Be careful about using references to God or Jesus when explaining death to children. They may believe that death is God's fault and develop a sense of anger toward God. I knew of a child who wanted to go to the hospital to see the hole in the wall where "Jesus came and took" her baby sister. Children cannot understand a literal heaven, especially when it reflects an earthly pain.

Don't put timetables on the emotional reactions. Grief work is individual and truly unending. We will never be "over it" or "our old selves again." Expect life to be different following the death of a loved one. Once our life has been touched by tragedy, we will never be the same again. As the parent, your job is to provide support and encouragement, allowing the sadness and heartache to surface. Special occasions such as birthdays, holidays, and anniversaries of a death bring back grief. This is a normal and predictable part of the grieving process. It will be helpful to include your children in planning something special to honor their loved one at those times.

Share your own feelings of loss with your child. Let your child know that you are sad, you miss the loved one, and you think about him or her often. It is okay for your child to see you cry. That lets them know that it is all right for them to cry as well. Just be cautious not to burden your child with your grief so that they shut down and don't want to add to your discomfort by letting you know how they feel. Some adults are afraid that if their child sees them cry, it may create further insecurities for the child. Many children will believe that a loss was not significant if they do not see their parents cry. Others feel they shouldn't cry about the loss because they haven't seen adults cry. Don't be ashamed of your tears, but try not to overwhelm them with displays of emotion.

Don't minimize your child's feelings with comments like, "You're a big girl; you can handle this"; "You don't need to feel that way"; or "Boys need to be strong." If the loss is that a pet has died, don't try to take the hurt away by saying, "We can get another dog." Don't buy a replacement pet immediately. Allow time for the grieving to take place. When we minimize our children's feelings, it sends a clear message that we don't understand what they are going through. Instead, validate their feelings by saying, "This is a very sad time for you"; "I know this is very difficult"; or "I love you and will be here for you." Comments like these let your children know that you are aware of their pain and it's okay for them to feel that way.

After a death, children need to be reassured of your love and your presence. They may feel abandoned or think the death was somehow their fault. Reassure children that the death wasn't their fault. Say "I love you" often and provide as stable an environment as possible. About two months after five-month-old Stevie died, three-year-old Emily was inconsolable. When she was finally calmed down, she said she was afraid "the men were going to come and take her away and she would have to go to heaven too." She was also afraid that one or both of her parents would die. This is a normal fear for young children. I would tell my children, "It is Mommy's plan to be with you for a very long time."

When it comes to feelings, don't use the words should or shouldn't. Don't say, "You shouldn't feel that way," or "You should be doing better by now." That indicates that there is a right or a wrong way to feel. Feelings aren't right or wrong. They just are. The more open you are to your children's feelings, the more willing they will be to share them.

Children feel that adults are at the funeral services for the other adults. Kids have a need to grieve too. When it is age appropriate, I encourage children to attend the funeral. My son had a friend in kindergarten who was killed in a tragic accident. Almost the entire class went to the funeral. They couldn't fully grasp the magnitude of his death, but they knew it was very sad and they would not see Chris again. It was so touching to see child after child pass the coffin and leave a small toy for Chris. Children shouldn't be isolated from their friends and childhood activities during the period of mourning.

A friend of mine recounts, "My son had a marvelous English teacher who had recently lost her son. Knowing my son's dad had died, she shared her experience with him. Although she didn't say, 'I know how you feel,' he clearly got the sense that she had some understanding of his situation. One day, she gave him a flyer for a Teen Age Grief (TAG) group on campus and he decided to go. He

participated in every activity, made new friends, helped other kids
in even more difficult circumstances than his, wrote essays, and put
together collages. It was great for him. I don't think children should
be left to their own devices to come to terms with loss. Sometimes
adults have to intervene, but I think it can be very important to
provide avenues for kids to take advantage of on their own, with the
right support." Look into support groups for your children. Never
suggest that the need for support or counseling is an indication of
weakness or shame. It takes tremendous strength and courage to
look for support.

*We want to assure our children they are a part of our family and
always will be.* A question children often ask is "Is _____ still in
our family?" I love what Maria Shriver wrote about her grandmother
in *What's Heaven?* "Everything she ever taught me is alive in me. She
taught me that it is really important to love my family, to treat others with respect, and to be able to laugh a lot. Most important, she
taught me to believe in myself."[1] Our loved one does live on in us if
we remember what he or she taught us and meant to us. Encourage
your children to keep their loved one alive by remembering what she
taught, how she lived, and letting it show in their lives.

*By observing our children, we can know the right times to share with
them.* The young mother who lost her five-month-old son, Stevie,
shared with me that her daughter was obviously distressed but not
able to put into words what was on her mind. By observing her play,
the mother could see that three-year-old Emily was using her dolls
to act out her concerns. She was playing with her dolls and playing
"hospital" when she said, "I'm very sad the doctors could not make
my doll well. My doll is going away forever and I am very sad." Her
mom told her that most of the time doctors do make us well, and her
doll was all better and wanted to play. By watching her closely, she
could get a sense of when the time was right to initiate a conversation
about Stevie with comments like, "I am really missing baby brother
today, and I know you are too," or "It is okay to talk about Stevie and
how much we miss him."

*Keep an open dialogue with your children about the loved one and the
feelings connected to the loss.* You don't ever want your children to think
that talking about the loved one will hurt you too much, that it is
better left alone, or that time marches on.

Never underestimate the impact a loss or crisis has had on a child. Children's attitudes and concepts about death and tragedy are related not only to their age but to their maturity and experience as well. The way we deal with children must be highly individualized. On the surface, they may seem to adjust to a crisis easily, but this may be a form of self-protection. I never let my parents know how much I was hurting because I didn't want to add to their pain. The real task of completing the grieving process may await children until later in life. If losses pile up on one another, resolution of a new loss will be more difficult.

Unresolved grief from childhood lies in wait for a time when we can deal with it. When my second brother, Larry, who had been in a children's home since he was two, died at twenty years old, I experienced all the emotion that accompanies a loss. It was much greater than I expected. I soon realized that I was reexperiencing the loss and accompanying grief from my childhood and my first brother's death.

Parental mood swings can be frightening to children if they're not discussed. It is appropriate for children to see their parents' sadness, but they need to know the reason for it. I remember one morning when Mom was in a terrible mood. Everything we did seemed to upset her. I was getting mad at her for being so upset with us when Dad asked to speak to me. "Mom is upset today because it is Larry's fifth birthday." He had been in a home since he was two. He had not been a part of our daily lives, and the doctors did not expect him to live to be five. Once I knew what was troubling Mom, I knew not to blame myself. Help the child understand the behavior of adults around them. Explain why Aunt Sally is tearful or Grandpa is silent. A little explanation will go a long way.

Expect some physical indication of your child's grief such as loss of appetite, difficulty falling asleep, or reverting to younger behaviors. You can help the appetite by preparing your child's favorite foods and serving smaller portions and offering quality food more often. To help with sleeping, give back rubs or comforting cuddles, read calming stories, or have gentle music playing in the background. Make the bedtime patterns longer, more relaxed, and with reassurances of your love and presence.

Help your child work through painful times. A friend of mine's husband died when her son was ten. He was very distressed about going to junior high school and having to tell new people that his dad had died, because he was afraid he would cry. She encouraged him to go into the bathroom, run the water, look in the mirror, and say over and over, out loud, "My dad died when I was ten," until the spoken words lost their trigger.

When a Loved One Is Dying

You will be surprised how children have a greater ease than adults do while they visit a terminally ill patient. Be sure to explain where they are going and what they will see. Don't discuss that the person is going to die, but that he or she is very sick, using the correct name of the disease to differentiate between a cold or flu and this condition. We want to show how much we love him or her by going to visit. Remind them they will need to be quiet and gentle, but their visit is very welcomed. Encourage your child to bring a special toy or doll to show the patient or even draw a picture for them. Having something with them will help break the ice and create a more relaxed atmosphere. If your child is a reader or is learning to read, bringing a book they can read to the patient is a good idea as well. The more open and honest you are about the situation, the more at ease your child will be. This time will be cherished by everyone. If your child learns early in life that visiting someone who is ill is a blessing and a comfort, it will help shape their attitudes for the future.

Keep the Memories Alive

Create a photo album or scrapbook that can be filled with special memories, events that were shared. My mother-in-law died before we had any children. I made a scrapbook with a beautiful eight-by-ten color portrait of her at the beginning and filled it with the cards and letters that were written about her. Another friend of mine made her sons "dad-books" the year after he died. There were lots of pictures and letters and condolence notes, as well as professional programs with his photo and biographies, to help them have a permanent impression of the man their dad was.

Provide a journal or sketchbook for writing and drawing remembrances. A journal is a great place to write letters to a loved one and document feelings and experiences. There is often a tremendous release when a child can see in print what they are feeling. Somehow, we don't have to carry our feelings or hold them as tightly once they have been put down on paper. An eight-year-old friend of mine has a workbook called *When Someone Very Special Dies.*[2] In the workbook are some gingerbread man–shaped outlines. Using different colors, she is asked to color what she is feeling in various parts of her body. It is an excellent tool to identify sadness, fear, anger, and happiness. It is also helpful for stimulating conversation. I have encouraged her to use the outlined figures on different days, realizing that some days one feeling is stronger and on other days we feel differently.

Have special keepsakes displayed in a prominent place. Many people have their children's baby booties and hospital bracelets framed or displayed. Try to do for one child what you've done for the others. Keep family photos hanging as an indication that the loved one will never be forgotten. Keep a trophy or award visible; perhaps a special toy or sports ball can be left out for display. These are all little indicators that the loved one is valuable and remembered. It also says, "It's okay to talk about them."

Plant a garden, a rosebush, or a tree in honor of the loved one. When you pick the flowers or vegetables, you can talk about what your child remembers or is feeling. When you work in the garden, you can share memories. One day my first-grade son was late to the pick-up area at school. When I asked what he was doing, he told me, "I was sitting on the bench under Chris's tree because I was thinking about him today." This was a year after Chris died, and the schoolchildren had planted a tree in his honor.

Here are some other things you can do:

- Include the special loved one in drawings.
- Encourage your child to write a poem about his or her memories, activities shared, and how much the loved one is missed.
- Go through pictures of your child with his or her loved one. Talk about special times they shared together so he or she will have positive memories of the deceased. Encourage your child

to tell you when he or she is thinking about the one who's gone and talk together about how much you both miss your loved one.

- Create handmade cards and letters for their loved one. Tell what they've been doing, what their life is like, how the loved one is missed.

- Light a special candle to represent the love you have for the person who has died, especially at holidays and anniversary dates.

- Find things the deceased kept that indicate his or her love for your child, such as the child's photo kept in a wallet, artwork framed or on display which may have been done many years ago, a personal greeting card that has been kept, newsletters or articles your child is mentioned in, a special tie or blouse your child picked out and gave.

- Name a pet or a stuffed animal after the loved one.

- Sing the loved one's favorite songs or watch a favorite movie.

- Celebrate special times like birthdays or holidays with a picnic or party in the loved one's honor. Launch balloons with messages attached to them, bake the loved one's favorite dessert, make a favorite meal, wear the loved one's favorite color, or hike to a special area that was enjoyed with the loved one.

- Encourage your child to continue learning or practicing something the loved one taught her or loved watching her do, such as play soccer, take art classes, or play a musical instrument. Again, this can be done in their honor.

- Another way of helping children cope with death is to create a storybook with them. The book can include their drawings, family photos, or magazine pictures. The book should tell the story of the loved one, how the death occurred, what their feelings are, and what life is like now. Younger children can dictate what they want the book to say. For example, the first page could be: "Molly was happy because she was getting a new baby sister." A middle page could be: "Molly is very sad because her baby sister died." A last page could be: "Molly is still sad sometimes when she thinks about her baby sister, but she is happy when she thinks about meeting her in heaven."

Conclusion

Whatever loss experience your child is facing right now, your reaction, guidance, and understanding are vital for his or her health and healing. Children's feelings need to be handled with compassion and tenderness. Conversations and explanations need to be simple and accurate. Reassure your child that his or her heart is hurting because he or she has so much love for the one who has died. Remember that we all grieve differently. Affirm your child's feelings and acknowledge how much he or she hurts. Never underestimate the impact the loss has on your child. You are the greatest role model your children will ever have. They look to you to learn how to handle these crises. When you invest your time in your children's lives, they will know you care. You can make a difference in their lives. While you can never undo the loss they face, you can hold their hands and walk the path with them, providing your love and support.

Questions to Discuss

1. Trying to stay in touch with your child's feelings is the primary focus following a death. When you feel the timing is conducive to a conversation, ask your child, "Can you tell me how you are feeling?" If their response is "I don't know," say, "Let's figure it out together." Start by asking if they feel mad, sad, scared, hurt, nervous, angry, or lonely.
2. As parents, ask yourselves what is different about your child's behavior. What is he or she struggling with? What seems to be more difficult now? Do you see some new or increased fears? What can you do to provide reassurances to your children?
3. Keep other adults who have contact with your children aware of what is happening with them. Make sure everyone is on the same page about how to answer questions, what your children know, and what fears they have. What is your explanation of heaven? Let others know how you have explained the loss. Include as broad a support team as possible.
4. Should you divert your child's attention anytime he or she brings up the loved one's name?
5. How are your feelings affecting your responses to your children?

For Further Reading

Resources for Adults

Briggs, Lauren Littauer. *The Art of Helping—What to Say and Do When Someone Is Hurting*. Colorado Springs: RiverOak Publishing, 2003.

Fitzgerald, Helen. *The Mourning Handbook*. New York: Simon & Schuster, 1994.

Heavilin, Marilyn Willett. *Roses in December: Finding Strength within Grief*. Eugene, OR: Harvest House Publishers, 1998.

Marshall, Sharon, and Jeff Johnson. *Take My Hand—Guiding Your Child through Grief*. Grand Rapids: Zondervan, 2001.

Yancey, Philip. *Where Is God When It Hurts?* Grand Rapids: Zondervan, 1997.

Resources for Children

Always read any book you select for your child before reading it to him or her.

Brown, Laurie Krasny, and Marc Brown. *When Dinosaurs Die—A Guide to Understanding Death*. New York: Little, Brown and Company, 1996.

Heegard, Marge. *When Someone Very Special Dies: Children Can Learn to Cope with Grief*. Minneapolis: Woodland Press, 1988.

Romain, Trevor. *What on Earth Do You Do When Someone Dies?* Minneapolis: Free Spirit Publishing Inc., 1999.

Sanford, Doris, and Graci Evans. *It Must Hurt a Lot—A Child's Book about Death*. Portland, OR: Multnomah Press, 1985.

Shriver, Maria. *What's Heaven?* New York: Golden Books, 1999.

Vigna, Judith. *Saying Goodbye to Daddy*. Morton Grove, IL: Albert Whitman & Co., 1991.

25

CHILDREN
AND DIVORCE

Archibald D. Hart, Ph.D.

Parents who divorce while they still have young children at home face monumental adjustments. Divorce is both an end and a beginning. It may be the end of a marriage, but it is the beginning of a new set of challenges and changes. Parents are in particular need of compassion and understanding, as the ordeals they face can have far-reaching repercussions. Very few parents who divorce are prepared for it. They find themselves in deep water before they even know what's hit them.

While the future might seem overwhelming, the good news is that there is clear evidence from research showing the effects of divorce that attention to some basic principles can aid recovery and facilitate a constructive experience rather than a traumatic one for all involved. This chapter is all about "transmuting" the tragedy of divorce and turning it into one of positive growth. If divorcing parents will give this recovery process the highest priority, they will most certainly reduce the magnitude of long-term damage—and become changed persons themselves. They will embrace new knowledge, new ideas and beliefs, and new relationship skills and will create a new sense of their own identity.

Divorce Is Never a Good Thing

While I feel very empathic toward those who divorce, I do want to say at the outset that I abhor what divorce does to people. I especially hate what it does to children when the divorcing parents don't take adequate measures to ensure that their children's best interests remain at the top of their agenda for change. I also hate how it makes enemies of those who once declared undying love for each other, and how many, because of the damage the "attachment injury" causes, are hindered in developing their future relationships. And I speak as one who, as a child, experienced the effects of divorce firsthand. However, as a clinician who has been particularly interested in the effects of divorce on children, I can assure my readers that they can influence the final outcome if, with God's help, they commit themselves to a healthy outcome.

Furthermore, let me say that I present here not an endorsement of divorce but a plea to limit the damage it causes for children. It is an unfortunate fact of life that divorce is sometimes unavoidable in a fallen and broken world. Everyone makes mistakes. People change or turn out not to be who you thought they were when you married them. While I believe that everything possible should be done to make marriage work, divorce will happen. Often divorce is forced on one of the parents. They did not instigate it, nor did they choose to be in this state. They are the innocent victims of someone else's sin or misguidedness and would have made any effort to work through their differences if given the chance. But the other party declined and withdrew. Regrettably, the innocent must sometimes suffer pain they don't deserve. However, you can take comfort in this: no matter how inconsiderate their actions, God makes it all right one day. This is the sort of God we worship!

So while marital dissolution is a tragic and sometimes unavoidable consequence for many, I am confident that God can give parents the power to turn their tragedy into something positive for all the innocent parties. So take God's provision for healing broken relationships and move on. He is the God of second chances. Try to focus on what you can do to bring healing to all concerned, especially the children.

The Damaging Effects of Divorce

Before embarking on a discussion of the important remedial actions that need to be taken to prevent the damaging effects of divorce on young children, we need to take an honest look at how and why divorce is not the benign life event that some modern-day soothsayers would have us believe. Divorce is never neutral, and the more you understand how it does its damage, the better equipped you will be to limit such damage.

Someone has described divorce as "the forever funeral." I can think of no more accurate description than this. It is a funeral that never seems to end, a death that never dies. You have to live with the consequences every day of your life. You may no longer be in a marital relationship with the other parent, but your joint parenting responsibilities don't end here, unless you are one of those deadbeat parents who abandon all responsibilities. If anything, parenting becomes more challenging and complex when you are divorced.

Why Does Divorce Hurt Young Children?

Famous child psychologist Dr. Lee Salk once said, "The trauma of divorce is second only to death. Children sense a deep loss and feel they are suddenly vulnerable to forces beyond their control." This statement agrees completely with the research literature, my experience as a clinical psychologist, and my own personal experience as a child. Never again will most of the children of divorce ever have to face as stressful a life event. The acute stress of the shock, the intense fears of the unknown, the feelings of anxiety created by uncertainty and insecurity, and the need to grieve the loss of the traditional family structure are enough to impact the psyches of the strongest of us.

While a small percentage of children of divorced parents might have a natural resilience bestowed by exceptional genes and early life training, and will, therefore, be capable of surviving any emotional trauma, most will need careful attention and intentional help in achieving this resilience. And the starting point is for both of the parents, or at least the parent closest to the child, to find out why and how divorce hurts children. If the parents are not willing or capable to provide this help, then extended family members need to become involved. For me it was the intentional involvement of my grandparents that saved me. Parents need to know where the potentially harmful land mines are hidden so they can chart a safe course across the divorce minefield. It's possible that the parents may have unwittingly planted some of these mines themselves!

Among the more important reasons why divorce, because of its very nature, is damaging to children are the following:

It signals the collapse of the traditional nuclear family. It is this family structure that I believe provides a young child with the safest haven within which the child can learn to be secure and loved. The family breakup makes a young child feel abandoned, lonely, and very frightened. This loneliness can become chronic and long remembered.

The divorce reduces the parents' capacity to parent. They are unavoidably distracted by their own emotions and easily become preoccupied with their own emotional pain and instinctively move to protect their own survival during the critical months (or years) before and after divorce.

The divorce creates conflicts of loyalty in the children, even very young children. Whose side do they take? Whose story do they believe? Often children feel pulled by their love and loyalty in both directions if they are not encouraged to go on loving both, exactly as before, and if parents don't present them with loyalty choices.

Uncertainty about the future causes deep-seated anxieties. The origin of several anxiety disorders can be shaped by how children are affected by the unpredictability of their perceived future. This is where the foundation of such disorders as separation anxiety (my nemesis), generalized anxiety (vague, persistent, and diffuse anxiety about everything), and even some phobias is formed.

The anger and resentment manifested by the parents toward each other, which exists in almost every divorce, intensifies fear in the child. The younger the child, the more damaging this climate of hostility can be. We now know that from a neurobiological point of view, such an environment creates increased stress hormones, especially cortisol flooding, that can impact two critical parts of the human brain: the amygdala (programming for increased fear response) and the hippocampus (diminished memory and new learning abilities). This means that such a child could easily develop learning difficulties and suffer from severe, long-term depression.

Most young children of divorce suffer from some degree of economic descent after divorce. Many literally move into the poor category. Divorce makes all parties poorer, but women and children become the poorest. Divorced women are the new impoverished members of our society. While very young children may not immediately be aware of the drop in their economic status, it begins to impact them as soon as they hit preschool.

Other More General Ways Divorce Affects Young Children

Common as divorce is in our society now, few children are really prepared for it when it happens. They expect it to happen to their friends, not to them. About 80 percent of children receive no warning that a divorce is about to take place. Even if the news is broken slowly and gently, the reaction is nearly always the same (and just as I personally experienced it when my parents divorced): shock, followed by denial, then anger, fear, lowered self-esteem, and depression. Many children also develop a haunting suspicion that they may have been responsible for their parents' problems. I know I did!

If the remaining family has to move, a child may fear losing contact with the other parent and feel the loss of the old home, school, neighborhood, church, and friends. Divorce presents children with a multitude of losses. As any psychologist will tell you, loss causes reactive depression. God has created children, as well as adults, in such a way that unless we are allowed to grieve such losses, there is an increased sensitivity to depression. (See my two books *Unmasking Male Depression* and *Unveiling Depression in Women* for further explanations and help.)

Young children take on much anxiety over their parents' well-being (a sort of role reversal). They worry intensely about their mother, in particular, with the departure of the father (or the father, if it is the wife who leaves), and could continue to be worriers into adulthood.

One of the clearest messages coming to us from the research is that the impact of divorce is selective. Both the timing of the divorce and the age of the children are important factors that determine the outcome. This makes sense. Maturity is a function of age, so the more mature a child is, the better he will be able to deal with the changes that divorce demands. Timing and age are crucial to the outcome. The most damaging age is somewhere around puberty. Children are maximally aware of what is going on but minimally equipped to deal with the stress and change of divorce. Very young children, say under age five, may be less aware but are almost totally dependent on a parent to facilitate the adjustment. If parents fail here, the damage will be lifelong.

How Do Children of Different Ages Respond?

Divorcing parents typically are so caught up in their own conflict that they don't consider when would be a more appropriate time for a divorce to take place. Knowing how children of different ages react can be helpful in deciding on the timing of a marital dissolution. Here is a summary of how divorce impacts children at different ages.

Toddlers

Children two to four years of age often show signs of regression to an earlier stage of development. They become more dependent and passive, engaging in babyish behavior. Rather than feeding themselves, they demand that you feed them, and they revert to a need for diapers even though they may already be potty trained. Some psychologists feel that the absence of the parent of the opposite sex at this stage may be detrimental to a child's sexual development.

Young Children

Children five to eight years of age also regress. In addition, these children tend to take responsibility for the marriage breakup. They tend to develop fears in general, but more specifically irrational fears of being abandoned and even of starving. (I remember at about six years of age, during some of the early threats by my parents to divorce,

I even considered hoarding some food just in case!) These fears need to be confronted and appropriate assurances given to the children that will reduce their fears of what might happen. Loss of sleep, bed-wetting, nail-biting, a deep sense of sadness (often a masked depression), and a retreat into fantasy as a way of solving the family crisis are all likely to occur at this age.

Some authorities believe that this age, when the child is just old enough to know what is going on but not old enough to have adequate skills for adjusting and dealing with it, is a most critical age for children to experience divorce. Special precautions need to be taken to protect the child at this age. These precautions will be discussed later.

Older Children

Children nine to twelve years of age experience anger as the dominant emotion. This anger is usually directed at the parent believed to be the initiator of the breakup, but it is easily scapegoated outside of the family and directed at peers just at a time when the support of loving friends is most needed. Children may alienate those close to them, including teachers and close relatives.

The spiritual development of the child is most likely to be damaged at this age. Disappointment, disillusionment, and rejection of the parents' spiritual values could easily occur. "They are just hypocrites and I don't want to have anything to do with their religion" is a very common reaction.

Teenagers

Children thirteen years of age and over have a different set of problems to deal with. They tend not to assume blame for the divorce as readily as younger children do because they have a better understanding of the reasons for the divorce. Nevertheless, they can also be deeply hurt and resent their parents for breaking up the home. They fear being separated from their friends, and as there is a natural tendency toward withdrawing and feeling depressed at this age, a divorce could accentuate these problems. It is common for them to isolate themselves and refuse to talk about what's bothering them. Teenagers also feel the loyalty dilemma acutely. They know their mother doesn't want them to like their father (or vice versa). "How can you like someone who has done this terrible thing to me?" or "Don't you know what a terrible person he (or she) is?" is typical of parental attitudes that create conflicts for teenagers. Keeping the peace with both parents can be emotionally draining for them.

Which of the Sexes Suffers Most?

Many psychologists believe that young boys are harder hit by divorce than girls. The reasons are not hard to discern:

It is usually the father who leaves and becomes the nonresident parent. With careful planning, the effect of this absence can be reduced, but the fact remains that "Daddy doesn't live here anymore." Boys feel the effects of this more than girls because of the expected boy-boy connection.

Boys are not taught in our culture how to show or experience their painful emotions. They are told, "Boys don't cry; boys have got to be *men.*" Boys, therefore, tend to deny their negative emotions more than girls do; this denial can be the source of the emotional constrictiveness many men exhibit later in life.

More is expected of boys in these circumstances, especially by fathers who feel guilty. They are expected to be stronger, more resilient, more capable of taking care of themselves, but this is not necessarily true. When their defenses break down, boys are often more devastated than girls are.

While boys are considered to be at greater risk, there is now a growing body of evidence that the risk is changing for girls. The disengagement of divorced fathers from their daughters, especially at an early age, is becoming a very serious concern. The daughters of divorce are now evidencing delayed effects, consequences that may only show up when they marry. In other words, they experience the onset of their problems much later than boys. *The truth is that girls need a father as much as boys do—no matter what their age. Never believe otherwise!*

Healing the Effects of Divorce

My discussion here will focus primarily on younger children because of their particular vulnerability, but the principles can be applied across the age board.

First, let me say that divorce is always a symptom of some larger relationship breakdown. It often involves a breakdown of trust or some serious betrayal on the part of one party. This being so, parents cannot bring healing to their children until they first have brought healing to their own conflict. Most divorcing parents don't get this point. Either they want to just forget the breakdown, or at the other extreme, they are still so hurt by the betrayal that they cannot let it go. Feelings run hot and cold, and the resentment fire is stoked by everything that happens. Divorce may temporarily ease the immediate pain associated with the marital conflict, but it is then replaced with a different sort of emotional pain. Very hard work lies ahead, and you cannot become an effective parent again until you have regained your footing and begun to repair the damage done to your person.

Most divorcing couples also don't understand that divorce follows a long emotional trajectory. What one feels now may not be what one feels a week from now. Your pain and grief will at times seem unbearable. When you think you've gotten over your resentment, it raises its ugly and painful head again. In addition, coparenting is very challenging when you are still fighting to survive. Because this chapter does not address these aspects of your healing, I would strongly recommend that you seek out either a divorce recovery group or individual counseling to help you through this task.

As you focus on your own personal healing, keep in mind the following important points:

While you may have failed in your marriage, you can still be tremendously successful in your parenting. The two are not related.

God's power to heal far exceeds the depth of your pain and confusion. "No temptation has seized you except what is common to man. And God is faithful; he will not let you be tempted beyond what you can bear. But when you are tempted, he will also provide a way out so that you can stand up under it" (1 Cor. 10:13).

Even if your former spouse was not a good partner, it doesn't mean he or she cannot be a good parent. Your responsibility is to ensure that he or she gets a fair shot at trying to be a good parent—which is one of the reasons your healing is so important—so that it doesn't get in the way of your child's adjustment.

The longer the conflict continues between your former spouse and yourself after divorce, the greater will be the risk that your child will suffer some long-term damage as a result of the divorce. It may not seem that the ongoing bitterness or arguments between the two of you have any direct effect on your child, but even if you continued this conflict out of their sight, it will show through in a thousand ways. Slips of the tongue, glances, subtle gestures, snide remarks, whatever, will maintain your child's stress at a high level.

Above all else try to avoid any feelings of helplessness. The human body and mind are designed to withstand an enormous amount of distress, but what they don't tolerate well is a feeling of helplessness. You need to put yourself, through faith in God, in the place of control. You and God, nobody else, determine your future, so claim control over it. Feelings of helplessness lead to hopelessness and depression. You'll have enough grieving to do as it is without compounding it with more depression.

Increasing Resiliency in Children

Building your child's resiliency (ability to roll with the punches, bounce back, get up when down) in this divorce period can go a long way toward making your child a healthier person, so keep in mind the following factors that are known to help children avoid long-term damage as a result of divorce:

The healthiness of each parent. The healthiness of one or the other or, better still, both parents, will shape the quality of the postdivorce bonding between each parent and the child. It is just a plain, simple truth that healthiness begets healthiness. When parents are open and honest with their emotions, the children learn to be honest with theirs. When parents model forgiving for their hurts, the children learn how to do so also. Make some special effort, therefore, to become a healthy person, even if it means undertaking a period of psychotherapy. Unfortunately, our society doesn't offer such help on a day-by-day basis.

The parenting styles of each parent. How each or both parents parent, their styles, also will shape their child's resiliency. Parents who are punitive in their style (always punishing, criticizing, angry, or resentful) will create a child who is so insecure that he or she will not know how to bounce back. They will get stuck in self-defeating behaviors for fear that if they deviate and try new behaviors, they will be punished. Accepting, unconditionally loving parenting styles are the breeding ground for resiliency because they allow the child to experiment and find new ways of behaving.

The protection and enhancement of the child's self-esteem. A healthy self-esteem (I never call it "high" self-esteem) requires two essential building blocks:

1. Accurate knowledge about oneself (we call this an accurate self-concept). To achieve this parents must be honest, realistic, and reassuring in all their dealings. When a child feels deficient in an area, explore other areas where a child can feel a sense of accomplishment. Don't force your child to be something he or she is not.
2. Complete self-acceptance. We all have to come to terms with our shortcomings. No one is perfect or competent at everything. Parents who help their child to accept their shortcomings, while at the same time helping them to stretch beyond their comfort zone, will maximize their child's healthy self-esteem, especially at a time when the family is no longer united.

Precautions to Keep in Mind

Young children, especially those under age five, are particularly vulnerable to the damaging effects of divorce. While they may not be fully aware of what is going on or what the implications of divorce are, they nevertheless are aware enough to be impacted by this disruption. Furthermore, the divorce is not instantly over the moment papers are signed. Judith Wallerstein, perhaps the most effective researcher in this field, has consistently found that the impact of divorce gets greater as the child gets older. The most difficult time for a child may not be at the time when the parents divorce, but when they grow up and face the many complications associated with blended families, divided loyalties, and the like. Parents can usually get over divorce in about three years, but children take much longer. Many suffer from such problems as alcohol and drug abuse, precocious sex, and school problems before they reach age fourteen. Special attention to the following can help to reduce these risks:

- Parents who are honest to admit that they are not good role models need to invoke the help of extended family members, especially grandparents. Speaking from personal experience, I believe it was my grandparents who saved my emotional life. I will forever be thankful for their presence in my life.

- Give your children permission to grieve and allow them adequate time to grieve. I believe that grieving the losses associated with divorce is perhaps the greatest challenge facing children. I trust that some of the resources listed at the end of this chapter will provide help here.

- If you are a custodial mother, do everything possible to facilitate and encourage the father to stay involved in the parenting task. Too often out of resentment, mothers want to exclude fathers or allow stepfathers to usurp the real father's role. Unless the father is a total deadbeat or psychotic, this can have disastrous consequences.

- Absent fathers, on the other hand, must make extra effort to be consistent in their parenting tasks. Keep your promises, show that you are a man of your word, make extra sacrifices if necessary, and make your children feel that they are the most important of all God's creation. If you do these things, they will bless you all the days of your life.

- Both parents must avoid using their children as pawns in the dirty game of revenge. Spying, tattletaling, sabotaging, squealing, or using one parent against the other will backfire every time.

Conclusion

In closing, I think that the most important advice I can give the reader is this: Spend a lot of time in prayer. No handbook, no matter how brilliantly conceived and written, can substitute for the wisdom that God can give you as he journeys with you through this dark valley. He can foster patience, give you the grace to be Christ-like in all your interactions, and instill in you a deep reassurance that one day he will make all matters right. Sometimes it takes supernatural power to overcome overwhelming obstacles. Accept that your task of aiding your children to turn their apparent catastrophe into a positive, growth-producing experience is a God-given task. Approach it as a spiritual discipline that not only will help your child but will draw you closer to God and foster your own spiritual growth in the process. Forge a partnership with God in this task of transmuting the devastation of divorce with the same determination as you would if you were embarking on some great missionary task. In other words, treat it as you would a spiritual task as holy as any calling, because that is what it is. Remain faithful in it, and God's response, "Well done my good and faithful servant," will await you as it does all who do his purposes.

Questions to Discuss

1. Why do you think some divorces are more damaging to some children than to others?
2. Of the reasons given early in this chapter for why divorce is damaging to children, which, for you, would be the top three? Rank them in order of seriousness, and give your reasons.
3. What are the primary factors that parents must address in themselves in order to be helpful to their children?
4. Discuss three specific precautions that parents can take to prevent their divorce from being harmful to their children.
5. From what you have read in this chapter, under what, if any, conditions do you think divorce could lead to a positive outcome for the children of divorce?

For Further Reading

Hart, Archibald D. *Helping Children Survive Divorce*. Nashville: Word Publications, 1996.

Hart, Archibald D. *Growing Up Divorced: For Adults Who Once Suffered the Trauma of Their Parents' Divorce*. Ann Arbor, MI: Servant Publications, 1991.

Todd, Karen, and Nancy Barros. *Parenting Through Divorce*. New York: Motivo, 1995.

Wallerstein, Judith S., Julia Lewis, and Sandra Blakeslee. *The Unexpected Legacy of Divorce*. New York: Hyperion, 2001.

Wallerstein, Judith S., and Sandra Blakeslee. *What About the Kids? Raising Your Children Before, During and After Divorce*. New York: Hyperion, 2003.

Weyburne, Darlene. *What to Tell Your Kids About Divorce*. Oakland: New Harbinger Publications, 1999.

26

CHILDREN IN THE SINGLE-PARENT FAMILY

Thomas A. Whiteman and Randy Petersen

I was eavesdropping the other day. Enjoying a business dinner at a local restaurant, I noticed a family I knew at another table. They were friends from church, and I knew I'd say hi later, but for now I just wanted to observe them. Sandy was the mom, and she had four kids: seventeen, fifteen, twelve, and nine. They all seemed well mannered at church, but how would they behave out in the real world? What was this family really like?

Shortly after the youngest was born, Sandy's husband left her. You can do the math. That left her with four kids under ten years of age. You would expect those children to grow up with major problems, to act unruly, to be in trouble at school. You'd forgive Sandy if her kids turned out to be holy terrors, even juvenile delinquents. Even the best mom would have difficulty rearing four youngsters by herself.

But here they were sharing a family dinner, showing kindness to one another, actively listening as one child after another had a chance to speak, even practicing good table manners. These were kids any parent would be proud of. I mentioned that to Sandy when I stopped by their table on my way out. I've spent my career helping people pick up the pieces of their lives and their families after the tragedy of divorce. It's encouraging to see a family that has survived, and not only survived but thrived.

"Well, we've had our hard times too," Sandy shrugged. Of course they had. Single-parenting is tough stuff, with many built-in obstacles, but Sandy's family demonstrates that it can be done. Parenting is clearly a job built for two, but if you're forced to go it alone, it is possible to succeed.

Surveying the Situation

How do people become single parents? Usually through tragedy. Divorce is the leading cause of single-parent situations, and of course marital breakups bring a host of emotional issues. So not only must you confront the built-in difficulties of the single-parent home, but everyone in that home is wounded, making it all the harder to succeed. The situation I've seen most often is when the husband leaves the wife and children, sometimes to start a new relationship elsewhere. Of course, the remaining family must deal with a sense of abandonment. In some cases, the wife walks out, leaving the husband to care for the family. This can be even more devastating. Sometimes the mother will take the children with her when she moves out. This creates an extra level of adjustment, as the children must get used to a new home as well as a fractured family. Increasingly we see parents splitting up by mutual decision and agreeing to share custody of the children in some way. While this might seem to be the least traumatic situation, it still leaves emotional wounds on everyone involved.

Some single-parent families are created through the death of one parent. In such cases, the remaining family members have to cope with their grief and probably considerable shock as well.

Nowadays we also see single people adopting children, and many single women are choosing to bear children to bring up by themselves, but these nontragic circumstances are still the minority of cases. Most single-parent families have gone through divorce, so forgive me if I focus on that situation primarily.

The problems of single parents fall into five major categories: energy, money, emotions, inconsistency, and new relationships.

Energy

"I'm just so tired all the time!"

I've heard that refrain sung again and again by single parents. It's not hard to figure out why. Children place substantial demands on single parents, and in addition most single parents are coming out of traumatic experiences themselves. Energy gets sapped quickly, and this can create a snowball effect: life gets tougher when you can't keep up with it, making it even harder to keep up. But there are some ways you can use your strength more efficiently, maybe getting ahead for a change rather than falling behind.

Let's look first at the reasons for this lack of energy, then at the consequences, and finally at some practical remedies.

Why Is Lack of Energy Such a Problem?

The emotional rigors of divorce or bereavement take their toll. In my divorce recovery counseling, I often speak of a slippery slope that people slide down as they deal with divorce. It's a series of emotions common to emotional trauma. You might know them as the stages of grief. Of course, the stages apply to single parents who are grieving the death of a spouse as well as those who are recovering from divorce.

Generally, people begin with denial and then progress through anger, bargaining, and depression, finally reaching a point of acceptance. (I also see a stage of forgiveness at the end.) This progression isn't clockwork, and people often slip back to a previous stage (hence the slippery slope), but I've seen this pattern again and again. The early stages can have high energy, as a person works to keep things the way they were (denial) or rails in anger against the former spouse. Bargaining is the hardest stage to understand, but it often consists of desperate attempts to change the circumstances and undo the divorce—again, high energy. But then comes depression. You come to the end of your efforts and just give up. You sink into the sadness of your situation.

The depression stage can last for a year or more. At this point, people are not only sad but *weary*. They've tried everything and nothing works. What's the use? They drag through their days doing the bare minimum, and still they feel worn out. They wouldn't mind staying in bed all day. Some do.

Well-meaning friends try to cheer you up. Or they might prod you to get moving, to get busy, to get your life back in gear. Some Christians preach to depressed folks about the joy of the Lord. Sometimes these approaches help, but not usually. They might serve to distract the depressed person, but they seldom supply the needed energy.

The fact is it's not a problem of the will or the spirit. The person has been wounded emotionally, and it takes time for those wounds to heal. A grieving person *needs* to be depressed for a certain time. If you rush that process, you can tumble back down the slope. No one really knows how long they need to be in depression, and some do languish longer than necessary, which is why the cheering up strategy sometimes works.

The physical requirements of divorce or bereavement can weary you. Especially in the immediate aftermath of a divorce/separation or the death of a spouse, there's a lot of stuff to do. There might be court appearances, visitation arrangements, perhaps a move to a new house, credit cards to change, financial arrangements, insurance settlements. All of these details pile up on you when you're least able to cope with them.

The household responsibilities previously shared by two parents are now loaded onto one. It's simply a matter of supply and demand. The demands of the household are just as great, perhaps greater, but the supply of parents has been cut in half. The single parent is trying to do the work of two people. Can it be done? Sure, but it's tiring.

"As a single parent of two preschool boys," one woman told me, "I found my life going through an overwhelming set of changes. At first, I was too depressed to be of any good to anyone, including my boys. But as I moved along, I became determined that I was going to overcome my circumstances. That led me to my superwoman role, where I tried to do everything by myself. I took a full-time job, arranged day care for the boys, ran the home, and tried to maintain a social life. I wanted to take the place of their missing father, but what I found was that I was becoming more and more frustrated, and the boys were usually mad at me. What a terrible feeling!"

The children are needier now because they have gone through this breakup too. They need more assurance and more attention, and they're more likely to act out. All of that puts an even greater burden on the parent.

Remember those stages of grief? Kids go through them too. They will deny and rage and bargain and sulk, perhaps for months at a time. The parent needs to play amateur psychologist, but that's hard to do when you get worn out just popping dinner into the microwave.

What Effect Does This Lack of Energy Have?

More than anything, it creates a downward spiral. You come home weary from work, so you don't have time to cook a balanced meal, so you and your kids snack on sugar products, which makes you all crazier and more exhausted. You don't feel like keeping your home in order, so it takes longer to find the things you need, which makes you more tired, and so on.

Children of an exhausted single parent can feel neglected. In the best cases, they step up and learn to fend for themselves, but of course this is difficult for younger children. One single mother told me of a time when she could hardly get out of bed. She put her baby daughter's crib next to her own bed and just fed the girl Ritz crackers whenever she cried. She shudders now when she thinks back on it, and she's amazed that her daughter grew up healthy, but her story isn't that rare. Many single parents sink into their lethargy, and the children suffer.

What Can You Do about This Lack of Energy?

Practice wise conservation of your personal resources. It's as if you have a quarter tank of gas in your car and a full day of errands to run. You have to plan things out, combine your trips, and make best use of every mile. Don't waste effort on pointless activities. I know people who get too tired to go to bed, so they sprawl in front of the TV until the wee hours of the morning. As much as possible, discipline your-self to eat right, sleep steady hours, and exercise regularly. (If you don't overdo it, a steady exercise pattern should stimulate your energy rather than sap it.) Say no to extra commitments at church or in the community, but hang on to one or two activities that will energize you. Be careful about addictions. In times of low energy, people are especially susceptible to temptation, whether that's alcohol, drugs, smoking, gambling, shopping, pornography, or something else. Those activities promise relief but only make matters worse.

Be satisfied with less. I already mentioned the single mom who tried to be Superwoman. Later she said, "I'm settling for doing the best I can and spending whatever time I can with the boys. It's like I wanted 100 percent before, and now I'm settling for 75 percent. But at least I might preserve my sanity this way, and who knows, maybe I'll even enjoy a few days." That's the secret. In this time of adjustment, you might have to lower some standards. The house won't be completely clean, you won't get all your work done, and you can't attend every soccer game your kids play in. Give yourself a break. Some newly divorced parents make it a personal challenge to live just as well after the divorce as before, in order to prove that they didn't need that partner anyway. That's a silly way to think, and it can be damaging. *Of course* your life will be tougher after your marriage is ripped apart! Don't try to pretend otherwise.

Delegate chores to your children. There's a long list of tasks involved in maintaining your household: cutting the grass, walking the dog, taking out the trash, maintaining the car, and so on. Quite simply, you need to find someone to do the things your spouse used to do. Go through the list and see how many might be capably done by your kids. A certain amount of responsibility is great for children, and you might even have to ask them to cut back on some of their outside activities. But be sure not to overburden your children. Make sure their tasks are age-appropriate and matched up with their own abilities. Your nine-year-old won't tune up the car, but could walk the dog. Allow for a learning curve as they get used to their new tasks. Demand an honest effort, but don't get too upset if things aren't done perfectly. Let them be children.

Get help from outside the home. The kids are not enough! You're going to need other adults to help you. Can you ask your parents or other relatives or neighbors or friends from church to baby-sit occasionally? Can you swap baby-sitting with other single parents in your church? As you go through that list of chores your spouse used to do, how many can you get outsiders to cover? And I know there are emotional issues involved, but is it possible to ask your ex-spouse to help out with certain needs involving the kids?

But we're not just talking about chores. You need a support network of adult friends who can cheer you on and counsel you in your neediest moments. I often see single parents leaning too hard on their children for emotional support. Yes, there is love and support within the family, but your son or daughter (especially under twelve) simply does not have the emotional resources to be your confidant or best friend or counselor. The oldest son does not become the man of the house. The oldest daughter does not become the homemaker. They may assume some responsibilities in the home, but be very careful about treating them too much like your former spouse. They might even want to fill those shoes, but they can't. Make sure you get the emotional support you need from other adults.

Money

Money isn't everything, but it is woven through our lives. The onset of

The Chores Game

Most children complain that they have too many chores to do. Try to make the chores that have to be done around the house as fair and fun as possible. Do this in a family meeting where everyone can discuss the chores they don't mind and the ones they hate the most. Allow free discussion without judgment. Once everyone (including you) has spoken, let them know that everyone has to help even though the task is not always enjoyable. You might start off by listing the tasks you are willing to do. Or you could even turn it into a game.

Write each chore on a three-by-five-inch card. For each chore card, write a privilege card (a trip to the mall, lunch at McDonald's, a back rub, one hour of video games—whatever you or your children might enjoy).

Then deal all of the cards to all of the players. Each player gets one chore card for every privilege card. Be sure each family member gets an equal number of chores and privileges.

The players can now look at their "hands" and go around the circle trading chores and privileges. To make the game more interesting, add additional privileges so that you can wheel and deal more. For example, offer someone two hours of video games and a back rub in exchange for doing the laundry.[1]

single-parenting, whether it's through divorce, death, or adoption, often creates new financial pressures in a home.

In the case of divorce, there is simply the fact that one major breadwinner is gone. Sometimes alimony and child support can make up for that, but often there is still an economic shortfall. Sometimes there are related adjustments in the practicalities of daily life. A family might move from a house to an apartment, might trade the minivan for a compact car, or might cancel a planned vacation.

What Are the Effects of This Money Crunch in Single-Parent Homes?

Children often feel disappointed when they have to adjust to a poorer lifestyle. They might have gotten used to some of the finer things in life. Perhaps they've always received whatever toys or gadgets they wanted, and now you can't afford them. Maybe they were looking forward to a family vacation or a new family car, and now that can't happen. It's natural for them to feel sad about these dashed hopes.

That disappointment can lead to a feeling of being cheated. And that might lead them to blame you. They'd be playing with the latest video-game system if it weren't for you and your divorce! This creates a dynamic of tension in the home, especially because you might already be feeling guilty. Actually, the money issue can serve to focus a lot of the anger brewing in children. They might find it hard to talk about the emotional pain they have suffered, but they can yell at you for depriving them of that trip to Disney World.

While it's difficult for you to bear the brunt of these angry outbursts, it's actually healthy for your children to express these feelings. But don't let them send you on a guilt trip. The whole household is suffering right now, and everyone's disappointed, but now is the time for the whole family to work together to create a good life for all.

In the school-age years, children tune in quickly to the economic divisions of society. No doubt the school has its rich kids and poor kids. The ones with the finest clothes and the latest accessories are often more popular, and your children might be afraid that they will now drop a few rungs on that socioeconomic ladder. They might be able to deal with their personal disappointments, but how will this affect their status? They are learning that it's a cruel world out there, and they don't want to lose their edge.

Certainly, all of these underlying emotions make your money troubles more complicated, but you also have a great opportunity to refocus your family's priorities. Jesus said, "Blessed are the poor." Wealth often distracts people from the things that really matter. It's impossible to serve both God and money. As we store our treasures in heaven, we can seek first his kingdom, and he will care for our basic needs. Your economic struggles will affect your children, but probably for the better. They now have the opportunity to grow into well-rounded people who will see past all the hot new gadgets and flashy clothes and truly honor God with their lives.

What Can You Do about These Financial Challenges?

Have a family meeting. Talk openly about the challenges you will all face. Let your children voice their disappointments, and apologize if promises have been broken. If you might need to move to a smaller home, prepare the kids for that. Do not fuel their fears, but model a sense of trust. They will be cared for; you will make sure of that. And together you will trust God to get you through this tough time.

Put money in its place. Keep teaching your children how trivial money is in the grand scheme of things. Money can't buy happiness, and you will find greater happiness as a family as you enjoy life's simpler pleasures together.

Downscale. You have some immediate financial needs, and you must do what it takes to meet those. Beg, borrow, or, well, don't steal, but you might have to rob your savings account. But you probably can't continue to live at your current level of expenses. (In some cases, single-parent families are well supported through alimony and child support, but if that's your situation, you're probably not reading this section. I'm assuming that you have a significant drop in your family income.) Look through your budget and cut the fat.

Be creative in low-cost alternatives. At a church in Baltimore, one Saturday each month a mechanic offers to check the cars of any single mothers in the congregation. He'll do simple tune-ups and oil changes free of charge. I wish more churches were that creative in meeting needs of single parents. What could be done with consortiums of parents sharing resources, games, toys, or hand-me-down clothes? You may need to create such programs in your church or neighborhood.

Get a long-term financial plan. Don't stop with your immediate stop-gap measures. Look at the big picture, five, ten, twenty years down the road. How will you make more money and save more money over that time period? Will you need to find a different job? Will you need training for that? Avoid get-rich-quick schemes that promise wealth within a year or two. You need to be patient, but plan for long-term solvency.

Seek help, but avoid con artists. You might need to see a financial adviser to put together your immediate budget or your long-term plan, but watch out for shysters. Ask church friends or relatives to recommend a financial adviser you can trust.

Emotions

Whether you are dealing with divorce or the death of a spouse, you are on an emotional roller coaster. At least for the first two years, and perhaps for as many as five, you will experience a wide range of emotions: anger, pain, depression, determination, frustration, and more.

Someone bumps you, and you fly off the handle. You don't always understand how you are feeling, but you are always on edge. Any little thing can set you off.

Adding to the problem is that your kids are also on this roller coaster, and they understand it even less than you do. So they might cry for no reason, which sets you off, which bothers them, which frustrates you—you get the picture. It's almost as if you carpeted your home with mousetraps. Any little misstep sets off a chain reaction.

One problem with emotions is that they aren't sharpshooters. Emotions fly free, and they hit anyone in their path. You might be angry with your ex, but then your child misbehaves, so you unleash your anger on your kid.

What's the Effect of All These Emotions?

People are amazingly resilient emotionally. God made us to deal with all sorts of situations and to heal from all sorts of pain. That includes kids. Earlier I mentioned the stages of grief, a pattern of emotional responses to trauma. These are natural and normal. Just as a broken bone heals in a month or so, our emotions are designed to heal in a year or two, following a certain progression of emotions. The problem comes when we get stuck in certain stages of our emotional recovery. You might get stuck in denial, or anger, or depression, and that will affect your children. Or they might get stuck in any of those stages.

There's no set timetable. Generally, a stage lasts as long as it needs to. When you are emotionally ready to accept the facts of the situation, you move out of denial. When you've let all your anger out, you move out of that stage. When you've grieved sufficiently in the depths of depression, you wake up one day and get on with your life. However, there are often rewards and obstacles that complicate that process, especially in a family situation. A child might be taught not to display anger, or a parent might withhold it for the sake of the children. A child might learn that living in denial makes life easier on Mommy, or that displays of anger attract some much-needed attention.

As a result, a family sort of crawls, amoeba-like, up the slippery slope of emotions, toward an eventual acceptance of the divorce (or the death). Individual family members can help one another forward or hold one another back.

Guilt is another factor that adds to the complexity of this emotional recovery in homes dealing with divorce. In some cases, children take on guilt for "driving Mommy or Daddy away." But even more common is parental guilt, especially as the custodial parent observes the effects of the breakup on the kids. "Have we scarred them for life?" is a frequent question, whenever a kid acts out on the playground or cries herself to sleep. Such guilt can hinder a parent from parenting normally. (Kids can also pick up on that guilt and leverage it to skew the family dynamics in their favor.) The whole truth is that you are always in a process of *shaping* your kids for life. All your decisions affect them, and the divorce will too. Everyone suffers hurt and bears certain emotional scars, but God has given us the ability to recover from the wounds of life. Your kids can recover nicely from the divorce if you continue to parent wisely.

What Can You Do about This Range of Emotions?

Relax, and let the emotional roller coaster run. Don't overreact to the normal ups and downs. There will be tears and tirades, false hopes and dashed dreams. Be there when necessary to comfort, discipline, and explain. Don't rush your kids through the stages. Let them move through at their own pace. And let yourself heal at your own pace. Don't be alarmed if you seem easily irritated or suddenly sad. That's all part of the process.

Be careful about how you express your emotions. Your emotions will swoop and career all over the place, but you need to be responsible for how you express them. "In your anger, do not sin," the Bible says. Your kids will fuel your ire, to be sure, but control your temper. Don't hit your kids in anger, and be aware of how deeply your words can wound them. Find other outlets for your angry feelings. Have a friend on call to hear your outbursts. Get a punching bag, or just beat the living daylights out of your mattress. When you hit depression, be sure your kids are cared for. You will have even less energy than usual, so ask a friend to check up on you. I repeat: These emotions are normal, but they can still be hurtful. You are still responsible for what you do with them.

Avoid the guilt trap with smart self-talk. Guilt feelings will clog up the whole process. You might need to give yourself regular pep talks. It won't help to pretend that you are guiltless; we are all sinners. In the case of divorce, you might bear a portion of the blame, whether five percent or fifty. Go to God with that. Confess whatever sins there are and then let go of them. What's past is past. Now trust God to work with you to redeem the present situation. Capsulize the truths you need as reminders and repeat them to yourself as necessary.

Learn to talk about your feelings with your kids. "I'm angry right now, so just tiptoe around me, all right?" "I'm really sad right now, so give me a hug and let me go to bed. Can you make your own sandwiches for dinner?" "I know you had a good time with your father, and I'm glad you did, but I'm feeling weird about him right now and I'd rather not hear all about it. Can we talk about that tomorrow?" If you learn to talk openly about your crazy mix of emotions, not only will your kids understand you better, but they'll learn how to talk about *their* emotions as well.

Find a friend who will listen. You need emotional support, and the best therapist is a good friend. Sometimes those who are recently divorced or bereaved find themselves without friends. Their spouse had been their confidant, and they didn't cultivate other friendships. And, sadly, some fair-weather friends drift away when you need them most. (I've seen this most often among other couples when their friends divorce, almost as if it's an infectious disease.) In any case, you might need to go looking for someone to support you in this time: a relative, a neighbor, a coworker, a friend from church. And you might find the greatest sympathy from someone who has gone through a similar struggle.

How Children React to Divorce

Reactions will vary according to the child's developmental level and personality, but generally you can expect some of the following:

Underreaction. This may be a form of denial and the beginnings of the grieving process. Don't be surprised when your child reacts with, "Can I go out and play now?" Some parents are happily surprised at this: "Brenda seems to be dealing very nicely with our divorce." Only years later the buried feelings emerge in a much more dangerous way. At some point, when your child is ready, you may need to urge him or her to let it all out, to express all the rage or sadness or fear that he or she feels. This may be painful for you, but it is important for the child to have opportunities to express feelings, even years after the event.

Preoccupation with egocentric thoughts. In certain developmental stages, children cannot help but react in self-centered ways. Your child may react with, "What about my birthday?" or "Who's going to take me to Disney World?" These are merely concrete expressions of fear for the future. Your child needs reassurance of how he or she fits into your new life.

Lack of interest in the details of the breakup. This reaction might reflect the child's inability to comprehend the news and fear of talking about it. They may have no questions. Keep the lines of communication open. After your initial discussion, create ongoing opportunities for the children to express their concerns.

Strong, hysterical reaction. It is possible for a child to respond with rage and flagrant misbehavior. The rage is a natural emotional reaction and this behavior is probably an attempt to manipulate the parents' decisions or at least to register a protest.

It takes courage on the part of the parents to understand the children's feelings and allow the children to express their pain. This will accelerate acceptance and growth on the part of the child.[2]

Find a therapist, if need be. You might not need expert help, but if you suspect that you or your kids are getting stuck in certain stages of recovery, or if you see serious symptoms in yourself or the kids (violence, extreme or extended lethargy, inability to face reality), see a pro. Your pastor might be able to do some basic counseling and could probably recommend a psychologist if necessary. Your health insurance might cover the costs, but even if you have to pay out of pocket, it's worth it. The best gift you can give your kids is a healthy parent.

You might end up with a psychiatrist who prescribes certain medication, probably an antidepressant. I know some Christian counselors who frown on medication, but I don't, especially in the case of single parents. You've got a job to do, and you have to do it. If an antidepressant can help you do the work of parenting your kids while you get through this tough time, great!

Inconsistency

Children want structure, rules, sureties. As they get to know the world around them, they count on certain certainties. Divorce, or the loss of a parent, shakes those certainties. They need to restore a kind of equilibrium as soon as possible.

That's tough with shared parenting. When kids are shuttled back and forth between two households, they have to make some major adjustments. They will. But it just takes some work. The two households might have different house rules, which they'll have to learn.

They also have to revise their expectations. Perhaps Mom and Dad promised a Disney vacation, and with the divorce, that won't happen.

Lack of energy on the part of the custodial parent can also mean that the parent doesn't follow through on promises, or threats. "Do that one more time and you're grounded for a week!" You can bet your kid will test you. If you're not ready for that fight, don't make that threat.

What's the Effect of Parental Inconsistency on the Family?

In the last several decades, researchers have studied children of divorce. The results are a mixed bag of positives and negatives.

Clearly, divorce affects children deeply, but it doesn't prevent them from living good lives. Still, there are certain common characteristics, and many of these can be traced back to the basic inconsistencies of parenting in a single-parent home.

Single-parent children have difficulty with trust. This can keep them from committing themselves fully in relationships as adults.

The single-parent family tends toward role reversals, a lack of clear boundaries, and constant transitions. Children take on parental responsibilities, and thus they rush into adulthood. They can feel pressure from those responsibilities, and they often lack a sense of safety and security in the home.

Children from single-parent families do not know how a normal family functions. As a result, their own relationships in adulthood can suffer.

Children from single-parent families have a tendency toward low self-worth and chronic underachievement. This occurs mainly in homes where blame is tossed around. Children feel responsible for the broken home, unable to hold things together.

Children from single-parent families have difficulty with open communication. The disappointments of their home life can lead them to a policy of "Don't talk, don't feel, don't trust."

The single-parent child can be irresponsible or rebellious. Lack of structure in the home leads to lack of personal discipline.

Scary, huh? Let me underscore that these are *tendencies*, not certainties. I have seen a number of fairly healthy single-parent homes in which children grow up to be loving, mature, expressive people. The tendencies can be overcome, but you have to work at it.

What Can You Do to Avoid Inconsistency in the Home?

Coparent with your ex. Unless there is the suspicion of abuse, the custodial parent should make sure the kids have an ongoing relationship with the noncustodial parent. This isn't always easy. You and your ex disagree on many things, no doubt, and childrearing might be one point of contention. But it's more important for the children to know two loving parents than for everything to be done exactly "right." Support that relationship even when you have disagreements.

Communicate thoroughly about family policies with your children and your ex. Maybe you have house rules in your home, and the rules are different with your ex. The kids will understand that if you make it clear. Compare notes with your ex about the rules of bedtime, homework, and behavior, but don't make a federal case of it. You can't control what your ex does, but you can make matters consistent in your home.

Watch your mouth. Be careful about making idle threats or promises. "If you do that, I'll ground you!" Chances are, you'll be tested. Don't make a threat unless you're willing to carry it out. And don't make a promise you can't fulfill.

Learn to apologize. You are going to screw up. Your kids need to know that. There will be times when you must swallow your pride and ask forgiveness for something. Not only should that diminish your children's anger, but it can serve as a model for their own apologies.

Be willing to practice tough love. Kids want discipline. They'll scream and holler when they get it, but they really appreciate the structure of a home with clear standards. Deep inside their psyche, they understand the concept of tough love. So don't be afraid to be the bad guy and administer punishment where necessary. It's an act of love.

You be the parent. Yeah, you're all in this together. You support one another. The kids are taking on some adult responsibilities. You and your kids are friends. But there are times when you just have to be in charge. Don't let it be forgotten that you are the parent. You have the final say.

New Relationships

What happens when you find someone new with whom you want to build a relationship, someone you might want to marry? This can unleash a whole new set of issues with your kids.

- Your children might resent the new person, because this relationship signals the end of their hopes of getting Mom and Dad back together.
- Your children might be jealous of the attention you show to the new person.

- Your children might be delighted with your new relationship and might harbor unrealistic hopes of restoring the family structure.
- Your children might form a personal attachment to this new person before you do, which will cause greater pain if the relationship fails.

This doesn't mean you can't pursue such relationships, but you must be very, very careful.

What Can You Do to Minimize the Ill Effects of a New Relationship on Your Children?

Go slow in the relationship. Your own sense of loss will propel you forward, but you have a lot at stake here. Be careful. Go slow in frequency of dates, in emotional commitment, and in physical involvement. Somewhere within your heart, you're hoping that this new relationship will solve all your problems. It won't. In fact, it might cause a whole bunch of new problems if it's not handled properly.

Go very slow in sharing this relationship with your kids. One expert says you shouldn't introduce a new partner to your kids until you're engaged. That's not a bad idea. I'd say it's all right to have some very casual interaction between your kids and someone you've been dating regularly, but don't get your children's hopes up. They will form attachments or fears quickly. They will assume your romance is hotter than it is. So you don't want to bring a new person into your family circle until you're fairly sure it's permanent.

Share your heart with your kids on a need-to-know basis. Your children might guess that you're going out on a date, and they might fear the consequences. Assure them of your love. (With younger kids, assure them that you'll *come back*.) But you don't need to give a lot of details. Think of your dates, and talk about them, as "going somewhere with a friend," which they are. Preteen daughters might be inordinately interested in the romance of your new relationship. That's sweet, but keep your romantic feelings private. Assure your children that you will tell them what they need to know when a relationship becomes important enough for that, but in the meantime, they need to back off.

Find long-term friendships that will meet your children's needs for pseudoparents. It's likely that there's a gap in your children's lives. They need a father, or they need a mother. Ideally, your ex is still in contact with them, but his or her role is certainly diminished. They need adults as role models, as mentors, as friends. That's why any new romance of yours is such a big deal. It seems to meet this need. But you can find safer ways to meet this need. Look for friends of the opposite sex in your church or neighborhood who can spend time with your family, filling a pseudoparental role. More than anything, you need someone who will be there for the long haul, which is why your latest boyfriend or girlfriend is not a good candidate.

Spend time with intact families. Not only do your kids need individual role models, but they need to see intact families functioning well. Maybe you have relatives you can spend time with, or families from church. Do not begrudge your children's time with such families. Yes, you might be jealous of their intactness, but get over that. Your kids need to experience that. You are still offering them your undying love and wise parenting, but you can make sure they see how functional families work. (Of course, not all intact families function well, so be choosy about which families you "adopt.")

Hope for the Future

Over the years I've seen many single parents struggling with the challenges of their situation. One who comes to mind is Barbara.

After her husband left her with two children, Barbara faced all the emotional and financial difficulties we've mentioned. Knowing that her minimum-wage job couldn't support her family, she went back to school for a business administration degree while doing some desktop publishing from her home. She arranged to share legal custody of the children with her ex-husband, but she retained physical custody. In this way, she hopes that her husband will be more involved in the children's lives. "I may not be married to him," she says, "but he is still their father. Even though he didn't turn out to be such a good husband, he was always a good father, and I believe he still is."

The children enjoy their visits with their father, and they don't hesitate to tell Mom all about their weekends away, because they know she genuinely supports their relationship with him.

Barbara has found a new group of friends who've been through similar life changes and remains friendly with a few of the married couples she knew before the divorce. She describes her life in this way: "I wouldn't wish divorce on my worst enemy, but I wouldn't trade anything for what I have learned having gone through a divorce. I have more self-confidence and feel more fulfilled now than ever before, because I'm no longer dependent on my husband. Sure, I get lonely sometimes, but . . . now I have much stronger friendships and a closer relationship with my kids." After a period of adjustment, Barbara's children are now doing better than ever in school and with their friends. They seem to be adjusting to the single-parent situation quite well.

Having led several groups and Sunday school classes for children and teens from single-parent families, I have concluded that some of the most difficult kids I have ever encountered have come from these homes. But I would also say that some of the most wonderful, responsible, and mature kids I have ever encountered *also* came from single-parent homes. The difference seems to be the attitude and adjustment of the custodial parent. Hope for your children comes from God's grace and unending work in your life to be the kind of parent you need to be. As you make choices and changes in your parenting, seek God's guidance, strength, and wisdom. Remember, in *our* weakness, *he* will make us strong. With God's help, you and your children can be living testimonies of God's healing power in the face of seemingly impossible tasks.

Questions to Discuss

1. How did you become a single parent?
2. What have been two or three of your greatest areas of adjustment? (For you personally and for your children.)
3. When it comes to your lack of energy, what situations tend to drain you the most? What steps have you taken to recharge your batteries?
4. Financial difficulties seem to be overwhelming for many single parents. Other than winning the lottery, what creative steps have you taken, or what ideas might help your situation?

5. When you talk to your kids about helping out with chores, or about financial cutbacks, how do they react?

6. What has been your predominant emotion over the past six months? Anger, guilt, depression, hope? What about the emotions of your children?

7. What help have you sought or received for these emotional concerns?

8. Consistency with your children is difficult even in an intact family. What has been your biggest struggle for consistency? Have you found anything that helps you?

For Further Reading

Burns, Bob, and Thomas Whiteman. *The Fresh Start Divorce Recovery Workbook*. Nashville: Thomas Nelson, 1998.

Cloud, Henry, and John Townsend. *Boundaries with Kids*. Grand Rapids: Zondervan, 1998.

Deal, Ron. *The Smart Step-Family*. Minneapolis: Bethany House, 2002.

Jones, Tom. *The Single Again Handbook*. Nashville: Thomas Nelson, 1993. (Available through Fresh Start Seminars.)

Whiteman, Thomas. *Your Kids and Divorce*. Grand Rapids: Revell, 2001.

Whiteman, Thomas, and Randy Petersen, *Starting Over*. Colorado Springs: Pinion Press, 2001.

Fresh Start Seminars, Inc.: 1-888-FRESH-ST, or www.freshstartseminars.org. Fresh Start provides seminars and educational materials for divorce recovery and single-parenting to individuals and churches throughout the United States and Canada.

27

RAISING CHILDREN IN STEPFAMILIES

Ron L. Deal, M.MFT.

Parenting is tough work. Parenting in stepfamilies is tougher. Maybe you can relate to the stepmother who said, "Being a stepmother is like setting your hair on fire and putting it out with a hammer!"[1] The good news is there are key lessons stepparents and biological parents can learn that make the challenges of raising children in stepfamilies easier. But first, there's prayer.

When Manoah and his barren wife first learned from an angel that they would conceive a son, Samson (Judges 13), they prayed, "O Lord, I beg you, let the man of God you sent to us come again to teach us how to bring up the boy who is to be born" (13:8). I don't know about you, but I've prayed that prayer: *Teach me, Father, how to raise up this child you have given.* But what if the child was born to someone else? What if the child is confused about your place in their life and doesn't want to obey? What then?

So did God send the angel back to answer all of Manoah's parenting questions? Not even close. The angel returned with only a few dietary restrictions for the child, but no parenting discipline plan. I doubt the Lord will hand us one either. Why? Because he wants us dependent on him in prayer, just as Manoah was. He wants our relationship with him and our attempts to be like Jesus to drive our parenting decisions. The same is true for stepparents.

Stepparenting is, at best, an ambiguous role. It calls for flexibility, tough skin, determination, and above all, prayer. Might I suggest, before you read any further, that together you as a couple bow before your God and say this prayer: "Dear Lord, we beg you, teach us how to bring up the child(ren) you have given us. And strengthen us with your wisdom as we strive to bring them up to know and serve you. In Jesus' name. Amen."

Biological Parents: Remarried with Children

In remarriage, children are definitely part of the package. But then, so are a lot of other people! Raising children in stepfamilies means dealing with multiple households, ex-spouses, grandparents and stepgrandparents, perhaps even former stepparents. While this complexity may at times feel impossible for a parent and stepparent to manage, knowing your roles, limits, and how to manage the coparenting issues between homes makes the journey manageable.

Biological parents hold a number of keys to successful parenting in a stepfamily. Even though children in stepfamilies frequently have three, four, or more caretakers, biological parents hold five keys that aid the stepparent in their new role.

Key 1: Declare Your Spouse (the Stepparent) Your Lifelong Partner

A healthy marriage paves the way for healthy parenting, but because your relationship with your children preceded the wedding, your marriage is the least bonded and most vulnerable relationship in your home. You must protect it, honor it with time and energy, and declare it a top priority. If you don't, your children might assume they can pull on your loyalties anytime it suits their selfish desires.

For example, if a child learns that acting sad over the losses they've experienced draws your sympathy, makes you soft in punishment, and makes you likely to defend them to the stepparent, they will use it to their advantage. Children need to know you sympathize with their grief, but they also need to know their place in the family.

Conflicting loyalties between children and your new spouse are exacerbated when everyone is together simultaneously. Therefore, balance separate time with your children and your spouse to decrease the tensions. Be sure each is getting your effort and attention. This strategy of compartmentalizing relationships in your home, that is, spending time with your children and spouse separately, is especially useful in a new stepfamily when steprelations are awkward. Sometimes the only person who is comfortable with both the stepparent and stepchildren is you. In addition, children appreciate exclusive time with their parent. It is reassuring, especially throughout the transitions from divorce to remarriage. Time for children with a stepparent can most comfortably occur around family activities and the daily routines of life (rides to school, soccer games, and church attendance).

Finding the balance between your children and your spouse means wrestling with what seems to be either/or dilemmas. Many parents feel they must choose between *either* their spouse *or* their children, but rarely is a parent forced to this ultimate extreme. The answer to this apparent dilemma is both/and; be devoted to *both* your spouse *and* your children. This is a balance first-marriage couples must find as well. You and your spouse together must see the value of this balance. A wise stepparent, for example, will not be jealous of your time with your children, because that is necessary nurturance for every child. But neither will you feel guilty giving time and energy to your marriage, even though it means not spending time with your children. A wise parent realizes that the investment they make in their remarriage relationship brings long-term stability to their child's home life. Declaring your spouse your lifelong partner leads to good parenting with your children.

Key 2: Pass Power to the Stepparent

Rules without relationship bring rebellion. The main challenge to stepparenting is earning or building a relationship with a stepchild that affords the stepparent the needed authority to make rules (and impose consequences for disobedience). Until such a relationship is built and trust between stepparent and stepchild established, how is a stepparent supposed to gain authority? They must live on borrowed power from the biological parent.

If you haven't yet, begin communicating to your children the expectation that they respect their stepparent. Say something like, "I know Bob is not your dad. However, when I am not here, he will be enforcing the household rules we have agreed on. I expect you to be courteous and respect him as you would any authority figure." Let's examine the key phrases in this statement to understand their meaning.

"I know Bob is not your dad." Children are put under unfortunate pressure when a parent expects them to like/love/honor a stepparent just as they would a biological parent. A stepparent cannot replace a deceased parent, nor should they try to move the nonresidential dad (or mom) out of the child's heart. For example, never insist that a child call a stepfather "Dad." If they choose to do so, fine. But insisting denies a child's loyalty to their biological parent and typically leads them to resist the authority of the stepparent as a way of protesting what is being expected of them. A wise parent and stepparent acknowledge that another parent exists and that there is no need to push them aside.

"He will be enforcing the household rules." Until they have bonded and established a trusting relationship with their stepchildren, stepparents enforce rules that biological parents make. The number one sabotage of healthy stepfamilies is a stepparent who claims authority they have not earned and tries to force it on their stepchildren. Tony believed that being "head of the house" meant respect didn't have to be earned, that it was something he just assumed when he married Micah. He ruled with declarations and heavy threats of punishment (which he had to carry out daily), only to alienate his children and his wife. He failed to understand that power cannot be claimed; it has to be earned through relationship.

Stepparents, until relationship is developed, are enforcers. Much like a baby-sitter who temporarily watches children while a parent is out, stepparents live on borrowed power. When a baby-sitter comes to your house, you probably communicate an expectation that your children obey him or her. How else can the baby-sitter manage the home if they have no power? It is not their power they rely on; it is the parent's power. The same is true for stepparents. When the rules and expectations of proper behavior are clear, a stepparent can enforce both rules and consequences when you are not present because your children know what you expect. You might communicate that there will be an added consequence from you when you return home if the child continually disobeys. This supports the stepparent's place in the home and allows him or her to build their own authority with time.

But there is something very different about a stepparent and a baby-sitter. The latter is not part of the rule negotiation process; baby-sitters don't get a say in what the rules should be or in what discipline strategies the parenting team will utilize. Stepparents do. They have full membership in the parenting team and therefore are part of the decision-making process. It is best if you and the stepparent can negotiate the household rules behind closed doors so that the children cannot influence the process. Then when a system of parenting is agreed on, you can communicate the rules and your expectation that they be kept, no matter who is enforcing them. The stepparent then functions as an equal part of the parenting team behind closed doors but allows you to be the heavy with the children, especially the first couple of years after the wedding. After all, you have the power to make things happen, and until they have built a relationship with the children, they don't. When both parents bring children to the marriage, each is the primary disciplinarian with their own children and a baby-sitter to the others. A unified set of household rules makes for equitable treatment of the children.

"I expect you to be courteous and respect him as you would any authority figure." Getting your expectations and your child's expectations about the stepparent's level of authority properly attuned is vital. Expecting your children to view the stepparent as they would a teacher, athletics coach, or camp counselor eases the acceptance of the stepparent. Children are accustomed to following the authority of teachers and Bible class leaders and are generally expected to respect older adults. Framing obedience to a stepparent as nothing more makes it more palatable. This is especially true for children who are caught in a loyalty conflict between their nonresidential biological parent and

stepparent, because cooperation with a stepparent doesn't feel like disloyalty to the biological parent. In effect, lowering the expectation takes children out of any emotional tugs-of-war and makes obedience and cooperation more likely. And that's good for everyone!

Key 3: Build Trust in the Stepparent

I have come to observe that one of the greatest barriers to entrusting your children to your spouse is a biological parent's fundamental lack of trust in the stepparent. In first-marriage two-parent biological homes, couples don't seem to question the motives of their spouse. They may not agree with the parenting style of the other or the punishment they impose at any given moment, but they don't question their spouse's love or commitment to doing what's best for the child. Parents generally assume the best about the other biological parent's motives. Stepparents are not always granted that same benefit of the doubt.

Roger loved Cheryl very much, but he just wasn't sure why she was critical of his two daughters. Cheryl complained that Roger was too easy on them and she feared they would grow up to be "spoiled, boy-chasing girls." Roger believed that Cheryl's real problem was jealousy; he interpreted her criticism of the girls as her attempt to step between Roger and his daughters. Therefore, he ignored her input and discounted her efforts at discipline.

To give your spouse the benefit of the doubt, you must force yourself to trust their motives. Sometimes stepparents are jealous, but that doesn't mean they are mean-spirited toward your children. If you don't strive for trust, you'll continually defend your children, even when ill-advised. Your children will learn that obeying the stepparent is optional (because you'll stick up for them) and your spouse will truly grow to resent your children. Open yourself to the stepparent's input. Listen to their outsider perspective and strive to see love behind their actions.

"*But what if my child complains about how their stepparent is treating them, and I kind of agree?*" Listen and affirm your child's concerns. Make neutral statements about the child's and stepparent's actions rather than feeling the need to defend anyone. Say, "I can see how she [the stepmother] hurt your feelings. I'm sorry that you're angry about this. Let me look into it, but you're still grounded." Later, discuss the situation with your spouse, but don't start with accusation. Allow them to explain the situation. If you have concerns, you might say, "I can see why you responded that way. I would be more comfortable if next time the agreed-upon response was . . ." Then negotiate what the plan will be next time and communicate the changes to your child. Try not to undercut the stepparent, but find unity in handling future similar situations.

Key 4: Strive for Cooperative Coparenting with Your Ex-Spouse

At a minimum, biological parents should contain their anger and conflict in order to cooperate and compromise on issues of the children's welfare. At a maximum, coparents can strive to enforce similar rules and standards of conduct in each of the children's homes. Most coparents find it difficult to accomplish the former; only a few are able to achieve the latter. Nevertheless, coparents should do everything they can to build cooperation between the two homes.

I cannot overemphasize the importance of this concept in regard to the well-being of children. Research clearly confirms that children successfully adjust to the ending of their parents' marriage and can fare reasonably well if (1) parents are able to bring their marital relationship to an end *without excessive conflict*; (2) children are *not put into the middle* of whatever conflicts exist; and (3) there is a *commitment from parents to cooperate* on issues of the children's material, physical, educational, emotional, and spiritual welfare.[2] Bottom line—children need their parents to work together whether married, divorced, or married to other people.

Furthermore, understand that children in stepfamilies live in two "countries."[3] They hold citizenship in each country and are therefore invested in the quality of life found in both. The parenting team should do everything it can to help children thrive and enjoy each of their two homes. Here are some practical suggestions taken from my book *The Smart Step-Family: Seven Steps to a Healthy Family*:

1. Work hard to respect the other parent and his or her household. Agree that each parent has a right to privacy, and do not intrude in his or her life. Make space for different parenting styles and

rules, as there are many healthy ways to raise children. Do not demean the other's living circumstances, activities, dates, or decisions, and give up the need to control your ex's parenting style.

2. Schedule a monthly (perhaps even more often) "business" meeting to discuss coparenting matters. You can address schedules, academic reports, behavioral training, and spiritual development. Do not discuss your personal life (or your ex's); that part of your relationship is no longer appropriate. If the conversation turns away from the children, simply redirect the topic or politely end the meeting. If you cannot talk with your ex face-to-face due to conflict, use email or speak to the answering machine. Do what you can to make your meetings productive for the children.

3. Never ask your children to be spies or tattletales on the other home. This places them in a loyalty bind that brings great emotional distress. Be happy when they enjoy the people in their new home ("I'm glad you enjoy fishing with your stepdad"). If children offer information about life in the other home, listen and stay neutral in your judgment.

4. When children have confusing or angry feelings toward your ex, don't capitalize on their hurt and berate the other parent. Listen and help them to explore their feelings without trying to sway their opinions with your own. If you can't make positive statements about the other parent, strive for neutral ones.

5. Children should have everything they need in each home. Don't make them bring basic necessities back and forth. Special items, like clothes or a comforting teddy bear, can move back and forth as needed.

6. Try to release your hostility toward the other parent so that the children can't take advantage of your hard feelings. Manipulation is much easier when ex-spouses don't cooperate.

7. Do not disappoint your children with broken promises or by being unreliable. Do what you say, keep your visitation schedule as agreed, and stay active in their lives.

8. Make your custody structure work for your children even if you don't like the details of the arrangement. Update the other when changes need to be made to the visitation

schedule. Also, inform the other parent of any change in job, living arrangements, etc. that may require an adjustment by the children.

9. If you plan to hire a baby-sitter for more than four hours while the children are in your home, give the other parent first right to that time (assuming they live close enough).

10. Suggest that younger children take a favorite toy or game as a transitional object. This can help them make the transition and to feel more comfortable in the other home.

11. Regarding children who visit for short periods of time or spend time in another home:
    - Sometimes it is tempting to do only "special activities" when all of the children are with you for fear that some children may feel that they aren't as special as others. Do special things with differing combinations of children (it's all right if someone feels disappointed that he or she wasn't able to go).
    - When other children come for visitation, let the lives of those living with you remain unaltered as much as possible.
    - Keep toys and possessions in a private spot, where they are not to be touched or borrowed unless the owner gives permission (even while they are in the other home).

12. Help children adjust when going to the other home:
    - If the children will go on vacation while in the other home, find out what's on the agenda. You can help your kids pack special items and needed clothing.
    - Provide the other home with information regarding your child's changes. A switch in preferences (regarding music, clothes, hairstyles, foods, etc.) or physical, cognitive, or emotional developments can be significant. Let the other home know what is different before the child arrives.
    - When receiving children, give them time to unpack, relax, and settle in. Try not to overwhelm them at first with plans, rules, or even special treatment. Let them work their way in at their own pace.[4]

13. If you and your ex cannot resolve a problem or change in custody or visitation, agree to problem solving through mediation rather than litigation.

Key 5: Understand Your Child's Issues with Loyalty

Stepfamilies and loyalty conflicts go hand-in-hand. Successfully defusing the loyalty binds felt by children and adults within stepfamilies is one of the most significant steps toward stepfamily integration. Loyalty speaks to where we put our allegiances.

Even in the best of circumstances, children feel caught between their biological parents and often feel as though they are in an emotional tug-of-war. Loyalty conflicts seem unavoidable from the children's perspective. They simply want to love everyone, without strings attached and in such a way that others don't feel hurt. Little do parents realize how trampled children feel when they battle for the children's time or attention.

Parents implicitly ask their children to "choose" and therefore put children in a no-win, tug-of-war when they

- badmouth the other parent or household;
- comment on or compare living conditions;
- cast blame on the other household for financial pressures or emotional pain;
- ask for the child's time when it takes time away from the other parent;
- coax the child into not visiting their other parent until child support payments are made or custody time is renegotiated;
- make children feel guilty for enjoying the people in the other home; and
- refuse to listen to their happy stories of life in the other home.

All of these situations and many more teach children to take their emotions underground and train them to play the game of "keep everyone happy by making them think I love them most." Children who internalize this tug-of-war become depressed, discouraged, self-destructive, and unmotivated. Children who externalize their pain become angry and oppositional, have behavior problems, and may turn violent. Children simply want to be connected to the people they love, no strings attached. Do your best to make this possible.

Keep these suggestions in mind as you seek to have a healthy coparenting relationship:

1. You will never lose your children's affections. Blood is very, very thick and nearly impossible to erase. Your children will not forget about you just because they have a new, rich, and/or entertaining stepparent. Don't worry or compete with the other household for loyalty; you already have it.
2. Never make children regret having affections for the other home. Remember that they have citizenship there, and forcing a loyalty battle only destroys them. Children need your permission to love their biological parent, and they need to see your psychological stability as they do so. Your permission helps to take them out of the emotional tug-of-war and relieves the pressure to take care of you. They also need your acceptance of the relationship they carve out with their stepparent. The more comfortable you are with children's relationships in the other home, the more likely it is that they will honor you (and *your* new spouse). Respect given is respect returned.[5]

Stepparenting: Growing into Your Role

Stepparenting is a two-person task. If the biological parent does not support the stepparent and is not willing to "play the heavy" while the stepparent develops a relationship with the children, it is likely that conflict throughout the home will escalate. Furthermore, just as in two-biological-parent homes, parents and stepparents must be unified in goals and work together as a team. What is needed most is a clear, working alliance so the adults stay in charge of the home. But the stepparent's role differs from the biological parent's. A summary of the mistakes of ineffective stepparents and the wisdom of effective ones is provided below.

Qualities of Ineffective and Effective Stepparents

1. *Ineffective stepparents try too hard to become an insider; effective ones enjoy the relationship they have now.* Stepfamilies are made up of insiders and outsiders. Insiders are blood rela-

tives, bonded by birth or adoption. Outsiders don't have this natural bond. Stepparents naturally want to be accepted into the family of insiders, but may try to force their way in only to discover resistance. Effective stepparents realize that building a connection and earning trust takes time. They accept the relationship as it is rather than worrying that it isn't more. Wise stepparents let the children set the pace for their relationship. If, for example, the children welcome affection, then give it. If, however, they remain formal and distant, don't panic or assume something is wrong. Honor their need for space and trust that the distance will diminish over the years that follow. Be patient and seek to grow with your stepchildren, but don't add too much pressure.

2. *Ineffective stepparents try to replace the nonresidential biological parent; effective ones encourage stepchildren to maintain contact with that parent.* When counseling stepfamilies, I frequently attempt to consult with the other home in which the children live in order to get a more complete picture of the interaction between them. While talking with Jeff, a nonresidential father of two, I discovered part of the reason he was so negative toward his ex-wife, Erin, and her new husband, Bob, was this: "I know I should be decent to Bob as my kids' stepfather," Jeff said, "but I can't get over him trying to take my place. He once told me that he was more of a father to my kids than I was, even though I see them each week and we talk regularly on the phone. He's just trying to push me out of the picture." I couldn't help but agree. And perhaps that was one reason Erin's children now wanted to go live with their dad. Effective stepparents not only respect a child's right to be with his or her parent; they encourage it. They allow pictures, mementos, and special reminders to be kept by the children. They invite the nonresidential parent to important ceremonies, recitals, and events. Wise stepparents do not compete with biological parents but recognize their role as an added parent figure rather than a replacement parent.

3. *Ineffective stepparents attempt punishment before having relationship; effective ones gradually move into disciplinary roles.* We've already established that parental authority comes through relationship. As a stepparent you gain the ability to lead and influ-

ence stepchildren the old-fashioned way—you earn it. Trust, respect, and honor grow out of a relational history that comes with time and experience. Effective stepparents are dedicated to relationship-building over the long haul, and they know the definition of their role will change. For example, stepparents begin in the baby-sitter role discussed earlier. Behind the scenes they are part of the household-rules negotiation, but in front of the children, they live on borrowed power acting as enforcers of the biological parent's rules. As relationships develop with time, stepparents can move into the uncle/aunt role, in which stepchildren view the stepparent as an extended family member. Eventually, some stepparents will take on a great deal of status with their stepchildren, moving into a bonus parent role.

Time with stepchildren is a significant factor determining whether a stepparent ever moves out of the baby-sitter role. Stepparents of children under the age of five will likely experience quick movement through the previously defined stepparenting roles. Stepparents of teenagers will find growth very slow, if at all. The challenge is to accept the role you currently have while remaining open to a gradual deepening of the relationship.

4. *Ineffective stepparents are critical and put up barriers to new relationships; effective ones find ways to connect.* Helen called to complain about her husband's parenting of her son. "Larry's not abusive, but he will always say no to whatever he asks, and when Tim walks in the room, Larry is always telling him to do chores or some task. He just won't open himself up to Tim. I feel like I am always running defense for my son, and it is the biggest cause of fights in our marriage." Larry was critical and unaccepting of his stepson, and it was pushing both his stepson and wife further away. The effective stepparent by contrast will learn about the child's interests, share talents and skills, compliment and show appreciation to each child, and engage in family group activities (like playing board games or going to the zoo). Researcher James Bray says one of the most important stepparenting skills after remarriage is *monitoring the children's activities.*[6] This involves knowing their daily routine, where the children are, whom they are with, and what

extracurricular activities they are involved in, but it does not necessarily include being involved in the child's emotional life. Stepparents who monitor check homework and daily chores and befriend stepchildren, yet refrain from emotional closeness that is unwelcomed by the child. Stepfathers should also seek to build relationship by establishing a culture of faith in the home. For example, wise stepfathers begin to show Christ to their stepchildren by influencing their mother (his wife). By working with her behind the scenes to establish an expectation of godly behavior in the home, rules that support honoring God, and involvement with a local body of believers, a stepfather can have dramatic impact. Leading the family in prayer, orchestrating family spiritual times (reading Scripture, singing worship songs, sharing stories of God's activity in his life), and reading Scripture at breakfast are just some ways a stepfather can gently lead his family while relationships are growing.

A Work in Progress

I often tell parents that raising children is a work in progress. No one ever has all the right answers, and all parents and stepparents yell, scream, plead, and lose their cool at some point. None of us is perfect. That's why we must rely on a perfect God for wisdom and guidance. Study the Scriptures on a daily basis. Seek to be transformed into the likeness of Christ, pray daily for wisdom, and you'll find the task of raising children in a stepfamily getting easier. Agree to honor one another before the other's children and support the household rules you negotiate together. And importantly, be sure the issues of parenting and stepparenting do not divide your marriage. Protect it and nurture it. Press on with your work in progress.

Questions to Discuss

1. How accepting of your marriage do the children seem to be? What barriers to marital intimacy have you experienced?
2. Biological parent: Have you created an expectation with your children that they respect and obey the stepparent as they would any other authority figure?

3. In what ways can you improve your working relationship with your ex-spouse(s)?
4. Stepparent: Which of the ineffective and effective qualities describe you at the present moment? Discuss a plan to make changes as needed.
5. Evaluate yourselves as a parenting team:
   - Are you cooperating poorly? Do you frequently disagree about rules and consequences? Does one of you feel sabotaged by the other? Do the same conflicts repeat because they aren't getting resolved?
   - If you answered yes to two or more of the above, you have a weak parental alliance and must work out a plan to act as a team.

For Further Reading

Barnes, Bob. *Winning the Heart of Your Stepchild*. Grand Rapids: Zondervan, 1992.

Broersma, Margaret. *Daily Reflections for Stepparents*. Grand Rapids: Kregel Publications, 2003.

Broersma, Margaret. *Stepparent to Stepparent: Answers to Fifty Common Questions Stepparents Ask*. Grand Rapids: Kregel Publications, 2003.

Deal, Ron L. *The Smart Step-Family: Seven Steps to a Healthy Family*. Minneapolis: Bethany House Publishers, 2002.

Erwin, Cheryl, Jane Nelsen, and Stephen Glenn. *Positive Discipline for Your Stepfamily: Nurturing Harmony, Respect, and Joy in Your New Home*. Roseville, CA: Prima Publishing, 2000.

Successful Stepfamilies (www.SuccessfulStepfamilies.com)—Christian resources from Ron L. Deal for church and home: articles, resources, videos, tele-classes, and seminars for stepfamilies and ministry leaders.

NOTES

Chapter 1: Giving Your Child Something to Rebel Against

1. Bruno Bettelheim, "Youth: Confused Parents, Confused Kids," *Time*, September 5, 1969.

Chapter 2: When Husband and Wife Become Mom and Dad

1. J. M. Gottman and N. Silver, *The Seven Principles for Making Marriage Work: A Practical Guide from the Country's Foremost Relationship Expert* (New York: Crown Publishers, 1999).

2. Carol Tavris, *The Redbook Report on Female Sexuality: 100,000 Married Woman Disclose the Good News about Sex* (New York: Delacorte, 1977).

Chapter 3: Raising Emotionally Healthy Sons

1. Herb Goldberg, *The New Male: From Self-Destruction to Self-Care* (Wellness Institute, 2001), 20–21, 44, 218; Aaron Kipnis, *Knights without Armor* (New York: Putnam, 1992), 11–34, 47, 57, 159; Daniel Evan Weiss, *The Great Divide: How Females and Males Really Differ* (New York: Poseidon Press, 1991).

2. *Arkansas Democrat-Gazette*, July 12, 2003, B1, 6.

3. Daniel Goleman, *Emotional Intelligence* (New York: Bantam, 1997), 131.

4. Michael Gurian, *A Fine Young Man: What Parents, Mentors, and Educators Can Do to Shape Adolescent Boys into Exceptional Men* (New York: J. P. Tarcher/Putnam, 1998), 36ff.

5. John Gottman, *The Heart of Parenting* (New York: Simon & Schuster, 1997).

6. Ibid.

7. Ibid.

8. Goleman, *Emotional Intelligence,* xiii.

9. Thomas Armstrong, *In Their Own Way: Discovering and Encouraging Your Child's Personal Learning Style* (Los Angeles: Jeremy P. Tarcher, Inc., 2000), 23.

10. David Mains, *Healing the Dysfunctional Church Family* (Wheaton: Victor Books, 1992).

Chapter 5: The Importance of Father

1. W. Horn and T. Sylvester, *Father Facts*, 5th ed. (Washington, DC: National Fatherhood Initiative. 2002).

2. J. Wallerstein and S. Blakeslee, *Second Chances: Men, Women, and Children a Decade after Divorce* (New York: Houghton Mifflin, 1996), 145.

3. Frank Furstenberg and Andrew Cherlin, *Divided Families: What Happens When Parents Part* (Cambridge: Harvard University Press, 1991), 10.

4. L. Silverstein and C. Auerbach, "Deconstructing the Essential Father," *American Psychologist* 54, no. 6 (1999).

5. W. Stanton, et al., "Sociodemographic Characteristics of Adolescent Smokers," *The International Journal of the Addictions* 7 (1994): 913–25.

6. D. Ferguson et al., "Parental Separation, Adolescent Psychopathology, and Problem Behaviors," *Journal of the American Academy of Child and Adolescent Psychiatry* 33 (1994): 112–31.

7. Rob N. Parsons, *The Sixty Minute Father* (Nashville: Broadman & Holman, 1996).

Chapter 6: How to Empower Your Children

1. Diana Baumrind, "The Discipline Controversy Revisited," *Family Relations* 45 (1966): 405–15.

2. See Rudolf Dreikurs, *The Challenge of Parenthood* (New York: Plume, 1992).

3. Eleanor Maccoby, *The Two Sexes: Growing Up Apart* (Cambridge: Harvard University Press, 1998).

4. Diane Ehrensaft, *Parenting Together: Men and Women Sharing the Care of Their Children* (Chicago: University of Chicago Press, 1990).

5. Carolyn Henry and Gary Peterson, "Adolescent Social Competence, Parental Qualities, and Parental Satisfaction," *American Journal of Orthopsychiatry* 65, no. 2 (1995): 249–62.

Chapter 7: Attachment Discipline

1. Adapted from Tim Clinton and Gary Sibcy, *Attachments: Why You Feel and Act the Way You Do* (Brentwood, TN: Integrity, 2002).

Chapter 8: The Good Enough Parent

1. Bruno Bettelheim, *A Good Enough Parent* (New York: Alfred A. Knopf, 1987), 5, 6.

2. Erik Erikson, *Childhood and Society* (New York: W. W. Norton, 1993).

3. Bettelheim, *A Good Enough Parent*, 41.

Chapter 12: Understanding Your Child's Personality

1. For more information on both the *Myers-Briggs Type Indicator* and the *Murphy-Meisgeier Type Indicator* for children, contact Consulting Psychologists Press, Inc., 3893 Bayshore Road, Palo Alto, CA 94303.

Chapter 13: The Importance of Play

1. This survey was conducted by Applied Research & Consulting; a quantitative telephone survey was conducted with a randomly selected sample of four hundred parents nationwide.

2. Garry Landreth, *Play Therapy: The Art of the Relationship*, 2nd ed. (Philadelphia: Brunner-Routledge, 2002), 14.

3. These categories, together with exhaustive material on play and development, come from James E. Johnson, James F. Christie, and Thomas D. Yawkey, *Play and Early Childhood Development*, 2nd ed. (New York: Addison Wesley Longman, 1999).

4. Charles E. Schaefer, *Therapeutic Use of Child's Play* (Northvale, NJ: Jason Aronson Inc., 1979), 16.

5. Landreth, 17.

6. Denise Chapman Weston and Mark S. Weston, *Playful Parenting: Turning the Dilemma of Discipline into Fun and Games* (New York: J. P. Tarcher/Putnam, 1993), 8.

7. Research shows that play therapy is statistically as strong as, and in many cases stronger than, other child therapy interventions. References to this research may be found at the Association for Play Therapy website (www.a4pt.org).

8. Daniel Sweeney, *Counseling Children Through the World of Play* (Eugene, OR: Wipf and Stock Publishers, 1997), 166.

9. Walter Kirn and Wendy Cole, "What Ever Happened To Play?" *Time* (April 22, 2001).

10. Harry Emerson Fosdick, "Living for the fun of it," *American Magazine* (April 1930), cited by Robert Neale, *In Praise of Play* (New York: Harper & Row, 1969), 175.

Chapter 15: Balancing Grace and Truth in Parenting

1. Jeff Jacoby, "The Road to Treason," *Boston Globe*, December 13, 2001.

Chapter 16: Teaching Values and Building Character in Your Child

1. Wilkinson, Bruce, *The Seven Laws of the Learner* (Sisters, OR: Multnomah, 1983).

2. *The Churched Youth Survey* (Dallas: Josh McDowell Ministry, 1994), 69.

3. From *Internet Modern History Sourcebook*, www.fordham.edu/halsall/mod/modsbook.html.

Chapter 17: Understanding and Reinforcing Your Child's Learning Style

1. Excerpted from Cynthia Ulrich Tobias, *Every Child Can Succeed: Making the Most of Your Child's Learning Style* (Colorado Springs: Focus on the Family, 1996).

Chapter 20: Defusing Anger

1. H. Norman Wright, *The Christian Use of Emotional Power* (Grand Rapids: Revell, 1986).

Chapter 23: Answering the Cries of the Spirited Child

1. National Symposium on Building Strong Families, *Building Family Strengths* (University of Nebraska, 1986).

2. T. Berry Brazelton, *Touchpoints: The Essential Reference of Your Child's Emotional and Behavioral Development* (Reading, MA: Perseus Books, 1992), 274–75.

3. Kevin Leman and Randy Carlson, *Parent Talk: Straight Answers to the Questions That Rattle Moms and Dads* (Nashville: Thomas Nelson, 1993), 17.

Chapter 24: Helping Your Child with Grief and Loss

1. Maria Shriver, *What's Heaven?* (New York: Golden Books, 1999).

2. Marge Heegaard, *When Someone Very Special Dies* (Minneapolis: Woodland Press, 1988).

Chapter 26: Children in the Single-Parent Family

1. Thomas Whiteman, Fresh Start Seminars, 1-888-FRESH-ST, www.freshstartseminars.org. Used by permission.

2. Ibid.

Chapter 27: Raising Children in Stepfamilies

1. Jean McBride, *Encouraging Words for New Stepmothers* (Fort Collins, CO: CDR Press, 2001), xv.

2. Carol R. Lowery, "Psychotherapy with Children of Divorced Families," in M. Textor, ed., *The Divorce and Divorce Therapy Handbook* (Northvale, NJ: Jason Aronson, Inc., 1989), 225–41.

3. Patricia L. Papernow, *Becoming a Stepfamily: Patterns of Development in Remarried Families* (New York: Gardner Press, 1993).

4. M. Engel, "President's Message," *Stepfamilies* 18, no. 2 (1998).

5. Adapted from Ron L. Deal, *The Smart Step-Family: Seven Steps to a Healthy Family* (Minneapolis: Bethany House, 2002), 110–17.

6. James Bray, *Stepfamilies: Love, Marriage, and Parenting in the First Decade* (New York: Broadway Books, 1998).

THE
COMPLETE
MARRIAGE
BOOK

Practical Help
from Leading Experts

- Set and achieve doable goals and priorities
- Communicate better
- Manage crisis in your relationship
- Find ever-constant ways to enjoy one-another
- Experience God together

Dr. David Stoop & Dr. Jan Stoop, editors

From in-laws to finances, romance to childrearing, spiritual growth to intimacy, *The Complete Marriage Book* shows you how to strengthen every area of your relationship.